THE

LAST TIMES

AND

The Great Consummation.

AN EARNEST DISCUSSION OF MOMENTOUS THEMES.

BY

JOSEPH A. SEISS, D.D.

AUTHOR OF

"THE GOSPEL IN LEVITICUS," "THE PARABLE OF THE TEN VIRGINS," "THE DAY OF THE LORD," "LECTURES ON THE EPISTLE TO THE HEBREWS," ETC. ETC.

REVISED AND ENLARGED EDITION.

PHILADELPHIA:
SMITH, ENGLISH & CO., 23 NORTH SIXTH ST.
NEW YORK: BLAKEMAN & MASON. BOSTON: GOULD & LINCOLN.
CINCINNATI: GEO. S. BLANCHARD.
LONDON: WERTHEIM, McINTOSH & HUNT.
TORONTO: W. C. CHEWETT & CO.
1863.

Οὐθὲν ανθρωπῳ λαβεῖν μεῖζον, οὐ χαρίσασθαι θεῷ σεμνότερον, ἀληθείας.—*Plutarch.*

"Man cannot receive, nor God bestow, a greater blessing than THE TRUTH."

I claim that liberty, which I willingly yield to others, in subjects of difficulty to put forward as true such things as appear to be probable, until proved to be manifestly false.—*Harvey.*

My determination with myself is, to follow neither men nor their opinions, but God and his word.—*Justin Martyr.*

Distinguite tempora, et concordabunt Scripturæ.

STEREOTYPED BY L. JOHNSON AND CO.
PHILADELPHIA.

PREFACE.

THIS book treats of the future destiny of the world and its population, as revealed in the holy prophecies. It was first published in 1856, since which time several editions and republications of it have appeared. It was originally designed to bear testimony against certain erroneous opinions extensively afloat in the popular mind, and to awaken attention to a subject too little appreciated and too much neglected by modern professors of Christianity. The favor with which it has met, and the blessing of God which has so largely attended it in many directions, together with the increased ominousness of our times, and the pressing importance of a right knowledge of what is coming upon the earth, have induced the author to revise, enlarge, and reissue it, and to enter into arrangements to bring it, in its revised form, simultaneously before the reading public of England, Canada, and the United States.

The views which it presents are somewhat in conflict with prevailing impressions and current opinions and prejudices; but they are the writer's honest convictions, produced by faithful study, and uttered under a full sense of the responsibility involved. They are also believed to be entitled to sober, candid, and careful consideration. They certainly have the sanction of high authorities, both ancient and modern, and are more and more commanding the belief of devout men of earnest hearts and eloquent tongues in all sections of the Church of Christ.

A few exceptions have been taken to former editions of this book. Its spirit was thought too positive, dogmatical, and severe. This criticism was not felt to be just. Strong, bold language was indeed employed; for it would be useless to think of making an impression in any other way; but as to dogmatical proscriptiveness, or disrespect to those entertaining different opinions, nothing was further from the author's feelings, or from the design of his book. Nevertheless, the revision has removed some passages, and modified others, which, perhaps, were liable to misconstruction in these particulars. If any thing remains which might reasonably disturb the most kindly feelings and relations with those who see things in a different light, the author is not conscious of it, and does not so intend it.

It has also been thought by some, that the book gave too unfavorable a picture of the present condition of the world,—that the moral and spiritual state of things now is not *worse*, but *better*, than in former periods. Seven years of additional study and observation, however, have only deepened the writer's belief in the truthfulness of the representations he has given. The difference between him and his critics, upon this point, may also, after all, be more apparent than real. The truth is, that the world is both *better* and *worse* than at any time since the days of the Apostles, and that it will continue to become better and worse until the "end." As the light increases, the shadows deepen. There is upon earth a kingdom of evil, and a kingdom of good; and both are expansive and growing. This is distinctly taught in the parable of the Wheat and the Tares. The great Lord of the field has said, "LET BOTH GROW TOGETHER UNTIL THE HARVEST; THE HARVEST IS THE END OF THE WORLD." Hence, Christ and Antichrist, holiness and iniquity, good and bad, are side by side, each advancing, the conflict between them increasing in intensity, the severest being the last, when the Lord of the harvest shall come with his reapers and make the everlasting separation. "The path of the just is as the shining light, that shineth *more and more* unto the perfect day," (Prov. iv. 18;) and yet "Evil men and seducers shall *wax worse and worse*, deceiving and being deceived." (2 Tim. iii. 13.)

The enlargements in this edition are considerable, amounting in all to more than one hundred pages. Some portions have been entirely rewritten. Notes have been added, to explain or further support the original text, and to bring up the work to the author's increased understanding of many important points. Pains have been taken and much labor bestowed to present a full analysis of Scripture References on the entire subject, and to give a full exhibit of the literature of the same from the days of the Apostles to the present. A complete Index to every thing important contained in the work has also been appended; all of which must materially enhance its value.

To appreciate this book as an argument for the system of doctrines concerning the future which it gives, it will be necessary to read all of it, and in the order in which it is presented. Its force is cumulative. Each part enters into the support of all the parts, and in its place contributes to the general conclusions of the whole. It is only by attention to this fact that the reader can do justice to the author, to the subject, or to himself.

As remarked in the preface to the first edition, the author of this volume does not presume to speak for his Church, or for any party, but only for himself. Nevertheless, he is happy to be able to say, that he speaks with Justin Martyr, Irenæus, Tertullian, and all the great divines of the first ages after Christ, as well as with many of the greatest lights of Protestant Christendom. And if he is to be censured or condemned for what he has here ventured to affirm, the Church of Christ itself, in the purest and brightest periods of its history, and in some of its most illustrious worthies, must also be censured and condemned.

With these remarks, the writer again sends out this volume, hoping that it may not be unfruitful of good, and praying that all who read it may be brought to share in the blessedness of those who shall have "part in the first resurrection."

PHILADELPHIA, U. S.,
March 18, A.D. 1863.

CONTENTS.

TWELVE DISCOURSES.

DISC.		PAGES
I.	THE SUBJECT PROPOUNDED—MATT. XXIV. APPLIED—CHRIST'S RETURN PROVEN—IMPORTANCE OF THE SUBJECT	9–35
II.	CHRIST'S COMING IN RELATION TO OTHER EVENTS—THE MILLENNIUM—WRONG VIEWS CORRECTED—THE ADVENT PRE-MILLENNIAL	36–61
III.	THE RESTITUTION OF ALL THINGS—"END OF THE WORLD"—PETER'S CONFLAGRATION—REPEAL OF THE CURSE	62–87
IV.	THE RESURRECTION—REV. XX.—TWOFOLD RESURRECTION—HOPES CONNECTED WITH THE RESURRECTION OF THE JUST	88–111
V.	MESSIAH'S KINGDOM—HOW PRESENTED IN THE SCRIPTURES—IS NOT YET SET UP	112–136
VI.	THE JUDGMENT—DAY OF—IS PROGRESSIVE—CONNECTS WITH THE MILLENNIAL REIGN—HOW INTRODUCED—ADMONITIONS	137–159
VII.	ADMINISTRATIONS OF THE JUDGMENT—UPON NATIONS—RESULTS OF	160–182
VIII.	RESTORATION OF THE JEWS—OBJECTIONS TO—NEW TESTAMENT ON—ANCIENT PROPHECIES—FACTS—EXPLANATIONS	183–208
IX.	THE WORLD TO COME—PICTURED IN THE TRANSFIGURATION—BLESSED CHARACTERISTICS OF	209–230
X.	TESTIMONY OF THE CHURCH—SUMMARY—THE FATHERS—AUTHORITIES—THE REFORMERS—CONTRAST BETWEEN PAST AND PRESENT	231–258

DISC. PAGES

XI. WHEN CHRIST WILL COME—WITH RELATION TO OTHER EVENTS—THREE METHODS OF COMPUTING THE TIME. 259–284

XII. RECAPITULATION—SIGNS OF THE TIMES WITH REFERENCE TO THE ADVENT OF CHRIST—SENTIMENTS OF DISTINGUISHED MEN—DESIRABLENESS OF CHRIST'S COMING 285–310

NOTES AND ADDITIONS.

NOTE PAGE

A. OPINIONS OF DISTINGUISHED MEN ON THE DAYS IN WHICH WE LIVE 316

B. THE MEANING OF γενεα—"GENERATION"—IN MATT. XXIV. 34. 323

C. THE AUGUSTAN AND HELVETIC CONFESSIONS AGAINST THE MODERN IDEAS OF THE MILLENNIUM........ 326

D. DOES THE AUGSBURG CONFESSION CONDEMN CHILIASM?.. 327

E. MILLENARIAN VIEWS OF THE SPIRITUALITY OF CHRIST'S KINGDOM 335

F. DECLARATION OF THE SAVIOR (JOHN XVIII. 36) IN REFERENCE TO HIS KINGDOM AND THIS WORLD 338

G. THE PERSONAL ANTICHRIST—IS IT LOUIS NAPOLEON?.... 341

H. THE TWO STAGES OF THE TRANSLATION OF THE SAINTS... 349

I. LUTHER ON THE MILLENNIUM 354

J. THE SCRIPTURE CHRONOLOGY OF THE WORLD 356

K. PROBABLE DATES OF THE SEVEN LAST VIALS 362

AUTHORITIES, BOOKS, AND REFERENCES.

CHAP. PAGE

I. ANALYSIS OF AUTHORITIES FROM THE HOLY SCRIPTURES 365

II. REFERENCES TO THE OPINIONS AND WORKS OF THE FATHERS 383

III. CLASSIFIED REFERENCES TO MORE RECENT WRITERS..... 400

GENERAL INDEX 433

The Last Times.

FIRST DISCOURSE.

THE SUBJECT PROPOUNDED—THE TWENTY-FOURTH CHAPTER OF MATTHEW APPLIED—CHRIST'S PERSONAL RETURN TO THE EARTH PROVEN—THE INTENSE IMPORTANCE OF THE THEME.

MATT. xxiv. 3: *And as he sat upon the mount of Olives, the disciples came unto him privately, saying, When shall these things be? and what shall be the sign of thy coming, and of the end of the world?*

FROM these words I begin a series of special discourses upon the holy prophecies concerning "The Last Times," and the winding up of the dispensation under which we now live.

It is agreed, by all believers in the Bible, that very mysterious scenes await our world. Christians and Jews concede, that we are approaching commotions and changes, such as never have been since time began. Indifferent to the future as we may be, and deep as are the church's slumbers upon the subject, God's purposes are fixed, and the wheel of his wonderful providence is rolling us on to the funeral of the "world" that now is. Every day we are coming nearer and nearer to a period, if we have not already entered within its margin, when the whole present arrangement of things shall be broken up and pass away.

No one acquainted with the existing aspects of the world, can have any doubt, that we have fallen upon very startling and critical times. All society, everywhere, with its politics, its philosophy, and its religion, is in a perturbed condition, indicating revolutions and occurrences which no mere human foresight can at all comprehend. The stream of earthly things is overflowing its old banks, and spreading out in every direction, in wild, disordered, ungovernable, and overwhelming volume. Old systems and modes of thought and belief, which have stood for ages, are everywhere tottering upon their thrones, and many of them reeling as for their final fall. Symptoms of a mysterious metamorphose meet us on every hand, causing some of earth's most far-sighted men, in church and state, to tremble with amazement and doubt. What these approaching changes are to be is differently given, according to the different points of observation which men occupy. But that changes are certainly coming, all admit.*

I propose, therefore, to enter upon a serious and honest effort to ascertain what light the Scriptures throw upon the momentous problem. Our heavenly Father has given us a "sure word of prophecy," and has been pleased mercifully to reveal therein what his great purposes are, and how things are to be ordered until those purposes are fulfilled; and it is my design to open the book of God, and to go with you to its unerring and inspiriting pages, to ascertain what the Lord hath made known concerning those "things which must shortly come to pass." I do not propose to take the prophet's chair, but to take the place of an humble student of the prophet's words. I am a learner, not a master—a seeker after what has been revealed, and not a revealer of what has hitherto been unknown. My purpose is, to keep close "to the law and the testimony." I will follow no guides but the inspired writers And I ask of you to test carefully all that

* See Note A, page 317.

I may present, beseeching you to reject all that I may by mistake utter at variance with God's word. I may err. I may not always hit upon the exact truth. All I claim of you is, to approach the subject with a prayerful and teachable spirit, ready to hear and weigh testimony without partiality or prejudice, sincerely desirous to learn what God the Spirit saith, and determined, at all hazards, to cleave to all that the blessed Scriptures really teach.

I know that there is in many a strong but morbid distaste for the discussion of these subjects. Some have even gone so far as to set it down to some mental defect for a man to touch the study of prophecy. But I suppose that there are among the men who have devoted their time, talents, and learning to this subject, some with quite as much soundness of mind and justness of taste as any of those who have decided not to open the seals which inexcusable neglect has put upon the prophetic Scriptures. Noah, also, was considered insane for his concern about what was coming upon the earth in his day. Jesus himself, with all his Divine gravity and wisdom, was pronounced a demoniac. And the apostle Paul, in the midst of some of his mightiest and brightest intellections, was branded as beside himself and mad. And who would not rather suffer reproach with such company, than to have that come upon him "which is spoken of in the prophets: Behold, ye despisers, and wonder, and perish: for I work a work in your days, a work which ye shall in no wise believe, though a man declare it unto you!" And those Christians assuredly have reason to blush and be ashamed to whom apology is necessary for an attempt to bring before them the wonderful and glowing prophecies of Scripture concerning things to come "in the latter days." Every thing dear and hopeful in the Christian faith stands inseparably connected with them. They include nearly all the grand motives to faith, obedience, watchfulness, and virtue. God also tells us, that *"All scripture is profitable,* for doctrine, for reproof, for correction, for instruction in righteousness;" that we have "a word of prophecy *whereunto we do well to take heed;*" and that "Blessed is he that readeth, and they that hear the words of this prophecy, and keep the things that are written therein." Where, then, do men get liberty to ignore one-half of the Bible as useless? Who has authorized us to seal and bury in oblivion those grand Apocalypses of futurity which God has given, and in reference to which he says, "If any man shall take away from the words of the book of this prophecy, God shall take away his part out of the book of life, and out of the holy city, and from the things which are written in this book!" Hath "the Lord God of the holy prophets sent his angel to shew unto his servants the things which must shortly be done," and we be under no obligations whatever to seek to find out the meaning of the heavenly communications? Shall he solemnly proclaim "these sayings faithful and true," and him "blessed" that keepeth them, and we call it piety and wisdom to put them aside as loose fables, and repudiate them as unmeaning riddles which can only addle our brains? How could we adopt a course more criminally indifferent, arrogant, and unbelieving? Is not such conduct a placing of ourselves with the scoffers of the last days, who say, "Where is the promise of his coming?" Shame, shame, to the skepticism of many professing Christians.

Let me suppose a case. Suppose that the blessed Savior should now appear in this assembly, and take this stand, and begin to discourse to you about the last times. Would you feel justified in stopping your ears to his words because he struck upon this particular theme? Would you not regard any one who should act thus as under some strange infatuation of the devil, and deserving of severe rebuke? But where is the difference, whether Jesus should thus come in person, or come to us in the written word, every sentence of which he has dictated, inspired, or delivered to us for our learning? And if you would feel bound to give him a reverent hearing in the one case, why not feel equally bound in the case which actually exists? Christ is here with his word to instruct us upon these very subjects; and it would not be worse to stop your ears to his personal voice, than it is to refuse to hear and consider his written truth.

Prophecy, it is true, is a somewhat difficult theme. Peter tells us, that it is "a light that shineth in a dark place." We must not expect everything to be as obvious and plain as in the noonday when all is luminous. Especially in unfulfilled prophecy, there must needs be some obscurity in the particular details of circumstances, "times and seasons." But, there are difficulties to be encountered and wildernesses to be traversed just as great and discouraging in other departments of learning; yet, instead of being deterred by them, men are rather the more stimulated to meet them, and are accustomed so constantly to triumph over them, that we cease to be surprised at the most astonishing strides of human genius. Does the astronomer cease to study and survey the heavens, because, with all his aids, he never can fully take in the tremendous sweep of God's universe, or tell what sort of inhabitants are in the sun, moon, and stars? Does the geologist cease to dig and bore into the bowels of the earth, or give over the study of its rocks and fossils, because he cannot find out all that lies hidden in its unknown centre, or tell how the strata of its crust were formed, or describe the appearance and habits of those monsters whose bones lie entombed under its surface? Does the physician throw aside all further inquiry into the anatomy and physiology of man, because he cannot discover "how the bones are formed in the womb," what life is, and in what part of the body the soul is? Why, then, should the Christian shun the study of the predictions which God has given, because there are some depths and mysteries about them which we cannot fathom? Nay, these very obscurities and difficulties, which deter so many from examining the prophetic word, are not without their wholesome effects. It is a real pleasure to the mind to know that something has been left for it to do. It luxuriates, and has its highest life in the exercise of overcoming obstacles, and bringing up the truth from regions which lie under the surface of ordinary observation. Only furnish to the human faculties the assurance of success, and it is their highest happiness and purest virtue to labor and to wrestle with difficulties. And so the glimmering twilight which hangs about prophecy, is just what we might expect, and what we need. There is light and plain certainty enough to guide, cheer, quicken, and excite; and just darkness enough to check the pride of speculation and the boasts of confidence, and to make us prayerful, humble, and inquiring. The difficulties are not insurmountable. They are not as great as many have agreed to regard them. They are more imaginary than real, and proceed rather from our slothfulness than from the prophecies themselves. People do not understand prophecy, simply because they do not study it; and then they refuse to study it because they do not understand it. There is no part of Scripture richer or more munificent in rewards for the faithful inquirer. It is a garden of flowers—a cabinet of wondrous jewelry. It is a vast and varied landscape, filled with beauty and grandeur, the horizon of which is fringed with the bright dawning glories of eternal day. Here, and here alone, we can see the real scope and magnificence of man's redemption. Here, and here only, we can trace God's providential plans to their ultimate consummation, and learn the real majesty of his counsels of love. At every step there is something to encourage and comfort us under the fatigues and trials of life, something to confirm our faith and to fill us with glorious anticipations. And if the limits of our knowledge can be extended, and the sum of human good augmented, by the study of rocks, and bones, and beasts, and birds, and stars, how can it be unprofitable to bend our attention a little more than we have done to what our Savior has revealed concerning "the signs of his coming, and of the end of the world"?

That the Lord Jesus, the Son of the Virgin Mary, will certainly return again to this earth, is a doctrine written in all the creeds, and sung about by Christians every week. It is an event the sublimest in coming time, the most largely treated in the Scriptures, and the most deeply involving all that relates to the destiny of our world. As Christ is the centre of history, his second coming is the centre of prophecy, which is history written beforehand. I have accordingly fixed upon this final advent of the Lord as the central thought of these investigations, and as the point from which to survey the great scenes of the last times. To attempt to prove to you that the Son of man will really and personally come again to this world, may seem quite superfluous. It is a doctrine which orthodox Christians universally admit. And yet, perhaps, there is not another article of Christian faith so coldly and indefinitely apprehended. Few men embrace it as a reality. Few men lay hold of it as an efficacious truth. People deny it not, but neither do they feel it. They have so much preoccupied their minds with imaginary figurative comings of the Savior, in providence, in his Spirit, in his word, and in his church, that his only real coming has well-nigh become obsolete—a mere dead letter. It no longer comes upon the heart and conscience with its proper awakening and commanding power. We recite it, and sing it; but we do not effectually receive it. It is in our creed, but it cannot be said to be our faith. If we entertain it at all, it is at a great distance off. It cannot therefore be a matter of small importance for us to review our position, and to endeavor to ascertain where we stand in regard to this great doctrine. If we have been unconsciously saying to ourselves, "the Lord delayeth his coming," it is time that we should wake up to the fact, lest that day should come upon us unawares. Christ bids us "Watch; for in such an hour as ye think not, the Son of man cometh." "The day of the Lord so cometh as a thief in the night." "As a snare shall it come on all them that dwell on the face of the whole earth." And amid the tremendous heavings of society in our day, we are the most solemnly admonished to look well to our hearts, and to keep close to the directions of our Lord.

The great original prophecy concerning the second advent, the principal storehouse from which the apostles and first Christians drew their faith and illustrations upon the subject, —is that glorious discourse of the Savior which he gave to Peter, James, John, and Andrew, in answer to the questions propounded in the text. Next to the sermon on the mount, that discourse is the longest and the most momentous of all that has been preserved of the Savior's communications. And yet, there is, perhaps, no part of Scripture that has been so much abused, confused, and obscured by professed interpreters. Though the Bible nowhere so pointedly, directly, literally, and plainly asserts and describes the final advent of the Lord, there is scarcely a commentary in existence which does not so *Jerusalemize*, spiritualize, and allegorize it, as to leave it the most indefinite and unmeaning of all the Savior's teachings. The prevailing impression is, that the twenty-fourth chapter of Matthew is a mixed prophecy, referring primarily to the destruction of Jerusalem by the Romans, and, *perhaps*, by a sort of typical implication, remotely touching upon the scenes of Christ's final personal coming. But what relates to Jewish troubles, and what relates to the transactions of the last times, no commentary in the hands of the people has told. Others, again, apply the whole to the taking of

Jerusalem only, and consider the coming of the Son of man nothing but the coming of the Roman legions into Palestine.

That there are difficulties connected with the exposition of this important portion of Scripture, is admitted; but that they are of a character to prevent us from using it as a basis of doctrine, or from understanding what the Savior in the main meant to teach by it, I am not willing to concede. The simple reading of it, with a few explanatory remarks, is all that is needed to exhibit its meaning with ample clearness for our present purposes.

That the passage, in part at least, was intended to foreshow the fate of Jerusalem, with the signs and accompaniments of the same, is not to be questioned. That the predictions which it contains were not meant to be limited to these particulars, but to include the last times and the period of Christ's personal return to the earth, appears to be equally well founded. And that the Savior does not speak first of the one application only, and then exclusively of the other, in regular historic and chronological order, is also pretty clear, from the difficulty of showing exactly where the point of transition is. The true key to the passage, and which relieves it of most of the troubles which expositors have found with it, I take to be this: that the fate of the ancient Jewish economy and its accompaniments was the commencement of a system of administrations which is at length to involve all nations,—a sort of first-fruits of the end,—the enactment on a limited scale of what is finally and more fully to be enacted on the theatre of the world at large.

It is a fact that history is continually repeating itself, and that the future is perpetually foreshadowed in the scenes and occurrences of the past. There is also a "latitude which is agreeable and familiar to Divine prophecies, being of the nature of their Author, with whom a thousand years are as one day, and therefore they are not fulfilled punctually at once, but have springing germinant accomplishments throughout many ages, though the height or fullness of them may refer to some one age." So in the case before us. The close of the Jewish economy was the earnest of a general closing up of the same sort for all nations. The destruction of Jerusalem, and the attendant particulars, constituted the starting-point; but the meaning of the prophecy goes quite beyond these, and grasps a much ampler scene of fulfilment. Both are embraced in one field of view, whilst the stress and fulness of the predictions reach the last times and the great consummation, and presently settle entirely in them.

The occasion of the discourse is set forth in these words:—

"And Jesus went out and departed from the temple: and his disciples came to him, for to show him the buildings of the temple. And Jesus said unto them, See ye not all these things? Verily, I say unto you, [the days will come in the which] there shall not be left here one stone upon another, that shall not be thrown down."

"And as he sat upon the Mount of Olives, the disciples [Peter, and James, and John, and Andrew] came unto him privately, saying, TELL US, WHEN SHALL THESE THINGS BE? AND WHAT SHALL BE THE SIGN OF THY COMING, AND OF THE END OF THE WORLD, OR AGE?"

I emphasize these last words, because they are the stem-words upon which the whole discourse is framed. Christ had spoken only of the destruction of the temple and the Jewish state. But with this the disciples associated the end of the whole earthly order of things, and the Messiah's entrance upon his glorious and heavenly dominion. Their inquiry, accordingly, had two leading subjects: *first*, the overthrow of the Jewish temple; and, *second*, the coming of Christ in his kingdom at the great consummation. They wished to know two things concerning these subjects; first, *when* these things should come to pass, and second, *what signs* should mark the time and manner of their occurrence. And, as they asked *two questions in one*, the Savior proceeded to answer them in the same double form.

"And Jesus answered and said unto them, Take heed that no man deceive you; for many shall come in my name, saying, I am Christ, and shall deceive many. [And the time draweth near; go ye not, therefore, after them.]"

The indication is here given, in the very first words, that the minds of the inquirers were in a somewhat confused and exposed condition. They expected the setting up of the Messiah's kingdom in connection with the fall of the Jewish temple, and hence were in great danger of being deluded by impostors, and of accepting antichrists and pseudo-christs for Christ himself. One of the punishments of the people of Israel for the rejection of the true Christ, was the relinquishment of them to false saviors and deliverers. In every period of corruption and consequent calamity, this symptom of lying consolations and promises repeats itself. It was so in the period of the captivity. (Jer. xxix. 8, 9, xiv. 13; Ezek. xiii.) It was so in the period of Jerusalem's overthrow, as Josephus has very fully shown. And it is elsewhere abundantly foretold that it shall be still more remarkably so in the end of the present dispensation. Hence the caution, to guard against deceivers and false hopes, which applied not only to the Christians of that time, but applies equally to us.

"And ye shall hear of wars, and rumors of wars: see that ye be not troubled: for all these things must come to pass; *but the end is not yet.* For nation shall rise against nation, and kingdom against kingdom, and there shall be famines, and pestilences, and earthquakes in divers places; [and fearful sights, and great signs shall there be from heaven.] All these are the beginning of sorrows."

How literally and completely all these things were fulfilled in the period of Jerusalem's fall, may be seen in Josephus, and the commentaries upon these verses. But they are equally predictions of what is to mark the period of the end. Indeed, they are here called "*the beginning of sorrows*," as if specifically to make known that their occurrence in the case of Jerusalem's trouble was but the commencement or first-fruits of a fulfilment which is to be still more amply realized by the world at large.

"[But before all these, they shall lay their hands on you, and persecute you.] Then shall they deliver you up [to councils, the synagogues, and into prisons], to be afflicted, and shall kill you. [And ye shall be brought before rulers and kings for my sake, for a testimony against them;] and ye shall be hated of all nations for my name's sake. And then shall many be offended, and shall betray one another. And many false prophets shall arise, and shall deceive many. And because iniquity shall abound, the love of many shall wax cold."

That these things literally came to pass in the times of the apostles themselves, may be seen in Acts iv. 1–3, v. 17, 18, 27, 40, 41, vii. 59, xii. 1–4, xvi. 19–23, xvii. 6, xxvi. 10, 11, xxviii. 30, 31, xx. 29, 30; 2 Tim. i. 15, iv. 10, 14; 2 Peter ii. 1; Jude 4; 1 John iv. 1, ii. 18; 2 John 7. They are also more or less fulfilling continually, preparatory to the still more complete fulfilment under the Antichrist of the last days. (See Dan. vii. 25; 2 Thess. ii. 3–8; Rev. xiii. 15.)

"But he that shall endure unto the end, the same shall be saved. And this gospel of the kingdom shall be preached in all the world for a witness unto all nations; and then shall the end come."

There is a threefold "*end*" spoken of in these words: the *end* of suffering, in the case of the individuals encouraged to endure; the *end* of the Jewish polity, as the first point inquired about; and the *end* of the whole present order of things, as connected with the coming of Christ, concerning which they also wished to be informed. That the gospel was very generally promulged before the fall of Jerusalem, is a fact of which we have very reliable testimony. Eusebius says of the apostolic age, "Under a celestial influence and co-operation, the doctrine of the Savior, like the rays of the sun, quickly *irradiated the whole world.*" And if Eusebius should not be sufficient authority, hear what Paul says on the subject. He died years before Jerusalem was destroyed; and yet he writes the Colossians, (i. 16,) "The word of the truth of the gospel is come unto you, as *it is in all the world.*" "Be not moved away from the hope of *the gospel* which ye have heard, and *which was preached* TO EVERY CREATURE WHICH IS UNDER HEAVEN." (i. 23.) "Have they not heard? yes, verily, their sound went into *all the earth*, and their words unto THE ENDS OF THE WORLD." (Rom. x. 18.) But that was only the type of a publication of the gospel which is now ever more and more going on, and which shall receive a still more marked and miraculous fulfilment as the end approaches and the judgment comes. (See Rev. xiv. 6.)

" [And when ye shall see Jerusalem compassed with armies, then know that the desolation thereof is nigh. Then let them which are in Judea flee to the mountains, and let them which are in the midst of it depart out, and let not them that are in the countries enter thereinto. For these be the days of vengeance, that all things which are written may be fulfilled. But woe unto them that are with child, and to them that give suck in those days; for there shall be great distress in the land, and wrath upon this people. And they shall fall by the edge of the sword, and shall be led away captive into all nations, and Jerusalem shall be trodden down of the Gentiles, until the times of the Gentiles be fulfilled.]"

It is remarkable that both the end of the Jewish economy, and the great consummation, are connected with the coming of foreign powers against Jerusalem, and disaster to the holy city; as also with a flight to the mountains on the part of those who are to escape destruction. (See Zech. xiv. 1–5.) The paragraph from Luke, which I have just given, seems to describe more especially the first, and the following from Matthew seems to describe more especially the second.

"When ye therefore shall see the abomination of desolation, spoken of by Daniel the prophet, stand in the holy place, (whoso readeth let him understand,) then let them which be in Judea flee into the mountains. Let him which is on the housetop not come down to take any thing out of his house: neither let him which is in the field return back to take his clothes. And woe unto them that are with child, and to them that give suck in those days. But pray ye that your flight be not in the winter, neither on the Sabbath day: for then shall be great tribulation, such as was not since the beginning of the world to this time, no, nor ever shall be. And except those days should be shortened, there should no flesh be saved: but, for the elects' sake [whom he hath chosen], those days shall be shortened."

The quotation from Daniel, respecting the desolating abomination, was understood by the Alexandrine Jews as referring to the profanation of the temple by Antiochus Epiphanes, as described in 1 Maccabees i. 43–60. And some have supposed a corresponding profanation under the bloody and sacrilegious zealots at the period of Jerusalem's overthrow. But, as the passage stands in Daniel, it connects with the scenes of the judgment and the end of the world. The Savior does not seem to quote it, either, in any other sense, or with any other application, than that which it has in its original connection. It is therefore altogether safest to understand it as referring above all to the terrible desecrations to be perpetrated by the Antichrist when his own image shall be set up for worship in the place of the services of God; for it is in connection with the setting up of that image that the great tribulation in its proper fulness is to begin. Hence its name, "the abomination of desolation," or, that maketh desolate. As to "the elect," or "chosen," different classes are perhaps meant. There were some, even unbelieving Jews, saved at Jerusalem's destruction; and not a Christian perished. Both these classes were therefore in some sense the elect. And there will be a corresponding election when these predictions come to their ultimate fulfilment in the great tribulation of the last days. Some shall pass through the terrible affliction, and entirely survive it; and others shall be caught up to their Lord in the air at the very commencement of these great woes, and thus entirely escape them, (Luke xxi. 36; Rev. xiv. 1–5,) being the elect of God to be the Bride of Christ. And when these straits and sorrows come,—

"THEN if any man shall say unto you, Lo, here is Christ, or there; believe it not. For there shall arise false Christs, and false prophets, and shall show great signs and wonders, insomuch that (if it were possible) they shall deceive the very elect. [Take ye heed.] Behold, I have told you before. Wherefore, if they shall say unto you, Behold, he is in the desert; go not forth: behold, he is in the secret chambers; believe it not. FOR AS THE LIGHTNING COMETH OUT OF THE EAST, AND SHINETH EVEN UNTO THE WEST: SO SHALL ALSO THE COMING OF THE SON OF MAN BE. FOR WHERESOEVER THE CARCASS [BODY] IS, THERE WILL THE EAGLES BE GATHERED TOGETHER."

Though the Savior may perhaps still have Jerusalem's overthrow somewhat in view, it is plain that the principal stress of this paragraph falls in the last days, and refers above all to what is to transpire in connection with the false pretences and lying wonders of the Antichrist and his minions, (2 Thess. ii. 3–12; Rev. xvi. 13, 14, xix. 20,) from which the people of God shall then be in peculiar peril. The last verses, particularly, do not refer to the Jerusalem troubles, but to Christ's literal and personal return, in contrast with all pretended saviors and usurpers of his place, whether coming as his rivals or in his name, in the days of Jerusalem's distress, or in the last days. Four things are contained in these verses: first, that false Christs and false prophets shall come; second, that the true Christ is also to come; third, that the coming of the true Christ will be after a manner and with demonstrations very different from those of usurpers and deceivers; and fourth, that we need give ourselves no anxiety about making our way into the presence of Christ when he comes, for that we shall as naturally find ourselves with him as eagles are where their prey is. To say that this coming of Christ as the lightning shineth, refers to his providential coming by the Roman armies, would require the invention of a similar fiction to correspond with the coming of the false Christs, and, indeed, divest the entire passage of meaning. The gathering of the eagles might be interpreted of the coming of an army which bore the eagle on its standards; but when we compare it with Luke xvii. 34–37, Isaiah xl. 31, Rev. iv. 7, xii. 14, the reference seems rather to be to Him who "was dead" but is "alive for evermore," and to the gathering of his redeemed people to himself in the clouds at his literal coming, according to 1 Thess. iv. 16, 17. So Theophylact, Euthymius, and many of the ancients took the passage; and Luther paraphrases it as if Christ had said, "As the eagles are gathered where the carcass is, so shall my people be gathered where I am."

It is also very noticeable how the subject of Jerusalem's overthrow, with which the discourse begins, gradually fades into the greater and more absorbing theme of Christ's coming and the end of the world. Especially from this on, it is quite lost in the intenser sharpness of the back part of the picture. It is of the judgment period that we now read,—

"Immediately after the tribulation of those days shall the sun be darkened, and the moon shall not give her light, and the stars shall fall from heaven;"—or, as Luke has it,—"[There shall be signs in the sun, and in the moon, and in the stars, and upon earth distress of nations with perplexity, the sea and the waves thereof roaring, men's hearts failing them for fear, and for looking after those things which are coming on the earth;] and the powers of the heavens shall be shaken."

It is no longer Jerusalem that we see in these graphic words. What is here spoken concerns all the families of man, and relates to the judgment-times in immediate connection with the glorious revelation of the returning Lord.

"*And* THEN SHALL APPEAR THE SIGN OF THE SON OF MAN IN HEAVEN: *and* THEN *shall all the tribes of the earth mourn, and they* SHALL SEE THE SON OF MAN COMING IN THE CLOUDS OF HEAVEN, WITH POWER AND GREAT GLORY."

What a shame, that learned men should spend their pains and talents in attempts to tie down this language to the destruction of Jerusalem by the Roman armies!

I take it as an axiom,—a settled verity which demonstrates itself,—that two events which are specifically described as successive—the one as coming *after* the other—cannot be the same. But, if this axiom had always been observed in the interpretation of this twenty-fourth chapter of Matthew, the students of the Scriptures might have saved themselves much inconsistency and confusion, and many a misapprehension of God's word. If we ask most of our popular commentators what is meant by "the tribulation of those days," described in the twenty-ninth and preceding verses, the answer given is, that it means the calamities and sufferings of the Jews, induced by the siege and overthrow of their city and state. And if we ask them, again, what is meant by the mourning of the tribes of the earth "*after* the tribulation of those days," the answer is about the same,—the calamities and sufferings of the tribes of Israel in connection with the fall of their city and state! If we inquire of them what is meant by the coming of the Son of man as the lightning in the clouds of heaven, with some twinges of uncertainty they nearly all finally agree upon the reply that it means the flashing judgments which were brought upon the rebellious people of Israel by the coming of the Roman armies against Jerusalem! The coming of which the Savior speaks was to be "out of the east" towards the west, and the coming of the Roman armies was out of the west and north towards the east and south; but the reply is, no matter for that; we are not to expect all the particular circumstances to hold! The coming of which the Savior speaks is specifically said to be "*after*" the tribulation induced by the invasion of Palestine by the Romans, as well as "*after*" that great unparalleled tribulation of which the Jewish troubles were the commencement and first-fruits; but no matter for that, we are told; as though effect could go before its cause, and as if priority or succession were nothing in the interpretation of a book such as the word of God! I question, indeed, whether the annals of learning can furnish a parallel to the absurdities which characterize the great mass of our popular disquisitions upon this portion of the inspired record. No wonder that the doctrine of Christ's personal return to our world has lost so much of its weight, certainty, and rightful importance in the minds and hearts of the Church, when its great foundation-text is thus sacrificed to a false and supercilious erudition.

One of the strangest things in the world is the manner in which some people read the Bible. It would almost seem as if they turned it upside-down, and read it backwards. "Eyes have they, but they see not." They praise it, and hold it in holy regard, and insist that everybody ought to have it; yet they look into it only as some recondite volume, which is a good text-book for preachers, but which is quite beyond the reach of their understanding. They adore it more for the unknown mysteries which they attribute to it, than from their personal appreciation of what their own eyes have beheld upon its pages. Many seem to view it as a sublime riddle-book, full of mystic poetry and unsearchable wisdom, rather than as a plain piece of information and advice given by a Father to his inexperienced and exposed children. And many who sit down to write commentaries upon it seem to be continually haunted with the idea that there is something recondite in every word, or that the real mind of the Spirit is not to be found in the plain import of the letter, but in some abstruse or mystic analogy which it is their business to dig after. I hold that the Bible is a book for everybody, in which God speaks for the purpose of being understood by everybody; that its language is conformed to the ordinary uses of speech; and that it is to be interpreted in the same common-sense way in which we would interpret the will of a deceased parent, or ascertain the meaning of a letter on business. It was not written to tax our ingenuity, or to test men's skill at learned exposition. Its design is to instruct, and in the most familiar way to express to men the mind and will of God. When Christ speaks of "the Son of man," he means the Son of man, and not the Roman armies. When he speaks of his "coming in the clouds of heaven," he means his coming in the clouds of heaven, and not the sailing of war-ships on the Mediterranean, or the march of soldiers over the fields of earth. When he says "*after*" the Jewish tribulations are ended, he means "*after*" those tribulations, and not before they began, or while they were yet in their incipiency. And when he says that all the tribes of the earth "*shall see the Son of man coming in the clouds of heaven with power and great glory*," expositors might as well attempt to demonstrate to me that day is night, or that white is black, as to attempt to make me believe that he means the march of an army of boorish heathen soldiers. Christ knew what he wished to say, and how to say what he meant; and I feel myself bound to understand him to mean just what he says. And what he here predicts respecting his coming in the clouds at the close of the tribulation no more refers to the coming of the Roman armies into Palestine than to the flight of Mahomet, or the next eclipse of the moon. He is describing the scenes of the judgment-period, and nothing else.

"And then he shall send his angels with a great sound of a trumpet, and they shall gather together his elect from the four winds, from one end of heaven to the other."

The elect, in this paragraph, I understand to be the same as the multitude which no man can number, described in Rev. vii. 9–17; the harvest of the earth described in Rev. xiv. 14–16.

"Now learn a parable of the fig-tree; when his branch is yet tender, and putteth forth leaves, ye know that summer is nigh: so likewise ye, when ye shall see all these things, know that it [the kingdom of God] is near, even at the doors. Verily I say unto you, THIS GENERATION SHALL NOT PASS, TILL ALL THESE THINGS BE FULFILLED."

Some have groundlessly supposed that this last remark requires the application of this whole prophecy to the times of the apostles, and consequently to Jerusalem's destruction. They take the word "*generation*" as meaning those who live in the same thirty years; thirty years being reckoned to a generation. But if this be the sense, then how shall we reconcile the prophecy with facts? Jerusalem was not destroyed until about forty years after the Savior uttered these words. And if he meant that a generation of thirty or even thirty-three years should not pass away till all these things should be fulfilled, his prediction cannot be verified. It is gratuitous, however, to insist upon that sense of the word generation. The original is γενεα—*a race, a class, a family of people;* as where it is said, "the children of this world are wiser in *their generation* than the children of light." The plain meaning of the Savior is, that the family of Abraham, the Israelitish people, should not pass out of existence, as a distinct class or race, before all these predictions should be verified. That the word will bear this sense must be admitted. Many of our most valuable critics and interpreters so understand it. The surroundings also seem to demand that we should here take it as meaning the Jewish people as a race. They are this fig tree which is to have a long winter of leafless barrenness, but which is to bud again when the summer-time of the kingdom approaches. And in this sense above all have the Savior's words thus far been most exactly and marvellously fulfilled, showing the truth of what follows,—

"Heaven and earth shall pass away, but my words shall not pass away."*

It is therefore as plain as language can make it, that this prophecy of the Savior runs through all time, from its delivery down to the end of the world that now is. Men may try to believe that he spoke only of the fall of Jerusalem and the Jewish constitution, but they deceive themselves; they distort, depreciate, and wrest the clear meaning of his words; and they bring endless confusion into one of the plainest, most literal, and most straightforward prophecies in God's word. The disciples asked him very important questions, and he answered them all that they inquired about. They wished to know when and how Jerusalem and the temple should be brought to desolation, and he told them when and how these things should be, tracing down the consequences upon the Jewish race to his final coming and kingdom. They wished to know what should be the signs and form of his final coming in glory and triumph, and he explained to them the whole matter with a fullness of detail which constitutes the great fund from which his followers ever afterward drew their information upon the subject. They wished to know when, and

* See Note B, page 323.

amid what circumstances, the end should come; and he answered them on that point too, as far as it was for them to know the facts; teaching them to look and watch for his coming in the clouds of heaven with power and great glory.

In this remarkable discourse, we are accordingly taught, and have the doctrine certified to us in a very peculiar and unmistakable manner, that OUR LORD JESUS CHRIST IS TO COME AGAIN INTO OUR WORLD. It is not only stated in various forms of language, but it is made the subject of a whole chapter of circumstantial particulars which connect with it, and is the central point in a vast field of predictions, many of which have already passed into historical facts. And one of the prominent reasons, perhaps, why the destruction of Jerusalem and the final consummation were embraced in the same prophetic view, was, that in looking back, and seeing how literally and fully the first part of it has already been fulfilled, we might be confidently assured that what remains to be fulfilled is just as certain as an unalterable fact of history. As part has already become history, so the remaining part shall also become. And thus, with a degree of certainty which excludes all possibility of mistake, the Savior has assured his church that HE WILL COME AGAIN to this disordered world. It is no mere fancy,—no poet's dream,—no mere fabulous device,—but immutable reality, as sure as the desolations which have been upon Mount Zion for these eighteen hundred years. Though men may think but little of it, and put it far away from them, it is one of the infallible verities of Almighty God. As the angels at his ascension said, so we may be satisfied, that "THIS SAME JESUS WHICH IS TAKEN UP INTO HEAVEN SHALL SO COME, IN LIKE MANNER AS YE HAVE SEEN HIM GO INTO HEAVEN." Henceforward, therefore, could his followers say, "THE LORD HIMSELF SHALL DESCEND FROM HEAVEN,"—"Our conversation is *in heaven, from whence also we look for the Savior, the Lord*

Jesus Christ." "*Behold,* HE COMETH WITH CLOUDS; *and every eye shall* SEE *him, and they also which pierced him.*" Henceforward could the disciples go forth, "looking for that blessed hope, even *the glorious appearing* of the great God our Savior Jesus Christ," and beseech men "by *the coming of the Lord Jesus Christ* and our gathering together unto him," and exhort their fellow-believers "to *wait for his Son from heaven,*" and proclaim the glad "rest, *when the Lord Jesus shall be revealed from heaven with his mighty angels,*" and encourage the fond hopes of the persecuted and desponding with the assurance that "*when he shall appear* we shall be like him, *for we shall* SEE HIM AS HE IS."

No, no; "We have not followed cunningly-devised fables, when we made known unto you *the power and coming of our Lord Jesus Christ.*" As certainly as the words of Jesus are true, as surely as the pillars of the Eternal throne are steadfast, Jesus himself, in glorified humanity, shall return again to this very world of ours. All the prophets have predicted it. All the pious, from the foundation of the world, have in some shape expected it. Jesus declared it, both before his death and after his resurrection. And the very last words in the holy Testament which he left us are, "He that testifieth these things saith, SURELY I COME QUICKLY. AMEN." Even apart from what the Scriptures contain upon the subject, with the account of his humiliation before us, reason itself might almost anticipate his return. We cannot suppose that such a glorious personage will always remain under the reproach and stigma of the cross. Natural justice seems to demand that he should come again, in the majesty that appertains to him, in order to sweep away the infamy which wicked men in every age have sought to heap upon him. As He whose right it is to reign, will reign; and as He whose "is the kingdom, the power, and the glory," will not forever leave his enemies to usurp his place; so we are driven to expect him yet to come, "glorious in his apparel, and triumphing in the greatness of his strength."

It must, therefore, be a matter of absorbing interest to every man, *how*, and *when*, and with what antecedents and results, the Son of man shall come. "*This*," says Charles Beecher, "*is the question now in the providence of God first claiming the solemn attention of the churches.*" What can be more momentous than the closing up of this whole present scene of things—the passing away of the world's present fashion and administration? What revolutions in government—what subversions of present social arrangements—what destruction of empires, thrones, principalities, and powers—and what shakings of the heavens and of the earth—are involved! What new and strange experiences shall pass over men when once the glorious King and Judge of quick and dead shall blaze forth his startling presence in the clouds, and summon the earth to answer for all its deeds! And shall we not seek to understand the revelation of God concerning these amazing scenes? Shall we not awake from our dreams of peace, and open our eyes to the startling things that are crowding thick around us, and our ears to what God has said about them? Have we not been allegorizing, and spiritualizing, and *Jerusalemizing* the prophetic word, until we hardly know where we are, or whether there is any thing more to be expected or not? Let us, then, rouse up upon this momentous subject. We have mighty interests staked upon it. There is more said about it in the Scriptures than upon any other single theme. And yet Christians now hardly cast a thought forward to the mighty occurrences which it involves. We say the prayer, "*Thy kingdom come!*" but so cold and lifeless is the petition on our lips, that we scarcely know what we are asking. Jesus says, "*Behold, I come quickly;*" but we fold our arms and answer, *No, no;* it will yet be a thousand years or more. He says "*Watch;*" but we say, There's no danger that he will come in our day. The midnight cry is being raised in every region and city of Christendom, "*Behold, the Bridegroom cometh; go ye out to meet him!*" but multitudes deride, and say, It is the raving of enthusiasts; it is the cry of fanaticism; and they heed it not. Alas, whose heart now thrills to the startling announcement, "*The Lord cometh*"? Who looks, and sighs, and prays now, for the return of the Savior to our world? Who is waiting for, as he is hastening unto, the coming of the day of God? Who is keeping himself in readiness for its solemn revelations?

My brethren, if the Son of man should come this week, this month, or this year, would he find faith on the earth? Would not the church itself be taken by surprise? Would not such an event now come upon the overwhelming majority of Christ's professed followers unawares? And yet, what guarantee have we that the chariot-wheels of the coming King are not already rumbling over the distant worlds? Has he not said, "In such an hour as ye think not, the Son of man cometh"? "the day of the Lord so cometh as a thief in the night"? and "as *a snare* shall it come upon all them that dwell on the face of the whole earth"? Who can say that we are not liable to have the great scenes of the judgment precipitated upon us at any moment? And shall we not be concerned to have our minds familiarized with what may any day occur, and which *must* occur sooner or later? Is there not something inconceivably dreadful in the thought of having that day come upon us at the very time we are saying, "My Lord delayeth his coming"? Would it not be better to be a little beforehand with our anticipations, and to bear the taunts that may be heaped upon us for our concern, than to accommodate ourselves to the wisdom and sobriety of this erring world, and be finally taken by surprise and perhaps lose our eternal all? Jesus says, that "the Lord of that servant" who shall be found faithless, sleeping, or scoffing, "shall cut him asunder, and appoint him his portion with hypocrites, amid weeping and gnashing of teeth." Of what avail will his worldly wisdom and his fruitless profession be to him then? What good will all his knowledge then do him? Better that we had never known the way of righteousness,—better that we had never been born,—than amid all our high privileges thus to come short of the approbation of the coming Judge.

And if judgment first begin at us, and many professing Christians lose the honors of the kingdom, "what shall the end be of them that obey not the gospel of God? If the righteous scarcely be saved, where shall the ungodly and the sinner appear?" With what surprise and discomfiture shall the day of Christ's coming overtake them!

My dear friends, these are solemn thoughts. It will not do to trifle with them. Momentous issues are involved. And we know not how soon the irrevocable decision shall be made. Let us, then, enter upon the study of this mighty subject with serious and prayerful hearts, anxious to know what God has been pleased to reveal, and earnestly set upon preparing to meet our God. And especially let us carefully lay to heart those impressive words of the Lord Jesus himself:—

"Of that day and hour knoweth no man, no, not the angels of heaven, but my Father only. [*Luke:* Therefore take heed to yourselves, lest at any time your hearts be overcharged with surfeiting and drunkenness, and cares of this life, and so that day come upon you unawares. For as a snare shall it come on all them that dwell on the face of the whole earth. Watch ye, therefore, and pray always, that ye may be accounted worthy to escape all these things that shall come to pass, and to stand before the Son of man:] [*Mark:* for ye know not when the time is.] But as the days of Noe were, so shall also the coming of the Son of man be. For as in the days that were before the flood, they were eating and drinking, marrying and giving in marriage, until the day that Noe entered into the ark, and KNEW NOT until the flood came, and took them all away: so shall also the coming of the Son of man be. Then shall two be in the field; the one shall be taken, and the other left. Two women shall be grinding at the mill; the one shall be taken, and the other left. WATCH, THEREFORE, FOR YE KNOW NOT WHAT HOUR YOUR LORD DOTH COME. But know this, that if the good man of the house had known in what watch the thief would come, he would have watched, and would not have suffered his house to be broken up. Therefore, BE YE ALSO READY: FOR IN SUCH AN HOUR AS YE THINK NOT, THE SON OF MAN COMETH. Who, then, is a faithful and wise servant, whom his Lord hath made ruler over his household, to give them meat in due season? Blessed is that servant, whom his lord, when he cometh, shall find so doing. Verily I say unto you, That he shall make him ruler of all his goods."

EVEN SO COME, LORD JESUS.

Yet once again thy sign shall be upon the heavens displayed,
And earth and its inhabitants be terribly afraid;
For not in weakness clad thou com'st, our woes, our sins to bear,
But girt with all thy Father's might, his vengeance to declare.

The terrors of that awful day, oh, who can understand?
Or who abide when thou in wrath shalt lift thy holy hand?
The earth shall quake, the sea shall roar, the sun in heaven grow pale;
But thou hast sworn, and wilt not change, thy faithful shall not fail.

Then grant us, Savior, so to pass our time in trembling here,
That when upon the clouds of heaven thy glory shall appear,
Uplifting high our joyful heads, in triumph we may rise,
And enter, with thine angel train, thy palace in the skies.

G. W. DOANE.

SECOND DISCOURSE.

HOW CHRIST'S COMING IS RELATED TO OTHER EVENTS—THE MILLENNIUM—WRONG VIEWS CORRECTED—THE SECOND ADVENT PREMILLENNIAL—THE POINT ARGUED.

LUKE xviii. 7, 8: *And shall not God avenge his own elect, which cry day and night unto him, though he bear long with them? I tell you that he will avenge them speedily. Nevertheless, when the Son of man cometh, shall he find faith on the earth.*

WITH these words to indicate the general sphere of my remarks, I now resume the subject which I introduced to your attention a week ago. I have tried to impress upon you that it is our duty, privilege, and a source of comforting edification, to study God's gràcious revelations concerning "the last times." Some have supposed that prophecy is mainly designed for the conviction of those who live when, or after, it is fulfilled, and that the investigation of it does not belong to those who live before that time. If it were even so, I would still insist that we ought to study these things, for the evident reason that we are at this very day in the midst of the incipient scenes of their fulfillment. And, apart from this startling fact, I hold that these revelations are for *us*, and for our learning, as well as for future generations. When once they have been fulfilled, redemption will be complete, doubts and unbelief will have no more place, the saints will be with their King in their rest, and no evidences from fulfilled prophecy will be needed to convince people of the existence and providence of God, or of the truth and faithfulness of his word. All this will be plain enough then in each one's heart without processes of reasoning upon the past to establish it. And if these impressive predictions are not intended for *our* "reproof, correction, and instruction," I am at a loss to know for whom or for what they are intended.

I have also endeavored to set forth the reality and certainty of the Savior's return to this world, by showing you the true and solid Scriptural basis upon which this glorious article of our faith reposes. Some say Christ comes at death, or when he manifests his secret providence by open judgment. Some say Christ comes when he manifests his grace in the conversion of souls, the revival of languid churches, and the victories of his truth. But it is very evident that neither of these is that coming of the Son of man of which the Scriptures say so much, and which is so distinctly embodied in all the creeds. Indeed, I very much doubt whether the sacred writers ever speak of these providential and spiritual manifestations as Christ's *coming*. I know of but two things to which the Bible applies this language: the one is the incarnation, when Christ was made man and born of the Virgin Mary; the other is his return from heaven in the last times to judge the world in righteousness. The New Testament tells of a first coming, and a second coming, and no more: the one was accomplished when "he came unto his own, and his own received him not;" and the other will be, when "he shall appear THE SECOND TIME without sin unto salvation." I find in all the Bible but these two personal advents of the Savior spoken of, the one of which occurred eighteen hundred and fifty years ago, and the other is to take place at the end of the present dispensation. And all the passages respecting the coming of the Son of man which have not been fulfilled in his first coming apply directly and only to his next coming at the judgment.

I proceed now to inquire at what stage in the progress of

the Messiah's earthly kingdom his second advent is to be expected. Is it to occur after his kingdom has run its entire mundane course, or does the ultimate consummation of his kingdom in this world depend upon his final coming? In other words, are we to look for the Savior's future personal advent *before* or *after* the millennium?

The word *millennium* is compounded from the Latin, and literally means *a thousand years*. Its theological import is not very clearly defined. Some use it to denote one class of ideas, others to denote another class, just as they adopt this or that system for interpreting the twentieth chapter of the Revelation. For the most part, however, it is used and understood to denote a future period of universal righteousness, liberty, and peace, during which Satan is to be bound, and Christianity be triumphant throughout the world. The question which I propose to consider is, whether Christ is to come personally to introduce and establish this glorious condition of things, or whether this triumph of all that is good is to be realized before he comes?

According to the popular belief, the final advent of the Savior is a far-distant event,—a mysterious and undefined something which is to transpire at some remote point in the revolutions of ages, long after the progress of Christian knowledge, the developments of science, and the march of intellect, have made the world universally pious, just, and happy. On the platform and in the pulpit, we hear men talking rapturously and hopefully of some golden, blessed age, which is to be ushered in under the operation of existing instrumentalities. By the preaching of the gospel, the work of Christian education, and the progress of reform, they expect the world to be converted, Antichrist destroyed, Satan cast out, and all the relations, occupations, and pursuits of men purified, ennobled, and regulated with justice. This is the hope which poets sing about, and orators preach about, as the great incentive to missionary effort, and the reward of self-denial, liberality, and prayer in the good work of propagating the gospel. And when once this glorious era has come, and continued through an indefinite period of duration, then, somewhere down among uncounted ages, the idea is, that Christ will appear in the heavens, join these terrestrial glories with glories celestial, and close the scene of grandeur amid songs and triumphs that die from us into the fathomless profound of eternity.

Now, all this may be very poetical, and answer very well to touch off platform speeches. It certainly is very flattering to human pride, and very pleasant for the fancy to dwell upon. But *is it the truth of God?* We are not inquiring now for what is captivating, and beautiful, and touching to the natural heart, or even to the Christian's imaginings. We want to know what Jehovah saith—what the Spirit of the Lord hath revealed concerning these things. And I am free to confess to you that my study of the Scriptures has taught me to expect a very different course and order of events. My Bible tells me of no millennium which existing processes are to bring about. Neither does it tell me of a millennium which is to *precede* the Savior's second advent. The only millennium I read of in the holy book is that which is to be *introduced* by the glory and power of Christ's coming, and the chief excellence of which is, his personal presence and reign with his saints upon the earth. It is not the reign of art, science, human culture, or free governments, for which the Bible teaches me to look; nor yet for the universal triumph of Christianity or the church as we now have it; nor yet for the reign of justice, holiness, or any mere abstract principle; but for *the personal reign of Jesus my Lord*, when "all people, nations, and languages, shall serve him," and shall "come up unto Jerusalem to worship the King, the Lord of hosts." And that this millennium may come, and this glorious reign be established, the Savior himself must *first come*, as he promised, and as the angels declared in the day that he was taken up into heaven.

The advent of Christ, then, for which I look, and for which I would have all men look, is not a *post*-millennial, but a *pre*-millennial coming; not a coming long hence, after an era of liberty and perfection such as orators and poets have dreamed of, but a coming which is to usher in and begin the promised age of gold, and introduce to the world the fruits of a consummated redemption. *It is Christ's coming that is to make the millennium*, and not the millennium which is to prepare the world for Christ's coming. Upon this point my mind is clear, and my faith too firm to be shaken. There is hardly another subject in the Bible upon which there is such a mass of varied divine testimony as upon this. And if you will be at the pains to search out and test the observations which I am about to submit, I feel satisfied that you will be obliged, either to repudiate the Scriptures, or to make up your minds to believe as I do.

1. I have examined the Scriptures with diligence and care, and have had this subject before me as a matter of study for more than a half-score of years; and to this moment I have not found one passage, and I do not believe that you can find one, which, by any legitimate construction, asserts a period of rest, triumph, and millennial glory *anterior to* the great personal coming of our blessed Lord. If there be such a passage, I will be obliged to any one who will point it out to me.

2. I find the Scriptures invariably representing the church of Christ as afflicted, persecuted, depressed, wronged, and reproached, until relieved by the coming and kingdom of the Savior to judge the world in righteousness. Daniel, in his vision, beheld the saints warred with, and prevailed against, *until the Ancient of days came*, and judgment was given: (vii. 21, 22.) The text distinctly identifies the avenging of

God's elect with the coming of the Son of man, and shows that his people shall be a suffering people until that day of avengement comes. And other passages to the same effect are numerous and strong. If we look at the laws and conditions of discipleship, we read, "ALL that will live godly in Christ Jesus shall suffer persecution." "If any man will come after me, let him deny himself, and take up his cross." "The servant is not greater than his lord. If they have persecuted me, they will persecute you." "In the world ye shall have tribulation." "We must through great tribulation enter into the kingdom of God." If we look at the accounts of the relative strength of the church, we always find it consisting of a depressed minority. "Strait is the gate and narrow is the way that leadeth unto life, and *few* there be that find it." "Fear not, *little flock*." "Many are called, but *few* are chosen." If we look at the promises of the gospel, we find them nearly all framed to a condition of suffering, temptation, and affliction on the part of those to whom they are addressed. "He that shall *endure* unto the end, the same shall be saved." "To him that *overcometh* will I give to eat of the hidden manna." "Think it not strange, concerning the fiery trial which is to try you, as though some strange thing happened unto you; but rejoice, inasmuch as ye are partakers of Christ's sufferings." "Rejoice, and be exceeding glad; for great is your reward in heaven; for *so* persecuted they the prophets which were before you." Are we to be rewarded for our toils and labors in the gospel? It will only be "when the Son of man shall come in the glory of his Father." Are we to inherit the kingdom? It is only "when the Son of man shall come in his glory, and all the holy angels with him." Is the church waiting in hope? It is "for the coming of our Lord Jesus Christ." Did Paul look for "a crown of righteousness?" It was only to be given him "at that day." It is only when "he shall appear a second time," that he will appear "unto salvation." Every thing of glad hope which the gospel gives us points to the final advent. "The whole creation groaneth and travaileth together in pain until now: and even we ourselves groan within ourselves, waiting for (the resurrection) the redemption of our body." There is no promise of rest, no Sabbath-keeping, for the dwellers upon earth, until our Joshua comes and gives us the glorious land. Every thing remains disjointed, sickly, afflicted, until then. And amid all these groans, reproaches, and troubles which roll and dash upon the church until they break against the throne of the returning Redeemer, we look in vain for that sunny continent of universal peace and jubilee of which men speak.

3. The Holy Scriptures, so far from promising to us a millennium of universal righteousness before Christ comes, invariably represent the world as *abounding*, if not *ever growing*, in wickedness, even up to the very moment of his coming. Look at the text. Though in the form of a question, it yet contains the strongest kind of asseveration, that the coming Judge shall find the world awfully apostate. "*When the Son of man cometh, shall he find faith on the earth?*" "That day shall not come except there be a falling away first." Many servants shall say, "My Lord delayeth his coming; and shall begin to smite their fellow-servants, and to eat and drink with the drunken; and the Lord shall come in a day when they look not for him, and cut them asunder, and appoint them their portion with hypocrites." "*Evil men and seducers shall wax worse and worse, deceiving and being deceived.*" "The Spirit speaketh expressly, that in the latter times some shall depart from the faith, giving heed to seducing spirits and doctrines of devils; speaking lies in hypocrisy, having their conscience seared with a hot iron." "This know also, that in the last days perilous times shall come. For men shall be lovers of their own selves, covetous, boasters, proud, blas-

phemers, disobedient to parents, unthankful, unholy, without natural affection, truce-breakers, false accusers, incontinent, fierce, despisers of those that are good, traitors, heady, high-minded, lovers of pleasures more than lovers of God; having a form of godliness, but denying the power thereof." "Remember ye the words which were spoken before of the apostles of our Lord Jesus Christ; how that they told you there should be mockers in the last time, who should walk after their own ungodly lusts. These be they who separate themselves, sensual, having not the Spirit." "Knowing this first, that there shall come in the last days scoffers, walking after their own lusts, and saying, Where is the promise of his coming? for since the fathers fell asleep, all things continue as they were from the beginning of the creation." "The mystery of iniquity doth already work: only he who now letteth will let, until he be taken out of the way; and then shall that Wicked be revealed, whom the Lord will consume with the spirit of his mouth, and shall destroy with the brightness of *his coming:* even him, whose coming is after the working of Satan, with all power, and signs, and lying wonders, and with all deceivableness of unrighteousness in them that perish; because they received not the love of the truth, that they might be saved. And for this cause God shall send them strong delusion, that they should believe a lie, that they all might be damned who believed not the truth, but had pleasure in unrighteousness." These are dark and awful descriptions, and they stretch down from apostolic times to Christ's own personal coming. In the Revelation also, under three distinct streams of prediction,—seals, trumpets, and vials,—we have a series of successive and ever-augmenting defections, revolts, apostasies, and usurpations, which are ended only with the tremendous judgments of the day of the Savior's personal appearing. Where, then, is that glowing period of universal righteousness, liberty and peace, which some are looking for previous to our Saviour's final coming?

4. The Savior's prophetic discourse, which is the fountain of all these prophecies concerning the last times and the second advent, allows no place for a period of millennial glory anterior to the personal arrival of the Son of man. That discourse, running through the twenty-fourth and fifth chapters of Matthew, gives us a luminous sketch, by the hand of the great Master of Prophets, of the leading aspects of the divine administrations from the destruction of Jerusalem to the consummation of all things. The Savior there describes most vividly and plainly all the great signs which are to precede, attend, and follow his coming in the clouds of heaven with great power and glory. And if it is true that his second advent is to be preceded by a thousand years of universal righteousness and peace, it is impossible to believe that he would have entirely omitted all allusion to it in a prophecy so comprehensive, and yet so minute in its details. Such an intervening millennium would have been a "sign" so notable that it could not have been passed by. And yet we search in vain through all that wonderful discourse for the smallest hint concerning it. Nay, he specifically describes a great and unprecedented tribulation, beginning with the siege and fall of Jerusalem, and stretching on "until the times of the Gentiles be fulfilled," and tells us that "IMMEDIATELY AFTER THE TRIBULATION OF THOSE DAYS shall the sun be darkened, and the moon shall not give her light, and the stars shall fall from heaven, and the powers of the heavens shall be shaken; and *then shall appear the sign of the Son of man in heaven;* and then shall all the tribes of the earth mourn, *and they shall see the Son of man coming.*" There can be no millennium of peace whilst "*tribulation*" lasts; but in this account "tribulation" only ceases at the point when the signs of Christ's immediate advent appear. The only space between the

tribulation and the terrifying signs of the judgment is described by the adverb ευθεως — *instantly, immediately, quickly*, without the intervention of any other event. To make that adverb include a millennium would be to contradict its whole meaning, and to adopt a principle of interpretation which would reduce all language to uncertainty. But we must do it to have the millennium before Christ comes. Nay more; as if forever to cut up by the roots all hope of a period of universal righteousness and peace prior to the judgment, the Savior adds, "*As the days of Noe were, so shall also the coming of the Son of man be.*" What were the characteristics that marked the last periods of the antediluvian world? Was the flood preceded by a millennium of righteousness and peace, or a millennium of universal apostasy, sensuality, wickedness and debasement? Let the word of God answer. "And God saw that the wickedness of man was great in the earth, and that every imagination of the thoughts of his heart was only evil continually. And it repented the Lord that he had made man on the earth, and it grieved him at his heart. The earth also was corrupt before God; and the earth was filled with violence. And God looked upon the earth, and behold, it was corrupt: for all flesh had corrupted his way upon the earth." Such is the awful portrait which inspiration gives of those early times; and He who cannot lie says, "So SHALL IT BE ALSO IN THE DAYS OF THE SON OF MAN!"

5. The Scriptures explicitly teach us that the world shall remain in a mixed condition, in which the good and the bad shall grow together and mature side by side until the day of judgment. Upon this point, the parable of the wheat and the tares is a perpetual demonstration. Much as men have controverted over that parable, no man can separate from its teachings this clear and strong prediction, that the wicked shall live and flourish as long as this present dispensation endures. Jesus himself has so explained and applied it. "*The field is the*

world." In that same field are both wheat and tares, the children of the Kingdom and the children of the wicked one. "*Both grow together until the harvest.*" "*The harvest is the end of the world.*" And, until that end comes, no man or angel can uproot or remove those tares. There they are, growing and bearing fruit; and there they will continue to grow and flourish until Christ comes with his reapers to wind up this present economy. There is no triumphing of the wheat over the tares; no monopolizing of the field by the righteous; no trampling down, subjugation, conversion or eradication of the hosts of the wicked, until then. What could more directly, positively and unequivocally prove, that there is to be no millennium of universal righteousness, liberty and peace, before Christ comes? In the millennium, the glory of the Lord is to "fill all the earth." "All people, nations and languages" are then to serve Jesus, "and all dominions shall serve and obey him." The knowledge of the Lord is to cover the earth as the waters cover the sea. "They shall not teach every man his neighbor, and every man his brother, saying, Know the Lord: for *all* shall know him from the least to the greatest." "Every knee shall bow, and every tongue confess, that Jesus Christ is Lord, to the glory of God the Father." And yet this selfsame holy record teaches us that the devil will have his children here, and that they shall grow and flourish until the day of Christ's coming to judge the world. Is not the demonstration complete, that the millennium does not commence until after Christ comes?

6. It is self-evident, that there can be no millennium of universal righteousness, liberty and peace, whilst the great antichristian powers, and the confederations of usurpation and wickedness, continue to defile and oppress the world with their foul presence and work. How can there be a millennium whilst "the mystery of iniquity" lives and operates "after the working of Satan, with all power, and signs, and lying won-

ders, and with all deceivableness of unrighteousness"? How can there be a millennium whilst the domineering, blasphemous and persecuting power in Daniel, which speaks "great words against the Most High," and wears out the people of God, continues making war with the saints and prevailing against them? How can there be a millennium whilst corrupt and oppressive governments still usurp the prerogatives of God, and array themselves against liberty and truth? How can there be a millennium whilst nations gather themselves to battle, and "the kings of the earth, and the great men, and the rich men, and the chief captains, and the mighty men," continue to make themselves obnoxious to "the wrath of the Lamb"? The thing is impossible. The very idea is preposterous. And yet I will prove to you that the Scriptures explicitly teach that these antichristian and usurping powers will live on till Christ comes, and that they shall only be destroyed when he shall judge the world.

Look at what is said of the duration and end of "the Man of sin," in the Second Epistle to the Thessalonians. The apostle tells us that it had already begun to work in his day. The paganism of the Roman government for a while stood in its way. But the Spirit said, that when this hindrance should be removed, "then shall that Wicked be revealed, whom the Lord shall consume with the spirit of his mouth, and shall *destroy*"—WHEN and HOW? By the gradual spread of evangelical religion? By the present processes of bringing men to the knowledge of the truth? No, no, no; "WITH THE BRIGHTNESS OF HIS COMING"—(*τῇ επίφανεία της παρουσίας αυτου*;) literally, BY THE APPEARING OF HIS OWN PRESENCE. Here, then, is positive proof from the word of God, that this Man of sin is to continue in existence until Christ's second coming, and is to be consumed and utterly destroyed only by the personal advent and appearance of the Son of God himself. It is useless to tell us that the "*coming*" here spoken of denotes a mere figurative or providential interposition of the Savior. The whole passage is sternly prosaic and free from metaphors, and the words employed are never elsewhere used figuratively in the New Testament. *Επίφανεία* is used in five other places, and is in each one universally understood as denoting *a real appearing,*—a personal and visible manifestation. *Παρουσία* is used in twenty-three other places in the Scriptures, and in every one of them denotes a literal *presence*—a *personal advent.* Both these words as strongly and directly describe a real, visible, and personal coming as any in the Greek language; and when used with reference to a person, they cannot mean any thing but a real presence and advent of that person. "The *coming* of Stephanus, and Fortunatus, and Achaicus," means the personal advent and presence of these men. "The *coming* of Titus" is the personal advent and presence of Titus. And so "*Christ's own coming*" is the advent and presence of Christ himself, in his own proper person. And if the words "*appearance of his presence,*" or "*the appearing of his own advent,*" do not mean the visible, literal and personal revelation or manifestation of himself, it is impossible to employ terms that can express it, and human language is incapable of being interpreted on any fixed and definite principles. Wherever else the word *επίφανεία* occurs in the New Testament, all men take it as conveying the unmistakable idea of *a real appearing.* Wherever else the word *παρουσία* occurs in the New Testament, there is no disputing the fact that it means *arrival, presence, advent;* and when applied to persons, *a personal arrival, presence,* or *advent.* Either of these words is held sufficient in other passages to prove a real and personal appearing and presence. And when both are united, as in the case before us, how is it possible that they should mean any thing less than the literal, real and personal arrival and presence of Jesus, with reference to whom they are used? The Man of sin, then, is to live on until Christ himself shall come, and shall be destroyed only by the appearing of the Savior's own personal advent. And so the most thorough and able interpreters have uniformly taught. Luther says, "*They* (the Man of sin and his rabble) *shall be preserved until the coming of Christ.* Let us therefore pray the God and Father of our Lord Jesus Christ, that he would hasten *that day of the glorious appearing of his Son,* which he has promised, in which he has declared that this Wicked one, this Man of sin and son of perdition, shall be destroyed." Archbishop Usher says, "The glorious appearing of the Son of God in the latter day shall be the overthrow of Antichrist, whence we gather that *before the last day he shall not be utterly consumed.*" Robert Fleming remarks, "Though the Lord will gradually consume or waste this great adversary by the spirit of his mouth, yet *he will not sooner abolish him than by the appearing of his own presence,* as I choose to render and understand the words, Thes. ii. 2–8." And Melancthon, Milton, Wesley, Watts, Chalmers, Bonar, Elliott, and other men of piety and learning, have expressed themselves to the same effect; all showing that there can be no millennium of peace and righteousness before Christ comes.

Look next at what is said concerning the destiny of the blasphemous and persecuting power denoted by "the little horn" in the visions of Daniel. Whether that presumptuous power is the same as Paul's "Man of sin," matters not in this connection. Its existence is certainly incompatible with the idea of universal righteousness, liberty and peace; and the epoch of its end is the epoch of the second advent and the judgment. The prophet distinctly states concerning the eleventh horn, "even of that horn that had eyes, and a mouth that spake very great (presumptuous) things, whose look was more stout than his fellows; I beheld, and the same horn made war with the saints, and prevailed against them, UNTIL THE ANCIENT OF DAYS CAME, AND JUDGMENT WAS GIVEN TO THE SAINTS OF THE MOST HIGH, *when the time came that the saints should possess the kingdom.*" This language is very plain; but to render it still more unmistakable, an angel interprets the vision to the prophet, and further says of this little horn, "He shall speak great words against the Most High, and shall wear out the saints of the Most High, and shall presume to alter appointed seasons and the law, and they shall be given into his hand until a time, times, and the division of time. *But* THE JUDGMENT SHALL SIT, WHEN *his dominion shall be taken away, to be wasted and destroyed.*" (See Wintle's translation.) Let the impious and persecuting power of the little horn, then, be what it may, the word of God says that it will live on till the Ancient of days comes, and the judgment sits, and the suffering saints enter into their kingdom.

Look also at the great ten-horned beast upon which this presumptuous little horn grew. Daniel says it was "dreadful and terrible, and strong exceedingly; and it had great iron teeth: it devoured and brake in pieces, and trampled upon the remains with its feet." The interpreting angel says that this beast is the fourth great kingdom upon the earth, which "shall devour the whole earth, and shall tread it down, and break it in pieces." Surely there can be no universal reign of righteousness, liberty and peace, while such a power remains and triumphs. And yet its end is particularly given as contemporaneous with the destruction of the little horn, and the second advent of the Son of God. The time when its thrones were cast down, as beheld in the vision, is the time when "*the Ancient of days did sit*, whose garment was white as snow, and the hair of his head like the pure wool, his throne the fiery flame, and his wheels the ardent fire. A fiery stream issued and trailed forth before him, thousand thousands ministered unto him, and ten thousand times ten thousand assisted before him; THE JUDMENT SAT, *and the books were opened.*" It was only then that "*the beast was slain, and his body de-*

stroyed, and given to the burning flame." And that this judgment and destruction is to take place in the period of the personal coming of the Savior, is also explicitly stated. "I saw," says Daniel, "and behold, *one like the Son of man came with the clouds of heaven,* and there was given him dominion, and glory, and a kingdom, that all people, nations and languages, should serve him: his dominion is an everlasting dominion, which shall not pass away, and his kingdom that which shall not be destroyed." The prophet here evidently refers back to a previous vision, and identifies this kingdom of the descended Lord with that referred to in the second chapter, where it is said, that "*in the days of these kings,*" the very powers symbolized by the ten-horned beast, "shall the God of heaven set up a kingdom which shall never be destroyed: and the kingdom shall not be left to other people, but IT SHALL BREAK IN PIECES AND CONSUME ALL THESE KINGDOMS, AND IT SHALL STAND FOREVER." Let any man look at these divine revelations with an unbiased mind, and he cannot escape the fact that the personal advent of Christ, the day of judgment, and the ultimate destruction of these great antichristian powers, are all connected together in one and the same great epoch of time, leaving no room for the millennium anterior to the Savior's coming.

If we look to the eleventh chapter of the Revelation, we again find the setting up of the reign of Christ over the nations, the great day of God's wrath, the time of the judging of the dead to give reward to prophets and saints, and *the destruction of them that destroy or corrupt the earth,* all connected together in the same period. The one is made synchronous with the other. And all belong to the epoch of the sounding of the last trumpet, when the whole mystery of God is to be finished, as he hath declared to his servants the prophets.

So also in the nineteenth chapter of Revelation. The ten

horned wild beast, which ascended out of the pit, and whose doom is to go into perdition, and "the false prophet that wrought miracles before him," both, with their deceived and infatuated followers, are still found alive and vigorous, and arrayed against the Lamb and his adherents, up to the very time when the heavens open, and the mighty Son of God comes forth to tread the winepress of the fierceness and wrath of Almighty God.

Let men dream, then, as they may, the revelations of God are certain and sure. Antichrist shall live till Christ comes. Sin, tyranny and usurpation shall continue as long as the present dispensation. And persecution and iniquity shall not cease until the Son of man cometh to judge the world in righteousness. IT FOLLOWS, THEN, THAT CHRIST WILL COME BEFORE THE MILLENNIUM.

7. But let me direct your attention to yet another Scriptural consideration bearing upon this subject. What I have said is enough; but the point is so momentous as to warrant the fullest accumulation of testimonies. It involves many matters of transcendent interest to the children of men, and we should spare no patience in probing it to its very depths. We can gain nothing by the indulgence of false hopes. It is the truth alone that shall not fail or disappoint us. Vast numbers of people believe that we shall have the millennium before Christ comes. In this I consider them mistaken. It accordingly becomes me to make a full exhibit of the grounds upon which I reject their dreams. I have shown, from the Scriptures, that the church is to remain in a depressed condition until Christ comes; that the world is to abound and grow in wickedness for the same length of time; that the Savior's great prophecy leaves no room for the millennium prior to the second advent; that the world is to contain a mixed population of good and bad until the great harvest of the last day; and that Antichrist and the great oppressing and

persecuting powers are to be destroyed only by the personal intervention of Christ when he shall come the second time. And I will yet prove to you, by the same divine authorities, that the general conversion of the world to obedience to the Son of God, which the idea of the millennium implies, is to be effected only when Christ comes.

There is, perhaps, no passage that is more frequently quoted in proof of the final and universal triumph of Christianity than the second chapter of Isaiah. God there says, "It shall come to pass in the last days that the mountain of the Lord's house shall be established in the top of the mountains, and be exalted above the hills; and all nations shall flow unto it. And many people shall go and say, Come ye, let us go up to the mountain of the Lord, to the house of the God of Jacob, and he will teach us of his ways, and we will walk in his paths. In that day a man shall cast his idols of silver, and his idols of gold, which they made each one for himself to worship, to the moles and to the bats. The Lord alone shall be exalted in that day; and the idols he shall utterly abolish." This is a grand and glowing promise; and, as surely as God lives, it will be fulfilled. But *when* shall these things come to pass? A thousand years before Christ comes? Not at all. It is to be when "*he shall judge among the nations;*" when men shall "enter into the rock and hide in the dust *for fear of the Lord, and for the glory of his majesty*"—in "THE DAY OF THE LORD;" when "the loftiness of man shall be bowed down, and the haughtiness of men shall be made low;" "WHEN HE ARISETH TO SHAKE TERRIBLY THE EARTH." How strange that men should throw out of this prophecy these plain and distinct allusions to the time, which unquestionably identify these glorious achievements with the day of judgment and the Savior's own personal manifestation! Why should men seek the caves and clefts of the mountains to hide from the Lord and the glory of his majesty, if he is not then to be personally revealed? What is "*the day of the Lord*" but the day of Christ's appearing for judgment? What is his rising to shake terribly the earth, and to bring the nations to account, but the coming of the great King with his rewards with him? And yet it is distinctly stated, that it is only THEN that the Lord's house is to be supremely exalted, and the nations learn war no more.

People also look and pray for the millennium as a time when Christ shall reign the King of nations, as he now reigns the King of saints. But the kingdoms of this world are to be the kingdoms of Jesus only when he shall really come. Daniel says, "I saw in the night visions, and behold, one like *the Son of man came with the clouds of heaven*, and came to the Ancient of days, and they brought him near before him; *and there was given him dominion, and glory, and a kingdom, that all people, nations, and languages should serve him.*" Here is a picture of the Savior's investiture with the universal sovereignty of the earth; but it is specifically connected with *his coming in the clouds of heaven.* John also "heard great voices in heaven, saying, The kingdoms of this world are become the kingdoms of our Lord, even of Christ; and he shall reign forever and ever." But it was only *after the last trump had sounded*, and the time of wrath, resurrection and judgment had come: (Rev. xi. 15–18.) He also saw thrones, and the martyrs and saints seated on them, Satan bound from deceiving the nations, and Jesus reigning with his holy ones; but it was only after the opening of the heavens, and the personal advent of Him who had on his vesture and on his thigh a name written, *King of kings, and Lord of lords:* (Rev. xix. 20.)

In the twenty-second Psalm we read that the son of David "shall have dominion from sea to sea, and from the river unto the ends of the earth. They that dwell in the wilderness shall bow before him. Yea, all kings shall fall down before him;

all nations shall serve him." But it is only when "*He shall judge the people with righteousness;*" when "HE SHALL COME DOWN."

In the second Psalm Jehovah says to his only-begotten, "I shall give thee the heathen for thine inheritance, and the uttermost parts of the earth for thy possession." But the time is also declared to be when "*I have set my King upon my holy hill of Zion.*"

In the sixty-sixth chapter of Isaiah, God says, "It shall come, that I will gather all nations and tongues; and they shall come and see my glory." But it is only when "THE LORD WILL COME WITH FIRE, *and with his chariots like a whirlwind, to render his anger with fury, and his rebukes with flames of fire.*" Zechariah also says, that "The Lord shall be King over all the earth." But it is only after "*the Lord shall* GO FORTH, *and his feet shall stand upon the mount of Olives, which is before Jerusalem on the east,*"—in the great "DAY OF THE LORD."

It is also given as one of the glories of the millennium, and essential to it, that the Jewish race is then to be entirely converted to the Messiah, and made a holy people. Paul says, "*All Israel shall be saved.*" The angel that announced the Savior's first advent said of him, "He shall be great, and shall be called the Son of the Highest, *and the Lord shall give unto him the throne of his father David.* AND HE SHALL REIGN OVER THE HOUSE OF JACOB FOREVER." And yet it is explicitly stated that this shall be only when he shall finally appear again in our world. Jesus says, "Jerusalem shall be trodden down of the Gentiles, *until* the times of the Gentiles be fulfilled; and *then* shall they *see the Son of man coming in a cloud with power and great glory.*" "They shall be mine, saith the Lord, IN THAT DAY *when I make up my jewels:*" (Mal. iii. 17.) When the Lord shall arise and have mercy on Zion, says the Psalmist, when the set time to favor her is come, "*when the Lord shall build up Zion,* HE SHALL APPEAR IN HIS GLORY." We read in Micah, "I will surely assemble all of thee, O Jacob; I will surely gather the remnant of Israel: I will put them together as the sheep of Bozrah, as the flock in the midst of their fold." But when this is to be done, we read, also, that "*their King shall pass before them, even* THE LORD *on the head of them.*" Jerusalem shall "arise and shine." "The Gentiles shall come to her light, and kings to the brightness of her rising." But it is only when "*the Redeemer* SHALL COME," *and* "*the Lord shall arise upon her, and his glory shall be* SEEN:" (Isa. lix. 60.) The Lord says, "I will pour upon the house of David, and upon the inhabitants of Jerusalem, the spirit of grace and supplication;" but, at that same time, "THEY SHALL LOOK UPON HIM WHOM THEY HAVE PIERCED:" (Zech. xii. 11.)

My brethren, is not this enough? Where is the foundation on which men expect a millennium of universal righteousness, liberty and peace, before the personal return of our ascended Lord? What do the most noted of scholars and saints tell you upon the subject? Hear our own Luther, whose name has been "ploughed into the hearts of millions, and on the brightest place in the roll of the illustrious dead." "Some say," says he, "that before the latter days, the whole world shall become Christians. THIS IS A FALSEHOOD FORGED BY SATAN, *that he might darken sound doctrine. Beware, therefore, of this delusion.*" So also thought the great Melancthon. "The true church," says he, "will always suffer persecution from the wicked to the end of time, and in the church itself the good and the evil will continue blended together." He expected Antichrist to live till the advent and resurrection. The intrepid Knox, the champion of the Scottish Reformation, says of this world's universal reform, "*It never was, nor yet shall be,* TILL THAT RIGHTEOUS KING

AND JUDGE APPEAR *for the restoration of all things.*" The masterly Confession of Augsburg, the foundation-symbol of Protestantism, and the acknowledged creed of the largest number of the greatest theologians in all the world, "CONDEMNS *those Jewish notions that,* PRIOR TO THE RESURRECTION OF THE DEAD, *the pious will engross the government of the world, and the wicked be everywhere exterminated.*" The idea of a millennium of universal righteousness, and of the triumph of the saints, previous to the second advent, is sternly denied a place in that glorious monument to the truth. The noble confessors of the Reformation refused to have any fellowship with it. They condemn it. They stigmatize it as a Jewish fable.*

The author of that great hymn, "*The Paradise Lost,*" the master as well of sacred learning as of song, says,—

> Truth shall retire
> Bestuck with slanderous darts, *and works of faith*
> *Rarely be found;* SO SHALL THE WORLD GO ON,
> To good malignant, to bad men benign,
> Under her own weight *groaning, till the day*
> *Appear,* of reparation to the just,
> And vengeance to the wicked, *at return*
> *Of Him—thy Savior and thy Lord.*

Thomas Hall says of the millennium, "*It cannot be before the day of judgment, for these reasons:—*

"The last days will be perilous days. *Wickedness will the most abound towards the end of the world.*

"The church of Christ on earth to the end of the world, is a mixt society, consisting of tares and wheat, good and bad, a Gog and Magog to molest the saints to the end.

"*It is a tenet contrary to the judgment of all the church of Christ.*

"It makes the ruin of Antichrist to be a thousand years or more before the day of judgment, when *the Scripture joins them together.*

---

* See Notes C and D, pp. 326, 327.

"It makes the church triumphant when Christ comes, contrary to the tenor of the Scripture."

Matthew Henry says, "As long as the world stands, there will still be in it such a mixture as we now see. We long to see all wheat and no tares in God's field; but *it will not be till the time of ingathering, till the winnowing-day comes:* both must grow together until the harvest." "Without doubt," says Cotton Mather, "the kingdoms of this world will not become the kingdoms of God and of his Christ, before the preordained time of the dead, in which the reward shall be given to the servants of God." "*They who expect the rest promised for the church of God to be found anywhere but in the new earth, or any happy times for the church in a world that hath death and sin in it,*—THESE DO ERR, *not knowing the Scriptures, nor the kingdom of God.*" "Christ's church, while in this world," says Whitefield, "will be a bush burning with fiery trials and afflictions of various kinds."

But I have not time to quote one-half of the testimonies I have at hand. This, however, I will say, that I have not found a respectable or acknowledged creed in all Christendom, from the beginning until now, that teaches the doctrine of a millennium before Christ's coming. I have not found one single passage in all the Bible that sustains the doctrine of a millennium before Christ's coming. But, on the other hand, I have found a long and unbroken line of witnesses from the days of the apostles until now, who testify with one voice, that the hope of a millennium of universal righteousness, liberty and peace before Christ comes, is a falsehood and a dream. I have found many eminent divines, who have blest the church and the world with their piety and wisdom, eagerly looking for the Savior's advent as the only thing that is to lift the church out of its present depression and gloom. And beyond and above all, I have found the word of God everywhere pointing to the same great and glorious event as the only hope of the pious, and as the great link which alone can connect us with or bring us into the joys and jubilations of the millennial era. Arrange it as you will, you shall not be able to put off the Savior's advent until after the millennium. Theorize and speculate as you please, when the Lord cometh he will find the world as now, full of vice, unbelief, sensuality and guilt. All society shall be chequered, varied, mixed and disordered as now, so that "one shall be taken, and the other left." We may impose upon ourselves, but God is not mocked. We may prefer our vague dreams, and set them up against his positive revelations; but his truth abideth. "He hath magnified his word above all his name." He "is not slack concerning his promise, as some men count slackness; but the day of the Lord cometh." It is not far off, at the end of thousands of years hence. It is near. We are "hasting unto it." Many years ago already it was said, by men who spake by inspiration of God, "The coming of the Lord *draweth nigh.*" "The end of all things *is at hand.*" And Jesus commands all, "Watch, *for ye know not what hour the Son of man cometh.*" All through the New Testament the coming of the Lord is spoken of as an event that may occur at any day. From this alone, I know that we have no right to expect a millennium first. It is useless to tell me that it is only a providential, spiritual, figurative coming that is to occur before the millennium. Providentially, and spiritually, Christ is already here. Wherever two or three are gathered together in his name, there he is. He is now and ever at work in his providence, controlling, arranging, overruling, moving every thing; and his Spirit is given to every man to profit withal. Figuratively, he comes every day. Every meal we take, every breath we draw, every new pulsation of our life, he brings to us, as it were, by his own hand. And if his coming before the millennium includes no higher, no more real coming than these things amount to, then I know not upon what ground Christians can hope that he ever will return in person to our world. The Bible has no terms expressive of a literal and real coming, but those which describe his premillennial coming. When we read of the coming of other persons, we never think of allegory or figure. We take the language for what it means. But when we read, in the same connections, of *Christ's coming—the coming of the Lord —the appearing of the Savior's presence*—theologians must rack their brains to find out some other meaning for the words; and that just to obscure that great and animating hope of the church, that "the Lord is at hand," and shall "*surely come quickly.*"

Oh, my brethren, let us beware how we torture and explain away the sacred words which God in mercy has given us for our guidance! Let us beware how we charge the Holy Ghost with saying what he does not mean. That servant who "says in his heart, My Lord delayeth his coming," the Savior calls an "*evil servant.*"

How is it, then, with you? Are you looking for, as you are approaching, the day of God? Have you made your peace with God? Have you your lamps trimmed, and burning, and well supplied with the oil of the grace of God? Have you committed yourselves fully into the only Savior's hands? Is he your portion, and the fixed hope of your souls? Do you believe that it is but "a little while, and he that shall come, will come, and will not tarry"? Or are you saying "Peace and safety" whilst unreconciled to God, or a Christian only in theory and in name? There still is hope. The doors of salvation still stand open to you. But, alas, how soon may the startling summons come to call you to your last account!

Awake, then, O careless one, and call upon your God, if so be that He will think upon you, that you perish not. There is no remedy and no hope but this. "I beseech you, therefore, brethren, by the mercies of God, that you present your bodies a living sacrifice, holy and acceptable to God, which is your reasonable service. And be not conformed to this world; but be ye transformed by the renewing of your mind, that ye may prove what is that good and acceptable and perfect will of God."

ANOTHER ADMONITION.

Awake! again the gospel trump is blown:—
From year to year it swells with louder tone;
From year to year the signs of wrath
Are gathering round the Judge's path;
Strange words fulfilled, and mighty works achieved,
And truth in all the world both hated and believed.

Even so the world is thronging round to gaze
On the dread vision of the latter days,
Constrained to own thee, but in heart
Prepared to take Barabbas' part:
"Hosanna" now, to-morrow "Crucify,"
The changeful burden still of their rude, lawless cry.

Thus bad and good their several warnings give
Of His approach, whom few may see and live;
Faith's ear, with awful, still delight,
Counts them like minute-bells at night,
Keeping the heart awake till dawn of morn,
While to her funeral pile this aged world is borne.

But what are Heaven's alarms to hearts that cower
In wilful slumber, deepening every hour,
That draw their curtains closer round
The nearer swells the trumpet's sound?
Lord, ere our trembling lamps sink down and die,
Touch us with chastening hand, and make us feel thee nigh.

JOHN KEBLE.

THIRD DISCOURSE.

THE GLORIOUS RESTITUTION — BELIEVED IN AND TAUGHT BY THE HEATHEN AND JEWS—THIS WORLD NOT TO BE DEPOPULATED OR ANNIHILATED—WHAT IS MEANT BY "THE END OF THE WORLD"—THE LAST CONFLAGRATION—THE WHOLE TERRESTRIAL SYSTEM OF THINGS TO BE DELIVERED FROM THE CURSE OF SIN.

ACTS iii. 20, 21: *And he shall send Jesus Christ which before was preached unto you: whom the heaven must receive, until the times of restitution of all things, which God hath spoken by the mouth of all his holy prophets, since the world began.*

THIS world is a disjointed and dilapidated fabric. The convulsions of sin have reduced it to a sad predicament. When God made it, it beamed with good, and was radiant with glory. Then man was holy, and every thing was peace. Pure happiness and harmony reigned universal. There was no sickness, no pain, no griefs, no fears, no death. There was nothing foul in humanity, and nothing grating or discordant in surrounding nature. Heaven shone benignantly on earth, and earth smiled gratefully on heaven. Man was in sweet companionship with angels, and wore upon his unwrinkled brow the crown of undisputed lordship over all this lower world. It is not so now. A dark eclipse has come over this mundane sphere. What was once bright in the smiles of its Maker has been blackened with the smokes of the pit. The garden which was fitted up as the abode of immortality has become a place of thorns, corruption and graves. Man disobeyed, and his disobedience has brought in all sorts of disorder, suffering and death. The soul rebelled against God, and, as the result, the flesh has revolted against the spirit, and the whole external creation has been thrown into resentful confusion. Cold, storms, earthquakes, volcanoes, barren fields, pestilential airs, smiting sunshine, tearing briars, and noxious things, combine in the terrific accusation against man, and utter the bitter manifesto of protestation against his unholy deeds. What was created to minister to our joy has become a disorderly servant, as if indignant to obey a convict sovereign. Aliens from God now by very nature, it would seem as if all creation around us viewed us with suspicion and abhorrence, and stirred in every part to shake us off, and groaned to rid itself of our tormenting presence. All the elements seem to have been jarred into discordance with each other, and inspired with a strange antipathy to us. Like Cain in his wanderings, we must now walk this fitful earth in continual fear lest we should find our death in every thing we meet. Plague is in the food we eat, the water we drink, and the air we breathe. Death comes in at our windows, and creeps through all the crevices of our dwellings. And however long or vigorously we may maintain the fight, the end of each one is to fall at last and to rot in the sepulchre.

Such is man, and the system with which he is connected. We contemplate the spectacle with sadness. We can find much that is lovely, but it is loveliness marred with sore distress. We see much that is venerable and majestic, but it is in connection with signs of some deep mysterious ailment. Goethe says, "When I stand all alone at night in open nature, I feel as though it were a spirit, and begged redemption of me. Often have I had the sensation as if nature, in wailing sadness, entreated something of me, so that not to understand what she longed for cut through my very heart." "Even in the things of the world of bodies which surrounds us," says Schubert, "there is an element of life, a yearning of what is bound, which, like that Memnon statue, unconsciously makes symphony when the ray touches it from above." And as we behold afflicted nature oppressed, blighted, disjointed, and sending up her deep-toned *miserere*, we ask, Is there no remedy—no relief? Is there not some deferred deliverance yet to come? Is there not some hope—some ray of promise to shine upon the gloomy wreck? We know that there is redemption provided for the spirit; is there none for the body? And if there is redemption for the body, is there none for the general system of which the body forms a part? Shall the sinner be visited with salvation, and that which suffers only for the sinner's sake be left without hope of deliverance? It cannot be. God, whose mercies are over all his works, in his own good time will bring relief.

The hope of some future general restitution of earthly things has been entertained and taught in all ages of the world. We meet with it in all the records of antiquity, both Gentile and Jewish. The sibylline oracles are full of it. They tell of the coming of one who shall yet fill the earth with blessing, raise the sleeping dead, restore all things, subdue all enemies, rebuild the city beloved of God, and introduce a time of glory when the East and the West shall celebrate the honor of God, and no more evils shall come. They point to "an age to come," and a "new birth of nature," and link the glorious Kingdom they predict with an exalted personage "from the heavenly heights," who is to "reduce all mankind to a single empire." Plato says, "In the end, lest the world should be plunged into an eternal abyss of confusion, God, the author of the primitive order, will appear again, and resume the reins of empire; then he will change, embellish, and restore the whole frame of nature, and put an end to decay of age, sickness and death." Plutarch gives it as part of the faith of the ancient Persians, that "there will come a time, appointed by fate, when Ahriman (the god of evil) shall be entirely destroyed and extirpated, the earth change its form and become plain and even, and happy men have one and the same life, language, and government." According to Strabo, the ancient gymnosophists had a similar tradition, and believed in a time when "the ancient plenty shall be restored." Virgil describes the renovation both of the physical and moral world. The Chinese philosophers entertained a belief in the present corruption and the future renewal of the entire world. (See Hort's Sermons.) It is also said that the Karens in Tavoy, in Asia, have a tradition "that God once dwelt among them, and that he has departed to the West, whence he is to return, and assuredly reappear;" and that "when God comes, the dead trees will bloom again; the tigers and serpents become tame; no more distinction exist between rich and poor; and universal peace bless the world." Dr. Wolffe relates that he heard a dervish of Hindostan express the belief that "the world will become so good, that the lamb and the wolf shall feed together; and there shall be general peace and fear of God upon earth; and there shall be no more controversy about religion, no more hatred, and all shall know God truly." Origen against Celsus says that the heathen authors did believe and teach the ultimate renovation of the world. According to Burnet, the Scythians, the Celts, the Chaldeans, the Indian philosophers, all say that the earth is to undergo a purgation and be renewed. And nearly all the heathen authors sang or wrote of some *great year* when all things should again return to beauty, order, and blessedness. The same ideas of future renewal were also entertained by the Jews. They looked for a grand millennial sabbath, in which the world should rest from all its tribulations, and holiness and peace be the portion of all its inhabitants. Philo gives it as their belief, that the earth shall be purified, and appear new again, even as it was when it first was made.

These, my brethren, are significant facts. What has been so universally believed, and so deeply ploughed into the minds and woven with the hopes of the most enlightened teachers of mankind, dare not be rashly discarded as a groundless fable. There must be some solid foundation for it somewhere. As Mede remarks upon another subject, so here, "all this smoke of tradition could hardly arise but from some fire of truth." And when we consider that many of the traditions and prophetic utterances of the heathen world are but the echoes and floating relics of God's own primitive revelations, we may safely refer this wide-spread notion of the earth's ultimate restoration and renewal to the same divine source. One thing is certain, that the Holy Scriptures do speak of a "time of restitution of all things," and assure us that God hath declared the same "by the mouth of all his holy prophets since the world began." Christ himself refers to a glorious "regeneration" which is yet to pass upon our world. Paul tells us of a "redemption" for which "the whole creation groaneth and travaileth together in pain," when "the creature itself shall be delivered from the bondage of corruption." And the Old Testament and the New point us to "new heavens and a new earth," which are to be formed by the purgation and change of "the heavens and the earth which are now."

This terrestrial system, then, is not an utter wreck—not a hopeless ruin. It shall yet be restored. God shall send Jesus Christ, even that same Jesus which the apostles preached, and under his wonderful administrations, Satan, with all his children and confederates, shall be cast out, and the sons of God shall shout over the complete redemption of a world the creation of which excited high songs of joy. Some have the erroneous notion, that the coming of Christ is to be attended, or speedily followed, by the entire destruction and annihilation of the earth. Some appear to believe verily that every thing in God's material universe is eventually to pass away, and space again become a blank such as they suppose it was before creation began. It is singular what a deep antipathy some evince towards all associations of materialism with our immortal destiny. How fond some have shown themselves of disrobing physical nature, and reducing her to smouldering ruins, as if she, and not man, were the offender! Indeed, we have all heard so much about

"The wreck of matter, and the crush of worlds,"

that we unconsciously set it down among the articles of our creed, not considering that there is not a word of truth in it. It has been so often repeated, that

"The great globe itself,
Yea, all that it inherits, shall dissolve,
And, like the baseless fabric of a vision,
Leave not a rack behind!"

that we are inclined even to contend that it must be so. A certain modern poem, among many foolish things, also has the following:—

"Behold now all yon worlds!
The space each fills shall be its successor,—
'Tis earth shall lead destruction; she shall end.
The stars shall wonder why she comes no more
On her accustomed orbit, and the sun
Miss one of his eleven of light; the moon,
An orphan orb, shall seek for earth for aye
Through time's untrodden depths and find her not!
HER GRAVE IS DUG!
And, one by one, shall all yon wandering worlds
Cease; and the sun, centre and sire of light,
Be left in burning solitude. The stars
. . . . shall pass!
The world shall perish as a worm
Upon destruction's path! THE UNIVERSE
EVANISH like a ghost before the sun,
Yea, like a doubt before the truth of God!"

Now, this may be fine poetry, and portray a sweep of fancy and power of diction fitting a better use; but it is nothing but sublime nonsense. There is nothing of the kind to which any known laws of nature can lead; and there is nothing of the kind predicted in the word of God. Suppose that Adam, instead of sinning, had gone on peopling the world with holy generations, as Jehovah commanded him; would not this earth have continued to be the happy home of the race, beautiful and "very good" forever? What other opinion will the Scriptures permit us to entertain? Yet Christ is "the second Adam," come down into this world for the expressed purpose to arrest the current of things which set in with the fall of the first: his whole mission and work looking to the restoration to the race exactly what the first Adam lost. And if the obedience of the first Adam would have exempted the earth from all trouble, danger and destruction, we may rest assured that the glorious redemption of the second Adam will not leave it in a condition less hopeful, secure, or blessed.

But the Scriptures have not left us to argue this point upon mere general principles. They have spoken respecting the duration of the fabric of nature, including this earth, in a manner which should put the question forever at rest in the minds of all believers. Hear what the Psalmist says:—"Let the *sun*, and the *moon*, and *all the stars* of light, praise the Lord: for he commanded, and they were created. HE HATH ALSO ESTABLISHED THEM FOREVER AND EVER." The same inspired singer, in another place, makes these material orbs of creation as permanent as the very promises and immutable oaths of Deity. He singles them out as the perfect emblems of the infallibility of God's covenant of mercy. "Once have I sworn," saith the Almighty, "that I will not lie unto David. His seed shall *endure forever*, and his throne *as the sun* before me. It shall be established *forever as the moon*." "One generation passeth away," says Solomon, "and another generation cometh; BUT THE EARTH ABIDETH FOREVER." "God laid the foundations of *the earth* that it should *not be removed forever.*" "God himself that formed the earth, and made it, he hath *established it;* he created it not in vain, he formed it *to be inhabited.*" "The righteous shall inherit the land, *and dwell therein forever.*" Daniel, in his vision of the last things, *after* the descent of the Son of man in the clouds of heaven, saw "the kingdom, and dominion, and greatness of the kingdom," not in some other world, but "*under the whole heaven,*" which is nowhere but upon this very earth, "given to the people of the saints of the Most High, whose kingdom is *an everlasting kingdom.*" And if these holy and divinely-inspired men knew any thing about the subject, and words have any meaning in them, I do not see that there is much ground for the apprehension that this orb, or any other, is likely to fall into oblivion.

Neither does the language of the New Testament on this subject differ from what is said about it in the Old. Jesus says, "*Blessed are the meek, for* THEY SHALL INHERIT THE EARTH." But where is the blessedness of inheriting the earth, if the earth is to be totally destroyed? This passage, as I take it, points directly to the fact, that the saints are to have this world as their final delightful home, when once the curse of sin has been rooted out of it. As things now are, it is not "the meek," but the proud, aspiring, ambitious and rapacious, who succeed to most of this world's possessions. And if the earth is not to continue, or is not to be the future home of immortality, I am at a loss to find any meaning in this saying of the Savior. According to Paul, (Rom. iv. 13,) the promise to Abraham, and to all his spiritual seed, is that they shall be "*heirs of the world.*" But is it not a poor sort of heirship which offers an inheritance that is to be eternally annihilated? Peter gives it as the promise of God, and the glad hope of the saints, that the earth, notwithstanding the fires that are to pass over it, is yet to be the home of righteousness, and hence of course also the possession of the righteous. But this cannot be if the earth is to pass away. According to John, the song of the ransomed spirits now in paradise awaiting the completion of God's mysterious plans, next to its ascriptions of praise to the Lamb that was slain, takes as one of its loftiest and sweetest strains, "WE SHALL REIGN WITH HIM ON THE EARTH!" What does that mean, if it does not contemplate the earth as enduring beyond the scenes of judgment, and furnishing the theatre for the sublimest joys and honors of our immortality? And as John looked down the pathway of futurity, beyond the day of judgment, he "saw a new heaven and a new earth," and "the new Jerusalem descending" upon it; and "heard a great voice out of heaven, saying, Behold, the tabernacle of God is with men, and he will dwell with them and be their God. And he shall wipe away all tears from their eyes; and there shall be no more death, neither sorrow nor crying, neither shall there be any more pain: for the former things are passed away."

Now, what is there in all this that looks like "the wreck of matter," "the crush of worlds," or the everlasting disappearance of "the great globe itself!" No, no; creation is not to be destroyed. The vast and splendid mechanism of the worlds is not to be broken up, and thrown aside, and consigned to oblivion. None of these great products of creative power and wisdom shall ever come to naught, or be forgotten. The footsteps of the Son of God upon this earth have consecrated it, and made it too sacred ever to be blotted from the page of being. And when I think that God hath condescended to be manifest in material flesh, and, in the person of Jesus, did actually unite himself with the dust of earth, and *wore it on him*, my contempt for materiality vanishes at once, and it seems to me like sacrilege to entertain the idea of this world's annihilation. Shall the clay which constituted the body of the blessed Christ pass over into the devil's hands, or go down to everlasting nothingness? Shall the soil that was saturated with the precious blood of his unspotted heart be consigned to irrecoverable ruin? Shall the theatre of his great labors, agonies, death and triumphs, disappear, "and leave not a rack behind" to mark the orb on which his mighty deeds of love were done? Shall men hold those spots sacred on which great patriots and benefactors lived and died, and the eternal God blot out the world on which his dear Son performed the sorrowful pilgrimage of human life, and accomplished the stupendous work of the redemption of its inhabitants? I do not, I *cannot* believe it. It goes against all my deepest conceptions of God and his great purposes of love.

Aside from all this, it seems to be a settled law of the divine operations, always to work out what is to be, from what already exists; and to bring in no new creations beyond what are absolutely necessary. You remember the miracle at the marriage in Cana. Jesus could just as easily have filled the waterpots with wine without requiring them first to be filled with water. But he preferred to take an existing element, and from that to develop the cheering fruits of his marvellous power. So in feeding the five thousand in the wilderness, he could just as easily have dispensed with the few scanty loaves and fishes; but he chose to take what they had, and to make that the basis of his wonderful provision. It would not be more difficult for him to create a new race of men upon earth than to redeem its present inhabitants; but it seems best to him to take the old materials, and out of them to effect his great ends of goodness. He is not prodigal in the use of his power, or wasteful of his creations. Every little fragment must be gathered, "that nothing be lost." He always takes the sinner to make a saint, and the dying and corrupt body to make an immortal and spiritual one. No matter how humble or unpromising the basis may be, so long as there is a basis on which to proceed, he invariably adopts it, and works from it, in preference to an entirely new creation. I do not know a single exception to this rule. I argue then, as he brings "the new man" out of "the old Adam," and the glorified body out of "the natural body," and the new harvest out of the old seed, so he will also assuredly bring the "new heavens and new earth" out of the old heavens and old earth, and thus make a paradise of God out of this very wilderness of our present dwelling-place. My faith is, that these very hills and valleys shall yet be made glad with the songs of a finished redemption, and this earth yet become the bright, blessed and everlasting homestead of men made glorious and immortal in body and in soul.

And why should we start back from such ideas, or wish that it were different? There is nothing essentially corrupt or degrading in matter. It did not detract from Adam's goodness or happiness that he stood in connection with a material system. It did not render Christ less pure, exalted, or adorable, that he took up his abode upon earth, and was manifested in the flesh. After all, there is much in this world that is beautiful, attractive and good. Though it has been much disfigured and disordered by reason of the sins of its inhabitants, we may still trace upon it the footprints of Deity, and behold in it many lingering relics of the smiles of its God. "Look," says Cumming, "at the floor on which you tread, so exquisitely carpeted with verdure, with fragrance and with blossom; look at the sky that is above you, where worlds are subservient as lamps and lights to ours; look at the whole economy in which you live, the ocean of air you breathe, the infinite provisions for your comfort; and why should you want this world destroyed? Go to some of its fair glens, its lovely scenes, its bright panoramas, and you will be constrained to say, Take away sin, take away corruption, take away head-aches, heart-aches, envy, malice, uncharitableness, and all the evils that sin has given birth to, and I could wish no lovelier heaven to dwell in forever and forever." Jesus himself points us to the humble lilies of the field, and tells us with emotion that "even Solomon in all his glory was not arrayed like one of these!" Just take from earth the curse of sin that has marred it; let its pristine beauty be renewed; plant in it the throne of the Redeemer's glory; consecrate and sanctify it with his holy and perpetual presence; and fill it with the happiness, love, peace and righteousness foretold in the Scriptures; and there certainly can be no reason why we should wish any better heaven, or ever think of its annihilation.

But some will be disposed, at this point, to remind me that the Scriptures do certainly speak of an *ending of the world*. The disciples asked Jesus what should be the sign of his coming, "and of *the end of the world*." The Savior says "the harvest is *the end of the world*;" that, "as the tares are gathered and burned in the fire, so shall it be in *the end of the world*;" and that he is with his ministering servants "always, even unto *the end of the world*." I had not overlooked these expressions; nor do they present the least embarrassment to the doctrine of the earth's eternal perpetuity. The word "*world*" often has no reference to the material earth, much less to the general material universe. When Jesus said that *the world* hated him, and that *the world* would hate his disciples, he certainly did not mean the inanimate globe. The word *world*, you will thus perceive, has different significations; and it is used in our English Bibles where very different words are used in the original Greek. The proper Greek word for the material earth is *γη*; but this word is not found in either of the passages which speak of the ending of the world. In two of them the word rendered *world* is *αιων*, which means a space of time, *an age*, an era, *a dispensation*. In the other two, the word rendered *world* is *κοσμος*, which denotes the exterior order, arrangements, investiture and embellishments of the earth. These shall end when Christ comes, and give place to something new; but the γη—the earth itself—has no end assigned it anywhere in all God's book of revelation. Ages shall terminate; dispensations shall be consummated and disappear; "THE FASHION of this world passeth away;" and present outward configurations of things shall vanish; but the earth shall abide. Already we have had at least one ending of the world since man's fall; and from that we may form some idea of what the next shall be. I refer to Noah's flood. Peter says of it, "By the word of God the heavens were of old, and the earth standing out of the water and in the water, whereby THE WORLD THAT THEN WAS, being overflowed with water, PERISHED." Now, what was it that *perished?*—the material earth? Not at all; when the flood was over, Noah still found it rolling in its accustomed orbit, where it has kept rolling until now, and where it will continue to roll forever and ever. Peter says it was the κοσμος that perished; that is, that outward order and constitution of things which existed in antediluvian times. There was no extinction of our globe, no missing of our planet from among the heavenly constellations; and yet inspiration says, "THE WORLD *that then was* PERISHED." May there not, then, be another ending or perishing of the world, without bringing oblivion upon the material orb on which we dwell? Nay, the Holy Scriptures authorize the remark, that "the end of the world" which is yet to come shall not be so destructive to the earth as the flood of Noah was. When Noah came out of the ark, "The Lord said, *I will not again curse the ground any more for man's sake,* NEITHER WILL I AGAIN SMITE ANY MORE EVERY LIVING THING, AS I HAVE DONE:" (Gen. viii. 21.) These are not human conjectures, but the words of the immutable covenant of Almighty God. And, as the perishing of "*the world that then was*" was not an annihilation or destruction of the globe itself, so neither will the ending of the world which now is any more damage or affect the existence of this planet.

But Peter says, "The heavens and the earth, which are now, are kept in store, reserved unto fire against the day of judgment and perdition of ungodly men;" that "the day of the Lord will come, in the which the heavens shall pass away with a great noise, and the elements shall melt with fervent heat; the earth also and all that is therein shall be burned up;" that "the heavens being on fire shall be dissolved, and the elements shall melt with fervent heat." Does not this teach the utter ruin and extinction of material things? Certainly not. The word translated *new* is often taken in the sense of *renewed*, made new, restored to original splendor, and cannot here mean *another* heaven and earth, but simply the present ones *renewed*. The whole passage taken together, then, is nothing more nor less than the assertion of a regeneration of the material world by fire, analogous to the regeneration of the natural man by the Holy Ghost. And as there is no extinction of existence, and no alteration in the essential constituents of the being, in the one case, so neither shall there be in the other. The earth shall not pass away. It shall live on—survive its baptism of fire—exist through the mysterious regeneration—and come forth, minus its curse, to flourish with all its sister orbs forever in its Maker's smiles. Fire cannot reduce matter to nothing. It may alter the modes and qualities of it; but it cannot destroy its substance. And when we come to examine what Peter says these last fires are for, it is plain that they shall not be such as to depopulate or make an utter end of this planet. Men of science tell us, that the deeper we penetrate towards the centre of the earth, the warmer do we find the temperature; and that, if we could carry our investigations deep enough, we would find the interior of the earth "one rolling, restless flood, like the burning lava that pours from Vesuvius, finding its occasional safety-valve in the volcano." It is evidently to this fact that the apostle speaks, when he says, (as some translate his words,) "the present atmosphere and earth are *stored with fire, reserved unto the day of judgment,* EVEN THE PERDITION OF EMINENTLY WICKED MEN." The last fires, then, are those which already exist, but which are imprisoned by the great Creator's word until the day of judgment, when they are to be let loose, not for the annihilation of the world, but for the destruction of the openly apostate, and the persecuting enemies of Christ and his kingdom. The scene which the apostle declares is not universal, but particular and local, and not greatly different from volcanic phenomena which have often been witnessed. Read the descriptions given of some of these terrific eruptions. Dana says of one which occurred at the great volcano Kilauea, Hawaii, "The stream (of fire) plunged into the sea with loud detonations, (with a great noise.) The burning lava, on meeting the waters, was shivered like melted glass into millions of particles, which were thrown up in clouds that darkened the sky, and fell like a storm of hail over the surrounding country. Vast columns of steam and vapors rolled off before the wind, whirling in ceaseless agitation; and the reflected glare of the lavas formed a fiery firmament overhead." Kinney says, "The intense heat of the fountain and stream of lava caused an influx of cool air from every quarter. This created *terrific whirlwinds,* which constantly stalked about, like so many sentinels, bidding defiance to the daring visitor. These were the most dangerous of any thing about the volcano. Clouds approaching were driven back, and set moving in wild confusion." Now, bring distinctly before your minds this terrific scene, the sky filled with flames, the loud roar and crash, the fused elements pouring forth from the earth, the disordered rush of winds and the dreadful danger of coming near, and then take up the literal words of Peter, and you will see that it is altogether a similar scene which he describes. The day of judgment is to unchain the imprisoned fires; and then the atmosphere will pass with a rushing noise; and the elements being kindled will melt; and the earth and the works on it will be burned. "As then all these are (to be) *loosed*, what manner of persons ought ye to be in holy deportment and piety, looking for and earnestly awaiting the coming of the day of God, in which the aerial regions shall be let loose, (to rush in fiery whirlwinds,) and the elements being fired shall melt." The picture is exceedingly awful, and, when realized, shall be dreadfully destructive to those upon whom God's vengeance shall thus fall; but what it portrays is evidently volcanic, and confined to particular regions. Hence, says David N. Lord, after a very thorough, critical and satisfactory examination of the whole passage, "The notion of the conflagration and dissolution of the heavens and earth at Christ's coming, is *without any ground whatever in the apostle's words*, and springs wholly from attaching to them a meaning which they do not involve. The fires by which the impious are then to be destroyed are to be but local and temporary, and are to offer, there is reason to believe, no more obstacle to the safety of the population of the globe at large than the volcanoes have that have already raged in the depths of the earth and ejected their burning elements into the atmosphere." And I cannot see how any man can take God's words to Noah, promising never again to smite every living thing, and yet believe that the last fires of which Peter speaks are to be the agents of a complete and universal destruction.

It is an inspired maxim, my brethren, that "no prophecy of the Scripture is of any private interpretation." We dare not take what one prophet says separate and apart from what another prophet says. We must take all together, contemplate the whole in the parts and the parts in the whole, and explain what is presented in one place by what is contained in another. The conflagration in the day of the Lord of which Peter speaks is the same as the fires of which other prophets have spoken in the same connection. But we search the Scriptures in vain for any corresponding prediction which describes a universal burning up of all earthly things. We read that "the Lord Jesus shall be revealed from heaven with his mighty angels, in flaming fire taking vengeance upon them that know not God and obey not the gospel." We read that "the beast and the false prophet," when the King of kings appears, shall be "cast alive into a lake of fire." We read that "the Lord shall suddenly come to his temple, and sit as *a refiner and purifier of silver*;" that "the day cometh that shall burn as an oven, and all the proud, yea, and all that do wickedly, shall be stubble: and the day that cometh shall burn *them* up;" that "our God shall come, and shall not keep silence: a fire shall devour before him, and it shall be very tempestuous round about him;" and that "a fiery stream shall issue and trail forth before him, and *the beast* be slain and given to the burning flame." But we find nothing to warrant the idea of a *universal* conflagration, much less such a burning as shall depopulate and annihilate the earth. On the other hand, it is explicitly stated in connection with these descriptions of the last fires, that the eminently and notoriously wicked alone are to be visited by them. Archbishop Usher says, they will take away "only the gross hypocrites and formal professors." Of other classes it is said, "But unto you that fear my name, shall the Sun of righteousness arise with healing in his wings; and ye shall go forth, and grow up as calves of the stall. And ye shall tread down the wicked; for *they shall be ashes under the soles of your feet* in the day that I do this, saith the Lord of hosts." Upon Gog and his hosts God will pour "*great hailstones, fire and brimstone.*" He "will send a *fire* on Magog, and among them that dwell confidently." But in the same connection we read of others who live on unharmed by all these avenging fires, whilst "the great globe itself" continues steadfast in its place.

Now, taking all these things together, I regard it as settled and certain, that Peter never meant to teach the utter depopulation and destruction of this planet. He tells us, in harmony with other prophets, that there shall be dreadful fires in the day of judgment. He tells us of the present existence of those fires, and whence they shall proceed. He tells us their object:—"the perdition of ungodly men." He also describes something of the terrific phenomena which shall attend them. And he exhorts us, in view of those awful revelations, to be devout and upright. But I do not find any thing in his language to contradict the declaration of the wise man that "*the earth abideth forever.*" There is immortality in the clods and rocks, as well as in the immaterial mind. There is something undying in the ground we tread beneath our feet, as well as in the soul with which we climb to the dwelling-place of God. There is no grave dug for the material world, any more than for the deathless spirit. And as there is redemption for man, so there is redemption for his smitten and dilapidated dwelling-place.

I know that the effects of human apostasy from God are very deep and far-reaching; perhaps much more so than we sometimes think. The whole earth has been involved in it. "The whole creation groaneth and travaileth in pain" in consequence of it. But with the deep depths of the distress which has been struck into all the pulsations of sublunary nature by reason of man's iniquities, the Scriptures do furnish the sublime hope that it shall all be again extracted. There is a time of restitution coming. There is a day of deliverance at hand. That universal wail, which has been going up for the past six thousand years, shall yet be hushed and lost amid strains of *halleluia* that shall never end. Luther says, "It is important for us to recur to Adam's original condition, as we expect all things to be brought back again to that." "All things are now disordered and decayed; whence Peter says that the heavens must receive Christ until the time when all things shall be restored again to what they were in Paradise; thus agreeing with Paul, that the whole creatureship has been made subject to vanity, and that it is to be hoped that not man only, but the earth and heaven, shall again be brought back to their Edenic state." Calvin says, "I expect with Paul a reparation of all the evils caused by sin, for which he represents the creatures as groaning and travailing." Charnock says, "As the world, for the sin of man, lost its first dignity, and was cursed after the fall, and the beauty bestowed upon it by the creation defaced, so shall it recover that ancient glory, when he shall be fully restored, by the resurrection, to that dignity he lost by his first sin. As man shall be freed from his corruptibility, to receive that glory which is prepared for him, so shall the creatures be freed from that imperfection and those stains and spots on the face of them, to receive a new glory suited to their nature, and answerable to the design of God, when the glorious liberty of the saints shall be accomplished." But let us hear what God himself has said. "In that day shall there be upon the bells of the horses, HOLINESS UNTO THE LORD; and the pots in the Lord's house shall be like the bowls before the altar." "He shall judge among many people, and rebuke strong nations afar off; and they shall beat their swords into ploughshares, and their spears into pruning-hooks; nation shall not lift up sword against nation, neither shall they learn war any more. But they shall sit every man under his vine and under his fig-tree; and none shall make them afraid." "And the floors shall be full of wheat, and the vats shall overflow with wine and oil." "The waters of the dead sea shall be healed by the waters which flow out of the temple; and by the stream of this water shall grow all manner of trees, whose leaves shall not wither, and whose fruit shall not decay; they shall yield their fruit monthly, and the leaves thereof shall be for the healing of the nations." "The creature itself shall be delivered from the bondage of corruption, into the glorious liberty of the children of God." "The wolf also shall dwell with the lamb, and the leopard shall lie down with the kid; and the calf, and the young lion, and the fatling together, and a little child shall lead them. The cow and the bear shall feed together, and their young ones shall lie down together; and the lion shall eat straw like an ox. And the sucking child shall play on the hole of the asp, and the weaned child upon the cockatrice's den. They shall not hurt nor destroy in all my holy mountain, saith the Lord." "Moreover, the light of the moon shall be as the light of the sun, and the light of the sun sevenfold, as the light of seven days, in the day that the Lord shall bind up the breach of his people and heal the stroke of their wound." "Then the eyes of the blind shall be opened, and the ears of the deaf shall be unstopped. Then shall the lame man leap as an hart, and the tongue of the dumb sing; for in the wilderness shall waters break out, and streams in the desert. And the parched ground shall become a watered place, and the thirsty land springs of water; in the habitation of dragons there shall be grass with reeds and rushes." "Instead of the thorn shall come up the fir-tree, and instead of the brier shall come up the myrtle-tree." "And the inhabitant shall not say, I am sick." "And there shall be no more death, neither sorrow, nor crying; neither shall there be any more pain: for the former things are passed away."

These are glad and glorious descriptions; and they are given by the Spirit of God. Whatever meaning people have attached to them, all agree that they set forth a condition of things which is yet to be realized upon this earth. Some say we must take them literally; others interpret them figuratively; and others understand them spiritually. But, no matter how we take them, one thing is settled and incontrovertible, that they include a *physical* as well as a moral redemption. They describe the lifting off of the curse from all creation around us, as well as from the souls within us. They exhibit suffering and disordered nature once more free, harmonious, congenial, restored, and forever at rest. They portray vast and happy changes in things spiritual and things physical, animate and inanimate, human, animal, vegetable and elemental. They show us the earth with its deserts fertilized, its elements harmonized, its inhabitants made congenial to each other, its products rendered abundant and sanatory, and its possessors invested with perfect happiness and immortality. Some have looked for their fulfillment in a fancied millennium previous to the Savior's coming. They would have us believe that these sublime predictions relate only to the universal triumph of political freedom, general wisdom, and exalted piety. But how will the mere reign of righteousness and love in the hearts and conduct of mankind extend redemption into the physical world, or work a deliverance to the animal and other kingdoms? Knowledge, holiness and liberty combined, and spread over the earth from one end thereof to the other, cannot save a man from bodily aches, decay and death. They cannot take the taint from the atmosphere, nor the malaria from the earth. They cannot cover Sahara with fertility, nor hush the storm and tempest, nor close the volcano's crater, nor stop the Maelstrom's whirl, nor stay the earthquake's giant tread, nor relieve the creature of its groans. Make every meal a sacrament, and every day a Sabbath, and every thought a prayer to God; and all that, of itself, cannot take away the curse with which God has cursed "the ground" for man's sake, nor relieve these dying bodies from their many ills. The case calls for greater changes in earth, air and sea, and in the whole present constitution of terrestrial things, than can by any possibility result from existing processes, or from mere natural developments. We must have special electric influences to quiet the atmosphere and adapt it better to the wants of humanity. We must have volcanic or some other action in and upon the earth, to change some of its surface, consume its impurities, and renew its wastes. We must have a complete revolution in the present order of things. In a word, we must have another putting forth of divine power upon this world. It must be retouched by the hand that made it. It must come under a renewing potency which can raise the dead. And all this shall be only when the Son of God shall again come from the heavens.

Accordingly, we read, that when the times of restitution come, "God shall send Jesus Christ." "And then shall they see the Son of man coming *with power*." And "he shall call to the heavens from above, and to the earth, that he may judge his people." "He shall have dominion also from sea to sea, and from the river to the ends of the earth." "He shall send forth his angels, and they shall gather out of his kingdom all things that offend, and them which do iniquity," and "destroy them that corrupt the earth." "He shall go forth as a mighty man, he shall stir up jealousy like a man of war; he shall cry, yea, roar; he shall do mighty things against his enemies." "The Lord also shall roar out of Zion, and utter his voice from Jerusalem; and the heavens and the earth shall shake." "They that are in their graves shall hear his voice, and come forth." "Them also that sleep in Jesus will God bring with him." "He shall change our vile body, that it may be fashioned like unto his glorious body, according to the working whereby he is able to subdue all things unto himself." "Then shall be brought to pass the saying that is written, Death is swallowed up in victory." "And there shall be no more curse." "And it shall come to pass in that day, that the mountains shall drop down new wine, and the hills shall flow with milk." "The ploughman shall overtake the reaper, and the treader of grapes him that soweth the seed; and the mountains shall drop sweet wine, and all the hills shall melt." "Then shall all the trees of the wood rejoice before the Lord; for he cometh, for he cometh to judge the earth; he shall judge the world with righteousness, and the people with his truth." "In his day there shall be abundance of peace." "The government shall be upon his shoulder; and of the increase of his government and peace there shall be no end." "He shall come down like rain upon the mown grass: as showers that water the earth. In his days shall the righteous flourish." "He will make a covenant for them with the beasts of the field, and with the fowls of heaven, and with the creeping things of the ground." "His name shall endure forever. All nations shall call him blessed, the Lord God who only doeth wondrous things. And the whole earth shall be filled with his glory; Amen, and Amen."

Thus, then, will He that sits upon the throne "make all things new." "There will be wonders in heaven above, and signs in the earth beneath, blood, and fire, and pillars of smoke." But out of trouble shall come joy, out of darkness shall go forth light; and in place of groans and tears and death shall be songs of joy and glorious immortality.

"The age of crime and suffering yet shall end;
The reign of righteousness from heaven descend;
Vengeance forever sheath the afflicting sword;
Death be destroyed, *and Paradise restored;*
Man, rising from the ruins of his fall,
Be one with God, and God be all in all."

"*Write,*" says the Son of God, "*for these words are true and faithful.*" It is not a poetic dream, but a divine revelation. God hath spoken it by the mouth of all his holy prophets since the world began. It was the hope of Adam as he went forth an exile from Eden. It was the light that illumined the tents of the pilgrims of old with a sweeter halo than the recollections of Paradise. It was the stay of faithful Abraham as he sojourned in tabernacles with Isaac and Jacob, the heirs with him of the same promise. It shone in the serene imagination of Isaac, and supported the dying head of Jacob, and caused Joseph to turn away from Egypt's mausoleums and ask that his bones might be carried up to the land of the redeemed. It shortened the centuries in which the Lord's chosen toiled in servitude, and cheered the house of affliction with songs. It kindled glad expectations amid the darkness of Gentile apostasy, and taught even the heathen to prophesy of deliverance. It fired the hearts and tongues of all Judah's minstrels, as they swept from the harps of inspiration those lofty anthems which filled the home of the Shekinah with praise. And thousands upon thousands have not counted their lives dear unto them for the excellency of this hope, and were tortured, not accepting deliverance, that they might obtain the better resurrection. Even irrational nature seems to be filled with the promise, and until now is earnestly expecting and waiting for "the manifestation of the sons of God," and the redemption which shall be effected when death shall be no more. It cannot, therefore, be a fable. A lie could not be so deeply graven. What has been so fondly believed, so long looked for, and so earnestly desired—what has been the hope of the good in every age, the theme of their songs, and the joy of their hearts—what has ever been pointed to as the solution of earth's enigma and Jehovah's great vindication — certainly cannot be a falsehood. No, no, no; it cannot be delusion. Creation's loosened strings shall again be screwed up to their primeval tone and concord, to accompany the songs of God's saints with immortal harmonies.

"The barren wastes shall rise,
With sudden greens and fruits arrayed,—
A blooming paradise.

"True holiness shall strike its root
In each regenerate heart;
Shall, in a growth divine, arise,
And heavenly fruits impart.

"Peace, with her olives crowned, shall stretch
Her wings from shore to shore;
No trump shall rouse the rage of war,
Nor murderous cannon roar.

"Lord, for those days we wait: those days
Are in thy word foretold;—
Fly swifter, sun and stars, and bring
This promised age of gold!"

"Wherefore, beloved, seeing that ye look for such things, be diligent that ye may be found of him in peace, without spot, and blameless." It would be a sad thing, if, after all these sublime arrangements of our Maker, we should eventually come short of the inheritance. Let me, then, exhort you to "give all diligence to make your calling and election sure." If you are prayerless, I beseech you to go and call upon God. If you have been thoughtless and careless, I entreat you to consider, and lay these great matters to heart. If you are a sinner, repent, repent *now*. And from this hour let each one who hears these remarks set out in full earnest to prepare to meet God. Soon your day of grace will be over. Soon your opportunities of becoming participants in the glad scenes of a restored creation will be at an end. "The end of all things is at hand; be ye therefore sober, and watch unto prayer. And above all have fervent charity among yourselves, for charity shall cover the multitude of sins. If any man speak, let him speak as the oracles of God; if any man minister, let him do it as of the ability which God giveth: that God in all things may be glorified.

WAITING FOR THAT DAY.

Waiting we stand,
And watching till our Savior shall appear,
Joyful to cry, as eastern skies grow clear,
"The Lord's at hand!"

But now the night
Presses around us, sullenly and chill;
Pain, doubt, and sorrow seem to have their will:—
Lord, send the light!

One after one,
Thou hast called up our loved ones from our sight;
For them we know that there is no more night,
But we are lone.

Weary we wait,
Lifting our heavy eyes, bedimmed with tears,
To skies where yet no trace of dawn appears:—
Lord, it is late!

But yet thy Word
Saith, with sweet prophecy that cannot fail,
That light o'er darkness shall at length prevail:—
We trust thee, Lord!

O Morning Star
Of heavenly promise! light our darkened way,
Till the first beams of the expected day
Shine from afar.

So will we take
Fresh hope and courage to our fainting hearts,
And patient wait, though every joy departs,
"Till the day break."

FOURTH DISCOURSE.

THE DOCTRINE OF THE RESURRECTION—ERRONEOUS INTERPRETATIONS OF THE TWENTIETH CHAPTER OF THE REVELATION REFUTED—THE FIRST RESURRECTION—WHAT THE ANCIENT JEWS TAUGHT UPON THE SUBJECT—CITATIONS FROM THE OLD PROPHETS—HOW THE MATTER IS PRESENTED IN THE NEW TESTAMENT—THE SUBLIME HOPES INVOLVED.

REV. xx. 4–6: *And I saw the souls of them that were beheaded for the witness of Jesus, and for the word of God, and which had not worshipped the beast, neither his image, neither had received his mark upon their foreheads, or in their hands; and they lived and reigned with Christ a thousand years. But the rest of the dead lived not again until the thousand years were finished. This is the first resurrection. Blessed and holy is he that hath part in the first resurrection.*

THAT the dead shall rise again, is the universal belief of Christians. As no historic fact was ever more invincibly established than the resurrection of our Divine Redeemer, so no article of our faith is more clear and indisputable than the doctrine of our rising again like him at our appointed time. It is hardly worth while, in this connection, to accumulate proofs and authorities to support what is so generally admitted and believed, and so clearly announced in the Holy Scriptures.

Certainly, no one will deny that the raising of the dead lies entirely within the reach of Divine power. No one will say that it is a thing impossible to Omnipotence. It involves no contradiction. It is prohibited by no foregone law or necessity. It is not rendered impossible by incapacity in the decomposed bodies of the departed for reorganization. God knows each atom, and where it rests. Our substance was not hid from him when we were made in secret. His eye saw it yet being imperfect. All our members were written in his book when yet there was none of them. He has his number for every hair upon each head. Wherever the particles of these dissolving bodies may be scattered or lodged, they lie completely within his knowledge and power. And He who could at the first so attemper the vulgar dust as to constitute a man can also again recover these attempered particles and restore them to their places. If he can bring a new and glorious ear out of the rotting seed, he can also bring a spiritual body out of the corruptible one.

And as the resurrection of the dead is not a thing impossible, so it is not a thing improbable. Faint analogies of it may be traced in the ordinary changes and revolutions beheld in nature around us. Clement, the contemporary and friend of St. Paul, says, "The Lord does continually show us that there shall be a future resurrection. Day and night manifest it. The seed sown in the earth displays it." The day fades and dies. It is buried in sleep, silence and darkness. In the morning it revives, opens its grave of gloom, and rises from "the dead of night." The summer dies, and lies down in its wintry grave. The winds of heaven sigh and weep over it as if they would not be comforted. In the spring, life begins to work again in the buried roots and seeds; the plants and flowers burst out of their dark cerements; and every thing arrays itself in newness and glory. The sower goes forth and casts his seed upon the earth. It falls down dry and naked, and in time dissolves. But the great power of the providence of the Lord raises it again from that dissolution; and from the old seed new germs arise, and bring forth fruit. The caterpillar builds himself a tomb, and then lies down in it and dies. But out of the grave of the ugly worm comes forth the butterfly which sallies forth in the sunshine like a living flower. And so there are many things in nature that are repaired by corrupting, preserved by perishing, and revived by dying. And as we behold man, the lord of these things, dying like them, it is but a fair presumption that he will revive again hereafter as we see them revive.

But God has not left us in the school of nature, nor given us over to settle our persuasions upon mere likelihoods. In the glorious record of his word, he has put the doctrine of the resurrection of the dead beyond dispute. Distinct glimmerings of it may be found all through the Old Testament; and it is predicted in the New in language which no one can misunderstand. Paul says there were many saints before his day who "were tortured, not accepting deliverance, that they might obtain a better resurrection." He says that the Jews allowed "that there shall be a resurrection of the dead, both of the just and unjust." The heroic Maccabees hoped for it. The sisters of Lazarus consoled themselves by thinking of it as they lingered at their only brother's grave. Christ explicitly pointed to a coming period, when "they that are in their graves shall hear the voice of the Son of man, and come forth." The great Apostle to the Gentiles argued it as a thing demonstrated by the resurrection of the crucified Savior. It was the great consolation of the noble army of the martyrs. And in every age of Christianity it has been cherished as the glad hope by which the believer triumphs over the gloom of corporeal dissolution.

God has also added a seal to this doctrine which cannot be counterfeited. He has actually restored deceased persons to life again. When Elijah prayed for the resuscitation of the dead child of the widow of Sarepta, God heard him, "and the soul of the child came into him again, and he revived." Elisha, in his lifetime, received power to raise the young Shunemite; and the mere touch of his bones caused a dead man to revive and stand upon his feet. When the daughter of Jairus died, Jesus "said unto her, *Tabitha, cumi*, and her spirit came again, and straightway the damsel arose." When he came "nigh to the gate of a city called Nain, there was a dead man carried out; and he came near and touched the bier, and said, Young man, I say unto thee, Arise; and he that was dead sat up, and began to speak." And not only in the chamber and in the street, from the bed and from the bier, did Christ call the dead to life. His voice was heard with equal effect even in the putrid grave. When Lazarus had been "dead four days," and so long buried that his sisters said, "Lord, by this time he stinketh," Jesus "cried with a loud voice, Lazarus, come forth; and he that was dead" and putrid obeyed and lived again. And the blessed Savior himself, after being "crucified, dead and buried," took to himself the might of his superior nature, and came forth from the sepulchre, and showed himself to hundreds with many notable signs. In these cases the problem has been solved, and the fact demonstrated forever, that there is such a thing as the resurrection of the dead. Though we may not be able to comprehend the processes by which it shall be effected, we may rest assured that it is no idle dream, no cunningly-devised fable, but a sublime and stupendous reality.

How far the resurrection-body is to be identical with the body which dies and wastes in the grave has not been revealed. It is enough for us to know that we shall rise from the dead, without being able to understand the philosophy of it. Doubtless we will leave much gross matter behind us in the grave. Not all those identical particles which, by that time, may be wrought over and over in nature's vast laboratory to supply still other bodies, will need to be recovered and replaced in order to bring about the resurrection. "That which thou sowest, thou sowest not that body that shall be, but bare grain; but God giveth it a body as it hath pleased him. So is also the resurrection of the dead. It is sown in corruption, it is raised in incorruption; it is sown in dishonor, it is raised in glory; it is sown in weakness, it is raised in power; it is sown a natural body, it is raised a spiritual body. There is a natural body, and there is a spiritual body." And yet, in the mysterious transition from the one to the other, identity is preserved. "For *this corruptible* must put on incorruption, and *this mortal* must put on immortality." Otherwise the whole idea of *resurrection* vanishes. "We believe in the resurrection of *the body;*" and, if it is not in some way the raising of the body that dies and is buried, the whole doctrine amounts to naught. The thing is so mysterious, and so far removed from our present experiences, that it is impossible for us to understand it fully; but this we must adhere to, that the transition from corruption to incorruption, and from mortal to immortality, is somehow accomplished in the same body. Identity does not necessarily imply the continuation of all and precisely the same parts. We may be corporeally identified as the same men ten years hence that we are now; and yet, according to what physiologists tell us, by that time there will hardly be a particle in our bodies which is now in them. Great changes may occur, but people will identify us as the same persons then that we are now. So, then, we may also lose the more earthy parts of our material organism, and still come from our graves with bodies refined and spiritual indeed, but still interiorly and in form identical with those which we now inhabit. The butterfly is the same animal with the caterpillar which preceded it. It has the same body. It has arisen out of the same elements which constituted the caterpillar; though it has left much gross material behind it. The seed which we plant is the same that afterwards shoots up into a stalk, with blades and blossoms; so that we point to it and say, "Here is the flower I planted;" although much of that seed decays in the ground and mingles with the dust.

And so the present mortal body is the germ or seed of the future heavenly body. The one rises out of the other. It is the same creature emerging in a new development. And when the signal for our reanimation comes, we shall gather to ourselves the interior essence of our slumbering dust, emerge in glory from our graves, and go forth amid the sublimities of a life in which body and soul shall enjoy unsullied and immortal union.

It has been made a question, however, whether the text before us refers to the literal resurrection of the dead. It is strange to see to what fancies men have resorted to do away with the plain, evident, and literal import of the apostle's words.

Some say that this "first resurrection," at the beginning of the millennium, is nothing more than the quickening and regeneration of sinners by repentance and faith in Christ. They take it as a spiritual resurrection, like that in the case of the returned prodigal. That the Scriptures do speak of the sinner's recovery as a resurrection, there can be no doubt. Whenever a wanderer from God is made thoughtful, prayerful and penitent, he rises out of moral inanity to spiritual activity. As John expresses it, he passes from death unto life. But this moral quickening will by no means meet the case before us. The resurrection of which the text speaks is the resurrection of such as had already been raised spiritually, and who partake of this resurrection because they were before "*blessed and holy.*" It is the resurrection, not of those who *sleep in sin*, but of "them that sleep *in Jesus*;" not of those who have never known Christ, but of "them that were beheaded for the testimony of Jesus, and for the word of God, and had not worshipped the beast." It is the resurrection of those who were saints without it, many of whom had so loved Christ as to lay down their lives for him and his gospel.

Others have supposed that this "first resurrection" is purely ecclesiastical, and that it was effected in the days of Constantine the Great, when the visible church was released from the cruel pagan persecutions, legalized, and elevated to the patronage of government. But every rightly-instructed man knows that the changes wrought by Constantine were rather a *burial* of the true church than a resurrection of it. So far from being attended with blessedness and holiness, it was rather the opening of the door for the worst degradations and wickednesses that ever despoiled Christendom. Instead of binding Satan, he was then first let fully loose upon the gospel to corrupt and tarnish it with his foul devices. In place of introducing the reign of Christ with his saints, it laid the way for the reign of the Man of sin with his corrupt adherents. And, so far from making men "priests of God and of Christ," it made them priests "after the working of Satan, with all power, and signs, and lying wonders, with all deceivableness of unrighteousness."

Others, again, are of opinion that this "first resurrection" denotes a great number of dissimilar changes relating to the prosperity of the gospel and the peace of the world, such as the general conversion of the wicked, the restoration of the Jews, the universal diffusion of liberty and light, and the revival of Christianity in the purity in which it was embraced by the martyrs. This notion was first set on foot by Whitby about 150 years ago, and has met with great favor from some classes of teachers. But it is filled with inconsistencies and surrounded by insuperable objections. The resurrection which the text speaks of is the resurrection of "them that were beheaded for the testimony of Jesus, and for the word of God, and whoever had not worshipped the beast nor his image." The wicked never were beheaded for the testimony of Jesus, or for the word of God. Their deadness in trespasses and in sins is not the result of their faithful adherence to the Son of God. The Jewish race, which now lies buried among the nations, was not denationalized and reduced to this condition in consequence of bearing testimony for Christ, but for denying and crucifying him. It is impossible, therefore, that these parties should be the subjects of the resurrection spoken of. And the idea that the resurrection of the martyrs denotes merely the revival of their spirit and moral qualities is at variance with the text in another respect. The apostle is speaking of *persons.* "I saw *the souls of them that had been beheaded for the testimony of Jesus;*—and *they* lived and reigned with Christ." The original term employed is ψυχας, which occurs nearly a hundred times in the New Testament, but which is never once used to denote characteristics or attributes. It invariably means *lives, beings, persons, souls;* as where we read there "were in the ship two hundred and seventy-six *souls;*"—there were added to the church "about three thousand *souls;*"—in Noah's ark "eight *souls* were saved." And so the living again and reigning of *those souls* that were beheaded for their fidelity to God, must mean the resurrection, not of their spiritual characteristics, but of these beings or persons themselves. As a patient student and learned critic remarks, "It is a literal resurrection that is predicted of them manifestly, inasmuch as that is the only resurrection of which disembodied saints are capable. It certainly is not a renovation of heart, as they were renewed while in this life, and are made priests of God and of Christ, and given to reign with him, because they were saints here. As their resurrection then cannot be a spiritual change analogous to a restoration of the body from death, it must necessarily be a corporeal change. That it is to be a corporeal resurrection is shown moreover by the representation that the rest of the dead lived not till the thousand years should be finished. The rest of the dead are the literally dead; not the literally living, though without spiritual life. To treat that term as a mere metaphor, is to deny to the vision the character of a symbol and to empty the whole passage of its meaning. If the death of those who are not partakers of the first resurrection be but metaphorical, then must the death of the martyrs be metaphorical also, and thence the resurrection which is ascribed to the souls be merely metaphorical. But that is to make the passage a mere assemblage of metaphors, without any thing literal from which the figures are drawn or to which they are applied, and to divest it of all propriety and significance. If the souls of the dead, as well as the resurrection, be mere metaphors, no agents whatever are left to be their subjects; and they are predicates without any thing of which they are affirmed,—metaphors with nothing which they metaphorize. As the souls exhibited in the vision then are real souls, so, also, for the same reason, the rest of the dead are the real dead, and the resurrection affirmed of the one and denied of the other a real resurrection." (Lord's Exp. of the Apocalypse, p. 519.) Professor Stuart also treats this text as "simple prose," and endorses "the exegesis which deduces from the whole passage *the reality of a first resurrection at the introduction of the millennium.*" (Com., *in loc.*)

The facts upon which those rely who interpret this first resurrection figuratively are,—that Ezekiel has the restoration and conversion of the Jews symbolized to him under the resuscitation of the dry bones, and that the Savior speaks of the repentance and recovery of the prodigal son as the making alive of him that was dead. With these two facts, they jump at the conclusion that the resurrection of the martyrs and holy ones at the beginning of the millennium is to be taken in a somewhat similar sense. But, when we draw the necessary distinctions between things that differ, this argument proves the exact reverse of what it is designed to establish. It must be taken as a settled canon of interpretation that where a resurrection is affirmed, it can be taken only in the sense of the presupposed death. So in both these instances the resuscitations are the exact counterparts of the previous deaths. The death symbolized by the valley of dry bones is plainly described as both a *national* and moral death; and the predicted resurrection is accordingly both a *national* and a moral resurrection. The death of the prodigal son was a moral and spiritual death; and his resurrection was of course of the same kind. And so it must also be in the case before us. But what sort of death is that which has passed upon the martyrs, and upon "those who were beheaded for the testimony of Jesus, and for the word of God" ? Was it a national death? Nationally the martyrs never lived, and of course could not nationally die. Was theirs a spiritual or moral death? No; for no one can be called Christ's witness, blessed and holy, and yet be dead in this moral sense. What was their death, then, but a literal, personal and individual death? Was it not a death in the real, natural and ordinary meaning of that word? Well, then, here, as in the other cases, as was the death so shall the predicted resurrection be. As these martyrs and saints literally, really and personally died, and in that sense alone are dead, so shall they again be literally, really and personally made alive in "the first resurrection;" whilst "the rest of the dead" sleep on "until the thousand years are finished." Spiritually the martyrs are not dead; nationally they never died; influentially they are not dead. They have had their successors in all ages, in whom their qualities and spirit have never become extinct. They yet speak. They are dead corporeally, and in no other sense. And when John tells us that they shall live again in the first resurrection, he can mean nothing but a corporeal resuscitation. The wicked who die in their sins are not to be spiritually raised, nor nationally raised, nor influentially raised. When they die, their probation ends, and judgment comes. When it is affirmed, therefore, that they shall live again, it can only be understood of a corporeal resurrection. Yet the same words, in the same verses, which assert the resurrection of *the unsanctified dead*, assert the resurrection of *the holy dead*, with only these two differences, that the holy rise to reign, whilst the wicked rise to burn, and that the one class rises a thousand years in advance of the other class. And as the resurrection of the wicked—"the rest of the dead"—at the final judgment can be taken only in a corporeal and literal sense, so the first resurrection—the resurrection of the "blessed and holy"—must also be received in the same corporeal and literal sense. I can see no escape from this conclusion.

I feel compelled, therefore, to understand the text as referring to the literal resurrection of the dead. I can find no other theory which will meet the necessities of the case, or which will conform to sound principles of interpretation. I find then a *duality* in the resurrection which the Scriptures teach. It is twofold. There is a "first resurrection" at the beginning of the millennium, and there is a resurrection at the end of the millennium. The one embraces the martyrs and saints,—the "blessed and holy,"—"them that sleep in Jesus;" the other the resurrection of "the rest of the dead." The one is *the* resurrection which we are taught to hope for and seek after; the other a something about which the Scriptures say but little, and which promises nothing to be desired. The one is a resurrection to all the glories, joys and honors of a perfected redemption; the other a resurrection to dismay, shame and everlasting contempt.

Nor is this a novel doctrine. Calmet says, "The ancient fathers acknowledged a twofold resurrection: first, that which is to precede the Messiah's reign of a thousand years upon earth; secondly, that which is to follow the reign of the thousand years. This sentiment is found clearly enough in the second book of Esdras, in the testament of the twelve patriarchs, and in several of the Rabbins." Professor Stuart declares that "the doctrine of a *first* resurrection as taught by John was not novel to the men of his time." "I have my doubts," says he, "whether the assertion is correct, that the doctrine of the *first resurrection* is nowhere else to be found in the Scriptures. That the great mass of Jewish Rabbins have believed and taught the doctrine of *the resurrection of the just*, in the days of Messiah's development, there can be no doubt on the part of him who has made any considerable investigation of this matter." Thus, Jonathan the Paraphrast, who lived thirty years before Christ, says of the people of God, "They shall be gathered from their captivity; they shall live under the shadow of Messiah; the dead shall rise, and good shall increase in the earth." This is based on the last chapter of Hosea. Rabbi Kimchi says, "The holy blessed God will raise the dead at the time of deliverance." This he draws from Isaiah xxvi. 19. The Sanhedrin, cited by Aruch, says, "There is a tradition in the house of Elias, that *the righteous* whom the holy and blessed God shall raise from the dead shall not return again to the dust; but for the space of a thousand years, in which the holy blessed God will renew the world, they shall have wings like the wings of eagles, and shall fly above the waters." Another says, "The benefit of the rain is common to the just and the unjust, but the resurrection from the dead is the peculiar privilege of those who live righteously." Chabbo says, "The dead in the land of Israel shall live or be quickened *first* in the days of Messiah, and shall enjoy the years of Messiah." Thus also in Zohar we read, upon Isaiah xxv. 8:—"The world cannot be freed from sin until King Messiah shall come, and the blessed God shall raise up those who sleep in the dust." These, and many like sayings, have been collected by critics from the most ancient of the Rabbinical writings. Corresponding passages have also been found in the sacred traditions of the heathen world. Of course no Rabbinical testimony or mere tradition is adequate to prove an article of religious faith; but these quotations are not without their significance. Where did these men get such ideas? They for the most part profess to receive them from the writings of the inspired prophets. · They refer us to Isaiah, Ezekiel and Daniel as their authority. Nor are their interpretations to be discarded as necessarily fanciful and erroneous because they belong to the records of Rabbinic lore. It is a sorry wit which takes for granted that a man cannot be guided to the truth of God because he is a Jew. These ancient Rabbins were the friends, countrymen, brethren and children of Jehovah's own inspired prophets, and may be our guides in many things.

The passage to which they refer us in Isaiah (xxvi. 19) certainly does describe a resurrection,—a *joyous* resurrection,—and therefore a resurrection of the just only,—and specifically connects it with the coming and glorious reign of the Lord Messiah. The place to which they point in Ezekiel (xxxvii.) certainly describes a national and moral resurrection, and surrounds it with promises which imply also the literal resurrection of all the faithful Israel to share the kingdom of him who shall be their Prince forever. And what they cite from Daniel, (xii. 2,) according to the best Hebraists, not only asserts a resurrection which all take to be literal, but draws a plain distinction between the resurrection of the just and the rest of the dead. Gaon thus paraphrases it:—"And many of them that sleep in the dust of the earth shall awake; *this* is the resurrection of the dead of Israel, whose lot is to eternal life; but *those* who do not awake (at that time) shall be an abhorrence to all flesh." This agrees with the translation of Professor Bush:—"Many from out of the sleepers in the dust of the earth shall awake; *these* (that is, those who awake, shall be) to everlasting life, and *those* (who do not then awake shall be) to everlasting contempt." Thus also does Professor Whiting render it:—"Many from the sleepers of the dust of the ground shall awake, *these* to everlasting life, and *those* to reproaches and everlasting abhorrence." The language of Daniel thus accommodates itself exactly to the language of the text. The martyrs and saints arise: "this is the first resurrection. But the rest of the dead lived not again until the thousand years were finished." Daniel is unquestionably speaking of a literal, limited and eclectic resurrection. As Dr. Hody argues, "if *many*, standing alone, could signify *all*, *many of*, which is the phraseology of this text, cannot signify all. Many *of* them that sleep in the dust of the earth cannot be said to be *all* they that sleep in the dust. *Many of* does plainly except some." And if there is to be a limited and eclectic resurrection when the great Prince shall stand up for Israel, and yet all men shall be made alive again, the point is settled that there must be a twofold resurrection, just as John teaches us in the text.

The state of the question, in the period in which the New Testament was given, was therefore simply this:—The ancient prophets speak of a resurrection from among the dead, a literal resurrection to eternal life, which embraces only the just, and leaves the wicked still in their graves. The more learned and devout Jews so understood these glorious predictions, and taught the doctrine of a first resurrection, or resurrection embracing only the just. The doctrine of a twofold resurrection was therefore no strange notion to those who lived in the time of Christ and his apostles, but familiar to the minds of many. If it was an error, we would naturally expect some contradiction of it from Christ or his apostles. The absence of such contradiction leaves room for the presumption that it was not an error. And if we can find language in the New Testament adapted only to this belief, and framed to it as the truth, the presumption in its favor will have all needful support to furnish ground upon which to insist upon it as a divine certainty.

Let us look, then, at what may be gathered on the subject from the New Testament.

1. I think you will find it invariably true, that wherever the resurrection of both the good and bad are spoken of, the resurrection of the righteous is always named first, and that of the wicked afterwards. "All that are in their graves shall hear his voice, and shall come forth: (1) they that have done good, unto the resurrection of life; and (2) they that have done evil, unto the resurrection of damnation." "There shall be a resurrection of the dead both (1) of the just and (2) unjust."

2. The resurrection of the righteous is specifically said to precede the resurrection of the wicked. "As in Adam all die, even so in Christ shall all be made alive. But every man in his own ταγμα,—*band, cohort, company:* Christ the first-fruits; afterward *they that are Christ's* at his coming; εἶτα το τελος,—*then the last band.*" "The dead in Christ shall rise *first.*" "The rest of the dead lived not again until the thousand years were finished."

3. The resurrection of the righteous is everywhere spoken of as a peculiar blessing, in which the wicked have no share whatever. Of every one that seeth the Son and believeth on him, Jesus says, "I will raise *him* up at the last day;" thus distinctly intimating that none but believers shall share in the resurrection here contemplated. He speaks of "the resurrection of the just" as something quite distinct from any thing in which the unjust shall have a part. He says that "the children of the resurrection are equal unto the angels, and are the children of God," and "are as the angels which are in heaven." Here he certainly speaks of a resurrection from which the wicked are quite excluded. See also Romans

viii. 23; 1 Cor. vi. 14; 2 Cor. iv. 14:—"*Blessed and holy is he* that hath part in the first resurrection."

4. The resurrection of the righteous is plainly spoken of as *eclectic.* One instance is in Luke xx. 35, where the Savior speaks of those worthy of heaven as destined "to obtain the resurrection"—not merely "*from the dead,*" as our version reads, but εκ νεκρων—"OUT OF, or FROM AMONGST *the dead ones.*" This certainly implies the raising of some, that is, the saints, whilst the rest of the dead remain in their graves. Another instance is in Philippians iii. 11, where Paul speaks of his strong desire and great exertions to "attain unto την εξ-αναστασιν των νεκρων,—*the resurrection* FROM AMONGST *the dead ones.*" What did Paul mean by this? "Of his resurrection at the end of the world, when *all* without exception will surely be raised, he could have no possible doubt," says Professor Stuart. "What sense then can this passage have, if it represents him as laboring and suffering merely in order to attain to A resurrection, and as holding this up to view as unattainable unless he should arrive at a high degree of Christian perfection? On the other hand, let us suppose a *first* resurrection to be appointed as a special reward of high attainments in Christian virtue, and all seems to be plain and easy. Of a resurrection in a *figurative* sense, *i. e.* of *regeneration,* Paul cannot be speaking; for he had already attained to that on the plain of Damascus." Both these passages bring before us the whole congregation of the really dead, and describe the resurrection of which they speak as a selection (εκ) *out of* or *from among* that great company, taking some, and leaving others. The second is particularly remarkable. For if the righteous and the wicked are all to be raised together, Paul might have saved his pains to attain to a resurrection of which he would have at all events been partaker. "Of like tenor," says Stuart, "is the implication in Luke xiv. 14, where the Savior promises to his disciples a sure reward

for kindness to the poor and suffering, *at the resurrection of the just.* Why the resurrection of *the just?*—What special meaning can this have, unless it implies that there is a resurrection where the just only, and not the unjust, will be raised? This would agree entirely with the view in Rev. xx. 5:—'But *the rest of the dead* LIVED NOT AGAIN, until the thousand years were finished.' "

Now, when we come to sum up all these facts, and assign them the force which belongs to the words of inspiration, the conclusion is to me unavoidable, that the doctrine of a two-fold resurrection has a solid foundation in the Scriptures. The resurrection of the holy is entirely separated, in nature and in point of time, from the resurrection of "the rest of the dead." Strike this doctrine from the Apocalypse, and we still have it in the epistles of Paul. Strike it from the epistles, and we still have it in the teachings of Jesus himself. Strike it from the whole New Testament, and we still have it firm and unshaken in the holy prophecies of Daniel and Isaiah. But let the hand be withered that attempts to strike it from any portion of the word of God. It is there, distinct and clear, authorizing all the saints to hope for the redemption of their bodies, and their corporeal transformation, so soon as the millennium shall begin.

Here, then, is another argument for the doctrine of Christ's premillennial coming. The resurrection of the saints is everywhere connected with his final advent. "All shall be made alive; *they that are Christ's at his coming.*" "Them that sleep in Jesus will God bring with him. For the Lord himself shall descend from heaven: and the dead in Christ shall rise first." "When he shall appear, we shall be like him." But the resurrection and glorification of the saints is just as clearly connected with the beginning of the millennium. There can be no millennium whilst the wilful king continues to "exalt himself, and magnify himself above every god, and speak marvellous things against the God of gods;" and the fall of this antichristian power, and the glorious resurrection proclaimed by Daniel, are contemporaneous. "He shall come to his end, and none shall help him. AND AT THAT TIME God's people shall be delivered, every one that shall be found written in the book; and many of them that sleep in the dust of the earth shall awake." So in the text, the millennium, or the period of the thousand years, is introduced by the rising and living again of "them that were beheaded for the testimony of Jesus, and for the word of God, and which had not worshipped the beast nor his image." These holy ones are to "live and reign with Christ the thousand years;" and so their resurrection must occur at the beginning of the thousand years. And as they that are Christ's arise "at his coming," *his coming must be before the millennium.*

Such, then, is the glorious hope of the Lord's people. Very soon shall Christ their deliverer come, and change them into a full likeness to himself. Then shall his victory over death be manifest. "Because he lives, we shall live also." "For if we believe that Jesus died and rose again, even so them also which sleep in Jesus will God bring with him." And how many sunny thoughts cluster around this doctrine!

There is nothing so repulsive to our natural instincts as death. There are few people who do not feel a cold shudder creeping through and through them whenever they realize the thought that they must die, and have the coffin-lid screwed down upon their foreheads, and be covered up with clods in the damp dark ground. But the hope of the resurrection of the just throws a radiance round the death-bed and the grave, and helps to reconcile us to the mysterious change. To a good man, the sepulchre is but the gateway to a better world, —the resting-place for the wasted and wearied body previous to going forth into the bliss and honors of a divine and eternal kingdom. Its shades are but a quiet night anterior to an everlasting day. Death is but *a sleep*, which presupposes a future awakening. "An eternal sleep" is a contradiction in terms,—a miserable solecism,—a mode of speech the very phraseology of which brands the atheistic invention with absurdity. Sleep is but the temporary suspension of animation for the purpose of refreshment and invigoration. It is always succeeded by a waking. And such is death to the Christian. Jesus has transmuted it into a refreshing *sleep*, from which we shall early arise, in renewed strength and glory, for the scenes and employments of a day which shall have no night. The New Testament nearly always speaks of the departure of the believing as a *sleep*. Jesus said, "Our friend Lazarus *sleepeth;* but I go that I may awake him out of *sleep*." "The saints which *slept*," is familiar phraseology to the reader of the Scriptures. "David, after he had served his own generation, *fell on sleep*." As the first martyr died, Luke said he "*fell asleep*." Paul comforted the mourning Thessalonians, by assuring them that their pious dead "are *asleep*,"—only "*asleep*,"—to be waked to life again when Jesus comes. And so all the saints that have departed this life are said to "*sleep in Jesus*."

Yes, Christian parent, that child which so suddenly sickened, withered and faded in your arms, and which with so much sadness you yielded to the cold dark grave, is not lost and gone eternally. It only sleeps—sweetly sleeps—in the arms of its Maker. You buried it; but you buried it looking for the resurrection of the last day, when it shall awake to be yours forever. Weep not, O daughter, as if that sainted mother whom you last saw dressed for the tomb shall never look upon you again with her wonted love and tenderness. She is thy mother still. She is not dead, but sleepeth. She will awake again, and take you to her heart as fondly as ever. Sorrow not as they that have no hope, O stricken one, mourning over a husband's grave. He has only laid him down to rest in soft slumber. God's eye is on that prostrate buried form. And when thy loved one's Savior comes he will shake off his sepulchral covering, and be thy constant friend as in the days gone by.

"Soon shall you meet again,
Meet ne'er to sever;
Soon will peace wreath her chain
Round you forever."

And what a reunion of hearts and exchange of happy gratulations shall crown and crowd that day! What glorious meetings and triumphs will then be celebrated! What devout and anxious hopes shall then be consummated! Then shall Jesus say, "Awake and sing, ye that dwell in the dust;" and they shall obey his call, and rise to praise him forever. Then will the once-afflicted saints of every age and clime "stand drest in robes of everlasting wear." Then shall those who denied themselves and took up the cross receive their crowns. Then shall the wisdom of their "respect unto the recompense of the reward" be vindicated forever. Then shall God glorify his Son by transforming millions into his glorious image. And "then shall be brought to pass the saying that is written, *Death is swallowed up in victory.*"

Earth, my brethren, has been the theatre of some splendid victories, the fame of which has filled the world and echoed along the corridors of ages. But never has earth beheld such a triumph as that which shall be realized at the resurrection of the just. Then shall be enacted another genesis, more glorious than the first. Then shall be performed another exodus, more illustrious than that which Moses led. Then shall truth triumph over error, and faith over unbelief, humility over pride, life over death, and immortality over the grave. Then shall the cross give way to the crown, and corruption to glory; and from the mold and ashes of every

Christian's tomb shall come forth an undying form, radiant with the transforming touch of Deity,—a dear-bought but sublime and imperishable monument to the resurrection and the life. The graves of the patriarchs shall open. The scattered dust and ashes of prophets, apostles and martyrs shall be gathered. Unknown saints of God that have died in garrets, and cellars, and barns, and dungeons,—and lowly and despised poor in Christ who sleep in potters'-fields,—shall spring forth from their unnoticed graves in sublimer glory than ever adorned the illustrious Solomon. Precious innocents, whose names were never heard, and lamented children, that molder in their little tombs, and pious afflicted ones, who spent their days in pain secluded from the gay world,—all, *all* shall then forsake their resting-places and shine as the stars for ever and ever. Then shall all the waiting saints of all lands and ages, mysteriously transferred to the bridal halls of heaven, join in holy fellowship to celebrate with untold joy the sublime epiphany of their redeeming Lord, with all their varied tongues in heavenly concord singing the triumphs of that salvation for which they lived, and hoped, and suffered.

> "Oh, scenes surpassing fable, and yet true!
> Scenes of accomplished bliss! which, who can see,
> Though but in distant prospect, and not feel
> His soul refreshed with foretastes of the joy?"

Not all the saints, indeed, may rise at the same instant, nor all the living be translated at once; there is progression and order in all the divine works;* but still the resurrection is for all that sleep in Christ, and the translation for all whom he shall find awaiting his coming. All shall share in the happy victory. And what adds to the peculiar joy of some is that they will never die at all, but shall be changed, in a moment, in the twinkling of an eye, at the last trump; for the trumpet shall sound, and the dead shall be raised

* See Note H, page 349.

incorruptible, and we shall be changed." "The dead in Christ shall rise first: then we which are alive and remain shall be caught up together with them." And what a thought is this, that there perhaps are some listening to me now who shall never know by experience what death is! Those of Christ's people who are living when he comes shall of a sudden feel the thrill of immortality careering through them, and find themselves transported to join the children of the resurrection. Not one of them that truly believe in Jesus shall be left behind. The humblest and obscurest, the lowest with the highest, all shall be taken together. For "he shall send forth his angels, with a great sound of a trumpet, and they shall gather together his elect from the four winds, from one end of heaven to the other." And they shall live and reign with Christ the thousand years. "And so shall we ever be with the Lord." And thenceforward forever shall this song be sung:—

"Behold, the tabernacle of God is with men,
And he will dwell with them,
And they shall be his people,
And God himself shall be with them,
And be their God.
And God shall wipe away all tears from their eyes;
And there shall be no more death,
Neither sorrow, nor crying,
Neither shall there be any more pain:
For the former things are passed away."

Verily, "blessed and holy is he that hath part in the first resurrection!" Was there ever conceived such a system of grace and glory as that which constitutes the gospel of Jesus? How precious are its promises! How transporting are its hopes! How it meets the vast desires of humanity, and pours consolation into the hearts of the children of sorrow! What is there to compare with it? Atheism, with its eternal sleep, may stupefy the soul, and render it somewhat callous to

10

the woes of life. But how sad and cheerless is the epitaph which it writes on the tomb! Heathen philosophy, with its transmigrations and feeble guesses, may excite some dull and low concern for futurity; but how gloomy is the destiny which it sets before man! It is only Christianity, with its resurrection and another life, that can at all rouse man into a proper consciousness of his dignity, or satisfy the lofty and mighty aspirations that well up from his heart. This is our glorious hope, the price of which cannot be equalled with gold.

And how devoutly thankful should we then be for what God has done for us and purposed concerning us! How should our hearts soften at the contemplations before us, and swell with emotions of love towards so great a Benefactor! How should we be concerned to find out the will of such a friend, and seek to approve ourselves unto him! How cheerfully should we hail him as the chief among ten thousand, and the one altogether lovely! How gladly should we set ourselves to do his gracious commands, and to keep his loving counsels! In him is our strength, our hope, and our joy. He is not ashamed to be our God, and surely we should not be ashamed to be his people, "looking for that blessed hope, even the glorious appearing of the great God, our Savior Jesus Christ." Let us, then, give ourselves to him, body and soul, as a living sacrifice, which is our reasonable service. Let us fully identify ourselves with Jesus, knowing that "when he shall appear, we shall be like him, for we shall see him as he is." And, especially, let us not forget that "every man that hath this hope in him purifieth himself, even as the Savior is pure." He hath prepared for us a city; but "there shall in no wise enter into it any thing that defileth, neither whatsoever worketh abomination, or maketh a lie." It is only "*the holy*" who shall have part in the first resurrection. "The fearful, and unbelieving, and the abominable, and murderers, and whoremongers, and sorcerers, and idolaters, and all liars, shall have their part in the lake which burneth with fire and brimstone, which is the second death." It is only "unto them that look for him" that "he shall appear the second time unto salvation."

WIRD DAS NICHT FREUDE SEYN!

Will that not joyful be,
When we walk by faith no more,
When the Lord we loved before
As Brother-man we see!
When he welcomes us above,
When we share his smile of love,—
Will that not joyful be?

Will that not joyful be,
When to meet us rise and come
All our buried treasures home,
A glorious company!
When our arms embrace again
Those we mourned so long in vain,—
Will that not joyful be?

Will that not joyful be,
When the foes we dread to meet
Every one beneath our feet
We tread triumphantly!
When we never more can know
Slightest touch of pain or woe,—
Will that not joyful be?

Yes! that will joyful be,
When we hear what none can tell,
And the ringing chorus swell
Of angels' melody!
When we join their songs of praise,
Hallelujahs with them raise,—
That, that will joyful be!

H. C. von Schweinitz.

FIFTH DISCOURSE.

THE MESSIAH'S KINGDOM—HOW SPOKEN OF BY THE ANCIENT PROPHETS—HOW APPREHENDED BY THE SAVIOR'S CONTEMPORARIES—HOW SPOKEN OF IN THE NEW TESTAMENT—SPECIFICALLY CONNECTED WITH THE SECOND ADVENT—THE PRESENT DISPENSATION NOT THE MESSIAH'S GLORIOUS REIGN.

DAN. vii. 13, 14: *I saw in the night visions, and behold, one like the Son of man came with the clouds of heaven, and came to the Ancient of days, and they brought him near before him. And there was given him dominion and glory, and a kingdom, that all people, nations and languages should serve him: his dominion is an everlasting dominion, which shall not pass away, and his kingdom that which shall not be destroyed.*

THAT this vision contains a prophecy concerning "the last times," will not be denied. That the "one like the Son of man" is Jesus Christ, in his glorified human nature, is admitted on all hands. That his "coming with the clouds of heaven" refers to his final advent in this world, is also the common belief of interpreters. His being led to the Ancient of days to receive dominion, plainly denotes his investiture with rulership, and his inauguration into the august office of the almighty Sovereign of the nations. This dominion is something more than his present spiritual reign in men's hearts; for he does not enter upon it until he comes in the clouds. It is also a kingdom the affairs of which are to be administered by Christ in person, or by those under his immediate control and direction; for it is given to him as the Son of man, and his personal descent at the time of receiving it is explicitly affirmed. It must also be a visible and terrestrial kingdom, for "nations" are mentioned as its subjects.

The doctrine which I accordingly deduce from this text, and which I shall aim to set forth in this discourse, is, That *the Lord Jesus Christ will return again to this world, and here set up a visible Christocracy, or empire of his own, and personally reign over the nations in the bliss and glory of a universal and eternal kingdom.* There are many good people who believe no such thing. My main object will therefore be to prove it by solid Scriptural arguments. And if I can show that it has a firm foundation in the word of God, I certainly have a right to claim for it the respect due to a doctrine of inspiration. Let us then approach the subject with humble reverence, sincerely desirous to learn the truth, and earnestly praying that God may give us a proper insight to this wonderful mystery.

I. I remark then, in the first place, that the prophecies of the Old Testament, when taken in their plain and natural sense, certainly predict the Messiah as a great prince who shall reign in this world. To establish this remark I apprehend to be no difficult task. The very first words that ever were uttered concerning Christ already imply it. When God reckoned with Adam, though he excluded him from Paradise, he left him this consoling promise:—*The seed of the woman shall bruise the serpent's head.* Satan had assailed our first parents, and overcome them. By that victory he became the reigning prince of this world, and to this day he holds his dark supremacy in nearly every department of the earth. The crushing of this serpent's head can mean nothing less than the demolition of Satan's empire, and the establishment of the empire of the woman's seed in its place. And if Christ, as the Son of man, is to displace Satan, and reign over the nations as Satan now rules over them, nothing short of a literal, real and universal empire can be the result.

The next distinct allusion to this "seed" is in God's covenant with Abraham, where it is said that he shall "*possess the gate of his enemies, and all nations of the earth be blessed in him.*" Paul tells us that this promise did not belong to Abraham's posterity at large, but only to "*one*, which is Christ." To possess an enemy's gate is to conquer that enemy,—to take his last defence. And when it is said of Christ, that he shall possess the gates of his enemies, and bless all nations, we have before us the idea of a great, victorious and universal prince, making himself the master and the benefactor of the world.

Another reference to the same thing we find in Hannah's song, where it is said, "*The Lord shall judge the ends of the earth, and he shall give strength to his King, and exalt the horn of his anointed.*" Here too we have the princedom of the Messiah in this world, and his universal sovereignty, pointedly asserted.

In God's promises to David we have the matter still more particularly amplified. God says to the monarch of Israel, "*When thy days be fulfilled, and thou shalt sleep with thy fathers, I will set up thy seed after thee, and I will establish his kingdom, and the throne of his kingdom, forever. And* THINE HOUSE, *and* THY KINGDOM *shall be established forever before thee:* THY THRONE SHALL BE ESTABLISHED FOREVER." If this promise refers pre-eminently to Christ "the Son of David," as all agree that it does, then he is to be a great earthly prince; for he is to occupy *a throne*, and possess *a kingdom*; and that throne and kingdom are identical with the throne and kingdom of his father David. Much as men may dislike to admit this, here is God's promise, in words as plain as any man can use. David had an empire in this world; and he reigned as a prince in this world; and God says that his promised Son shall take David's place, and establish David's throne forever. David himself certainly so understood the promise, and by divine inspiration so prophesied of it in the Psalms. As he had his court in Mount Zion, so he represents his illustrious Son as "*King upon the holy hill of Zion,*" with the heathen given to him for his inheritance, and the uttermost parts of the earth for his possession. "He shall have dominion from sea to sea, and from the river to the ends of the earth. Yea, kings shall fall down before him: *all nations shall serve him.*" Who can listen to such language with an unbiassed mind, and not gather from it the idea, that the prophet is here speaking of some great and mighty king, who is to sway the sceptre of literal empire over the inhabitants of this world?

Turn now to Isaiah, the great evangelical prophet, and see how he describes the Messiah. "Unto us a child is born, unto us a son is given, and his name shall be called, Wonderful, Counselor, The mighty God, The Father of the everlasting age, The Prince of peace." Nobody misunderstands this. All take the words just as they are written, without looking after some mystical or allegorical meaning. By what authority, then, shall we reject the literal acceptation of what follows? "*And the government shall be upon his shoulder. Of the increase of his government and peace there shall be no end,* UPON THE THRONE OF DAVID, AND UPON HIS KINGDOM, *to order* IT, *and to establish* IT *with judgment and with justice from henceforth even forever.*" What could more unequivocally describe the Messiah as a great prince, reigning in David's place in this world?

If we turn to Jeremiah, we find the Savior spoken of in the same manner. "Behold, the days come, saith the Lord, that *I will raise* UNTO DAVID *a righteous Branch, and a* KING *shall reign and prosper, and shall execute justice and judgment* IN THE EARTH. *In his days* JUDAH *shall be saved, and* ISRAEL *shall dwell safely.*" "And they shall serve the Lord their God, *and David their King* (*in his promised Son*) *whom I will raise up unto them.*"

These are very plain and positive predictions. Others of like import might be presented. Here and elsewhere, the Messiah is again and again called *a king*. He is to possess and occupy David's throne. He is to be a conqueror of his enemies and the possessor of their cities. He is to reign over the nations. He is to be the commander around whose banner the Gentiles shall be gathered. His kingdom is to be in a sense the kingdom of David, re-established, exalted, extended over all the earth, and made forever permanent. This is the natural and obvious meaning of the words; and there is no reason why we should understand them differently, or seek for some other remote and occult meaning. Professor Stuart has justly said that "it is one of the plainest and most cogent of all the rules of hermeneutics, that every passage of Scripture, or of any other book, is to be interpreted as bearing its plain and primary and literal sense, unless good reason can be given why it should be tropically understood." Vitringa gives it as "an unerring canon, and of great use," that "we must never depart from the literal meaning of the subject mentioned in its own appropriate name, if its principal attributes square with the subject of the prophecy." Ernesti says, "Theologians are right when they affirm the literal sense to be the only true one." And Hooker declares, "I hold it for a most infallible rule in expositions of sacred Scripture, that when a literal construction will stand, the farthest from the letter is commonly the worst." What then are we to do with the prophecies to which I have referred? The literal meaning is evident. There is not only no necessity for departing from it, but we cannot depart from it without violence and inconsistency. I therefore claim it as a fact, that the Old Testament writers have predicted Christ as a great prince who is literally to reign upon the throne of David in real empire over all the world

II. It is also true, in the second place, that when the Savior came into the world, as the Son of Mary, he was expected as a great prince who should set up a literal empire in this world. This is a point so notorious, and so much dwelt upon by theologians and preachers, that it is hardly necessary to do more than state it.

Knapp says, "At the time of Christ, and previously, the current opinion of the people in Palestine, and indeed of most of the Pharisees and lawyers, was, that he would be a temporal deliverer and a King of the Jews, and indeed a universal monarch, who would reign over all nations. *The apostles themselves held this opinion.*"

Neander says, "The Jews expected a Messiah who should be armed with miraculous power in their behalf, free them from civil bondage, execute a severe retribution upon the enemies of the theocratic people, and make them masters of the world in a universal empire, whose glory it was their special delight to set forth."

Schaf says, "The Jews conceived of the Messianic kingdom as a glorious restoration of the throne of David."

Brooks says, "It is quite notorious that the Jews did, in the time of our Savior, look for a King who should, in an illustrious and glorious manner, inherit the throne of David, reign over Israel, and obtain dominion and possession over all nations."

And so uniform is the testimony on this point, that it is unnecessary to argue it. When Herod inquired of the chief priests and scribes where Christ should be born, "they said unto him, In Bethlehem of Judea; for thus it is written by the prophet, And thou Bethlehem, in the land of Juda, art not the least among the princes of Juda: for out of thee shall come A GOVERNOR *that shall rule my people Israel.*" This shows how the Jews understood the ancient prophets, and what were their expectations at the time. Herod certainly acted under the apprehension that the coming Christ was to be a great prince, when he gave orders "and slew all the children that were in Bethlehem, and in all the coasts thereof." Why adopt measures to slay the infant Savior if he did not fear that Christ would again restore the Jewish throne? Nay, we read that even from far beyond the limits of Palestine, certain "wise men came, saying, Where is he that is born *King of the Jews?*" It would seem that whithersoever a knowledge of the Hebrew prophecies had gone, it was uniformly expected that the promised Messiah would be a sublime and triumphant Jewish king, whose dominion would absorb all other kingdoms, and stand forever.

That extravagant and unfounded notions were entertained by many, I have no doubt. Some looked for Christ only as a military hero, and conceived of his reign too much after the style of ambitious tyranny. They sometimes spoke of him only as a conquering leader, whereas he is at the same time a divine spiritual Savior. They surrounded him too much with their own carnal and resentful feelings, and overlooked that meekness and holiness of spirit which is indispensable to a blissful participation in his princely ministrations. They failed to apprehend that great foundation-fact, that he was first to suffer ere he should reign, and bear the cross before reaching the crown. But, with all their narrow bigotries and carnal hopes, they did not misconceive this one prominent feature of the matter, that the promised Messiah was to be a great prince, who should reign upon the throne of David his father, and extend his royal dominion over all the earth. So the prophets had spoken, and so they understood what the prophets said.

III. I proceed, then, to a third remark, viz.: that the New Testament nowhere contradicts what was thus expected of the Messiah. There are, indeed, a few passages which seem to conflict with these expectations; but when attentively considered, and their real meaning ascertained, they will be found entirely accordant with the doctrine which I am endeavoring to set forth.

That Christianity is an eminently spiritual religion, all who understand it must admit.* The fundamental principle of the Messiah's kingdom is his reign over the heart, bringing all its affections and impulses into subjection to the will of God. This is the germ on which every thing else depends. He who is not spiritually renewed, and morally assimilated to Christ, has neither part nor lot in Christ's kingdom, whatever may be his birth, blood, or external relations. "However different the extent and outward form of the kingdom," says a distinguished author, "however great its ultimate triumph and glories, this is still its peculiar feature and character,—God, the Savior, reigning supreme in the heart of the once-alienated and rebellious sinner, and all dispensations are but hastening on this great result the more fully over all the earth." We would ignore the most glorious and most distinguished feature of Christianity, if we were for a moment to think differently. It is therefore to be presumed that the Savior and his inspired servants should set forth this point with marked perspicuity. And we would especially expect them to express themselves strongly on this feature of the kingdom, as there were many of their hearers who had quite lost sight of it. It was the most serious mistake of the Jews, not that they expected Christ as a triumphing Lord, but that they did not comprehend how he was at the same time to be a spiritual Redeemer, and that the blessings of his glorious reign were to extend only to those who should be inwardly subjected to his holy will. They thought their lineal descent from Abraham, and their formal submission to the Mosaic ritual, presented all that was needful to secure for them the full benefit of the sublime achievements of their expected King. This was a disease needing to be cauterized. Hence, when the Pharisees

---

* See Note E, page 335.

asked Jesus "when the kingdom of God should come," he at once struck at the root of their false hopes, and called them back from their dreams of glory to those first rudiments without which neither Jew nor Gentile shall ever see the kingdom of God. "He answered and said, The kingdom of God cometh not with observation." That is, the essence of the Messianic reign does not lie in the pomp, show and outward demonstrations of power for which they were looking. "Neither shall they say, Lo here! or, Lo there!" as if it were to be set up with mere physical victories. "*The kingdom of God is within you.*" Its seat is in the heart; and unless first found in the heart it will never be found at all. This is what they had overlooked; and this is all this passage teaches. It is to the same point that Paul speaks, when he says, "The kingdom of God is not meat and drink, but righteousness, peace and joy in the Holy Ghost." The antithesis which he presents is not between a visible personal reign of Christ, and a mere reign by his Spirit and grace, but between the true prerequisite spiritual submission to Christ, and that mere ceremonial righteousness upon which the Jews so much boasted and relied. But the fact that a man's heart must be renewed and purified as a condition of participation in the blessings of the mediatorial kingdom, by no means proves that that kingdom is not hereafter to take form, and be outwardly manifested in a triumphant personal reign of the Savior in this world. For if we interpret these words so as to confine the divine kingdom to the heart, and to righteousness, peace and joy in the Holy Ghost, we necessarily exclude from it the outward church, the sacraments, and a future home in heaven. And yet, if we dare extend the limits of the divine kingdom beyond the mere inward experiences of the soul, there is nothing to prevent us from extending it so as to embrace also the future personal reign of the Messiah upon earth. For if the present existence of the kingdom in men's hearts is reconcilable with the hope of a more glorious form of the kingdom in the heavenly world, it is equally reconcilable, and on the same grounds, with the doctrine of the future princely reign of Christ over the nations.

Another passage often misquoted upon this subject is that where Christ says, "*My kingdom is not* (ἐκ) FROM *this world.*" When he uttered these words, he was on his trial before Pilate. He had been accused of treasonable purposes. Pilate, therefore, asked him whether he was a king. He boldly affirmed that he was a king. But to quiet their apprehensions that he was about to undertake to subvert the existing authorities by carnal violence, he qualified his avowal; and these words contain the qualification. He does not say that his kingdom is not to be located upon earth; for it is located here. His church and all its ordinances are on earth. The children of the kingdom live and operate in this world. He only says, his kingdom is not *from* this world, that it is of heavenly origin, and that it is to be set up by supernatural means, and not by human prowess or the might of earthly arms. That this is what he means, and all that he means, is evident from all the circumstances of the case, and is made abundantly clear from the additional words:—"*Else would my servants fight, that I should not be delivered to the Jews.*" Why did he not allow his servants to fight? Because his kingdom was not to be built up in that style. He is to enter upon his throne by a different process. He is to receive his dominion from above, and not from beneath. The Lord will give it to him. It will not come *out of* this world.*

I may therefore say, with perfect safety, that there is nothing in the New Testament to contradict the cherished expectations, that the Messiah is to reign as a great prince on David's throne in this world.

IV. Nay, I go further, and say, that there is much in the New Testament tending directly to confirm and deepen these

* See Note F, page 338.

prevailing expectations. Look for a moment at what the angel said to Mary, when he came to announce to her the birth of the expected Christ. Gabriel there says to the Virgin, "Thou shalt conceive in thy womb, and bring forth a son, and shalt call his name JESUS; he shall be great, and shall be called the Son of the Highest." These are plain words. All understand them just as they stand. And what follows is equally plain, and by all sound principles of interpretation must be taken as equally literal:—"*And the Lord shall give him the* THRONE OF HIS FATHER DAVID. AND HE SHALL REIGN OVER THE HOUSE OF JACOB FOREVER; *and of his kingdom there shall be no end.*" Now, what effect could such an announcement have upon those who were looking for the Christ as a great reigning prince, but to establish and fix all their prepossessions concerning him in that respect? And when his virgin mother first brought him as a babe to the temple, Simeon and Anna, by direct divine inspiration, spoke of him as the consolation for which Israel was looking, and as the one to accomplish *in Jerusalem* the very redemption which Judah was expecting. What could be the tendency of such utterances, but to make the people who heard them still more enthusiastic in the hopes they were cherishing? When Nathanael first recognized the Savior's Messiahship, and addressed him as "Rabbi, the Son of God, *the King of Israel*," he evidently conceived of that kingship according to the prevailing belief of the time. And yet Christ passed it as a proper conception, and replied to it in a way which could only give intensity to the anticipations that were entertained. When the five thousand, who had been miraculously fed in the wilderness, would have taken him by force, and placed him on the throne, he withdrew himself; for his time for that had not yet come; neither was that the way in which he was to obtain his crown. But he uttered not a word of censure to indicate that they were wrong in looking upon him as he who should hold earthly dominion, and reign with authority like that with which they desired to invest him. When he made his triumphal entry into Jerusalem, and the people around him shouted, "*Blessed be the King!*" "*Blessed be the kingdom of our father David which cometh in the name of the Lord!*" "*Hosannah to the Son of David!*" what did they mean? Did they not thereby point to him as their expected Messiah, who should break the power of their enemies, renew the Jewish throne, establish an earthly empire, and reign as a mighty prince? What else could they have meant? And yet Jesus received it all with approbation, and never once so much as hinted that they were the least mistaken. Nay, when the enraged Jewish officials came to him, angrily complaining of what had been said of him by the shouting multitude, he not only sided with the applauding people, but declared that if these held their peace, the stones themselves would cry out! What more impressive endorsement could he possibly have given to what the exulting crowd had uttered? Did he not thus acquiesce in their views? Did he not thus most effectually set his seal of sanction to the proclamation, and emphatically declare himself the King of the Jews, who should restore and occupy the throne of David, and reign in Mount Zion according to the letter of prophecy? And so again, when the mother of Zebedee's children asked him that her two sons might sit, as ministers of state, the one on his right hand and the other on his left *in his kingdom*, she doubtless conceived of that kingdom as a princely reign in this world. Her request is amply indicative of this. But, if she was wrong, the Savior's answer certainly went much further to confirm her views than to undeceive her. True, he did not agree to grant her desire; but he left her under the belief that there are such places to be filled in his empire, and that they are reserved for those for whom the Father has prepared them. Are we to suppose the holy Jesus capable of encouraging delusion? He knew what sort of views that woman had of his kingdom; and if it were not in his purpose to establish that kingdom as she apprehended that he would, his conduct and answer are quite inexplicable. The prayer of the penitent thief on the cross presents a similar case. That heart-broken sufferer besought the Savior to remember him when he came *in his kingdom*. His ideas of that kingdom were doubtless, in the main at least, just what were generally entertained. And the Savior answered him without intimating that he was at all mistaken, and left him to die under the impression with which he uttered the prayer. See, also, with what firmness the Savior expressed himself when before Pilate. He was there charged with conspiracy and treason. The question of Pilate was addressed directly to his political pretensions. His accusers were standing by, eagerly watching for the smallest intimations on which they might secure his condemnation. But his great spirit did not quail. Rising up in the sublime dignity which belonged to his high nature, he boldly affirmed his claim to royal appointment and power. And then, at the last, having spent forty days with his disciples after his resurrection from the dead, "speaking of the things pertaining to the kingdom of God," how impressive is the sanction which he gave to the fond expectations concerning his earthly princedom! Certainly, all these special instructions to his disciples upon this particular subject left them no room for any further misunderstanding. And yet, at the last hour of his stay on earth, we find them still identifying the Messiah's reign with the restoration of the Jewish throne, and Christ himself still replying to them in a way which could only deepen and strengthen their ideas of the matter. If there were nothing else upon the subject in the New Testament but this account of Christ's last interview with his disciples, it would be enough upon which to base the belief, that it is his purpose, at the appointed time, to revive the throne of David, and to reign personally upon earth. They expected him to "restore the kingdom to Israel," and wished to know the time; and all he said, and the last he said, was, that they were not "to know the time."

There is also another class of New Testament passages, equally, if not still more strongly, corroborative of the common expectations of the Messianic reign. When the disciples asked the Savior what they should have in return for their sacrifices in his cause, he replied, "*When the Son of man shall sit in the throne of his glory, ye also shall sit upon twelve thrones, judging the twelve tribes of Israel.*" "I appoint unto you *a kingdom, as my Father hath appointed unto me,* that ye may eat and drink at my table *in my kingdom, and sit on thrones, judging the twelve tribes of Israel.*" "Jerusalem shall be trodden down of the Gentiles, until the times of the Gentiles be fulfilled. . . . . When ye see these things come to pass, know ye that *the kingdom of God is nigh at hand.* Verily, this γενεὰ—this Jewish race—shall not pass away—not cease from being a distinct people—TILL ALL BE FULFILLED."* He here appropriates to himself a future kingdom. He says that it is to be set up at the expiration of the Gentile dominancy, and while the Jews still continue as a distinct race. He says that the apostles are to share in the administrations of that kingdom, as judges of the twelve tribes of Israel. And what effect would such declarations produce upon the minds of men who contemplated the Messiah's reign as a literal kingdom upon earth? What language could have been framed that would more certainly have been interpreted in favor of their views? May we not then set it down as settled and clear, that the New Testament, so far from contradicting the literal statements of the old, or the expectations founded thereon, speaks in the same strain, and fans those anticipations into greater brightness and intensity?

---

* See Note B, page 323.

V. But again I remark, that the Scriptures explicitly speak of the setting up of a kingdom in connection with the Savior's final advent, which answers exactly to the literal predictions of the ancient prophets which I have quoted, and to the expectations of the Jews and his first disciples. Upon this point the text itself is conclusive. All agree that it refers to the Savior's coming in glory to judge the world,—to his personal coming at the end of the present dispensation. And it is here affirmed, with an explicitness which cannot be evaded, that at the period of his coming there is to be "*given him dominion, and glory, and a kingdom, that all people,* NATIONS *and languages* SHOULD SERVE HIM: *his dominion is an everlasting dominion, which shall not pass away, and his kingdom that which shall not be destroyed.*" And that there might be no misunderstanding or mistake about the matter, an angel explains the vision, and says that the blasphemous and persecuting power denoted by the little horn is to prevail against the saints until "*the judgment shall sit,*" and THEN "*the kingdom, and dominion, and the greatness of the kingdom* UNDER THE WHOLE HEAVEN, *shall be given to the people of the saints of the Most High, whose kingdom is an everlasting kingdom, and* ALL DOMINIONS SHALL SERVE AND OBEY HIM." These words describe a literal kingdom, a universal kingdom, a kingdom *under* the heavens, over the nations and tribes of this world, and which is only to be set up at the session of the judgment, and the coming of the Son of man in the clouds.

Look also at the vision of the great golden-headed image, and the stone cut from the mountains without hands, which smote the great image, broke it and filled all the earth. We have there an epitome of this world's history: first, the four great monarchies beginning with Babylon, and extending down to the sovereignties which now occupy the territory of the ancient Roman empire; second, the utter extinction of these monster powers during the regency of the ten kingdoms into which the Roman empire was ultimately divided; and third, the setting up in their place of a divine, universal and eternal empire, symbolized by the stone from the mountains. Daniel thus interprets the vision :—"*In the days of these kings*" —that is, in the days of the kingdoms denoted by the ten toes of the great image, during the existence of the Roman empire in its last form of ten kindred regencies—"*shall the God of heaven set up a kingdom which shall never be destroyed: and the kingdom shall not be left to other people, but it shall break in pieces and consume all these kingdoms, and it shall stand forever.*" Some have supposed that the introduction of Christianity is here meant; but Dr. Berg has justly remarked that "*this view is not tenable.*" When Christianity was introduced, the Roman empire was yet *one.* It was not divided into its ultimate ten parts for hundreds of years afterwards. Besides, Christianity is not *a kingdom* in the sense in which the prophet is here using that word. This kingdom denoted by the mystic stone, which God is to set up, and which is to stand forever, is so related to the other kingdoms mentioned that we must necessarily assign to it something of a similar nature. Tillinghast says, "In respect of nature, it is the same with the kingdoms represented by the great image; *i. e. it is outward as they are outward;* which appears: (1.) From the general scope and drift of the prophecy, which runs upon outward kingdoms. All the first four kingdoms, or monarchies, are outward, as none can deny; why then the Holy Ghost, in speaking of the fifth and last, should so far vary the scope as to glide from the outward kingdom to the inward, ought, besides the bare say-so, to have some solid and substantial reason brought for it by those, whosoever they are, that either do or shall assert it. (2.) Because it is not proper to say that a bare spiritual kingdom, considered only as spiritual, should break in pieces, beat to very chaff, grind to powder, the great image, *i. e.* destroy the very being of worldly kingdoms, which work is yet, notwithstanding, done by this stone. Indeed, Christ's spiritual kingdom may, by that light and life which it gives forth, much refine and reform outward kingdoms; but when once the work comes to breaking, and breaking in pieces, *i. e.* subverting kingdoms, razing their very foundations and destroying their very being, as they the kings of this world are here, unless we conceive God to do it by a miracle, must we also conceive some other hand besides a spiritual put to the work. (3.) Because the stone, to the end there might not be a vacancy in the world, comes straightway in the place and room of the great image, so soon as the same is totally broken. For as the great image, while standing, bears rule over all the earth, so the same being broken, the stone becomes a mountain and fills the whole earth, *therefore must the kingdom of the stone be such a kingdom as was that of the great image, viz.:* OUTWARD; or otherwise, the coming of that, in the place of the other now taken away, could not supply the want of the other."

This quotation is long, involved and robed in the quaintness of two centuries ago, but it is perfectly conclusive upon the point that the stone-kingdom which God is to set up, and which is to consume and destroy all other kingdoms and stand forever, is a literal, real, outward, terrestrial empire. The time when that kingdom is to be set up is the time when the last forms of usurped dominion, denoted by the ten toes of the great image, are to be broken in pieces. The ten toes of that image are acknowledged on all hands to be the same as the ten-horned wild beast of John. The ten-horned wild beast is only to be taken and destroyed when the heavens shall open and the Son of God come forth to tread the winepress of God's wrath, and give judgment to the martyrs and saints. *Therefore the coming of Christ is to be attended with the setting up of a visible, outward, universal, divine and eternal empire,* such as the Jews associated with the Messianic reign.

The Savior himself has spoken of the matter to the same effect. Hear his words:—"WHEN *the Son of man* SHALL COME IN HIS GLORY, and all the holy angels with him, THEN SHALL HE SIT UPON THE THRONE OF HIS GLORY; *and before him shall be gathered all nations; and he shall separate* THEM (THE NATIONS) *one from another*, as a shepherd divideth his sheep from the goats; and he shall set the sheep on his right hand, but the goats on the left. THEN *shall* THE KING *say to them on his right hand, Come, ye blessed of my Father*, INHERIT THE KINGDOM *prepared for you from the foundation of the world.*" In the same strain he elsewhere says, "*They shall see the Son of man coming in a cloud, with power and great glory. . . .* WHEN *ye see these things come to pass, know ye that* THE KINGDOM OF GOD IS NIGH AT HAND." Paul also says to Timothy, "I charge thee therefore before God, even the Lord Jesus Christ, who shall judge the quick and dead AT HIS APPEARING AND KINGDOM." All these passages unequivocally connect the setting up of the glorious Messianic kingdom with the Savior's final coming.

Elsewhere Paul connects the final advent with the sounding of "the last trump;" and when we turn to John's vision of what attends the sounding of the seventh or last trumpet, we read, "There were great voices in heaven, saying, THE KINGDOMS OF THE WORLD ARE BECOME THE KINGDOMS OF OUR LORD AND OF HIS CHRIST; AND HE SHALL REIGN FOREVER AND EVER!" And that there might be no misapprehension of *the time* to which this vision relates, the four-and-twenty elders respond with thanksgiving that it is "*the time of the dead that they should be judged,*"—the time of giving reward to the servants of God, the prophets, saints and all that fear him,—the time that Christ shall "destroy them that corrupt the earth:" (Rev. xi. 15–18.)

Paul also connects the resurrection of the saints with Christ's final coming:—"The Lord himself shall descend from heaven, and the dead in Christ shall rise first." In this he agrees exactly with John's vision of "the first resurrection." But in that vision John saw *thrones*, and the martyrs, the blessed and holy, seated on them; and they were made kings and priests of God, "*and they lived and reigned with Christ a thousand years.*"

In all these passages we have a literal, universal and abiding kingdom ascribed to Christ in connection with his second coming. It is not a kingdom far off in the remoteness of unknown space, but here in this world. It is to be "*under heaven.*" It is to embrace "the kingdoms of the world." Its subjects are to be "people, nations and languages." To take possession of it, Christ is said to "descend from heaven," "come," "appear," and stand again upon the earth. It is then of necessity just such a kingdom as the prophets foretold, and as the Jews and apostles expected. It is to be outward, literal, universal, glorious and eternal. It is not "*from* or *out* of *this world*," just as John's baptism was not "*from* or *out* of *this world.*" It comes *from God.* It originates from above, not from beneath. It is not set up by earthly means, but by divine power. But as John baptized on earth, although his baptism was not "from this world," and as the church is located on earth, although not of the earth, so Christ will reign in this world in the sublimities of visible empire. We never read of his return to heaven after he once comes to this world a second time. He remains here. His tabernacle is then to be "*with men, and he will* DWELL *among them*, and they shall be his people, and *God himself shall be with them.*"

This reign of Christ, then, is also to be a *personal reign.* He was "made in the likeness of men." He must therefore have a local dwelling-place. As the Son of man he is now in heaven. And when it is said that he will come again to earth, and *dwell with men*, we must believe that this world will be his home. He cannot dwell and reign on earth as the son of David and not be personally present on the earth.

Every point, then, at which the Scriptures touch upon this subject, furnishes something to corroborate and strengthen our doctrine that the Lord Jesus Christ will return again to this world, and here set up a literal empire or Christocracy, and personally reign over the nations in the bliss and glory of a universal and eternal kingdom. The prophecies of the Old Testament, taken in their plain natural sense, teach it. When Christ was on earth, both Jews and Christians held it. The New Testament nowhere condemns it as an error, but in many places refers to it as a matter well and correctly understood; and in the Old Testament and the New we find many passages which cannot be consistently interpreted without admitting it as a true doctrine of God. We cannot, therefore, escape from the conclusion that the blessed and adorable Son of the Virgin is yet to reign in this world as a great and glorious divine prince, whom all the nations shall obey and the world hail as its only King. All the Scriptures proclaim it; the whole creation groans and longs for it; and I cannot but believe it. Next to the doctrine of atonement for the world's guilt, it is the dearest of all the revealments of God.

To this hour, the greatest desideratum of our race is good government,—government freed from the frailties and unrighteousness which have ever adhered to that department of human interest. The church, too, is crippled, torn and disordered, for want of some present divine umpire to judge between its contending sects, purge out its ambitious disturbers and quell its feverish perturbations. All nature seems to have heard the promise concerning the seed of the woman and his restorative empire, and has stood in anxious expectancy ever since. All the world, in all its departments, has been longing and prophesying for ages, for a divine Deliverer, and the age of gold which his administrations are to bring with them. And yet he has not come. I do not, indeed, deny that Christ now reigns in the hearts of his children, or that he exercises a providential control over the affairs of the world. I know and rejoice that there is a sense in which he is present now, even where but two or three are assembled in his name; and that wherever a sinner turns to God, there something of his regal authority and power are felt. But I also know, that, with all his spiritual and providential presence and rule, as now in the world, every thing is *imperfect* as compared with the promises of what is to be hereafter. Satan, for the most part, is yet the king and master of this world, and not the illustrious Son of David. Every thing in church and state, public and private, is more or less disjointed, weak, sickly, and failing of what we most desire. Remedies only multiply wants and defects. "That which is crooked cannot be made straight; and that which is wanting cannot be numbered." The best-planned institutions and the wisest laws are constantly disappointing us. The holy law itself was "weak through the flesh;" and the same is to be said of all that we now have. No one adequately fulfills or can fulfill his relations. The consciences even of the best Christians, if properly enlightened, continually reproach them. Every thing seems to feel the absence of its redeeming Lord. He does not yet reign as it is necessary for us that he should reign. "*We see not yet all things put under him.*" Matters now are only in a stage preparatory to something still beyond us. The throne of David is yet less than a cipher. The promised Son has not yet lifted it out of its degradation. Mount Zion is still trodden by the vile foot of the destroyer. Israel, that is to be redeemed and become the standard-bearer of ransomed nations, is still scattered over all the earth. The enemies of God still vaunt themselves over his Anointed. Ignorance, fanaticism and infidelity still stalk abroad, even through the church. The man of sin, who opposeth and exalteth himself above all that is called God, still sits in the temple of God. Great Babylon still stands, drunk as she is with the blood of the saints. The wild beast and the false prophet are still allied against the Lamb, and against the witnesses of Jesus. Evil men and seducers are still waxing worse and worse. Despotism and tyranny still hold the places which justice and charity alone should fill. War and bloodshed still devastate and deluge this poor fallen world. Rapine and plunder still press their foul trade on land and on sea. Ambition, intrigue, finesse and deceit still hold disgraceful sway in the best parliaments and legislatures on earth. Scoffers abound everywhere, walking after their own lusts, and saying, Where is the promise of His coming? . The wails of suffering and wretchedness still float on every breeze; and the cries of wronged millions still go up into the ear of Jehovah.

Oh, tell me not that this is the glorious reign of Messiah! Tell me not that these are the scenes to which the saints of old looked with so much joy! I will not so disgrace my Savior or his word, as to allow for a moment that this dispensation is the sublime Messianic kingdom. No, no, no; Christ does not yet reign in the kingdom which he has promised and for which he has taught us to pray. Isaiah and Gabriel have said, that he should occupy the throne of his father David, and reign over the house of Jacob, and establish his government in eternal peace and righteousness; but David's sceptre he has never held, over Jacob's house he has never ruled, and the whole world is yet full of iniquity and wo. The Psalmist has taught us that "all nations shall serve him, the Gentiles be his inheritance, and the uttermost parts of the earth his possession;" but there is not a nation in all this wide world that is thoroughly Christian, and not a people who unanimously acknowledge that Christ is Lord. Of the ten hundred millions of souls that now constitute the family of man, not two-fifths are even professedly Christian! Take from the most Christian community—take from among the highly-favored inhabitants of our own city—all who are not of the household of faith, and what a scanty population would remain! Take the most enlightened and cultivated of the nations: take England—take Saxony—take our own country—take the model nation of Christendom, containing the most churches, and the greatest number of devout people: examine the structure of its government, test the operations of its laws, sift the character of its inhabitants, weigh it in the balances of Scripture truth and divine requirements, aggregate its good and its evil, strike the balance between righteousness and iniquity, and then tell me whether there is a nation on all the globe that does not gravitate towards hell rather than towards heaven! The church itself, enclosing within its pale all the purest and holiest specimens of humanity, after the toils and prayers of eighteen centuries, is still a feeble craft, working against wind and tide! Where, then, is that universal righteousness, peace and glory which gave inspiration to the songs of the prophets and hope to the souls of the dying saints of old? The reign of Messiah is to be a reign of glory, power and triumph, where vice is unknown and iniquity at an end,—where the branch from the root of Jesse is to strike all enemies dead and the Sun of righteousness disperse all darkness forever,—where all nations shall serve, worship and obey the King of Israel, and the earth shout the alleluia of her ultimate redemption; and it is worse than useless to try to persuade ourselves that such a condition of things belongs to this dispensation.

Nor is there any thing by way of inference from the past, or from indications of the present, or even in the sublime promises of the word of God, by which to assure ourselves that such a condition of things ever will be realized until the personal return of the blessed Christ for whom we wait. It is only *when he shall come*, that he will sit upon the throne of his glory. Antichrist shall not die till then. The world will not be fully redeemed till then. The glorious kingdom will not come till then. That is the grand climacteric of our faith; that is the sublime ultimatum of all our hopes.

Long, long has this great consummation been delayed,—so long that even pious men begin to doubt whether it ever shall come. But the word of Jehovah is out; he cannot recall it; he must fulfill it. Soon it will be here. Soon shall Messiah come in his glory, and set this imprisoned and down-trodden world at liberty. Soon shall the Son of Mary stand upon the Mount of Olives and plant his throne upon the hill of Zion. Soon shall the glorified saints supplant besotted politicians, and the swelling tide of righteousness and peace overflow the earth. Soon shall the new-born nations send up their delegations to Jerusalem to worship the King in his beauty, and go forth with joy in the blessedness of obedience to him.

Men may scoff, and say that we are degrading the blessed Savior to a level with earthly monarchs, and surrounding him with the miserable trappings of their foul courts. They may ridicule us, and say that we are dragging down the throne of Heaven's King to place it amid graves, almshouses, hospitals, penitentiaries, labor-prisons, sickly cities, and worn-out states. But they forget that the promise is that Christ shall "MAKE ALL THINGS NEW," and banish forever all these evidences and emblems of depravity and sin. They forget that death is to be swallowed up of life, and the whole sentence of the world's curse forever rescinded. They forget that all tears are to be dried, and that there is to be no more death, nor sorrow, nor crying, nor tears, nor any more pain, nor any more sin, within all the domain of Messiah's eternal dominion. Oh, that Christians did but look at these things as God has presented them, and lay hold of the promises which he has given to encourage us. Then would they go forth to duty with greater earnestness and intenser joy. Then would they pray, with fonder hope, *"Thy Kingdom come!"* and ever and anon respond, "AMEN, EVEN SO COME, LORD JESUS!"

MARANATHA!

Christ is coming! let creation
  Bid her groans and travail cease:
Let the glorious proclamation
  Hope restore, and faith increase:—
      Maranatha!
  Come, thou blessed Prince of Peace!

Earth can now but tell the story
  Of thy bitter cross and pain;
She shall yet behold thy glory,
  When thou comest back to reign:—
      Maranatha!
  Let each heart repeat the strain!

Though once cradled in a manger,
  Oft no pillow but the sod,
Here an alien and a stranger,
  Mocked of men, disowned of God,—
      All creation
  Yet shall own thy kingly rod.

Long thy exiles have been pining,
  Far from rest, and home, and thee;
But, in heavenly vesture shining,
  Soon they shall thy glory see:—
      Maranatha!
  Haste the joyous jubilee!

With that "blessed hope" before us,
  Let no harp remain unstrung;
Let the mighty advent-chorus
  Onward roll from tongue to tongue:—
      Maranatha!
  Come, Lord Jesus, quickly come!

J. R. MACDUFF.

SIXTH DISCOURSE.

THE JUDGMENT — SCRIPTURAL IDEA OF A JUDGE — THE DAY OF JUDGMENT NOT AN ORDINARY DAY OF TWENTY-FOUR HOURS — THE JUDGMENT PROGRESSIVE—CONNECTION OF THE JUDGMENT WITH THE MILLENNIAL REIGN—IS THE EXECUTION OF ADJUDICATIONS ALREADY GOING ON — HOW IT WILL BE INTRODUCED—ADMONITIONS TO THE CARELESS

ECCLESIASTES xii. 14: *For God shall bring every work into judgment, with every secret thing, whether it be good or whether it be evil.*

WE now approach one of the most difficult subjects in the Bible, and one which, perhaps, is the least understood, and the most imperfectly apprehended, of all the great revelations of God. Poetry and imagination have undertaken to portray its imposing sublimity; but all such efforts have tended to bewilder and deceive rather than to instruct. The truth is, that poets for theologians, and painters for commentators, are about the poorest guides that a Christian can select. There is a spirituality and supernatural vastness in divine things which cannot be given in pictures, and which no earthly imagery can reach. The external groupings and drapery with which fancy deals very often have little or no connection with the truths they are designed to illustrate. I propose, therefore, to dispense entirely with the popular, pictorial and poetic method of contemplating the great theme of the text, and to approach it more in the style in which the Scriptures present it.

Long has the cry, "A day of judgment! a day of judgment!" been heard in our world. Even before the death of Adam, there rose up a prophet, saying, "Behold, the Lord cometh, with ten thousand of his saints, to execute judgment upon all." Few, indeed, regard the solemn prediction. Many live as if it were all a fable. Thousands scoff at it as an idle dream. But the truth is not altered by man's forgetfulness or unbelief. Refusing to think of the subject cannot retard the chariot-wheels of the avenging King of Zion. He moves on steadily to the accomplishment of his great designs, undismayed and unmolested by the thoughtlessness, the skepticism or the rebellion of mortals. Some will not believe that the earth revolves on its axis, or that it moves in a circuit round the sun; but that does not change the facts, or stop the world in its revolutions. And whether men believe it or not, judgment will come. Accountability is woven in with our very being. It is a primordial condition of our nature. It grows out of the necessities of our very existence. It surrounds the child from its first consciousness. It lies upon us in the circle of friendship. It cleaves to us as citizens of the state. And we certainly cannot rid ourselves of it as members of the great household of God's rational creation. And where there is accountability, there must be adjudication. Every family, social circle, church, state, or empire, must needs have its tribunal, in effect if not in form, by which decisions are decreed and judgment executed. And surely it is not to be supposed that the great Father and King of all has failed to establish this indispensable requisite to all government.

We also find in man, either as the result of common reason, or an original implantation in human nature, a something which is ever reminding us that we must encounter righteous retribution somewhere, at some time or other. We bear with us, in the deep recesses of our souls, a sort of premonitory sense of coming judgment. Every man has his spiritual fears, apprehensions and misgivings, which are most solemnly prophetic. A good man feels that it must be well with him in the end; and a bad man cannot be at peace in his own heart, or rest with abiding composure upon his confidence of safety. Reason as we may, there is still some deeply-seated conviction of the soul, which seems to be a part of itself, which rises up to assert our responsibility with a power that no argument can resist and no logic overcome.

We may therefore take it as a fixed verity, not only asserted in the Scriptures, but abundantly confirmed by the nature of things, that "God shall bring every work into judgment, with every secret thing, whether it be good, or whether it be evil."

We are not, however, to conceive of this judgment as a mere assize, or court, sitting only at a specific time, for the hearing and determination of causes that have been long accumulating. Something of this sort is remotely implied in what the Scriptures say of the matter; but such an assize furnishes a very imperfect and inadequate idea of the great judgment. The Scriptural conception of a *judge* is not simply that of a jurist on the bench, but that of a ruler or king reigning in righteousness, guiding and blessing his loyal subjects, and avenging them of their enemies. Just call to mind the reign of "*the judges*" in the time of Sampson, Gideon, Jephtha, Eli, Samuel, and others, who are said to have "judged Israel." In what did their office of judging consist? Brown, in his Dictionary, has evidently given it correctly, where he says, "These judges had the sole management of peace and war, and decided causes with an absolute authority. *They executed the laws, reformed or protected religion, and punished idolaters and other malefactors;* and were much the same as the archons of Athens, the dictators of Rome, the suffetes of Carthage, and the governors of Germany, Gaul and Britain before the Roman invasion." They were, then, *sovereign princes;* and in that sovereignty we have the Scriptural idea of a *judge.* He is one who rules the people, subdues their enemies, punishes evil-doers and administers the affairs of government. Hence, when the Hebrews appointed a king to reign over them, they called him a *judge,* and called his administration *judging.* Read the eighth chapter of the First Book of Samuel. You will there find that "all the elders of Israel" said, "*Make us* A KING TO JUDGE US;"—"We will have *a king over us,* that we also may be like all other nations, and that *our king may* JUDGE US, *and go out before us and fight our battles.*" Their conception of judgeship was that of kingly rule. Hence, when the Scriptures speak of judgment, they very often add expressions which show that they connect with it the general idea of government, and identify it with sovereign control and gubernatorial administrations. "Let the nations be glad," says the Psalmist, "and sing for joy; for thou shalt *judge the people righteously, and* GOVERN THE NATIONS *upon earth.*" Isaiah says, "Unto us a Son is given, and the *government* shall be upon his shoulder. . . . Of the increase of his *government and peace* there shall be no end, *upon the throne* of David, and upon *his kingdom,* to order it, and to establish it WITH JUDGMENT *and with justice forever.*" "Behold, *a king shall reign and prosper, and shall* EXECUTE JUDGMENT IN THE EARTH. In his days Judah shall be saved, and Israel shall dwell safely; and this is the name whereby he shall be called:—The Lord Our Righteousness. And he *shall judge among many people,* and rebuke strong nations afar off: and they shall beat their swords into ploughshares, and their spears into pruning-hooks." Jesus says, "Ye which have followed me, in the regeneration when the Son of man shall sit on the throne of his glory, ye *also* shall sit upon twelve *thrones,* JUDGING (governing) the twelve tribes of Israel." Paul says, "The saints shall *judge the world;*" and this judgeship of the saints is explained in the Apocalypse, where the Saviour says, "He that overcometh, and keepeth my works unto the end, *to him will I give power over the nations, and he shall* RULE THEM." All these passages evidently refer to the last grand administrations of God,—to *the judgment.* And you will readily perceive from them that the Scriptural idea of *a judge* is one who exercises sovereign rule, one who administers the laws, governs the people, avenges them of their enemies, guides them in peace and safety, and punishes evil-doers.

In a general sense, then, and as presenting a key to this whole subject, we might say that *the judgment of God is the administration of the government of God.*

It is, therefore, also erroneous for us to conceive of the judgment as limited to one day of twelve or twenty-four hours. We indeed read of "*the day of judgment,*" and that the Lord hath "appointed *a day* in the which he will judge the world." But the word "*day*" is often used, both in the Old and New Testaments, and also in common conversation, to signify much larger periods of time than the seventh part of a week. In the first chapter of Genesis it is used six times, to denote six different epochs of the creation. In these cases, some take it to mean an ordinary day; but the majority of learned men think that it means a thousand years, or six thousand years; and that the six days of the creation include six, thirty-six, or even a much greater number of thousand years. How this is we know not; but in the next chapter we read of "*the day* that the Lord made the earth and the heavens, and every plant of the field." Here the whole period of the creation, which geologists think includes myriads of years, is called *a day.* So the forty years of wandering in the wilderness is called "the *day* of temptation,"—"the *day* that God brought them up out of Egypt." Isaiah calls the whole period of the Messiah's reign "*his day*" And Peter, in direct reference to "the day of judgment," exhorts us not to be ignorant "that *one day* is with the Lord as a *thousand years*, and a thousand years as one day." I make these remarks to show that nothing can be inferred from the word *day*, as applied to the judgment, by which to limit it to twenty-four hours, or to any other brief period of time. The *day* of creation means simply *the time* of the creation. The *day* of Israel's pilgrimage is the *time* of the pilgrimage. The *day* of the Messiah is the *time* of the Messiah. And so "*the day of judgment*" is merely *the time of judgment*, whether it be a week or year, a hundred or a thousand years, or as many years as there are days in a thousand years. Hence, Joseph Mede, whom Professor Bush pronounces "one of the profoundest Biblical scholars of the English church," remarks, that "it is to be remembered that the Jews, who gave to this *time* the name of *the day of judgment*, and from whom our Savior and his apostles took it, never understood thereby any thing but *a time of many years' continuance*."

The truth is, that the Scriptures present the judgment as a progressive thing, which began with the expulsion of Adam from Paradise, which is to some extent continually going on, and which will finally reach its entire consummation in the advent and administrations of the Son of man, when an utter end shall be made of all disorder and sin, and the pious of all ages enter upon the full fruition of the honors and joys which God has covenanted unto them. Paul calls it "*eternal judgment*," not only because its results shall be permanent, but more particularly because it continues perpetually. God is ever and anon dealing out retributions and deliverances, which are the steps and preludes to the more complete and ever-augmenting awards of eternity. The Bible distinctly teaches this. Jesus says, "He that believeth on the Son *is not* condemned; but he that believeth not *is condemned* (IS JUDGED) ALREADY, because he hath not believed in the name of the only-begotten Son of God." All agree that whenever a sinner repents and accepts of Christ as the great and only Savior, he is at that moment justified; but justification is altogether a judicial transaction. When the Savior was yet on earth, he said, "Now *is the judgment of this world;*"— "The prince of this world *is judged.*" When God went through Egypt, and smote all the first-born of man and beast, it is said that he executed judgment upon them: (Gen. xv. 14; Ex. xii. 12.) The revelation of his avenging arm against proud Babylon, and the deliverance of Israel from its power, is described in the same way: (Jer. li. 47; Ezek. xxxix. 21.) And so every interposition of God to enforce the principles of his government, either by way of punishing his enemies or delivering his people, is called *judgment*, and is really a part and earnest of the one great eternal judgment which is to be consummated in the coming and administrations of the blessed Jesus. Thus the immediate consequences of death are also called "the judgment," (Heb. ix. 27,) because there is then a broader line of distinction drawn between the good and the wicked, and God's government goes into further effect in giving over the one class to wander in the darkness of their alienation from holiness, and taking the other class into peace and rest.

But all these adjudications are but the beginnings of *the judgment*, whilst there is reserved a still future series of administrations by which they are to be carried on to eternal completeness. Hence, we read that "God hath appointed a day, in the which he will judge the world in righteousness, by that man whom he hath ordained, whereof he hath given assurance unto all men, in that he hath raised him from the dead." The Lord Jesus himself is to return again to the earth, to take the entire dominion of the world, and to administer justice and judgment to the quick and to the dead according to his gospel. In this great judgment, of which all others are but the foretastes and the earnest, "the Father judgeth no man, but hath committed all judgment to the Son, that all men should honor the Son even as they honor the Father." "For, as the Father hath life in himself, so hath he given to the Son to have life in himself, and hath given him authority to execute judgment also, because he is the Son of man."

Considering, then, that the Scriptural idea of *a judge* is that of a sovereign prince administering righteous government, that the ultimate administrations of judgment are given entirely into the hands of Jesus as the Son of man, and that Jesus is to return to this world to reign here in a glorious and universal empire, under which iniquity is to be finally expunged and made to give place to eternal righteousness and peace, we are prepared for the announcement, that the time of the judgment is the time of Christ's coming and reign upon earth, and that the final judgment itself is nothing more nor less than the sovereign ministrations of the descended Jesus as the sovereign of the world.

Now, this reign of Christ is really eternal. It is everywhere so spoken of in the Scriptures. "Of the increase of his government and peace there shall be no end." "His kingdom is an everlasting kingdom." "It shall stand forever." But there is one period in this sublime reign which is especially marked in the prophecies of God. That period is the first thousand years of its existence, or the millennium. Until these first thousand years are over, the divine purposes will not be entirely fulfilled. It is only at the expiration of this thousand years that the last rebellion is to be put down, and the second resurrection accomplished. It is this thousand years, then, and especially the adjudications by which they are to be introduced and concluded, which constitute the day of judgment. It will have its morning and its evening, like every other day. Its morning is the period of Christ's "coming and kingdom," when he will raise the sleeping saints, change the pious living, assign all the faithful their places in his holy and eternal empire, and break down and destroy every thing that stands in the way of the establishment of his princely reign over all the nations of the earth. Its evening is the close of the millennial era, when the last revolt under Gog and Magog shall be destroyed, the devil cast into the pit of destruction, and all the unsanctified dead delivered over to the second death. In other words, there is a duality in the judgment of the great day, just as there is a duality in the resurrection, in the law, in the book of Revelation, in the nature of Christ, in the destiny of men, in the Savior's advent, and in many other things of which the Bible speaks.

After long and prayerful study of the subject, then, it seems to me that the first thousand years of the Messiah's personal reign is the period which the Scriptures style by eminence "*the day of judgment*," and that the great judgment itself is nothing more nor less than those wonderful administrations of the coming Son of Mary, by which he will set up his visible kingdom, and eventually shut up all its enemies in everlasting death.

It is certain, my brethren, that the Scriptures do unequivocally connect the judgment with Christ's occupancy of the throne which he is to receive at his second coming. Maton has remarked, that "we may justly doubt whether our Savior hath as yet executed the office of king." He exercises, indeed, a partial sovereignty in men's hearts; "yet, that he doth not now reign in that kingdom which he shall govern as man, and consequently in that of which the prophets spake, his own words in Rev. iii. 21 do clearly prove: 'To him that overcometh I will grant to sit with me in my throne,' &c., from whence it follows that the throne which he here calls *his own*, and which he hath not yet received, (Heb. ii. 8, 10, 12, 13,) must needs belong to him as man: because the place where he now sits is the Father's throne,—a throne in which he has no proper interest but as God. Again, it follows, that seeing he is now in his Father's throne, therefore neither is this the time nor the place in which *his own throne* is to be erected." I have shown you, in a previous discourse, that Christ's throne is the throne of his father David, which is in this world. I know of no Scripture which assigns to Christ any throne as *his own* but this. And the judgment is specifically connected with his sitting upon his own throne at his coming. He says himself, "When the Son of man shall come in his glory, and all the holy angels with him, THEN *shall he sit upon the throne of his glory*, and in his presence shall all nations be placed together, and he shall separate them (*the nations*) one from another, as a shepherd divideth his sheep from the goats." Here are judicial administrations; and those proceedings are attributed to Christ *as the Son of man*, seated upon *his own throne*, and dealing with *nations* in this world, to whom as the Son of man he is present.

In Daniel we read of the coming of the Son of man, to be invested with a kingdom, in which "nations and languages" are to serve him; which kingdom is to break in pieces all other kingdoms, and take away, destroy and consume the dominion of the blasphemous power that made war with the saints; yet these administrations of the enthroned Jesus are called "the judgment,"—the sitting of the judgment.

Of this same Messiah that was born of Mary, Isaiah says, that he shall bear rule "*upon the throne of David*, to order it and establish it"—how?—"WITH JUDGMENT." The judgment, then, and the Messiah's reign are things which go together. Again, he says of Christ, "*A King shall reign and prosper, and shall execute judgment in the earth.*" Here the reign of Christ is set forth as the judgment of the world by him. So also says the Psalmist:—"*He shall judge the people righteously*, EVEN GOVERN THE NATIONS UPON EARTH."

What do these passages mean, if they do not speak of the judgment of the world by Christ as identical with the administrations of his personal reign as the Son of man? Consider, also, once more, what he himself said to the apostles:—"When the Son of man shall sit on the throne of his glory, *ye also* shall sit upon twelve thrones, *judging* the twelve tribes of Israel." It is evident that this judgeship of the apostles and saints is rulership. The Savior here says that their judgeship is to be of the same kind, nay, an actual part of his own. As, then, the judgeship of the apostles and saints is their reign with Christ over the nations, so his judgeship and his reign are one and the same thing, and the judgment and the administrations of the Messianic kingdom are identical.

Hence, also, Christ's coming to judge the world is called the coming of his kingdom. Jesus says, "There shall be signs in the sun, and in the moon, and in the stars, and upon earth distress of nations with perplexity, the sea and the waves thereof roaring, men's hearts failing them for fear, and for looking after those things that are coming on the earth; and the powers of the heavens shall be shaken; and when ye shall see all these things come to pass, know ye that *the kingdom of God is nigh at hand.*" And in the Apocalypse it is distinctly announced that "the time of wrath, and the time of the dead, that they should be *judged* and reward given to the prophets, saints and all that fear God," is identical with the time when "the kingdoms of the world become the kingdoms of our Lord, and of his Christ;" all of which goes to show that the judgment is the same with the establishment of the Savior's reign upon earth as the Son of David.

Joseph Farmer argues the same thing from Rev. xx. 4. He says that "the kingdom wherein the saints reign with Christ a thousand years, is the same with the kingdom of the Son of man, and the saints of the Most High in Daniel; therefore, it also begins at the great day of judgment, which is not consummated till Gog and Magog's destruction at their end; *therefore, the whole thousand years is included in that great day of judgment.* The resurrection of the just will take place in the morning of the day of judgment, or beginning of the thousand years."

Dr. Thomas Goodwin, one of the great patriarchs of English Independency, also has this remark, that "there is a special world, (which is the present world in its future renewed form,) called *the world to come*, appointed for Jesus Christ eminently to reign in, between this world and the end of the day of judgment," and that "*the day of judgment itself is part, if not the whole, of the time wherein our Lord and Savior Jesus Christ shall reign.*"

And Mede, from 2 Pet. iii. 8, considers it settled, that the day of judgment is the thousand years' reign of Christ. He thus paraphrases that passage:—"Whereas, I mentioned the day of judgment, lest ye might take it for a short day, or a day of a few hours, I would not, beloved, have you ignorant that one day is with the Lord as a thousand years, and a thousand years as one day."

I feel myself, therefore, fully warranted, by the infallible authority of Holy Scripture, and by the authority of men who have gone most profoundly into the investigation of this subject, in maintaining that the great consummating judgment is nothing more nor less than the administrations of the Son of man, in taking to himself the throne of his father David, and establishing his sublime kingdom triumphant over all his foes.

And this judgment is just the carrying into full effect of all previous administrations of God with man. The righteous are now justified, accepted and adopted as the children of God; and the wicked are condemned already; but these things are not yet fully manifest. The sentence is not yet entirely enforced in either case. As to those who have passed into the world of departed spirits, there is a greater enforcement of the present divine adjudications than we have in this life. But still Paul tells us that the full manifestation of the sons of God is reserved until the period of the resurrection and redemption of the body; and that the full perdition of the ungodly is deferred to the same or some subsequent period. The sentence upon good and bad is already passed; but it will not be fully executed until the great day of Christ's coming and kingdom. Paul did not expect his crown until then. Peter did not look for the perdition of ungodly men until then. And the great administrations of that day will consist in the distribution of blessings and curses already awarded. It will simply be the consummation of adjudications already existing,—the completion of processes even now begun. The resurrection of the saints is not so much a resurrection for the purpose of being judged, as the execution of judicial decisions which already exist. The same is true of the resurrection of the wicked. The one class are to rise in glory, and the other class in shame and contempt. The resurrection of the saints is to occur a thousand years previous to the resurrection of the wicked. The resurrection itself, then, is a judicial administration; and the judgment, instead of being confined to scenes after the resurrection, is going on now, and takes in a long series of transactions already begun, but which will only be consummated by the awards of eternity. And when these eternal awards are made, it will be but the ultimate effect of proceedings which are at present in progress.

From these considerations, it follows that the introduction of "the day of judgment" will be very different from what is often supposed. As the judgment consists in the administrations of the glorious Messianic kingdom, and that kingdom is to extend over nations and men in the flesh, its first symptoms and manifestations will be found in the existing living world. The Savior plainly tells us that "there shall be upon the earth distress of nations, with perplexity; the sea and the waves thereof roaring;" great popular and revolutionary disturbances; "men's hearts failing them for fear, and for looking after those things that are coming upon the earth; for the powers of heaven shall be shaken." These words describe scenes of the judgment, which are to be witnessed before the visible manifestation of Christ,—scenes which will glide in upon the world without the least suspicion on the part of men generally that they are the beginnings of the great judgment.

By looking at the various changes that have already occurred in God's earthly administrations, we find that when one dispensation was exchanged for another they overlapped each other. The new always began before the old reached its conclusion. The two interpenetrated each other, so that the new began within the old, and the old ran far into the new. The Jewish system was not overthrown when Christ was born, nor yet when the dispensation of the Spirit commenced at the day of Pentecost. The old system still stood for many years, so that many were both Jews and Christians at the same time. And so it will doubtless be when the millennial or judgment era begins. It will commence within the world that now is. David was an exact type of that future Son of his who is to execute justice and judgment on his throne. But David was the anointed king long before Saul's power was broken and taken from him; and the processes by which he ultimately came to possess the throne which God had given him in Saul's stead consisted of wars, slaughters and destructions. And so in the setting up of the judgment-throne of Christ, our David, there will be corresponding troubles and devastations. All other kingdoms must be broken in pieces and consumed before the kingdom of God will be fully set up. They must be broken with a rod of iron, and dashed in pieces as a potter's vessel. All existing orders of things must be shaken down and destroyed. "Babylon" must fall. "The vials of the wrath of God" must be poured out upon the earth, overwhelming mankind with trouble, deluging empires in blood, and gathering the kings of the world to the war of the great day of God Almighty, when they shall come to their end, and none shall help them. He that is called "Faithful and True" must "judge and make war," and "smite the nations," and "tread the winepress of the fierceness and wrath of Almighty God." And all these things relate to *nations*, tribes and confederations of men as they now live in the flesh, and will doubtless be felt and manifested long before men generally are at all acquainted with what is going on. Thoughtful people will wonder at the amazing upheavings of society around them; they will tremble at the mighty agitations which trouble and confuse every thing in church and state; they will grow pale at the gigantic moves of revolutionists and military despots; and their hearts shall fail them as they attempt to look forward to what the results of all shall be. Some will call it progress; some will call it the result of wrong education of the masses; some will look upon it as the work of ambitious or mistaken legislation; some will think it is liberty rising from her sleep of ages to take dominion of the world. And a thousand theologians, philosophers and jurists will have as many different solutions of the great problem of what is coming upon the earth, without once striking upon the real truth that the day of judgment has begun. Signs and wonders shall exist on every hand; but unsuspecting mortals will point to a thousand natural causes as explanations, and bigoted sectarians will refuse to believe even their own senses. And the world, in all its departments, with here and there a few who are faithful to what God hath written for our learning, shall drift on to dissolution without knowing what is actually transpiring.

But some one will ask, Shall we not see Christ when he

comes, and thus be advised when the great day of judgment begins? Yes, "every eye shall see him;" but not necessarily at the same time, and only when he shall come "*with all his saints with him;*" and all his saints cannot be with him until after the pious dead are raised, and the pious living translated. I have found no Scripture which, when construed with its corresponding passages, says a word about Christ's visibility or appearance previous to the resurrection of the saints. On the contrary, we are repeatedly told that the day of judgment shall come "*as a thief in the night.*" And how does a thief come? He not only comes stealthily, and at such an hour as we think not, but he is already on the premises, in the house and doing his work, before we are aware of his presence. And so shall it be with the coming of Christ and the day of judgment. He will be here gathering and removing his elect before the world shall have become aware of it.

But another will ask, Shall not the trumpet sound, and will not that tell us when the judgment begins? Yes, "the trumpet shall sound, and the dead shall be raised incorruptible, and we shall be changed;" but it is not such a trumpet as all men shall hear and understand. Paul calls it "*the last trump.*" A *last* trumpet implies other trumpets before the last, just as the Scriptures elsewhere tell us. In the tenth chapter of Revelation, it is announced that "*in the days of the voice of the* SEVENTH ANGEL, *when he shall begin to sound*, the mystery of God shall be finished, as he has declared to his servants the prophets." To understand what is meant by this "seventh angel," and his "voice," we must look at the eighth chapter, where John says, "I saw seven angels which stood before God; and to them were given *seven trumpets.*" He then heard each of these angels, one after another, sound his trumpet. The sounding of the seventh is therefore "*the last* trumpet." And that this seventh trumpet of John is "the last trump" of Paul is evident from the events which are attributed to the sounding of both. Paul says of "the last trump," that when it sounds "the dead shall be raised and we shall be changed." All agree that it refers to the period of the judgment. And so also when John's "seventh angel" sounded his trumpet, "there were great voices in heaven, saying, The kingdoms of the world are become the kingdoms of our Lord and of his Christ; and he shall reign forever and ever. And the four-and-twenty elders worshipped God, saying, *Thy wrath is come, and the time of the dead that they should be* JUDGED."

The last trumpet, then, or the trumpet which is to usher in the scenes of the judgment, is just such a trumpet as were the six that preceded it; and its sounding is to be understood in the same way that they sounded. And, fortunately, these six trumpets have already sounded. We can point directly to the several events to which they refer. The first four relate to the several invasions of the Goths, Vandals and Scythians who laid waste the Roman empire. The fifth refers to the Saracenic wo, inflicted by Mohammed and his fierce armies. The sixth introduced the woes inflicted by the Tartar tribes or Turks in their furious devastations. Such, at any rate, are the applications which the best interpreters have made of these parts of the Bible, and I see no reason to doubt their correctness. They certainly refer to occurrences of this kind that have already transpired upon earth, none of which have been ushered in by audible signals from the heavens. The trumpets belong simply to the scenery on the panorama by which these events were brought before the apostle's view, and not to the events themselves. And, as there was no audible, startling, miraculous, wide-sounding, celestial bugle-note to announce to the world the fulfillment of the predictions connected with the six trumpets, so I infer and conclude that there is to be no audible trumpet-blast from mid-heaven to inform the world when the day of judgment has come. For aught you or I know, the last trump has already sounded, or is now sounding, in the changes which have been occurring within the last fifty years, in the mysterious symptoms of revolution which are everywhere so ominously manifest, in the judgments of God, and the sermons and books of his servants, crying, "*Behold the Bridegroom cometh!*" Commencing as it probably does with the end of the 1260 year-days of the dominancy of the Papal Antichrist, we must now be near, if not within, the period of its sounding. It does not connect with a mere instant of time, but, like the other trumpets, takes in a space of years, which begins with the fall of Papal power, and includes the seven last vials of the wrath of God, under which Christ comes as a thief, gathers his saints from their graves, translates his waiting people, and inflicts upon Satan and his adherents his terrific judgments.

But shall we not see the dead rising when the day of judgment comes? It may be that the resurrected saints shall appear to the saints then living, and converse with them, before they are caught up into the clouds; but there is no proof in Scripture that men generally will see or know of their resurrection. No one saw Christ rise; and his saints may come from their graves as quietly and invisibly as they now sleep in them. And when the process of the translation of the living commences, it will no doubt be like the resurrection to which it corresponds. It will not be with great pomp and public demonstrations, but quietly and in a manner hardly understood by those that remain. The unbelieving multitudes may be startled at accounts of the missing here and there, who, like Enoch, shall not be, because God took them; but sage skeptics will soon invent some new theory of spontaneous combustion, or something else, to account for the mysterious disappearances, and but few men will, perhaps, suspect what is really going on. Unsanctified preachers will, perhaps, continue preaching, and unconverted congregations continue to visit the sanctuaries upon which God has written *Ichabod.* Lawyers and doctors, scribes and Pharisees, may, perhaps, continue to talk learnedly about Christianity, which none of them understand, and contend earnestly for the faith which none of them ever experienced, and chuckle complacently over the delusion and fanaticism of those who told them that the day of judgment had come. I do not say that things will occur just in this way; but what I have said is certainly much more like the truth than the conceptions which men usually form of these matters.

Of this one thing, my brethren, I am well assured, that the stupendous occurrences of the day of judgment will glide in upon the world as by stealth, and before a great number of even pious people shall be aware that these great scenes have commenced; whilst the great mass of worldlings and politicians will not believe it to the very last, when the Son of man will blast them forever with his terrific indignation. "As it was in the days of Noe, so shall it be also in the days of the Son of man. They did eat, they drank, they married wives, they were given in marriage, until the day that Noe entered into the ark, *and* KNEW NOT *until the flood came and took them all away.*" Perhaps it had rained a month before those wicked scoffers began to feel any special alarm. Perhaps many of them beheld the ark taken up by the swelling waters, and yet stood upon the hill-tops laughing at the old preacher's folly. Though the valleys were all covered, and the waters rose higher and higher every hour, "*they knew not*" until all were swept away by the shoreless waves. And "so shall it be also in the days of the Son of man." The nations shall be undergoing their judgment, the sainted dead shall be raised, the sainted living shall be translated, and the whole earth shall heave with the throes of judgment already present; and yet multitudes will go on as they did before, and refuse to believe what is transpiring. Nations in their desperation will continue to declare war, and make treaties, and form alliances, and join their armies, and gather together their warriors against the Lamb and his people, until at last, to their everlasting consternation, the Son of man shall appear with his sainted hosts, and hurl upon them the mighty thunders of his eternal wrath. If it is not to be so, why have Peter and Paul told us that "the day of the Lord will come as a thief in the night?" If it is not to be so, why has the Savior told us so earnestly to *watch*, and pointed out so many signs by which we are to be guided, and so repeatedly admonished us to take heed lest that day come upon us unawares? All these things prove that the judgment will come upon the world unknown except to the devoutest and most watchful of the children of men. How important, therefore, that we should study with the profoundest care what the inspired prophets have written upon this subject for our learning! With what solemn concern should we contemplate the mysterious movements of the age in which we live! With what absorbing interest should we ponder the given signs by which we are to know when the great day of the Lord shall come! Would it not be an awful calamity for the church, which professes to be waiting for Christ, to be plunged into the midst of the scenes of that great day without so much as knowing that that day has come? Wo, wo, wo, to them whom Christ, when he comes, shall find ignorant of the times, and faithless to their duty! "For behold, the Lord will come with fire, and with chariots like a whirlwind, to render his anger with fury, and his rebuke with flames of fire. For with fire and by his sword will the Lord plead with all flesh, and the slain of the Lord shall be many." No man can tell the painful surprises, sufferings and scenes of dread and horror which shall then be enacted. All the prophets have spoken of them. Christ has again and again warned us respecting them. Ever and anon they rise before us on the inspired pages to admonish us of our danger. And yet men go on in their sins, and even Christian people remain unmoved, not thinking that we may even now be upon the very margin of the awful day!

O, careless, prayerless, thoughtless child of Adam, whoever you may be, let me warn and entreat you this day not to trifle any longer with your soul, or with the requirements of Jesus! Here God hath placed me upon the watch-tower, to keep you advised of threatening danger; and I now give you the cry of alarm. In the name of that Jesus who will soon come, I bid you escape to the mountains, tarry not in all the plain, lest you be consumed. Retribution may appear slow in coming, but it will come. Cold unbelief and unconcern may seem good enough now, but the ways thereof are the ways of destruction. Lot will soon have passed out of Sodom, and "the salt of the earth" have vanished; and then the souls of the rebellious and the careless shall be like stubble to the fire. The trampled law will rise at last to assert its dignity and vindicate its honor. Christ will not bear the taunts, and thongs and mockery of Pilate's hall forever. For every soul and for every sin there is a judgment. We may not consider it, but that will not change it. We may be but little alarmed with reference to it, but that will not soften its terrors or disrobe it of its awfulness. We may argue, and equivocate, and wish it were not so; but it will not reverse the settled decree of that God who hath said he will bring every work into judgment, with every secret thing, whether it be good, or whether it be evil.

Young man, those sports and gayeties for which you are putting Christ and his word aside will all confront you again hereafter. Those midnight suppers, rank with profanity and intoxication, shall have their reward. Those gatherings in the drink-shops of Satan, those witty jests levelled at sacred things, those fiery lusts burning on the altar of pleasure, all are written down in the book of doom which shall soon be opened. That scene of riot, that broken pledge, that visit to the haunts of profligacy supposed to be known only to yourself, each has its appropriate recompense in the distributions of coming wrath.

Yes; the blood of murdered innocence will not always cry from the earth in vain. The wails of trampled helplessness will not go unheard forever. The widow's wrongs, and the orphan's robbery, will not go perpetually unrequited. The unknown assassin, and the secret sinner, will yet be found out. The malicious incendiary, and the dishonest clerk, the mother who strangled her babe, and the boy that cursed his parents in his heart, and every violater of law or despiser of the truth, shall yet have to confront their crimes, and answer for them to the Lord their Maker. And when once the fearful inquisition begins, and the chained thunders are let loose, and the long arrearages of wrath come to be paid off, and violated law, abused goodness, despised mercy, and outraged justice, all combine in the demand for vengeance, oh, who shall tell the doom of him who is found uncovered by the Savior's righteousness and unsanctified by the Savior's blood? Who can tell the greatness of his wretchedness? Who can weigh his torment? Who can fathom the depth of his hell? Is there before me a soul so hardened as to resolve to encounter it?

Awake, then, O sleeper, and call upon thy God, if so be that you perish not! Your race will soon be run. The day when God will put his terrific adjudications in force upon you will soon arrive. It is stealing upon you as a lion crouching to spring upon his prey. The great judgment is close at hand. Already we hear the mutterings of the approaching tempest. Before you think it possible, the Lord will arise and say, "*It is done.*" Why, then, sleep, and sport, and fold your arms in indifference? "Behold, now is the accepted time! Behold, now is the day of salvation!" And I entreat you, by all the awful perils that surround us—by the preciousness of the immortal soul—by the untold peace and blessings of eternity,—do not waste your time, nor neglect your opportunities. Haste to the arms that are stretched out to save you. Fly at once to the refuge set before you. Take sanctuary in Jesus, who now offers to save you. And may he who came into the world to save sinners be your portion forever! Amen, and Amen!

DIES IRAE.

Day of anger, day of wonder,
When the world shall roll asunder,
Smote with fire and smoke and thunder!

Death astonied, nature shaken,
See all creatures, as they waken,
To that dire tribunal taken.

Lo! the book where all is hoarded,
Not a secret unrecorded:
Every doom is thence awarded.

So the Judge, when he arraigneth,
Every hidden thing explaineth:
Nothing unavenged remaineth.

In that fiery revelation
Where shall I make supplication,
When the just hath scarce salvation?

Fount of love, dread King supernal,
Freely giving life eternal,
Save me from the pains infernal!

This forget not, sweet life-giver,
Me thou camest to deliver:
Cast me not away forever!

Kneeling, crushed in heart, before thee,
Sad and suppliant I adore thee:
Hear me, save me, I implore thee!

From the Latin of Thomas de Celano, 13th cent.

SEVENTH DISCOURSE.

THE ADMINISTRATIONS OF THE JUDGMENT, WITH RESPECT TO THE DEAD, WITH RESPECT TO THE LIVING—THE UNSANCTIFIED LIVING TO BE JUDGED NATIONALLY AT THE SECOND ADVENT—THE RESULTS OF THESE NATIONAL JUDGMENTS.

ACTS xvii. 30, 31: *And the times of this ignorance God winked at; but now commandeth all men everywhere to repent: because he hath appointed a day, in the which he will judge the world in righteousness, by that man whom he hath ordained: whereof he hath given assurance unto all men, in that he hath raised him from the dead.*

I HAVE already given you one discourse upon the judgment; but I feel that another is necessary to furnish you with a clear and full conception of what is revealed concerning it. In my last, I endeavored to disabuse your minds of some wrong impressions which prevail respecting it, and to present what I regard as the more Scriptural views of the subject, reserving a more detailed account of its particular administrations for the present occasion. You were then shown that, in a general sense, the judgment of God is the administration or enforcement of the government of God, and that "the day of judgment" is that notable period, when the Son of man shall take his great power, complete the redemption of his saints, destroy all his enemies, and set up his glorious kingdom over the nations. That day will include at least a thousand years, as Peter says. It will have its morning and its evening. Its morning will be the period of Christ's coming, and include all the great "signs" which immediately precede, attend and follow the second advent. Its evening is the period when the last rebellion in the mystic Gog and Magog shall be defeated, the wicked dead raised, and they, the devil, death, and all that ever disturbed and polluted the earth, given over to the ever-burning lake of the second death. It is tho morning of that day of which the Scriptures say the most, and of which I desire now more particularly to speak. And may God dictate to your hearts and mine, and so enable us to comprehend his mysterious purposes, that we may be found of him in peace, without spot and blameless!

You have doubtless observed in your reading, that the Scriptures distinguish between the judgment of men in the flesh, and the judgment of the dead. Christ is "ordained of God to be the Judge of *quick and dead.*" He "shall judge *the quick and the dead* at his appearing and kingdom." He is "ready to judge *the quick and the dead.*" By "the quick," we are of course to understand *the living,*—those who, not yet having died, live in the body at the period when Christ comes. We will therefore be under the necessity of distinguishing between the judgment as respects the living, and the judgment as respects the dead. The one is evidently very different from the other; and, without treating of them separately, we can have no clear conception of what God has revealed upon the subject.

As respects the dead, the matter is plain enough from what was presented on the subject of the resurrection of the just. All "them which sleep in Jesus" shall be raised from among the dead, glorified, exalted, gathered to Christ in the clouds beyond mortal sight, and assigned their places in the heavenly kingdom according to their works. "The rest of the dead live not again until the thousand years are finished." These are the administrations of the morning of the judgment-day as respects the dead.

But even among those who live in the body when Christ

comes, we find two classes,—the righteous and the wicked, with regard to whom two distinct proceedings will take place. As to the pious living at that time, they will be translated, and undergo a sudden change analogous to the resurrection, and be taken up to the risen saints, to be dealt with in the same way as those who have been raised from the dead. Paul says, "The Lord himself shall descend from heaven with a shout, with the voice of the archangel, and with the trump of God; and the dead in Christ shall rise first; then *we which are alive and remain shall be caught up together with them in the clouds, to meet the Lord in the air: and so shall we be ever with the Lord.*" "We shall not all sleep, but *we shall be changed,* in a moment, in the twinkling of an eye, at the last trump: for the trumpet shall sound, and the dead shall be raised incorruptible, *and we shall be changed.*" Thus, all the really pious, who live till the day of Christ, shall be changed and caught up, as Enoch and Elijah, their great types, were changed and caught up, and go to join the glorious resurrection-host,—"the Bride of the Lamb,"—"the church of the first-born." Their judgment then will be personal and final, introducing them into the fruition of their rewards in the eternal kingdom.

We come now to the unsanctified who shall be found living upon earth when Christ appears. How is the introduction of the day of judgment to affect them? Of course they will not be translated. Their pious friends and associates shall be taken, but they shall be left. Neither will they then receive their judgment in full. The final judgment of the wicked is not until the end of the millennium. Whatever, therefore, shall befall them on the morning of the day of judgment will only be their judgment in part. It will be a judgment in the flesh only, and consist of the dispensation of temporal troubles and calamities. It will be more national than personal, and concern them more as states, societies and confederations, than as individuals. It will doubtless be a judgment of the same kind with those judgments which have heretofore been administered to wicked powers and apostate nations and churches. Upon this point the Scriptures are very plain.

There is a very remarkable passage on this subject in the twenty-fifth chapter of Jeremiah. The prophet there sets forth this judgment of the nations one after another as time progresses, until it reaches its grand consummation in the administrations which are to attend Christ's final coming. He says, "Thus saith the Lord God of Israel unto me: Take the wine-cup of this fury at my hand, and cause *all the nations*, to whom I shall send thee, to drink it. And they shall drink, and be moved, and be mad, because of the sword that I will send among them. Then took I the cup at the Lord's hand, and made all the nations to drink, unto whom the Lord had sent me: to wit, Jerusalem, and the cities of Judah, and the kings thereof, and the princes thereof, to make them a desolation, an astonishment, an hissing and a curse; as it is this day; Pharaoh king of Egypt, and his servants, and his princes, and all his people; and all the mingled people, and all the kings of the land of Uz, and all the kings of the land of the Philistines, and Ashkelon, and Azzah, and Ekron, and the remnant of Ashdod, Edom, and Moab, and the children of Ammon, and all the kings of Tyrus, and all the kings of Zidon, and the kings of the isles which are beyond the sea, Dedan, and Tema, and Buz, and all that are in the utmost corners, and all the kings of Arabia, and all the kings of the mingled people that dwell in the desert, and all the kings of Zimri, and all the kings of Elam, and all the kings of the Medes, and all the kings of the north, far and near, one with another, AND ALL THE KINGDOMS OF THE WORLD, WHICH ARE UPON THE FACE OF THE EARTH: and the king of Sheshach shall drink after them. Therefore, thou shalt say unto them, Thus saith the Lord of hosts, the God of Israel, Drink ye, and be drunken, and spue, and fall, and rise no more, because of the sword which I will send among you. And it shall be, if they refuse to take the cup at thy hand to drink, then shalt thou say unto them, Thus saith the Lord of hosts, *Ye shall certainly drink.* For lo, I begin to bring evil on the city which is called by my name, and should ye be utterly unpunished? Ye shall not be unpunished: for I will call for a sword *upon all the inhabitants of the earth,* saith the Lord of hosts. Therefore, prophesy thou against them all these words, and say unto them," —and here comes a description of this universal judgment of the nations as it shall be consummated when Christ shall be manifested,—"The Lord shall roar from on high, and utter his voice from his holy habitation; he shall give a shout, as they that tread the grapes, *against all the inhabitants of the earth.* A noise shall come even to the ends of the earth: for the Lord hath a controversy with the nations, he will plead with all flesh; he will give them that are wicked to the sword, saith the Lord. Thus saith the Lord of hosts, Behold, evil shall go forth from nation to nation, and a great whirlwind shall be raised from the coasts of the earth. And the slain of the Lord shall be at that day from one end of the earth even unto the other end of the earth: they shall not be lamented, neither gathered, nor buried; they shall be dung upon the ground."

And it is in perfect harmony with this, that the Savior himself tells us, that in the period of his coming there will be "upon earth *distress of nations* with perplexity;" and that "when the Son of man shall come in his glory, and all the holy angels with him, then shall he sit upon the throne of his glory; and before him shall be gathered *all nations,* and he shall separate *them* (THE NATIONS) one from another, as a shepherd divideth his sheep from the goats." And when that solemn reckoning comes, as the Scriptures abundantly teach, there is but one people on the face of the whole earth which, as a nation, shall not fall among the goats, and be doomed as the uncharitable persecutors and neglectors of the brethren of Jesus. Daniel tells us, that when the Son of man shall come in his kingdom, "it shall break in pieces and consume all these (goat) kingdoms." Yea, "he cometh with clouds, and every eye shall see him, and they also which pierced him, *and all the kindreds* (φυλαι—*tribes*) *of the earth shall wail because of him.*" He shall "judge and make war." He shall be "clothed with a vesture dipped in blood." He shall "with a sharp sword *smite* THE NATIONS, and RULE THEM *with a rod of iron;* treading the winepress of the fierceness and wrath of Almighty God. And all the fowls that fly in the midst of heaven shall eat the flesh of kings, and the flesh of captains, and the flesh of mighty men, and the flesh of horses and them that sit on them." "Behold, the day of the Lord cometh,—his feet shall stand in that day upon the Mount of Olives,—for I will *gather all nations* against Jerusalem to battle. . . . Then shall the Lord go forth and fight against those nations, as when he fought in the day of battle. . . . And it shall come to pass that a great tumult from the Lord shall be among them." "In that day the Lord shall punish the host of the high ones that are on high, and the kings of the earth upon earth; and they shall be gathered together as prisoners are gathered in the pit; *when the Lord of hosts shall reign in Mount Zion, even* IN JERUSALEM, and before his ancients gloriously." Again, it is said, "Come near, *ye nations*, and hearken, ye people: for the indignation of the Lord is upon all nations, and his fury upon all their armies: he hath utterly destroyed them, he hath delivered them to the slaughter; and the mountains shall be melted with their blood. For it is the day of the Lord's vengeance, and the year of recompenses for the controversy of Zion:" (Is. xxiv. and xxxiv.) The word of the Lord by

Zephaniah is, "Wait ye upon me, until the day that I rise up to the prey: for my determination is to *gather the nations*, that I may assemble the kingdoms, to pour upon them my indignation, even all my fierce anger; for all the earth shall be devoured with the flaming fire of my jealousy." And all, when "he shall *appear* to the joy" of those that "tremble at his word."

John's vision of the opening of the sixth seal refers to the same events, in which he beheld, "and the kings of the earth, and the great men, and the chief captains, and the mighty men, and all their adherents, hid themselves in the dens and in the rocks of the mountains; and said to the mountains and rocks, Fall on us, and hide us from the face of him that sitteth on the throne, and from the wrath of the Lamb: for the great day of his wrath hath come, and who shall be able to stand?"

Do you ask me, then, what the judgment is with regard to the unsanctified who live upon earth when Christ comes? Here you have it described, not by the fancies of poets who wrote to make themselves a name, but in the words given by the Spirit of the great Judge himself. And what a sublime and terrific picture it furnishes of the final vindication of the reality and righteousness of that divine Sovereignty which every nation and confederation on earth, both civil and ecclesiastical, has been usurping, invading and denying ever since man first departed from God! Where is the nation, state, kingdom, or hierarchy under the broad heavens that has not been built and sustained more or less by injustice, oppression, ambition and unrighteousness? Where is the policy that has reigned, or that now reigns, in church or state, that is not crooked, perverse, and mixed up with vast and wicked invasions of the rights of Him whose is the kingdom, and who alone is the rightful governor among the nations? And wheresoever the carcass is, there will the eagles be gathered together. It was upon that generation of the Jews who lived when Jerusalem finally fell, that all the blood of prophets and martyrs shed by their fathers was visited; and so the nations still living when Christ comes shall be dealt with for all "their ungodly deeds which they have ungodly committed," and which have been accumulating for ages. The ploughshare of destruction shall then run deep; and the furrow it shall turn will bury forever all the proud works of rebellious man. In all the Scriptures, there appears to be but one exception to the general crash of earthly establishments; and even that shall not be an entire exception. There is an exemption proclaimed in favor of the Jewish race, which, as a distinct nationality, has had its judgment. Jeremiah says, "These are the words that the Lord spake *concerning* ISRAEL, *and concerning* JUDAH. . . . Alas! for that day is great, so that none is like it: it is even the time of Jacob's trouble;" which extends from Jerusalem's fall to the period of the final advent: (Luke xxi. 24.) "*But he shall be saved out of it.* . . . Therefore fear thou not, O my servant Jacob, saith the Lord; neither be dismayed, O Israel; for lo, *I will save thee from afar,* and thy seed from the land of thy captivity; and Jacob shall return, and shall be in rest, and be quiet, and none shall make him afraid. For I am with thee, saith the Lord, to save thee; *though I* MAKE A FULL END of ALL NATIONS WHITHER I HAVE SCATTERED THEE, YET WILL I NOT MAKE A FULL END OF THEE: *but I will correct thee in measure,* and will not leave thee altogether unpunished. . . ." (See also Zech. xiv. 2.) "They that devour thee shall be devoured; and all thine adversaries, every one of them shall go into captivity; and they that spoil thee shall be a spoil, and all that prey upon thee will I give for a prey. For I will restore health unto thee, and heal thee of all thy wounds, saith the Lord. Behold, I will bring again the captivity of Jacob's tents, and have mercy on his dwelling-places, and the city shall be builded on her own little hill. Out of them shall proceed thanksgiving and the voice of them that make merry: and I will multiply them, and they shall not be few; I will also glorify them, and they shall not be small. Their children also shall be as aforetime, and their congregation shall be established before me, and *I will punish all that oppress them.* . . . Behold, the whirlwind of the Lord goeth forth with fury, a cutting whirlwind: it shall fall with pain upon the head of the wicked. The fierce anger of the Lord shall not return until he have done it, and until he have performed the intents of his heart: *in the latter days* ye shall consider it:" (Jer. xxx.)

My brethren, some people contemn the Jews, and speak despisingly of them. For eighteen hundred years they have been a hissing, a byword, and a reproach. The nations have dealt most unjustly towards them; and many to this day never look upon them but with derision and with scorn. But every Jew that moves upon the face of the earth is a living token of the coming wrath of God. All God's prophets were Jews; and there is a sense in which all the Jews are God's prophets. Superstitious, obstinate, blind, derided, as the Jew is, he is a herald of the fierce judgment of Almighty God, which is to make "a full end of all nations" wherever he is found. He stands in our luxurious cities, and before our churches, as Jonah amid Nineveh, summoning us to repentance and mourning. And instead of feeling contempt and scorn when we come into his presence, we should rather be humbled and solemn, as if God's prophet were before us predicting trouble. He is the harbinger of disturbances and desolations which he alone, of all the races living, shall escape. His day of tribulation has been great and long, without a parallel. His Jerusalem is "trodden down of the Gentiles," and will remain trodden down "till the times of the Gentiles be fulfilled." But he shall be saved out of his troubles. All his wounds shall be healed. He shall yet live. And when the time of his nation's resurrection comes, which has been so long foretold by his holy prophets, then shall the nations mourn. "In that day, saith the Lord of hosts, I will make Jerusalem a cup of trembling to all nations that are round about. And I will make Jerusalem a burdensome stone to all nations, and *they shall be cut in pieces and broken, though all the people of the earth be gathered together*." It is useless for us to shut our eyes to these awful announcements. God himself has made them, and no man can alter the thing that is gone out of his mouth. The despised Jew shall yet look forth from Zion and behold the grave of every kingdom upon earth.

But let us now endeavor to draw out, and set forth in greater particularity, some of the things comprehended in these more general statements.

He that will be at the pains to put together all that has been revealed concerning the judgment as it respects the living when Christ comes, will not fail to see that it is to be a scene or succession of terrific social agitations, irruptions and revolutions. It will be a time of wars and rumors of wars; of political perplexities and disasters; of ferments and precipitations in the whole existing order of things; of civil storms, earthquakes, commotions, overturnings and devastations. People are to rise up and overthrow governments, slay their rulers, prey upon each other, and involve the world in bloody and inextricable broils. Ambitious and godless men will spring into places of power, array their followers against each other, trample down national and international law, and rush to certain destruction. Infidels and socialists of a thousand hues shall disorganize, undermine, subvert and destroy with bloody hands, and spread ruin in their path. Schisms and feuds of all sorts shall break forth to cripple and desolate. Great powers, which think themselves secure, shall be suddenly overwhelmed. Infatuated zealots, secular and ecclesiastial, shall lead men into scenes of terror and ruin. Great alliances and combinations shall be formed and swelled into the most gigantic proportions, until they unexpectedly fall by their own weight and crush every thing beneath them. And the whole earth shall heave, and reel, and start, and stagger, with agony and delirium; for it is "the great day of the fierceness and wrath of Almighty God."

In this condition of things, all present forms of government shall be modified, if not wholly dissolved. All emperors and kings shall be divested of their power; for "the sun shall be darkened." All orders of corrupt nobility, princedoms, dukedoms, premierships, and such like, shall be cast down; for "the stars shall fall." Kings, great men, rich men, chief captains, mighty men, and all their adherents, shall be stripped of their possessions, and driven to terrible extremities and desperation; for God hath said it in just so many words. Every sceptre shall break in the hands of him who holds it; every crown shall tumble from the brow of him that wears it; the mightiest armies shall be utterly routed, and the greatest navies brought to naught. Worlds shall not rush upon each other and be no more, but thrones and human magistracies will. Matter will not wreck and vanish, but all political combinations will. The great orbs of immensity shall not be annihilated, but all whom those orbs symbolize in this world will; for God will "*break in pieces and consume all these kingdoms.*" The whole body and framework of Nebuchadnezzar's image, from its golden scalp to its toes of clay, every particle of it, shall be "like the chaff of the summer threshing-floors," driven by the four winds.

A similar destiny also then awaits all present church organizations,—at least all establishments and hierarchies. As they stand connected with the world's politics, they shall share the same fate. "The moon shall be confounded, and become as blood." The ecclesiastical as well as the political heavens shall have their powers shaken, and be rolled up as a scroll; and the stars in the one shall be cast down as the stars in the other. There is not a church system or denominational organization now on earth that shall ever find its way into the millennial times, or survive this period of the wrath of God. They are all provisional and temporary. They are all wood, hay and stubble, which the fires shall consume. They are all tainted. They are all founded too much on the wisdom of man, and consist too entirely of works of human authority and power to live. They shall all wither and die; and they that build their salvation on them shall die with them. There are many church politicians who are as bad and as obnoxious to the judgment as any state politicians; and one doom is reserved for them all. My hope is in Christ Jesus and his infallible word, and not in any lauded church system under the sun. I am sure that there will be neither Protestantism, nor Romanism, nor High Church, nor Low Church, nor Lutheranism, nor Methodism, nor Presbyterianism, nor any other kind of *ism*, in the glorious millennium. What then shall become of all these *isms*, and the systems founded on them? There is no alternative; they shall all perish forever in the storms and fires of wrath which are beginning to be felt, and which shall soon sweep over all the earth; and they that adhere to these systems to the neglect of Christ and his pure gospel shall perish with them.

Brethren, strange as these things may seem to some, they are the sober truths of Divine revelation. Study carefully the word of God, think for yourselves, only adjust in your own minds some of the great facts which we all admit, and you will not fail to arrive at the same conclusions. Your beautiful ceremonies, your magnificent rituals, your boasted democracy of church order, your vast and unique organization, all constructed by human wisdom, must be changed and come to naught. Your unsanctified and defiant denominational champions, and your sectarian Goliaths, shall all fall dead before the sling-stone of that David who cometh to judge the world in righteousness; and all their marshaled hosts, who have been rallied under the battle-cry of mere party, shall be scattered in confusion, and scorched by the hot flames of God's retribution.

Understand me rightly. I am not exhorting any one to forsake his denomination, or to stand aloof from the church in the forms in which it now exists. That would only augment partyism, and increase needless contention or fatal indifference. Let him who would approve himself unto his Lord do the best he can under the circumstances. Keep diligently to your Bible, make the most of your opportunities, and meekly wait and watch for the coming of the Savior to set all things right by making all things new. If you are a Lutheran, work as a Lutheran; but let the Scriptures and not Lutheranism be your guide. If you are a Methodist, work as a Methodist; but work, not for Methodism, but for Christ. If you are an Episcopalian, work as an Episcopalian; but rest not your hope and aim in Episcopalianism, but in the simple gospel of the blessed God. Let the *ism* be to you as though it were not, and embrace Christ with all your heart, and lay hold of him as your all in all. For as certain as the judgment, all these isms must die. The great day shall make an end of them. And if you have no Christianity but them, alas for your hope!

These judicial visitations, however, will fall much more heavily upon some nations and combinations than upon others. Some are deeper in apostasy and guilt than others; and the righteous Judge shall apportion the punishment to the crime. There are some nations, confederations and hierarchies specially singled out in the prophecies as the objects of Jehovah's most terrific indignation. Conspicuous among these are,—

1. The ten-horned wild beast of Daniel and John;
2. The image of the beast; and,
3. Great Babylon.

I cannot, in this connection, present and reason out the processes by which the objects denoted by these symbols are to be identified. A vast amount of criticism and comment are involved, through which I have tried to wade, but which are of too intricate a character and too voluminous and conflicting to be brought forward in this connection. There are conclusions to which I have come, however, which I will announce, remarking at the same time that I believe them to be at least plausible, and not without some solid foundation.

The ten-horned wild beast of Daniel and John is the representative of the Roman empire. Its ten horns are the ten kingdoms which took the place of the old Roman empire, and now occupy its territory. It is, therefore, the symbol of the supreme civil power of the ten kingdoms into which the Roman empire was divided. These ten kingdoms originally embraced the Huns, the Ostrogoths, the Visigoths, the Franks, the Vandals, the Sueves, the Burgundians, the Herulians and Thuringians, the Saxons and the Longobards. At present, they perhaps embrace the three Papal States, Naples, Tuscany, Austria, Great Britain, France, Portugal and Spain. The supreme civil power, then, of these and, may-be, a few other countries, is the wild beast of whom we are now speaking.

The image of the beast may represent the ecclesiastical rulers and teachers which princes and people have been deluded to erect into a vast church hierarchy under the pope, who exercises over it a sway and jurisdiction analogous to, or *the image of*, that which the civil rulers exert over their political empires. This image of the beast derived its existence and power from the false teachings and lying wonders of the papal beast on the one hand, and from the misled political authorities on the other: (Rev. xiii. 14, 15.) It is, therefore, that empire of priests and church officials, presented in what is falsely called "the Catholic church," and who are feared and worshipped by their millions of subjects with an idolatry as debasing as it is wicked.

But what is meant by great Babylon—that mother of harlotry and source of earth's worst abominations? Some have thought that this symbol denotes the city of Rome. Some have taken it as the representative of the Romish church. Some have given it still other applications. But I know of no explanation which so completely meets the case, as that which takes great Babylon as the symbol of that base and corrupting system known as the union of church and state. The city of Rome cannot be meant; for great Babylon is presented as a living agent; and living agents do not represent inanimate objects. She is represented as borne by the wild beast; and must therefore be something different from the mere secular power, and yet entirely dependent upon the secular power. The Romish church, as such, does not wholly depend upon the secular power; but all state churches do. I therefore take great Babylon as the symbol of the living, seductive and corrupting body of nationalized hierarchies, both Papal and Protestant, whether in the Old World or in the New.

Now, then, let us glance at the destiny of these three monsters, intertwined as they are, for the most part, the one with the other, and see how they will be affected by the introduction of the day of judgment.

As to great Babylon, her doom is sealed. She shall fall; and great shall be her fall. In the visions of John, as soon as one angel announced that "*the hour of judgment is come,*" another followed, saying, "Babylon is fallen, is fallen, that great city, because she made all the nations drink of the wine of the wrath of her fornication:" (Rev. xiv. 7, 8.) Whatever may be said in their favor, these state churches and nationalized hierarchies are an abomination in the sight of God. They are "full of names of blasphemy." They have ever arrogated to themselves the rights of God, and assumed unwarranted authority over his legislation and over the consciences of his people. They are august and splendid establishments, "robed in purple and scarlet, and decked with gold, and precious stones, and pearls." They have seduced millions into spiritual fornication, by their elegant attire and their bewitching flatteries. But all their pompous decorations and lofty pretensions will not hide their impurities from the eye of a jealous God. They are all "drunk with the blood of the saints, and with the blood of the witnesses of Jesus." Sustained as they are with more than princely revenues, and shielded by the sword of secular power, they have been the agents of the bloodiest persecutions that the world has ever seen since the days of the pagan emperors. Ask a Papist who were the authors of those disgraceful inflictions in various countries professedly Christian, by which thousands upon thousands lost their lives for their religious opinions, and he will tell you, the civil government. Ask rabid Protestants, and they will tell you, the Romish church. But consult the truth, and it will tell you, it was the union of church and state. Even in the most enlightened Protestant countries where such union exists, the skirts of its robes are clotted with the blood and saturated with the tears of wronged and oppressed dissenters. I say this with shame and sorrow; but so it is, and God has noted it all in his book of doom. There never has been a state church, in any age or any country, that has not been more or less an intolerant and a persecuting church. And where the papal hierarchy has enjoyed this relation to the secular power, God alone knows all the wrongs that have been perpetrated, and the streams of martyr-blood that have been spilled. It was not the state, as Rome would persuade us; it was not the Romish church, as such; but it was the product of church and state united,—the result of the blasphemous undertaking on the part of the civil power, with the consent of those who called themselves the church, to legislate in things which belong only to the individual conscience and its God. Religion is not a subject for human legislation. It is not for man to say how we are to be held in communion and allegiance with our Maker. Some tell us that it is our duty to obey the state; and others insist that it is our duty to obey the church; and from these two things it is argued that it is pre-eminently our duty to obey where church and state speak together. But the whole argument is sophistical and unsound. No man, or combination of men, has any right to impose laws between the soul and its God. Jehovah himself is the only Lord of the conscience. When Nebuchadnezzar commands his subjects to fall down and worship an image, it is an inalienable right in us, like the three Hebrew children, to disobey. When Darius forbids calling upon God, Jehovah is with every Daniel who sets the prohibition at defiance. When the Sanhedrim pronounces a ban upon the preaching of Peter and John, the Lord God of the holy prophets commands them to trample it under their feet. The human soul is obliged by no law which meddles with its relations to its Creator. And the great, crying, and unpardonable sin of great Babylon is, that it everywhere undertakes to legislate for God, and forges chains to shackle the free-born soul.

But Babylon shall be "remembered before God, to give to her the cup of the wine of the fierceness of his wrath." All these state hierarchies shall be shaken down and overwhelmed. The very governments which now support and make use of them shall turn against them. God says, "The ten horns upon the beast shall hate her, and make her desolate and naked, and shall eat her flesh, and burn her with fire." States in their straits shall rob her of her wealth, confiscate her goods, divest her of her possessions, appropriate her benefices and revenues to other purposes, and reduce the whole system to distress and desolation. Such is to be her fall; and after her fall shall come her punishment. Her lord-bishops, her high superintendents and all her officials shall yet have a dreadful road to travel. God will yet say to those whom she has wronged, impoverished and oppressed, "Give to her as she also gave; and double to her according to her works. Into the cup which she has poured, pour to her double. As much as she has glorified herself and lived luxuriously, so much torment give her and sorrow." "In one day shall her plagues come, death, and sorrow, and famine; and she shall be burned with fire: for mighty is the Lord God who shall judge her. And the kings of the earth"—the civil powers—"who have committed fornication and lived luxuriously with her, shall bewail her, and lament for her, when they shall see the smoke of her burning; and standing afar off for fear of her torment, shall say, Alas, alas! that great city Babylon, that mighty city! for in one hour is thy judgment come. And the merchants of the earth"—the nobles and dignitaries that held the patronage of her benefices—"shall weep and mourn over her. . . . . And they that were made rich by her shall stand afar off for fear of her torment, and cast dust on their heads, crying, weeping and wailing," whilst all heaven shouts, ALLELUIA! that her judgment is come: (Rev. xviii.) Her destruction shall be entire. As a millstone, when thrown into the depths of the sea, sinks forever out of the sight of men, so shall this great harlot be swept from the earth, without leaving so much as a rack behind.

As to the wild ten-horned beast,—the civil powers that have grown out of the Roman empire,—all of which are but branches and modifications of the old Roman monster, with great iron teeth and claws of brass, devouring, breaking in pieces and trampling under foot,—its destiny is also announced. There is not a throne upon the territory of the Cæsars that is not a nuisance in the face of heaven. They are all built in usurpation and wrong. They are all sustained by tyranny and stained with blood. They have deceived, and they shall be deceived and lured to perdition. By the pressure of the times, and by the cunning of demons, they shall yet be brought into one grand coalition, and go forth to the war of the great day of God Almighty, when the hand of the descended Jesus shall strike them to the earth to rise no more.

I have intimated, that the Jewish race is to be restored to its ancient home and the Jewish nationality rebuilt. I will illustrate this point at greater length hereafter. In connection with this restoration of the Jews, much offense will be taken by some of the reigning powers. The prophet says, "Jerusalem shall be made a cup of trembling to all nations that are round about, and a burdensome stone to all nations." There shall be great controversies about the occupation of the Holy Land. Politics will become inextricably involved. Strange alliances shall be brought about, until at length all the powers of Earth shall find themselves involved in one great confederation, under the last head of the beast,—most likely the Emperor of the French,—and involved in a great Eastern war, of which Palestine will be the centre. This vast combination, under its infidel leader, shall overflow the whole world, destroy many countries, have power over the treasures of Egypt, enter into the glorious land, plant its tents between the seas in the glorious holy mountain, and there encounter the fierce wrath of God: (Dan. xi. 40–45.) Plague unprecedented shall seize the invading hosts. "Their flesh shall consume away while they stand upon their feet; and their eyes shall consume away in their sockets; and their tongues shall consume away in their mouth; and great tumult from the Lord shall be among them:" (Zech. xiv. 12–16.) The beast shall be "slain, and its body destroyed and given to the burning flame:" (Dan. vii. 11.) The heavens shall open; the Son of man shall appear; his kingdom shall be revealed; the beast and false prophet shall be taken and given to the fires; and thus shall God "break in pieces and consume all these kingdoms:" (John xix. 11–20; Dan. ii. 44.)*

And as to the image of the beast,—the ecclesiastical empire of popery,—its destiny is so closely identified with great Babylon and the beast itself, that when we read the fate of the one we have in substance the fate of the other. Stroke after stroke shall fall upon it, wasting, crippling, denuding, consuming it, until the brightness of the Savior's presence shall bring it to everlasting destruction: (2 Thess. ii. 8.) "And if any man worship the beast, and his image, and receive his mark in his forehead or in his hand, the same shall drink of the wine of the wrath of God, which is poured out without mixture into the cup of his indignation, and he shall be tormented with fire and brimstone in the presence of the holy angels, and in the presence of the Lamb:" (Rev. xiv. 9, 10.)

Let men beware, then, how they tamper with these objects of God's distinguishing and extinguishing retributions. Let them beware how they approve, justify, defend and abet the cause of state churches, lest they involve themselves in the whoredoms of great Babylon. Let them beware how they admire, applaud and revere the tyrannical and blasphemous systems and policies of European legislation and dominion; for they that "worship" this ten-horned monster, or receive his mark, shall go down into the pit. And especially let men beware, that they give not their reverence to the image of this beast, or bow their knees or necks to the ecclesiastical empire of popery, or in any way identify themselves with its abominations; for they that bear its insignia shall "have no rest day nor night; and the smoke of their torment ascendeth up forever and ever." It is upon these systems, their adherents and

---

* See Note G, page 341.

abettors, that the heaviest and thickest woes of the judgment of the great day shall fall.

From these statements it appears that there is after all a wise and mighty overruling providence in the affairs of men. Whatever skeptics and politicians may say, "The kingdom is the Lord's, and he is the governor among the nations." "He setteth up kings, and he putteth them down." "He ruleth in the kingdoms of men, and giveth them to whomsoever he will." He "frustrateth the tokens of liars, and maketh diviners mad; he turneth wise men backwards, and maketh their knowledge foolish." This world is not a fatherless thing, cast off to everlasting orphanage. It may seem endlessly confused now; but God hath appointed a day in the which he will judge it in righteousness, by that man whom he hath ordained, whereof he hath given assurance unto all men, in that he hath raised him from the dead. Its affairs are not things of chance, nor its destinies without control. Wise men may plan, and wicked men may plot, and mighty men may execute; but the ultimate disposal of every thing is of the Lord. The mightiest and the weakest, the vastest and the minutest, are equally under his omniscient eye and equally within his almighty power. He is in the senates and cabinets of nations, in the battle-field of conflicting armies, at the desk of the author, and in circles of the designing everywhere, and always moulding, directing, restraining all things for the consummation of his own great purposes, and making even the wrath of man to praise him. People may rage, and nations disregard his laws, and men act out their villany; but they shall never press Jehovah to extremities, or defeat that holy arm which stands pledged for the everlasting defence of the righteous. He knows the end of all things from the beginning, and his inscrutable arrangements are all made accordingly. There is not a turn in human things which he has not taken into his sublime calculations. Matters may be very dark to us, but they are all plain to him. Wisdom, order, righteousness and glory shall yet come out of the mighty riddle of human history. The day of judgment shall solve the problem that has puzzled men so long. Confusion, injustice, falsehood and wrong may seem to triumph for a while; but the result is certain. Their grave is dug. Their doom is at hand. They may be too mighty for us; but Christ is Lord, and he must reign until he hath put all enemies under his feet. Antichrist shall die; tyranny shall die; error shall die; sin shall die; and at last death itself shall die. The world has a ruler who will subdue all evil and set things right in the end. The sublime wisdom and rectitude of all his administrations will yet be the glory and delight of the saints, and the rapture of his holy ones forever and ever.

And in view of the commotions and distresses, the overturnings and the desolations, that await the unsanctified world, how precious are the hopes of the devout! If we are in Christ Jesus, there is no more condemnation. The true people of God are safe. They are enclosed in everlasting arms. The broad shield of Omnipotence is over them. Some may pass through a sharp night, but it will be short.* Though the powers of the heavens be shaken, and the foundations of the earth be moved, they that put their trust in the Lord shall never be confounded. Wars may come, and bloody revolutions may come; famine may come, and plagues may come; thrones may fall and empires may dissolve, and all the proud works of human genius may be dashed to desolation; but, if our hope is fixed on God, and our souls are united with his Anointed, we shall sing, amid the turmoil and the wreck, "*Alleluia! for the Lord God omnipotent reigneth!*"

Only let us see to it, then, that we be indeed the disciples and friends of Jesus. Let us not rest satisfied with peradventures, but give the most earnest heed to the things which we have heard, lest at any time we should let them slip.

---

* See Note H, page 349.

Signs of the approaching judgment are already being manifested on every side. All fingers are pointing to the great crisis as near at hand. The days in which we live are freighted with intense and exhaustless issues. We stand upon a point where the last rays of a fading world mingle with the dawn of an opening eternity. Nations and churches, superstitions and errors, are heaving and tottering for their final fall. The time is come that judgment must begin. The fires stored away so long are beginning to beat against their prison-walls, and to clamor for their promise of release. And may kind Heaven help us to prepare to meet our God!

AROUSE FOR DUTY.

We are living, we are dwelling,
  In a grand, eventful time;
In an age on ages telling,—
  To be living, is sublime.

Hark! the waking up of nations,
  Truth and Error to the fray.
Hark! what soundeth? 'tis Creation
  Groaning for its latter day!

Will ye play, then? will ye dally
  With your music and your wine?
Up! it is Jehovah's rally!
  God's own arm hath need of thine.

Hark! the onset! will ye fold your
  Faith-clad arms in lazy lock?
Up! O, up! thou drowsy soldier;
  Worlds are charging to the shock.

Worlds are charging, Heaven beholding;
  Thou hast but an hour to fight;
Now, the blazoned cross unfolding,
  On!—right onward, for the right.

A. C. COXE.

EIGHTH DISCOURSE.

THE RESTORATION OF THE JEWS—OBJECTIONS ANSWERED—NEW TESTAMENT ALLUSIONS TO THE SUBJECT—ANCIENT PROPHECIES—HISTORICAL FACTS—PARTICULARS EXPLAINED.

Ez. xxxvii. 21: *Say unto them, Thus saith the Lord: Behold, I will take the children of Israel from among the heathen, (nations,) whither they be gone, and will gather them on every side, and bring them into their own land.*

It is to be borne in mind that our inquiries in this series of discourses relate to but one great epoch in human affairs, the consummation of the age, and what connects with it. All that I have thus far said appertains to this wonderful and critical period. The personal return and manifestation of Christ in our world, "the restitution of all things," the resurrection of the sainted dead, the transfiguration of the pious living at the time, and the terrific administrations of the enthroned Messiah upon the guilty nations and confederations of the earth,—all, to a great extent, are contemporaneous. They all synchronize, or happen together in the same general period. But there are still other great occurrences predicted for that time of wonders. Among these is the conversion and final restoration of the Israelitish race.

That the great bulk of this astonishing people will yet be converted to Christ the Messiah, and be again grafted upon the olive-tree of the spiritual Israel from which they have been measurably broken off, is pretty well agreed on all hands.

Whitby says, "This hath been the constant doctrine of the church of Christ, owned by the Greek and Latin fathers, and by all the commentators I have met with." The inspired declarations upon this subject are too explicit to be evaded. "*All Israel shall be saved:* as it is written, There shall come out of Sion the Deliverer, and shall *turn away ungodliness from Jacob:* FOR THIS IS MY COVENANT UNTO THEM."

But that this scattered family of Jacob shall again be gathered, and nationally restored to the land of their fathers, is not so generally admitted. Some have no patience at all with such a theory, and sneeringly ask, What can be the object of such a restoration? What end is it to answer? What purpose can it subserve? But to all such methods of reasoning, it is enough to reply that our business is with the word of God, and that if God has announced it as his purpose so to restore the Jewish nation he certainly has adequate reasons to justify his purpose. No Christian will refuse to defer to the rectitude of Jehovah's doings. The only question is, whether God has said that he will restore the Jewish nation; for, if he has so said, no reasonings of ours can invalidate his promise or throw uncertainty upon his word. Whether we can foresee the objects to be subserved or not, there is not a "jot or tittle" of his revelation which is not more reliable than all the whims or reasonings of all the wisest thinkers that ever lived.

Others tell us that the restoration of the Jewish nationality would be contrary to the spirit of the gospel; that all such distinctions and differences as are implied in the re-establishment of that nation have been superseded by the new covenant; that "the middle wall of partition" between Jews and Gentiles has been broken down in Christ; and that therefore we cannot hope for Israel's restoration. But what of that, if God has clearly declared that he will rebuild Jerusalem and the Jewish state? We dare not set aside the positive declarations of the Lord by human inferences. But it is not true that the gospel has abolished all national distinctions. The wall of partition has been broken down only so far, that the offers of forgiveness and eternal life are now made equally to Jews and Gentiles, so that either may embrace them and be numbered with God's redeemed ones. Receiving Christ as the Savior does not make Englishmen Americans, nor Frenchmen Greeks. These national distinctions still remain, however eminent may be our saintship, and will perhaps remain forever. Converting a Jew to Christianity will not make him a Gentile. And if there can be an English or American nationality without subverting the spirit and nature of the gospel, there may also be a Jewish nationality equally exempt from all contravention of the Christian economy. I can see no more difficulty in the one case than in the other.

Again, some say if we admit that the Jews are to be restored as a nation, we must also admit that they will occupy an enviable place and possess peculiar prerogatives, which it would not be well for us to concede. But shall we bend and modify the word of God to make it harmonize with our whims and jealousies? Are we to explain away the positive statements of revelation because they disagree with our tastes and conflict with our vanity and pride? Away with such unworthy feelings upon a subject like this! What if the Jews shall be put into the front ranks in the glorious kingdom of the Son of David? If God sees fit to give them that place, will it not be right? They have not abused their original calling any more than the Gentile church has abused the gospel. The most illustrious of the saints belonged to the Jewish race. The adorable Redeemer himself was a Jew. "He took on him the seed of Abraham." For more than two thousand years the Hebrew people were nurtured as God's own favorites; and for all that time were the only people under heaven who worshipped the one living and true God.

And had it not been for them, where would be the Bible in which we glory, or those glad promises of life through which we hope? Then why murmur and seek to turn the point of Jehovah's prophecies, because, perchance, these descendants of Abraham, Isaac and Jacob may yet be blest for their fathers' sake and be made to stand high in the millennial kingdom? For my own part, I am heartily willing to acquiesce in any arrangements which the blessed Savior may make; and I will at the same time persist in holding as the truth of God whatsoever I find clearly stated in his holy word, no matter where it may lead me.

And yet again it is said that the New Testament is the key to the Old, that the New Testament says nothing about the restoration of the Jews, and that therefore we are to seek for some other interpretation of those Old Testament predictions which seem to declare it. Now, I deny that the New Testament is silent on the subject, and will presently show to the contrary. But, if the Gospels and Epistles never once alluded to it, I would still deny the inference which the objector would have us draw from such a fact. The announcements of the prophets are just as reliable and authoritative as those of the apostles and evangelists; and it is a mistake to suppose that, because we have the New Testament, we have nothing further to do with the Old. The one is no less the word of God than the other. Each department of the Scripture has its own peculiar importance, and was given to meet its own peculiar emergency. And if a thing asserted in one part, given for one purpose, is not reiterated with equal explicitness and fullness in a subsequent part, given more directly for another purpose, to conclude therefrom that what was first asserted is no longer the divine intention, would be to treat the immutable Jehovah as a child. I know that the New Testament contains but little on the subject of Israel's restoration. But it has allusions to it, and encouraging allusions, which are enough to show that God's purpose in that direction still stands.

The first passage to which I refer you in the New Testament respecting the restoration of the Jewish race, is one uttered by the Savior himself, where he says, "*Jerusalem shall be trodden down of the Gentiles, until the times of the Gentiles be fulfilled.*" Take a plain common-sense view of this passage, and what does it mean? The treading down of Jerusalem can be nothing more nor less than the destruction and desolation of the Jewish metropolis and state by the deportation of the Jewish people. And what is the cessation of this treading down of the Jewish metropolis and state but the restoration of the Jewish people? Who can make any thing else out of it? Commentators have been wrangling and racking their wits for ages about what is to be understood by the fulfilling of the times of the Gentiles; but, if we recur to what has been developed in our preceding inquiries, who can have any difficulty with it? The fulfilling of the times of the Gentiles is simply the winding up of the affairs of the present Gentile church at Christ's second manifestation,—the day of judgment to the Gentile nations and church, as Christ's first coming brought after it the day of judgment to the old Jewish nation and church. And when this day of judgment to the Gentiles comes, and the period is fulfilled when the present economy of Gentile ascendency is to be closed, then the Savior says, Jerusalem shall be trodden down no longer; that is to say, it will be restored, and the nation whom it represents, and whose heart it was, is and ever shall be, shall again occupy its ancient place in more than its ancient grandeur.

A second New Testament passage on the subject is that which I have already quoted, where Paul says, "*All Israel shall be saved*, as it is written, There shall come out of Sion the Deliverer, and shall turn away ungodliness from Jacob."

This is generally understood as a *spiritual* salvation by conversion to Messiah. And a spiritual deliverance is certainly a prominent and controlling idea in the passage. It is expressly stated that one feature is the removal of ungodliness. But this interpretation by no means exhausts the passage. It has an appendage in the succeeding verse which throws much additional light and consequence upon the predicted deliverance. Paul says that this salvation is just what was included in God's ancient covenant with the Jewish fathers. "All Israel shall be saved, *for this is God's covenant unto them when he shall take away their sins.*" Now, if we can ascertain in full what that covenant is, we will have in full what this salvation and deliverance includes. We go back, then, to the Old Testament, where this covenant is repeatedly announced and recorded. We read the fifteenth chapter of Genesis. We there find that, by sundry miraculous manifestations, "the Lord made *a covenant* with Abraham, saying, Unto thy seed have I *given this land, from the river of Egypt unto the great river, the river Euphrates:* the Kenites, and the Kenizites, and the Kadmonites, and the Hittites, and the Perizzites, and the Rephaims, and the Amorites, and the Canaanites, and the Girgashites, and the Jebuzites." In the next chapter we read again :—"God talked with him, saying, As for me, behold, *my covenant* is with thee, and thou shalt be a father of many nations, (or multitudes.) . . . . And I will establish my covenant between me and thee, and to thy seed after thee, in their generations for *an everlasting covenant;* to be a God unto thee and to thy seed after thee. And I will *give unto thee, and to thy seed after thee,* THE LAND wherein thou art a stranger, (sojourner,) *all the land of Canaan for an everlasting possession;* and I will be their God." To Isaac it was subsequently said, "Sojourn in *this land,* for unto thee and unto thy seed will I give *these countries,* and I will perform the oath which I sware unto Abraham thy

Father." And so the dying Jacob testifies:—"God Almighty appeared unto me and said unto me, Behold, *I will . . . . give this land to thy seed after thee* FOR AN EVERLASTING POSSESSION:" (Gen. xlviii.)

And if any one supposes that this is not the covenant of which Paul speaks, then let us turn to what God calls "a new covenant with the house of Israel," and see whether the same features are not included. We read the latter part of the thirty-first of Jeremiah. A glorious spiritual renewal is there promised. They shall know the Lord, and he will forgive their iniquity and remember their sin no more. But this is not all. The language is as strong as words and imagery can make it. Jehovah points to the enduring orbs of immensity, and declares that "*the seed of Israel*" shall no more "*cease from being a nation before him forever*" than the sun, moon and stars shall disappear from the universe. Nay, more:—"Behold, the days come, saith the Lord, that *the city shall be built to the Lord from the tower of Hananeel unto the gate of the corner. It shall not be plucked up nor thrown down* ANY MORE FOREVER." This prophecy cannot refer to the return from Babylon, for all were not then converted and pious; and since then their sin has been remembered, and their city rendered more awfully desolate than ever it was left by Assyrian kings. Nay, I take the broad ground, and no man can overturn it, that God's covenant to Abraham and his seed has never yet been even nearly fulfilled. Its great fullness is still matter of promise, to be verified hereafter, when Christ shall "come a second time unto salvation." That covenant charters to them *the land* from the river of Egypt to the great river Euphrates, for their everlasting possession; which has never yet been made good. That covenant guarantees unto them a national existence and glory as lasting as the great orbs of heaven; which yet remains to be fulfilled. Wherever the terms of that covenant are given, from first to last these are two of its prominent and immutable features. And if "all Israel is to be saved," according to that covenant which Paul explicitly declares to be unchangeable,—"without repentance,"—it is demonstrated to an absolute certainty that they will yet be gathered and replaced in that "goodly land and large" in which they dwelt when David controlled their triumphant armies and Solomon and his court were the admiration of the world.

A third reference to this subject in the New Testament is contained in the first of Acts, where the disciples put to the Savior their last question:—"*Lord, wilt thou at this time restore the kingdom to Israel?*" What did they mean by that inquiry? Every preacher, commentator and thoughtful Bible-reader will tell you that the Jews looked for the Messiah as a reigning prince. For many years they had been a dependent and oppressed people. In the period of the Savior's stay on earth, they were subject to the dominion of the Cæsars. And their great hope was, that when Christ came he would judge their oppressors, deliver them from their national dejection, and restore their state and kingdom to former independence and glory. The disciples shared in the common expectation. Hence their despondency at his crucifixion, saying, "We trusted that it had been he which should have redeemed Israel." They felt all their fond hopes crushed in the Savior's death. But as soon as he arose from the dead and reappeared among them, their old hopes revived, and they looked anew for the Messiah's deliverance of their nation. And this was the burden of their question as here presented. They wished to know if Christ was then about to effect the expected national redemption, and "restore the kingdom to Israel." The question then arises, Were their anticipations respecting this redemption right or wrong? I maintain that they were right. If they were not right, then I am at a loss to account for the fact that these anticipations retained their full force through three or four years of special daily instruction from the Savior himself, and continued uppermost in their minds to the very last moment of Christ's stay upon earth. Then again, if they were all this while cherishing erroneous expectations in this matter, would not the Savior have set them right now that he was at the point of leaving them until his final "coming and kingdom"? But look at his answer. Not one word did he utter against the views implied in their question. All he said was, "It is not for you to know the times and the seasons which the Father hath put in his own power." They did not ask him whether he would restore the kingdom to Israel; they took all that as settled; and the Savior answered them upon the same assumption. They simply wished to know whether that was *the time*, and the answer was that they were not to know the time. As regards every thing but the time, the reply leaves it just as it was apprehended by the inquirers. And, taking the circumstances and all together, it is to me perfectly conclusive that it is the divine intention to "restore the kingdom to Israel" in the exact sense in which the disciples expected it; and that the blessed Savior, in his last words, meant to throw his solemn sanction upon the hope of Israel's restoration. I have no interest in forcing or perverting the Scriptures from their plain and obvious meaning, and if I did not solemnly believe what I here state I would not utter it.

A fourth allusion which the New Testament contains upon this subject, is in the fifteenth of Acts, where James says, "Simeon hath declared how God at the first did visit the Gentiles, *to take out of them a people for his name.* And to this agree the words of the prophets, as it is written, *After this I will return, and will build again the tabernacle of David which is fallen down; and I will build again the ruins thereof, and I will set it up:* that the residue of men might seek after the Lord, and all the Gentiles, upon whom my name is called, saith the Lord."

Two things are here to be specially noted. The first is the object of the present dispensation; which is, *to take out of the Gentiles a people for God's name.* I have heretofore shown that there is nothing in the Scriptures to warrant the hope that the world is to be converted before Christ comes the second time. The whole object of the present economy is, to take out from among men a people for the Lord. This is here pointedly declared. But James goes further. He assures us that it is the purpose of God, as announced by the prophets, to return after the object of this dispensation has been attained, and then to "*build again the tabernacle of David which is fallen down.*" And in order to understand what is meant by this rebuilding of David's tabernacle, we need only revert to the original prophecy in the ninth of Amos, which treats of Israel's dispersion for their sins, and their redemption in the latter days, "that they may possess the remnant of Edom, and of all the Gentiles, *and be pulled out of their land no more.*" Surely the matter is as plain as words can make it, that, at the end of this dispensation, Christ will come and restore the scattered Jews to their own land, and reign over the house of Jacob forever upon the throne of his father David.

There are still other allusions to this subject in the New Testament; but I have not the time to give them now. It is more especially in the Old Testament that we are to seek the amplest details of Israel's hopes. That is peculiarly the gospel of the Jews. The prophecies there on record respecting the conversion and restoration of Jacob's seed may well be pronounced by Bishop Newton to be innumerable. There is hardly a chapter from Psalms to Malachi which does not in some way bear upon it. To give all, we would have to recite about half of all that the prophets have written.

Let me refer you to a few specimens.

Look at the text and its contiguous parts :—" Thus saith the Lord : Behold, I will take the children of Israel from among the Gentiles, whither they be gone, and will gather them on every side, *and bring them into their own land.*" What could be plainer than this ? It is useless to say that it refers to the deliverance from Babylon ; for this prediction relates to "*the whole house of Israel,*" whilst only parts of Judah and Benjamin ever returned from the Babylonian captivity. The restoration here predicted is to be attended with the everlasting reunion of the two wings of the great Israelitish schism, so that they shall "not be divided into two kingdoms any more at all ;" which to this day has not taken place. This restoration is to be perpetual, "*forever ;*" the restoration from Babylon was only temporary. This restoration is to be attended with the ultimate entire conversion of the whole nation, and an everlasting release from all their filthiness and sins ; but they have involved themselves deeper in crime since they came back from Babylon than before, and even murdered the Messiah.

Neither will it answer to say that the restoration here predicted is to be understood *spiritually*, as referring to the final conversion of the Jewish people, and their incorporation into the Christian church. The church is no more *their* land than it is the land of Gentile believers. The prophecy sets forth their spiritual renovation in words sufficiently plain to need no further spiritualizing ; thus leaving us to infer that the other particulars are to be understood in the same plain and obvious sense. The prophecy also contains a promise of the multiplication of man *and beast,* which certainly cannot apply to the church unless our sanctuaries are yet to be filled with the brute creation. The same prophecy promises to Israel their old estates,—"*I will settle them after their old estates,*"—which, whether taken in a spiritual or a literal sense, necessarily implies their restoration to a condition of isolation and distinctness from all other orders or races of men. But this is not all. If the regathering and restoration of the Jewish people into their own land is to be understood spiritually, then their deportation from that land and dispersion must be understood spiritually too. The one must correspond to the other. The same prediction contains both sides, in the same strain of discourse; and the promise of the restoration is founded on the predicate of their previous dispersion. Hence, if the one is spiritual, the other is equally spiritual; and if the one is literal and outward, so also must the other be. God himself, speaking upon this very subject, has settled this point forever. "It shall come to pass, that LIKE AS I have watched over them to pluck up, and to break down, and to destroy, and to afflict; so will I watch over them to build, and to plant, saith the Lord:" (Jer. xxxi. 28.) Here, then, I take my stand with unflinching firmness, and upon the immutable basis of God's own word, demand of you either to show that the spoiling was only spiritual, or else admit that their final restoration is to be national and literal. If Titus only took the church, and not the literal city,—if he only cast the Jews out of the church, and did not kill them or carry them away captives,—if he did not devastate and depopulate Palestine, but only intercepted God's spiritual blessings by desolating the ways to eternal life,—*then*, but *only* then, can this promised regathering of Israel into their own land be interpreted so as to preclude their national restoration. "*I will gather them*," saith God, "*and bring them into their own land.*"

The same literal restoration of the exiled descendants of Jacob is foretold by Moses, in his farewell address to that people. We there have a graphic delineation of the whole history of Israel up to the present and still future times. Moses there foretells a sore and wide dispersion; but he predicts with equal explicitness a final and complete recovery from it. "The Lord thy God will turn thy captivity, and have compassion upon thee, *and will gather thee from all the nations whither the Lord thy God hath scattered thee.* If any of thine be driven out unto *the uttermost parts of heaven, from thence will the Lord thy God* FETCH THEE : *and the Lord thy God will bring thee into* THE LAND WHICH THY FATHER POSSESSED, AND THOU SHALT POSSESS IT : *and he will multiply thee above thy fathers:*" (Deut. xxx.) Never, to this day, has there occurred to Israel such a deliverance, from such a dispersion. And the idea that this prediction is to be fulfilled by the simple incorporation of the Jews into the existing church, is worse than ridiculous. They are, therefore, to be restored.

Isaiah, also, has spoken most pointedly upon this subject. In his eleventh chapter we have a glowing prophecy, which all treat as referring to the millennial times. And in that prophecy we find it written, "It shall come to pass IN THAT DAY, that *the Lord shall set his hand again,* THE SECOND TIME, *to recover the remnant of his people which shall be left from Assyria, and from Egypt, and from Pathros, and from Cush, and from Elam, and from Shinar, and from Hamath and from the isles of the sea,* and he shall set up an ensign for the nations, *and shall assemble the outcasts of Israel, and gather together the dispersed of Judah*"—the whole Jewish race—"*from the four corners of the earth.* . . . . And there shall be an highway for the remnant of his people which shall be left from Assyria; LIKE AS IT WAS TO ISRAEL IN THE DAY THAT HE CAME UP OUT OF THE LAND OF EGYPT." Will any man say that such a prophecy as this has ever been fulfilled, or includes no more than the conversion of the Jews to Christianity? Was the deliverance from Egypt a mere joining of the church? Yet here we have God's solemn promise a second time to recover the remnant of his people, to gather Israel and Judah from the four corners of the earth, and to provide a way for them, "*like as it was to Israel in the day that he came up out of the land of Egypt.*"

Brethren, what you think of these things, I know not; but I am fully persuaded that it is God's immutable purpose to bring back the Jewish race to its ancient home. The passages which I have given more than prove it; whilst the great mass of prophecy upon the subject has not been touched. And if even all these solemn statements of God were to pass for nothing, the simple but significant facts of history furnish ground enough upon which to infer that Israel is yet to be restored to that land where Abraham lived and the Savior died.

Look at that wonderful race! For nearly two thousand years, scattered all over the face of the earth, oppressed, despised, persecuted, unmercifully butchered; yet still existing, as distinct in manners, feelings and hopes, as when Moses was their leader and Aaron was their priest. Since God shook them out of their ancient dwelling-places, nations, thrones, kingdoms, have risen, flourished, fallen, and lost their proud subjects in the ever-varying stream of human affairs; but Israel still stands apart, unshaken by earth's mutations, with the accents of David and Isaiah still upon their lips, and still looking for the promised Shiloh to take them back in triumph to their father-land. The Christian church herself, glorious as she is in her list of martyrs and attirements of grace and truth, has, since then, been depressed, diminished, enfeebled, by violence and defections which she has found it hard to survive; but the house of Jacob, with all their wrongs and spoliations, have only strengthened with their trials, whilst all the bitterness of their great cup of sorrow has never made them forget that they were Hebrews, or loosened the tenacity with which they cling to God's peculiar covenant unto them. Kings have issued severe edicts and commissioned bloody executioners against them, and the seditious and spiteful multitudes have afflicted them with outrages still more violent and tragical. Princes and people, civilized and savage, Pagans, Mahometans, and professing Christians, disagreeing in so many things, have more than once made common cause for their extermination. But still they live and thrive. Though for nearly twenty centuries without a temple, prophet, king, country, or home, they still bear the same marks which characterized them before Vespasian set foot on their sacred land or Titus invested their lovéd Jerusalem.

Look, again, at their holy city. "Captured, ravaged, burnt, razed to the foundation, dispeopled, its deported citizens sold into slavery, and forbidden by severest penalties to visit their native seats;" yet, even in its mournful desolations, it stands forth, a thing to itself, and altogether distinguished from all other ruins. Who now weeps over the fall of Troy? What people pays pilgrimages of devotion to the ruin-piles of mighty Nineveh or Babylon? These great monuments of human pride and glory sleep their last sleep, and no tear falls upon their unhonored graves. But Jerusalem, even in her ashes, is still dear to the hearts of millions, and the mere mention of that name awakens pangs of mingled grief and hope as deep as those that weighed upon her captive sons when they mourned under the willows by Babel's waters. Beautifully has it been said, that "ever and anon, and from all the winds of heaven, Zion's exiled children come to visit her, and, with eyes weeping sore, bewail her widowhood. No city was ever honored thus. None else thus receives pilgrimages from the fiftieth generation of its outcast population. None but this, after centuries of such dispersion, could, at the first call, gather beneath its wings the whole of its wide-wandering family. None but this has possessed a spell sufficient to keep its people still distinct, even in remotest regions, and in the face of the mightiest inducements. And none but itself can now be repeopled with precisely the same race which left it nearly two thousand years ago."

Now, what mean these anomalous, I might say, *miraculous*, facts? Why are the Jewish people still distinct, and Jerusalem's walls still dear, as ever? Why have Jacob's seed always refused to hold lands anywhere but in Palestine, and Jerusalem always refused to give permanent habitation to any but them? Meet a Jew where you will, he is a mere wanderer or sojourner, ready to move at the shortest warning. Scattered over all lands beneath the sun, he has never taken root in any. And of all that have ever tried to fix themselves in the Holy Land,—Romans and Persians, Saracens and Turks, Egyptian Caliphs and Latin Christians, Mamelukes and Ottomans,—none have ever been able to gain a permanent foothold in it. WHY IS ALL THIS? Men of political science may try their skill at explanation; but, after all, the problem will reduce itself to this: that God has his own settled purpose with this people and this place, holding the one in reserve for the other until each shall be forever satisfied with its own. Here, history is prophecy. And if all the holy seers were silent, the very stones themselves cry out for Israel's restoration. The rocks of Palestine will have no lord but Jacob.

I am, therefore, prepared to adopt the statement of David N. Lord, a very profound and able American expositor of sacred prophecy, that "those who assent to the true laws of language and symbols will no more deny or doubt that the prophecies teach that the Israelites are to be restored, than those who assent to the definitions and axioms of geometry will deny the demonstrations that are founded on them. There is not a proposition in the whole circle of human knowledge of more perfect certainty than that God has revealed the purpose of regathering that scattered nation, establishing them as his chosen people, and reappointing a temple-worship at Jerusalem that is to embrace some of their ancient rites. It is not merely certain, but is taught with a frequency, an emphasis and an amplitude, and invested with a dignity and grandeur that are proportionable to the vastness and wonderfulness of the measure in the great scheme of his administration over the world." The descendants of Jacob are specifically, and in many places, spoken of as the subjects of a long and painful dispersion and depression, which we see literally verified before our eyes. The same passages, with the same explicitness, affirm of this same people, that they shall be delivered from their oppressions, regathered from their dispersions, restored to the land which their fathers possessed, and forever secured against any similar calamity. The countries from which they are to come; the manner in which they are to come; the very methods of their conveyance, on horses, and mules, and dromedaries, in chariots, in litters, and in ships, and in swift-moving vehicles, which some have taken as a description of railroads; all are specifically noted. And how any student of these things can rise up and say that the doctrine of Israel's restoration is a fable, I cannot understand.

The return of this wonderful people will doubtless begin, in a small way, under what some will call the natural course of things. There are even now already thousands of Jews in Jerusalem and its vicinity. A goodly portion of the Holy Land is at this moment under mortgages in the hands of those rich Jewish bankers, the Rothschilds, of Europe. The effects of the peace just concluded between the great powers of the Old World, in securing toleration of other religions under the Turkish laws, is at once the signal for the downfall of the Ottoman empire, and the opening of the door for Israel's return. Many religious associations in all parts of Protestant Christendom are in efficient operation with and for the Jews, all looking more or less to their ultimate restoration. These things, all working in the line of Israel's intense desires, cannot but work mighty consequences. They are the preliminaries of the second Jewish exodus.

But it is not by these alone that Israel shall be redeemed.

According to the eighteenth of Isaiah, and other passages, there will yet be great national movements upon the subject. We there read of a great maritime power, spreading wide its wings, existing somewhere in the Far West from Palestine, and which must either be the United States, Great Britain, or perhaps both, as one in religion, language and laws. This power, accustomed to send messengers by sea, is to become interested in behalf of the Jews, and to aid them with contributions, embassies, treaty-stipulations, fleets and other ways. The prophet himself calls to this power, (I use Horseley's translation,) "Ho! land spreading wide the shadow of thy wings!" and he gives it its commission, "Go;" which would seem to indicate that it will be from the study of prophecy, and from the will of God as thus presented, that men shall be roused up to this work. "Go, as a swift messenger, to a people wonderful from the beginning hitherto, a nation expecting, expecting, and trampled under foot, whose land rivers (invading armies) have spoiled; *and all the inhabitants of the world, and dwellers upon earth, shall see the lifting up, as it were, of a banner upon the mountains; and shall hear the sounding, as it were, of a trumpet.*" That is, as I understand it, when these movements in favor of the Jews begin, there will be an extraordinary waking up upon the subject, and a very deep interest felt, so that men generally will regard themselves as specially called to help in the great work. And it is a singular fact, in this connection, that the United States government, without any assignable cause for it, did, only a few years ago, send out Lieut. Lynch and his party, to explore the Jordan and obtain detailed and authentic descriptions of the condition and topography of Israel's land. England has done the same, as if these countries, so closely allied in so many particulars, were already laying the foundations for their work and mission in bringing back the dispersed children of Abraham.

But I have no expectation that any thing very decisive or extraordinary will occur in the line of the Jewish restoration, until God's judgments shall begin to tear asunder the nations. There is first to be a "pruning," "a taking away of luxuriant branches," "a leaving to the mountain-birds of prey;" and only "*at that season a present shall be led to Jehovah of hosts, of a people dragged away and plucked; even of a people wonderful from their beginning hitherto; a nation expecting, expecting, and trampled under foot, whose land rivers have spoiled, unto the place of the name of Jehovah of hosts, Mount Zion:*" (Isa. xviii. 7.) When the "distress of nations with perplexity" shall have fully set in, and the day of earth's troubles has come, then the people of Israel shall flock home, like doves to their windows; and the Lord himself shall show wonders in their favor, like to the day that he brought them up out of Egypt. The last chapter of Isaiah tells of manifestations of divine power, mercy and consolation, and says, "When ye see this, your heart shall rejoice, and your bones shall flourish like an herb; *and the hand of the Lord shall be known toward his servants, and his indignation toward his enemies.* For behold, the Lord will come with fire, and his chariots like a whirlwind; to render his anger with fury, and his rebuke with flames of fire. For by fire and by his sword will the Lord plead with all flesh, and the slain of the Lord shall be many. . . . *And I will set up a sign among them, and I* WILL SEND THOSE THAT ESCAPE OF THEM UNTO THE NATIONS, to Tarshish, Pul, and Lud, that draw the bow, to Tubal and Javan, to the isles afar off, that have not heard my fame, neither seen my glory; *and they (that escape God's terrific judgment upon Israel's enemies) shall declare my glory among the Gentiles;* AND THEY (THE GENTILES) SHALL BRING ALL YOUR BRETHREN (the prophet's brethren, THE JEWS) *for an offering unto the Lord out of all nations,* upon horses, and in chariots, and in coaches, and upon mules, and upon swift beasts, (rapid vehicles,) *to my holy mountain Jerusalem, saith the Lord.*"

The accompaniments and great results of this final restoration of the Jewish people are so wonderful and miraculous, that it is hardly possible for us to form a proper conception of them. Within fifty years from this present time, perhaps the whole story will be told. One thing is certain, that Israel's restoration is not for Israel alone, but for the whole world. It is one of those means, in the wonderful arrangements of God, for letting forth his mercy and salvation upon all the inhabitants of the earth. It is in the seed of Abraham that all nations shall be blessed. Israel's restoration shall be the world's resurrection. Paul says, "If the fall of them be the riches of the world, and the diminishing of them the riches of the Gentiles, how much more their fullness? If the casting away of them be the reconciling of the world, what shall the receiving of them be, but *life from the dead?*" (Rom. xi. 12, 15.) This return will itself be a fulfillment of prophecy so startling that it will open men's eyes as they never have been opened, and make them feel the power of divine truth and the reality of Jehovah's sovereignty as they never have felt them. The Bible will suddenly become a new book, and beam forth a new light and speak with a more potent authority. In the language of Hamilton, "The moment the vail is rent from Israel's eyes, the vail will be rent from a thousand prophecies; and, read in the light of restored and regenerated Judah, the word of God will sparkle with unwonted coruscations, and, like deep-colored gems that look dusty in cloud-light, many of its dark sayings will brighten up into its divinest truths when the beams break forth from Salem."

The thorough cleansing and renewal which will pass upon the Jewish people, and God's wonderful manifestations in their behalf, shall speak like a new revelation to the hearts and consciences of men; and "many people, and strong nations, shall come to seek the Lord of hosts in Jerusalem, and to pray before the Lord; and ten men out of all languages of the nations shall take hold of the skirt of him that is a Jew, saying, We will go with you, for we have heard that God is with you:" (Zech. viii. 12.) All Israel shall then own the Messiah, and be fully and forever converted unto him, not by the slow processes of present evangelization, but by wonderful manifestations from God, as in the case of Paul, their distinguished type: (1 Tim. i. 16.) Noble saintship and Davidic zeal shall again be found in Judah. "He that is feeble among them shall be as David; and the house of David shall be as Elohim, the Jehovah angel, before them:" (Zech. xii. 8.) The times of the Gentiles being fulfilled, Jacob's trouble shall be over and the grand Sabbath of the world begin. Christ shall sit upon the throne of his father David, and reign over the house of Jacob forever; and "they shall call Jerusalem *the throne of the Lord.*" According to "the word that Isaiah the son of Amoz saw," not concerning *the church*, but CONCERNING JUDAH AND JERUSALEM, "the mountain of the Lord's house shall be established in the top of the mountains, and shall be exalted above the hills, and all nations shall flow unto it. And many people shall go and say, Come ye, and let us go up to the mountain of the Lord, to the house of the God of Jacob, and he will teach us of his ways, and we will walk in his paths; *for out of Zion shall go forth the law, and the word of the Lord from Jerusalem:*" (Isa. ii. 1–3.) "AND THE LORD SHALL BE KING OVER ALL THE EARTH:" (Zech. xiv. 8.) This world shall then have embraced its rightful Sovereign, and the hearts of its great nations shall beat in unison with heaven.

Nor need you be surprised, my brethren, when, in the light of these prophecies, I declare the conviction that Jerusalem is yet to become the metropolis of the world, just as it was the metropolis of Judea in the days of Solomon. All the nations of this world are yet to come under one universal government,—the kingdom of Christ and his glorified saints. "God hath highly exalted him, and given him a name that is above every name; that at the name of Jesus every knee should bow, and every tongue confess that *Jesus Christ is Lord:*" (Phil. ii. 10.) "*Now we see not yet all things put under him:*" (Heb. ii. 8.) But "*He must reign* until he hath put all enemies under his feet:" (1 Cor. xv. 25.) "The Gentiles must be given him as his inheritance, and the uttermost parts of the earth for his possession:" (Ps. ii. 8.) He has declared himself to be appointed *King of the Jews, and Prince of the kings of the earth:* (Matt. xxvii. 11; Rev. i. 5.) "The *kingdoms of the world* are to become the kingdoms of our Lord and of his Christ; and he shall reign forever and ever:" (Rev. xi. 15.) And the centre and seat of this great kingdom is JERUSALEM. "The Lord of hosts shall reign"—*where?*—"IN MOUNT ZION, AND IN JERUSALEM, and before his ancients gloriously:" (Isa. xxiv. 23.) "The Lord also shall roar"—*from whence?*—"*out of Zion*, and utter his voice FROM JERUSALEM, and the heavens and the earth shall shake; but the Lord will be the hope of his people, and the strength of the children of Israel. So shall ye know that I am the Lord your God, DWELLING IN ZION, my holy mountain: then shall *Jerusalem* be holy:" (Joel iii. 16, 17.) Nay, as there is to be a literal reign of the Son of man on earth, where is it most likely that his imperial seat will be? What locality does the mind most naturally turn to? The holy associations and the very geographical position of Palestine mark it out with signal felicity as the place where the Son of Mary shall hold his sublime court. As remarked by one who has looked carefully at the matter, "Palestine is so remarkably situated, that it forms the bridge between two continents and a gateway to a third. Were the population and wealth of Europe, Asia and Africa condensed into single points, Palestine would be the centre of their common gravity. And with the amazing facilities of modern intercourse, and the prodigious extent of modern traffic, it is not easy to estimate the commercial grandeur to which a kingdom may attain, planted as it were on the very apex of the old world, with its three continents spreading out beneath its feet, and with the Red Sea on one side to bring it all the golden treasures and spicy harvests of the East, and the Mediterranean floating in on the other side all the skill and enterprise and knowledge of the West. For the sake of higher ends it seems the purpose of God to make the Holy Land a mart of nations, and, by bringing the forces of the Gentiles to Jerusalem, to send the blessing of Abraham over all the earth."

It is also well known that ever since the Jews first entered Canaan, it has been the battle-ground of nations. To this hour it is mixed up with the mightiest disputes that disturb the world. The Assyrian, the Egyptian and the Roman of old, the Arab, the Turk, the Greek, the Papist and the Rabbi of our times, all have claimed it as if the earth contained not another prize like it. The late war, which converted the Crimea into a Golgotha and made the world tremble, had its beginning in Jerusalem, in disputes and altercations about its shrines and holy places. And the history of the world is filled with illustrations of the desirableness that has ever adhered to that "goodly land," and of the interests involved in its occupation. Ages have rolled around it as the spot of decision on which the question of supremacy is suspended. And divine prophecy, sounding through the long galleries of centuries, proclaims the fact that all the nations shall yet be governed from that point.

Men may think I dream, but I must take God's word as meaning what it says. The day is coming when the world shall join in that glad song of David, "*Beautiful for situation, the joy of the whole earth, is Mount Zion,* THE CITY OF THE GREAT KING!" That wonderful people, the scattered relics of a mighty nation, shall come back to their ancient home. From the North and the South, from the East and the West, they shall come with singing unto Zion. "And they shall build the waste cities, and inhabit them; and they shall plant vineyards, and drink the wine thereof; and they shall no more be pulled out of their land which I have given them, saith the Lord:" (Amos ix. 14, 15.) Jehovah Elohim shall come down again, more glorious than when of old he dwelt in cloud and flame in the Holy of Holies, even Jesus in his own glorified humanity; and they shall say, "*Lo! this is our God! we have waited for him, and he will save us: this is the Lord; we have waited for him, we will be glad and rejoice in his salvation:*" (Isa. xxv. 9.) Jerusalem's light shall then have come and the glory of the Lord have risen upon her, and she shall arise and shine. Gentiles shall come to her light, and kings to the brightness of her rising. Her sons shall come from far, and her daughters shall be nursed at her side. The abundance of the sea shall be turned to her, and the wealth of the Gentiles shall come unto her. The multitude of camels shall come up,—the dromedaries of Midian and Ephah; all they from Sheba shall come; they shall bring gold and incense, and they shall show forth the praises of the Lord. All the flocks of Kedar shall be gathered together unto her. The rams of Nebaioth shall minister unto her; they shall come up with acceptance on God's altar, and he will glorify the house of his glory. The nation and kingdom that will not serve her shall perish, and be utterly wasted. The glory of Lebanon shall come unto her, the fir-tree, the pine-tree, and the box together, to beautify the place of God's sanctuary; and he will make the place of his feet glorious. The sons of them that afflicted her shall come bending unto her, and all they that despised her shall bow themselves down at the soles of her feet; and they shall call her, "THE CITY OF THE LORD, THE ZION OF THE HOLY ONE OF ISRAEL!" (Isa. lx. 14.)

But Jerusalem below, radiant in all its untold glory, shall be but a type and earthy picture of the higher and sublimer Jerusalem that is above,—that firmly-founded city for which Abraham looked, whose builder and maker is God,—that city which John saw "descending out of heaven from God, having the glory of God, and her light like unto a stone most precious, even like a jasper-stone, clear as crystal." The one is earthly, the other is heavenly. The one is built by human hands, the other is the workmanship of God himself. The one has a population composed of men holy and happy, but men *in the flesh;* the other is the glorious residence of the glorified saints. The one shall rest upon the earthly mount; the other shall be above the mountains and the hills." The one will need clouds and rain, sunshine and peaceful night; the other has no need of the sun nor of the moon to shine in it, for the glory of God shall lighten it, and the Lamb is the light thereof. The one shall have its temple and its altars; the other has no temple therein, for the Lord God Almighty and the Lamb are the temple of it. And whilst the sons of Abraham in the flesh shall possess Jerusalem that is below, the sons of Abraham by faith in Christ, who have come out of great tribulation, and washed their robes and made them white in the blood of the Lamb, shall, in their glorification, have their everlasting bliss and home in "the Jerusalem that is above." The relation of the one to the other is like that of the Sanctuary to the Holy of Holies. The one is the metropolis of the "new earth;" the other of the "new heavens." The one is suspended in the clouds to pour its radiance on the saved nations below: (Rev. xxi. 24;) but both belong to the one sublime and wonderful economy which is to encompass this planet when once its redemption is complete.

All hail to the day when these things shall be fulfilled! The cross shall then give place to the crown, and gladness supplant our sighing and tears. Hope shall then change into fruition, and the exile reach his eternal home. Oh, let us rejoice and give thanks that such promises have been left us. Let us stay ourselves upon them and feed upon their preciousness. They are "well-ordered and sure," and cannot disappoint us. They are all as immutable and abiding as God's own eternal nature. Time may intervene and great changes may occur before they are fulfilled; but, as Jehovah lives, if we are Christ's we shall be glorified with him and dwell in the city he has prepared.

THE DAY IS COMING.

The day is coming—yea, is now at hand—
When wars shall struggle on the Syrian plains,—
Wars such as ne'er before have been on earth,
Nor the sun seen in all his ancient reigns:—
The day is coming—yea, is now at hand—
When, urged by Heaven, to her old hallowed ground
Shall beauteous Solyma lead back her tribes,
While with sweet tones her Hebrew camps resound.
Then shall stand still Euphrates; then shall stop,
In fierce affright, Nile's many-founted river,
Then, too, with whirl gigantic, shall the way
Of the Red Sea cleave wide apart and sever.
Day of revival! then shall festal Zion
To her eternal God build shrine on shrine,—
High Lebanon and Hermon shout with singing,
While flowering olives crown their cliffs divine!

Poem on the return of Napoleon's ashes to France.

NINTH DISCOURSE.

THE WORLD TO COME—ILLUSTRATED IN THE SCENES OF THE TRANSFIGURATION—THE BLESSEDNESS OF CHRIST'S PERSONAL PRESENCE—THE MINISTRATIONS OF THE GLORIFIED SAINTS—THE ABSENCE OF ALL POWERS AND AGENCIES OF EVIL—THE BLESSING OF THE WORLD THROUGH ISRAEL—THE CURSE REPEALED.

HEB. ii. 5: *The world to come, whereof we speak.*

THESE words occur in connection with the apostle's endeavor to impress his Jewish brethren with a sense of the greatness and glory of the Lord Jesus and of the salvation which is preached in his name. He begins the epistle by announcing the Savior to them as the Son of God,—the appointed heir of all things,—the Maker and upholder of the worlds,—the brightness of the Father's glory and the express image of his person, who has been exalted to the right hand of the Majesty on high. These were sublime statements, and needing to be well substantiated to be made acceptable. He, therefore, instituted various lines of argument, adapted to the Jewish mind and founded upon the Scriptures, which all held to be divinely inspired. And as the Jews regarded angels as the highest created orders, and as standing next in the scale to the eternal Father himself, Paul's first effort was to prove from prophecy that Christ is superior to the angels. He introduces three points in which this super-angelic dignity is shown. The first is, that Christ is assigned a higher *name* than the angels; the second is, that he is clothed with a sublimer *honor* than the angels; and the third is, that

Christ is invested with a sublimer *office* than the angels,—they being only ministering spirits, whilst he is spoken of as a *divine King*, whose throne is forever and ever, and the sceptre of whose kingdom is a sceptre of righteousness. The princely investiture and reign of the Messiah is thus distinctly deduced from the Old Testament, and used by the apostle as the sublimest demonstration of the Savior's personal dignity. And this Messianic dominion he applies particularly to what is hereafter to grow out of the gospel economy. He tells us that it is peculiarly "*the world to come*" over which the Messiah's reign is to be exercised. "*For unto the angels hath he not put into subjection the world to come, whereof we speak;*" thus proceeding upon the implied assumption that it has been, by promise, put into subjection to Jesus Christ; and that all those allusions to the Savior as *a King* have their chief application and ultimate fulfillment in that "world to come." The Messiah's reign and this world to come accordingly belong together, and coexist in the same period and locality. By determining, then, what is meant by this "world to come," we may form an idea of what is included in the Messianic kingdom; or, if we already know what the consummated Messianic reign is, and where it is to be, we have it already decided what we are to understand by this "world to come."

If any stress is, therefore, to be laid upon the conclusions evolved in the preceding discourses, there is no alternative left but to understand this world to come as *the millennial world*, or the world as it shall be when Christ shall have restored the throne of David, and entered upon his glorious dominion as the sovereign of the nations and Lord of the whole earth. And to this agrees exactly the original word, *οἰκουμενη*, which means *the habitable earth,—the domiciliated globe on which we dwell,*—and not some remote supernal region, as we sometimes imagine. The world to come, then, or the οἰκουμενην την μελλουσαν, as the apostle calls it, is nothing more nor less than this selfsame world of ours in its final or millennial condition. This earth is not to be annihilated. God never obliterates his own creations. The dissolving fires, of which Peter speaks, are for "the perdition of ungodly men;" and not for the utter depopulation and destruction of the whole world. They may consume cities, destroy armies, and effect some important meteorological and geological changes; but men and nations will survive them and still continue to live in the flesh. The earth is to be renovated and restored from its present depression and dilapidation, and thus become "the new earth" of which the Bible speaks. It is to pass through a "regeneration" analogous to that through which a man must pass to see the kingdom of God; but there will be a continuity of its elements and existence, just as a regenerated man is constitutionally the same being that he was before his renewal. It will not be another earth, but the same earth under another condition of things. It is now laboring under the curse; but then the curse will have been lifted off, and all its wounds healed. At present, it is hardly habitable,—no one being able to live in it longer than a few brief years; but then men shall dwell in it forever, without knowing what death is. It is now the home of rebellion, injustice and guilt; it will then be the home of righteousness. It is now under the domination of Satan; it will then come under the blessed rule of the Prince of peace. Such, at any rate, is the hope set before us in the word of God; and this I hold to be "*the world to come*" of which the text speaks. It cannot be any thing else. It cannot be what is commonly called heaven; for the word οἰκουμενη cannot apply to heaven. It is everywhere else used exclusively with reference to our world. Neither can it be the present gospel dispensation, as some have thought; for that began long before this epistle was written, and could not, therefore, have been spoken of by

Paul as yet *"to come."* We are consequently compelled to understand it to mean our own habitable world in its millennial glory. And as the prophecies concerning the Messiah's eternal kingship are here referred to as having their fulfillment in the subjection of the millennial world to his dominion, we are furnished with another powerful argument of Scripture in favor of the doctrine of Christ's personal reign as a great Prince in this world. Indeed, the Bible is so full of this subject, and its inspired writers are so constantly and enthusiastically alluding to it, that I am amazed to find so many pious and Bible-loving people entirely losing sight of it. Ever and anon the Scriptures return to it as the great and animating hope of the church in all her adversities and depressions; and it does seem to me that we are depriving ourselves of much true Christian comfort by the manner in which we have been neglecting and thrusting aside that glorious doctrine. But, as I have already spoken on that subject and given some idea of the manner in which the Scriptures present it, I will not return to it now. My present object is to show, from the Scriptures and by just inferences from them, what sort of a world this "world to come" is, and to describe, as far as I can, what we are to look for when once this earth has been fully subjected to that divine King whose throne is forever and ever, and the sceptre of whose kingdom is a sceptre of righteousness.

That "the world to come" is a highly blessed world, and a vast improvement upon the present scene of things, will be inferred on all hands without argument. It could not be a subject of hope if it were not. The Savior himself exhibited a model of it when in the Mount of Transfiguration; from which, perhaps, we may obtain as deep an insight of its glories as from any other portion of Scripture. That he designed that scene as a miniature model of what his future coming and kingdom is to be, is obvious. A week before it occurred, he told his disciples that "the Son of man shall come in the glory of the Father, with his angels or *messengers* with him;" and that there were some standing there when he made the declaration who "*should not taste of death till they saw the Son of man coming in his kingdom.*" This coming in his kingdom, which some of the disciples were to live to see, is not the final advent; for the disciples are all dead, and the final advent is still future. Neither is it the destruction of Jerusalem; for but one of the apostles lived to see that catastrophe, and the Son of man did not then come in his kingdom. And yet some of the apostles were to have ocular demonstration of the Son of man's coming in his kingdom before tasting of death. Search through apostolic history as we will, we shall find nothing but the transfiguration to which the Savior's words will apply. That, then, was, in some sense, the coming of the Son of man in his kingdom. It was not, indeed, the coming itself, but it was an earnest and picture of it. It was the coming of the Son of man in his kingdom, as the bread and wine in the Eucharist are Christ's body and blood. Peter says "the power and coming of our Lord Jesus Christ" are not "cunningly-devised fables." He declares that he was certified of their reality by the testimony of his own senses. We were *eye-witnesses*, says he, "*when we were with him in the holy mount.*" We thus have clear inspired testimony that the scene of the transfiguration was a demonstrative exhibition of the coming of Jesus in his kingdom. Hence, whatever we find in the descriptions of that scene, we may confidently expect to be realized in that "world to come whereof we speak." As Christ appeared in that glorious scene, so he will appear when he returns to this world. As he was then personally present as the Son of man, so he will be personally present in the millennial kingdom. And as he was there attended by different classes of persons, so will his glorious kingdom consist of similar classes. The first will be the risen and glorified saints, represented by Moses; the second will be the transformed saints, represented by Elijah who was caught up without tasting of death; and the third and most numerous class will be those who shall live in the body, represented by Peter, James and John, as they bowed before his mighty power, and looked with transport and wonder on his ineffable glory.

Let us, then, endeavor to draw out before us some of the more striking features of "the world to come," and, by the contemplation of its attractiveness, endeavor to school our hearts into more ardent thirst to participate in its blissful scenes.

I do not wish to depreciate in the least those gracious arrangements of heaven under which we now live. It is a blessed thing to have the Bible, and to attend properly on the means of grace, and to enjoy the renewing and comforting influences of the Holy Ghost. In giving to us these things, God has endowed us with mercies for which we never can be sufficiently thankful. But he authorizes us to look for greater things than these. The present economy is only preparatory to something higher and more blessed.

"We're now but in creation's vestibule,
And acting the mere prelude unto joy
Immortal, universal."

There is another and more exalted scene of things to follow after the present. If we are faithful to our Lord, there remains for us "a new earth, wherein dwelleth righteousness." And one of the most remarkable and sublime features of that "new earth" is, that it is to have in it the personal, visible and illustrious presence of the Son of God, its great King. It was the presence of Jesus in his glory that made Peter wish to stay in the mountain rather than return again into the cold and heartless world below. That glorious presence was more than all earth beside. We may thus gather some idea of the preciousness of that promise that "the pure in heart shall *see God*." The mere vision of Christ in his glory will be heaven to the soul that leans on him as the Redeemer.

There is no thirst in man more craving than the desire to *behold God*. All the images in heathen temples, and all the idolatries of the world, are but expressions of this perpetual sigh of humanity. Moses himself coveted most of all things to *see* Him who was accomplishing such wonders by his hand. And very few, if any, can pray without first forming to the mind some image of God. We are creatures of sense. Abstract spirit is a cold and uninviting conception. All our deepest impressions, and all our ideas, are received by means of the outward senses. And there is no glory of God of which we can conceive that can possibly be so satisfying and transporting as that of *beholding* him, and for ourselves *seeing* his glory. All Christ's sublime teachings did not so impress and rejoice the hearts of Peter, James and John, as that one short vision of the Savior, as he was transfigured before them. Not all the sublime experiences of Moses so satisfied him, as when God gave him some visible manifestation of his glory. When John sums up the highest prospects of believers, he makes their fullest satisfaction and rapture depend on *seeing* Jesus as he is. And Peter, when he came to his strongest reason for holding Christianity to be a reality, referred to what he had witnessed on the holy mount. It was a glad thing to see Jesus, even in his humiliation. We sometimes wish that we had lived in those days, that we might have looked upon his face and heard the tones of his voice. If we could refer to but one slight glimpse of him, we would treasure it as a blissful thing. We would ever recur to it with pleasure. If there were now a spot on earth where we could see him even as he then was, millions would spare no expense or pains to gain a look upon him, and multitudes would throng to the place, crying, "*Sirs, we would see Jesus!*" And if it would be a high and lawful gratification to see Christ as he once lived on earth, how sublime would be the portion of seeing him in the glory of his kingdom! Would it not afford a certainty to our faith, and a rapture to our hearts, worth living for? Look at the case of the queen of Sheba, when she came to see the glory of Solomon,—the type of the greater than Solomon. She had "heard of his fame concerning the name of the Lord," as we have heard of Christ and his glory; but there was an air of romance about it which made her doubtful, just as many even Christian people are with respect to revelation. There was something wanting to complete her enjoyment. She needed yet to see the reality of which she had heard. To secure this, a journey of months through exposure and dangers she deemed of small account. "And when she had *seen* all Solomon's wisdom, and the house that he had built, and the meat of his table, and the sitting of his servants, and the standing of his ministers, and their apparel, and his ascent by which he went up to the house of the Lord, there was no more spirit in her;" she fainted for very ecstasy. Now she could say that it was a true report which she had heard, and that the half had not been told her. Never could she have forgotten that visit. Never could that vision of Solomon's glory have passed from her delighted memory. Never did it cease from being a sunny spot in her recollection to which to recur as the happiest event of her life. And if the sight of the glory of the mere human type of the Messiah was thus transporting and overpowering, what a joy would it be for the Christian to see the blessed Jesus himself in the glory of his ineffable kingdom? If to see Solomon's grandeur was an event worth living for, who shall estimate the heavenly rapture of beholding the Savior on his high throne of glory, clothed with light as with a garment, crowned with all the sublime beneficence of heaven, thousands ministering unto him, ten thousand thousands standing before him, and multitudes of celestial spirits ever shouting to his praise, "Holy, holy, holy, Lord God Almighty!" Would it not be a high privilege to see all this? Would it not fill out the believer's joy, and establish him in the certainties and raptures of his faith, as nothing else can? Would it not set his whole nature in a glow with heavenly inspiration, and consecrate him as a new apostle just from the third heaven? Would it not impart a richer pleasure, and a more satisfying joy, than all the gifts of Pentecost?

From this we may, then, infer something of the bliss of millennial times, when Christ shall be upon earth, arrayed in all the glory of his kingdom. Then *we shall see him as he is.* The glorified saints shall ever be near him, in the closest communion with him, for he is their brother as well as their Redeemer and King. And those who live in the flesh shall not be excluded from near visions of his glory and rapturous approaches to his person and presence. The ransomed nations shall continually send up their streams of worshippers to Jerusalem, where they shall "*see the King in his beauty,*" and receive his communications, and be made glad in his favors. Then, with overflowing hearts, shall men say, "It was a true report which we heard; our eyes now have *seen;* and, behold, the half was not told us!" Doubt and unbelief will then be no more. Harassing fears will be cast out. Christ's existence, triumphs and unspeakable glories will then be visibly demonstrated, and the world shall be lifted out of the grave of its darkness and misgivings into the glorious light and liberty of the sons of God. For if Christ's presence in the transfiguration converted the rugged mount into all that Peter could desire of heaven, his sublime and gracious presence in his kingdom cannot make this world less than a paradise of God.

"Oh, the delights, the heavenly joys,
The glories, of the place
Where Jesus sheds the brightest beams
Of his unveiled face!"

A second great feature of the "new earth," or "world to come," is the exaltation, presence and ministrations of the church of the first-born. Paul tells us, that when Christ comes, the holy dead shall be raised, and the pious living changed, and both these classes together enter into their high and peculiar estate. These will the Savior bring with him, and have associated with him in the princedom and sublimities of his glorious empire. They shall then have spiritual and glorified bodies, like the glorious body of their Lord. They will not return to the earthy life which they once lived in the flesh; but they shall live a life like that which Jesus lives. They shall be in the closest union with Christ, for they constitute his Bride, and are to "be ever with the Lord." His delight shall be in them, and their delight shall be in him. They will share in his glories, and be partakers of his throne. They are to "*reign with Christ.*" They are to judge angels and judge the world. The twelve apostles are to have twelve thrones, judging the twelve tribes of Israel. Having overcome, and kept the Savior's sayings to the end, they shall have power over the nations. He that has been faithful over five talents shall have dominion over five cities; and he that has been faithful over ten talents shall have dominion over ten cities; every man according as his work has been. And so "the kingdom and dominion, and the greatness of the kingdom under the whole heaven, shall be given to the saints of the Most High." They are to sit on thrones, and judgment shall be given them, and they shall be priests of God, even of Christ, and shall reign with him the thousand years. They are to wear crowns of righteousness, which God the righteous Judge will give unto them at that day. Having exercised meekness, they shall inherit the earth; and, by the righteousness of faith made "heirs of the world," they shall enter upon their inheritance. Jesus is the heir of all things, and the saints are joint-heirs with him. Having suffered with him, they shall be glorified with him. They shall have a city of habitation becoming their high nature,—"a firmly-founded city, whose builder and maker is God." They are to eat and drink with Christ, at his table, in his kingdom. "They shall see his face, and his name shall be in their foreheads, and they shall reign forever and ever." They shall neither marry, nor be given in marriage, but shall be as the angels of God. "Oh, what untried forms of happy being, what cycles of revolving bliss, await the just! Conception cannot reach it, nor experience present materials for the picture of its similitude; and though thus figured out with the choicest emblems, they do no more represent it, than the name of Shepherd describes the watchful guardianship of Christ, or the name of Father the unspeakable love of God." "It doth not yet appear what we shall be." What shall be the precise nature of the authority, priesthood, heirship and glory of the saints, cannot now be told. But this "we know, that when he (the Savior) shall appear, we shall be *like him, and shall see him as he is.*" A world of wonders is in every word of this promise. But how great shall be the believer's happiness, what his peculiar circumstances, how large his possessions, and what the exact nature and dignity of his employments, tongue cannot tell, nor heart conceive. We cannot understand the soul's faculties now; and they shall be greater hereafter. Sublime are the Christian's relations now; and they shall be sublimer then. Wonderful are the offices and mission of good men now; and they shall be a thousand times more wonderful then. A thoroughly-converted and enlightened man, even whilst in the corrupt flesh, is a noble object to behold. Even the angels are not ashamed to become ministering spirits to him. What then shall be his glory when he shall come to occupy his throne with the adorable Jesus in the dignity of eternal empire!

That the glorified saints will, to some extent, mingle with those who live in the body, and at times unveil their radiance to them, I think there is reason to believe. Their offices would seem to imply it. If they are to govern, direct and minister to those in the flesh, it is natural to suppose that they will also be visible, at least occasionally. Angels, in the performance of similar offices, have often been manifested to living men; and why should it not be so with Christ's servants, in the wonderful administrations of his glorious kingdom? The earth will then be much nearer to heaven than ever it was before, and the intercourse between them will doubtless be much more free and intimate. Glorified or spiritual bodies are, perhaps, in their nature, invisible to our earthly senses. Christ, after his resurrection, was not visible except at certain times when he manifested himself. The angels are invisible, and yet we have many instances in which they were revealed to the view of mortals. And in that new world in which the glorified saints are to be enthroned, and commissioned, as the ministers of Christ the great King, to execute his orders and administer his government over the nations, we may reasonably expect that they will often appear, and converse with those who live in the flesh; and that intercourse between them and those in the body will be as real, familiar and blessed as that which Adam enjoyed with heavenly beings in Paradise

But whatever may be the specific nature of the kinghood and priesthood of the glorified saints, or in whatever way they may discharge their sublime ministrations, we may rest assured that their relation to the world will be for good and blessing. Christ will thus associate them with him in his kingdom only the more gloriously to fulfill his grand designs of love and mercy. He came into this world to seek and to save that which was lost. He came to reveal God to man, and to lift up man into harmony with God. He came amidst the groveling, the selfish and the earthly, to tell a tale of disinterested love at which selfishness might hang its head. He came amidst the guilty, the wretched and the lost, to reveal a design of mercy at which angels rejoice with exceeding joy, and before which the aching and the burdened heart may throw off the load under which it labors. He suffered, died, rose again, now lives in heaven, and will soon return to earth, all to cast out the evil which has come upon man, and to bring this world back to the Paradise it once was. And this espousing to himself of an elect, ransomed and glorified church can be for no other purpose than that which he has already manifested in his wonderful doings hitherto. Much of the great plan of redemption yet remains unfulfilled; and this church of the first-born is exalted to its high place, not only for its own glory and the Savior's praise, but as another great link in the chain of agencies and administrations by which the entire world is to be yet restored to the high sphere for which it was destined. These children of the resurrection are to constitute an elect and immortal college, connected with the Savior's own glorified humanity, that he may thus consummate his wonderful designs in the ultimate and entire repeal of the curse under which the earth groans, and the recovery forever of the lost heritage of man. Why does he call and constitute the church as we now have it? Certainly not only that those who enter it may be justified and accepted. There is another object. It is that he may work in and through the church, and carry light, civilization, truth and hope to the children of men. And Christians are not done with this world when they die. When this elect church shall have been completed, and its members come to be priests and kings with Christ in the glorious Messianic kingdom, the same general calling which they now fill will continue. These sublime princedoms of the eternal empire are a part of God's great plan to let forth his love, wisdom and blessing upon earth's future generations. Blessed, blessed, shall it then be for the world, when once the saints shall be installed with their promised dominion, and sit with Christ upon his throne!

Another characteristic of the millennial world will be the entire absence of all the confederations and powers of wickedness. When the Savior comes, Antichrist, in all its shapes, will be destroyed. The wild beast and the false prophet, and all their supporters and adherents, are to be taken and cast into the bottomless abyss. The last renovating fires which are to be kindled in the day of the Lord shall carry all the confederates in usurpation and wrong to their merited perdition. The dragon, that old serpent, which is the devil, even Satan, shall then be seized, and bound, and confined in the pit, to deceive the nations no more till the thousand years be fulfilled, and after a brief release consigned to eternal death. Instead of despotism and tyranny shall be justice and charity. Those that now corrupt and destroy the earth will then have been destroyed. The filthy dreamers, who despise government and speak evil of dignities, will then have passed away. The raging waves of popular revolution, foaming out their own shame, shall have been stilled, to rise no more. Those wandering stars in church and state, by whom so much disturbance is now experienced, will then have gone to the blackness of darkness appointed for them. Might shall not then trample any more upon right. The course of nature, now set on fire of hell, shall then be made to flow in all the smoothness and tranquility of heaven. "The Son of man shall send forth his angels, and they shall gather out of his kingdom all things that offend, and them which do iniquity, and shall cast them into a furnace of fire." False prophets and false teachers, with all their "damnable heresies," shall then have gone to their destruction. Nations shall cease their fierce works of war, and armies no more butcher each other upon the bloody field of battle. Violence will no more be heard in the land, nor wasting and destruction within its borders. Satan will be deprived of his power to stir up rankling passion, and the sway of oppression and iniquity will be ended. The greatest of the world's burdens will thus be lifted off, and the mill-stone that has weighed it down so long will be loosed from its neck forever.

A fourth feature of the millennium, or new earth, will be the great exaltation, piety and glory of the Hebrew nation, and of the world through them. I have shown that this people is to be restored to Palestine; that Jerusalem is to be rebuilt in more than its former glory; that the throne of David is to be re-established; and that the Prince Messiah is to be their King. "For lo!, the days come, saith the Lord, that I will bring again the captivity of my people Israel and Judah, and I will cause them to return to the land that I gave to their fathers, and they shall possess it. *And they shall serve the Lord their God and* DAVID THEIR KING, *whom I will raise up unto them:*" (Jer. xxx. 3–9.) "They shall all of them be righteous, and shall inherit the land forever." Their land that was desolate shall become like Eden, and even its desert like the garden of Jehovah. "In that day shall the branch of the Lord be beautiful and glorious, and the fruit of the earth shall be excellent and comely for them that are escaped of Israel. And he that is left in Zion, and he that remaineth in Jerusalem, shall be called holy." God says of the house of Jacob, "The Gentiles shall see thy righteousness, and all kings thy glory. Thou shalt be *a crown of glory* in the hand of the Lord, *and a royal diadem in the hand of thy God.* Ye that make mention of the Lord, give him no rest till he make Jerusalem a praise in the earth. Say to the daughter of Zion, Behold, thy salvation cometh. And they shall call them, *The holy people, The redeemed of the Lord.*" "Rejoice ye with Jerusalem, and be glad with her; for thus saith the Lord, Behold, I will extend peace to her like a river, and the glory of the Gentiles like a flowing stream." "At that time *they shall call Jerusalem* THE THRONE OF THE LORD; *and all the nations shall be gathered unto it, to the name of the Lord, to Jerusalem.*" "I the Lord will be their God, and my servant David a prince among them. And I will make them and the places round about my hill a blessing. And I will raise up for them a plant of renown. Thus shall they know that I the Lord their God am with them, and that they, even the house of Israel, are my people." "I will be as the dew unto Israel; he shall grow as the lily, and cast forth his roots; his branches shall spread, and his beauty shall be as the olive-tree, and his smell as Lebanon." "And many nations shall come and say, Come, and let us go up to the mountain of the Lord, and to the house of the God of Jacob; and he will teach us of his ways, and we will walk in his paths; for the law shall go forth of Zion, and the word of the Lord from Jerusalem." Jesus himself shall descend among them, and be their King. He shall fight for them in the day of battle, and slay all their enemies. For "God shall give unto him the throne of his father David, and he shall reign over the house of Jacob forever," and "before his ancients gloriously."

These are glowing promises. Well may they cause the Jew to be hopeful amid all his long-continued spoliations, and to sing still, "If I forget thee, O Jerusalem, let my right hand forget her cunning! If I do not remember thee, let my tongue cleave to the roof of my mouth!" And when these glad predictions shall be fulfilled, all the nations shall share in the sublime exaltations of God's ancient people and their glorious King. Then all the nations of the earth shall be blessed in Abraham's seed. "Israel shall blossom and bud.

and fill the face of the earth with fruit." "The remnant of Jacob shall be in the midst of many people as a dew from the Lord, and as showers upon the grass." "They shall be called the priests of the Lord; and men shall call them the ministers of our God." When Zion, the city of the Lord, shall arise and shine, the Gentiles shall come to its light, and kings to the brightness of its rising. When the New Jerusalem appears, "the nations of them which are saved shall walk in the light of it." In that day, Israel's King, even "the Lord, shall be King over all the earth." "All people, nations and languages shall serve and obey him." "The heathen shall be given to him for his inheritance, and the uttermost parts of the earth for his possession." "Kings shall fall down before him, and all nations shall serve him." "He shall reign and prosper, and his rest shall be glorious." "The world to come, whereof we speak," has been put into subjection unto him. The kingdoms of this world are to be his kingdoms. Every knee shall bow, and every tongue confess that he is Lord. He must reign until he hath put all enemies under his feet. Morally, spiritually and politically, all people must be eventually subjugated unto him. "For the earth shall be filled with the knowledge of the glory of the Lord, as the waters cover the sea."

All these are God's own revelations. They are full of mystery, but full of hope. How they are to be fulfilled may be a subject of wonder; but that they will be fulfilled is as certain as the existence of God. It may not all be done at once. It will be an achievement of moral force, and not of mere arbitrary coercion. It may require years upon years to accomplish all; but He who has promised knows how to perform what he has uttered. The new, august and momentous personal manifestations of Christ for which we are taught to look, the enlarged gifts of the Holy Ghost which are yet to be bestowed, the appointment of other, better equipped and more efficient ministerial agencies, the probable revival of miracles, the shaking of the nations with the terrors of coming judgments, the increased power of the Bible derived from the fulfillment of its prophecies, and the removal of Satan and all his treacherous opposition, certainly will leave it no difficult task to make a speedy conquest of all the great nations to the glorious dominion of the Son of David, come down from heaven to be their King and Lord forever. At all events,—

> "Jesus shall reign where'er the sun
> Does his successive journeys run;
> His kingdom stretch from shore to shore,
> Till moons shall wax and wane no more."

But the new earth has yet another blessed characteristic. It is to present the glorious spectacle of the entire repeal of the curse of sin. It is true that the complete and entire repeal of the curse will not be consummated until the end of the thousand years, when all wickedness and the wicked shall finally be cast out from the earth forever. But, from the time Christ comes and takes dominion of the world with his glorified saints, every thing will advance closer and closer until it reaches this final and transcendent consummation. His coming is styled "the regeneration,"—"the day of the restitution of all things,"—the time when God shall "make all things new,"—"the manifestation of the sons of God," for which the creation groans and waits,—the day of redemption, when "the creature itself shall be delivered from the bondage of corruption, into the glorious liberty of the children of God." Christ is the Redeemer and Lord of the whole creation, as well as of the human soul. When God made man, he said to him, "Have dominion over the fish of the sea, and over the fowl of the air, and over the cattle, *and over all the earth*, and over every creeping thing that creepeth upon the earth." This dominion Adam lost. The rebellion of the soul against God brought with it the rebellion of the flesh against the spirit, and of nature against the entire man. Discords, antipathies and a thousand evils ensued. Christ is the second Adam, and by subverting the empire of Satan he regains the dominion which Adam lost, and carries his redemption as far as the consequences of the fall have reached. Otherwise, the entire breach is not healed, and salvation is imperfect. The whole earth under the Messiah must then ultimately become all that it was under Adam, and what it always would have been if Adam had never sinned. The curse that was put upon the ground for Adam's sin, filling it with thorns and thistles, infusing sweat and pain into all our participations of its products, must be taken off. The evils and confusion which sin has brought into the world must be driven out. And this is exactly what is promised under the reign of Christ and his saints. "The Spirit shall be poured from on high, and the wilderness be a fruitful field, and the fruitful field be counted a forest. And the work of righteousness shall be peace; and the effect of righteousness, quietness and assurance forever." "The mountains and the hills shall break forth into singing, and all the trees of the field shall clap their hands. Instead of *the thorn* shall come up the fir-tree, and instead of *the brier* shall come up the myrtle-tree: and it shall be to the Lord for a name, for an everlasting sign that shall not be cut off." "Then the eyes of the blind shall be opened, and the ears of the deaf shall be unstopped. Then shall the lame man leap as an hart, and the tongue of the dumb sing; in the wilderness shall waters break out, and streams in the desert. And the parched ground shall become a watered place, and the thirsty land springs of water; in the habitation of dragons there shall be grass, with reeds and rushes." *"And the inhabitants shall not say, I am sick."* There shall be no more thence any dying in infancy, or of men who have not filled out their days. "They shall build houses and inhabit them; and they shall plant vineyards and eat the fruit of them. They shall not labor in vain, *nor bring forth for trouble.* The wolf and the lamb shall feed together, and the lion shall eat straw like the ox: and dust shall be the serpent's meat. They shall not hurt nor destroy in all my holy mountain:" (Isa. lxv. 17–25.) "The waters of the Dead Sea shall be healed." Trees shall grow which shall "yield their fruit monthly, and the leaves thereof shall be for the healing of the nations." "They shall not hunger nor thirst, neither shall the heat nor sun smite them." "AND THERE SHALL BE NO MORE CURSE." "And God shall wipe away all tears from their eyes; AND THERE SHALL BE NO MORE DEATH." "The last enemy that shall be destroyed is death." He may linger through a brief and feeble existence in some of the outskirts of the millennial world; but he must be entirely destroyed. "Then shall be brought to pass the saying that is written, *Death is swallowed up of victory;*" and earth's redeemed and undying generations shall take up the song, "O death! where is thy sting? O grave! where is thy victory? Thanks be to God, which giveth us the victory, through our Lord Jesus Christ!'

Such, then, is the glorious consummation to which the works of Providence and grace are tending. Such is the finishing of the mystery which God hath spoken by the mouth of all his holy prophets. This battle-field of hell and heaven shall rise up out of all its desolations. The bliss of Paradise shall yet dwell in its valleys and the glory of God shine on all its hills. Though a lazar-house for so many ages, it shall be the home of righteousness and peace and a temple of blessing and glory, whose vaulted dome shall echo forever with redemption's songs. Things may look unpromising now; but everywhere heaven is pouring into it. Tyranny, war, distress and wickedness may seem to be triumphant; but their end is near, and the Desire of nations approaches. Satan and his emissaries may struggle in their desperation;

but they shall not be able to keep the world from the resurrection to which it is moving. The sore travail of the Savior's soul shall yet be seen in an everlasting equation between it and heaven. Jesus himself shall set up his throne in it and brighten it with the glories of his ineffable personal presence. The holy ministries of the children of the resurrection shall cover it with a mantle of peace and light. Satan and all his works shall be rooted out of it forever. All its long-erring nations shall be reclaimed, and all its discordant elements recovered to harmony and rest. Over all this place of graves the flowers of immortality shall bloom. Instead of the coffin shall be Elijah's chariot, and in place of the death-struggle shall be Enoch's rapture. And from all God's great universe shall break forth the song of joy and praise over a world that was lost but is found; over this blasted earth made new again and glorious forever.

Region of life and light!
Land of the good whose sweaty toils are o'er!
Nor frost nor heat may blight
Thy vernal beauty, fertile shore,
Yielding thy blessed fruits for evermore!

There, without crook or sling,
Walks the Good Shepherd. Blossoms white and red
Round his meek temples cling;
And, to sweet pastures led,
His own loved flock beneath his eye are fed.

He guides, and near him they
Follow delighted; for he makes them go
Where dwells eternal May,
And heavenly roses blow,
Deathless, and gathered but again to grow.

He leads them to the height
Named of the infinite and long-sought Good,
And fountains of delight;
And where his feet have stood
Springs up, along the way, their tender food.

"From lips divine flow forth
Immortal harmonies, of power to still
All passions born of earth,
And draw the ardent will
Its destiny of goodness to fulfill.

"Might but a little part,
A wandering breath, of that high melody,
Descend into my heart,
And change it, till it be
Transformed and swallowed up, O Christ, in thee!

"YET A LITTLE WHILE."

Beyond the smiling and the weeping
I shall be soon;
Beyond the waking and the sleeping,
Beyond the sowing and the reaping,
I shall be soon.
Love, Rest, and Home!
Sweet hope!
Lord, tarry not, but come.

Beyond the blooming and the fading
I shall be soon;
Beyond the shining and the shading,
Beyond the hoping and the dreading,
I shall be soon.
Love, Rest, and Home!
Sweet hope!
Lord, tarry not, but come.

Beyond the parting and the meeting
I shall be soon;
Beyond the farewell and the greeting,
Beyond this pulse's fever-beating,
I shall be soon.
Love, Rest, and Home!
Sweet hope!
Lord, tarry not, but come.

H. BONAR.

TENTH DISCOURSE.

THE TESTIMONY OF THE CHURCH — SUMMARY OF OUR DOCTRINE—CERINTHUS—THE ANABAPTISTS—MILLER—IMPROPRIETY OF CLASSING US WITH THESE PARTIES—TRUE CHURCH TESTIMONY—BARNABAS—CLEMENT — PAPIAS — JUSTIN MARTYR — IRENÆUS — TERTULLIAN—CYPRIAN — ACKNOWLEDGMENTS AS TO THE FAITH OF THE EARLY CHURCH—HOW MILLENARIAN DOCTRINE WAS SUPPRESSED—ORIGEN'S SYSTEM—REVIVAL OF THE PRIMITIVE FAITH—LUTHER—MELANCTHON—THE FRUITS OF OUR BELIEF — DIFFERENCE BETWEEN THE EARLY AND PRESENT CHURCH.

DEUT. xxxii. 7: *Remember the days of old, consider the years of many generations: ask thy father, and he will show thee; thy elders, and they will tell thee.*

THE past is one of our best teachers. History is one of the storehouses of wisdom. "Not to know what transpired before we were born," says a classic author, "is to remain children."

In matters of religious faith it is particularly important to recur to the testimony of those who lived before us. Novelty is sometimes the best proof of heresy. That cannot be Christianity which cannot stand the test of history. Antiquity alone is no evidence of orthodoxy. A creed may be old and yet be false; but it cannot be new and yet be true. The Christian religion is a written tradition, just as complete at its first delivery as it is now. All the advances of science, though they may have assisted in preparing men the better to appreciate it, have not added to it a single jot. In some things the children may be accounted the fathers, and the fathers the children; but even in those instances "the child is father of the man." We cannot be independent of what has gone before us. In every thing wisdom bids us "remember the days of old." Yea, "*Thus saith the Lord*, Stand ye in the ways and see, and *ask for the old paths*, where is the good way, *and walk therein*, and ye shall find rest for your souls."

I propose, therefore, to make some inquiry into the testimony of Christians of former ages respecting the doctrines which I have been putting forth in these discourses. If the church in its first and purest periods held them as the teachings of the Scriptures, that fact must go very far to confirm them as the truth of God. The saying of Tertullian, that "whatever is first is true; whatever is later is adulterate," may not always hold good. Neither are we to rest our faith upon the mere opinions of men, whether ancient or modern. "The Bible, the Bible alone, is the religion of Protestants;" and upon the Bible do I rest for the truth of what I have been teaching.* But it is not very likely that the most enlightened Christians who were the pupils and hearers of the inspired apostles and their immediate successors were mistaken as to what are the hopes which Christianity presents. If it can be satisfactorily shown that they believed and taught the Scriptures as I have been interpreting them, it will be hard for a reasonable man to conclude that I am wrong. Whilst, then, we take the Scriptures as our only and infallible standard, and accord to every man the right to examine and decide for himself as God shall judge him, the light of antiquity cannot be discarded as useless. It is one of our helps to a right understanding of God's revelation, which we are not safe in despising. And though we are not to receive the testimony of anybody where that testimony conflicts with

---

* See pp. 365–380.

the Bible, we will do well to "remember the days of old," and to "consider the years of many generations." The fathers had some advantages which we have not. Let us then avail ourselves of these advantages in our search for truth. Let us ask them, and they will show us, and inquire of the elders, and they will tell us.

The principal points which I have thus far presented, as my apprehension of God's revealments concerning "the last times," are as follows:—

1. That Christ Jesus, our adorable Redeemer, is to return to this world in great power and glory, as really and as literally as he ascended up from it.

2. That this second advent of the Messiah will occur before the general conversion of the world, while the Man of sin still continues his abominations, while the earth is yet full of tyranny, war, infidelity and blasphemy, and consequently before what is called the millennium.

3. That this coming of the Lord Jesus will not be to depopulate and annihilate the earth, but to judge, subdue, renew and bless it.

4. That in the period of this coming he will raise the holy from among the dead, transform the living that are waiting for him, judge them according to their works, receive them up to himself in the clouds, and establish them in a glorious heavenly kingdom.

5. That Christ will then also break down and destroy all present systems of government in church and state, burn up the great centres and powers of wickedness and usurpation, shake the whole earth with terrific visitations for its sins, and subdue it to his own personal and eternal rule.

6. That during these great and destructive commotions, the Jewish race shall be marvelously restored to the land of their fathers, brought to embrace Jesus as their Messiah and King, delivered from their enemies, placed at the head of

nations, and made the agents of unspeakable blessings to the world.

7. That Christ will then re-establish the throne of his father David, exalt it in heavenly glory, make Mount Zion the seat of his divine empire, and, with the glorified saints associated with him in his dominion, reign over the house of Jacob and over the world in a visible, sublime and heavenly Christocracy for the period of "the thousand years."

8. That during this millennial reign in which mankind are brought under a new dispensation, Satan is to be bound and the world enjoy its long-expected Sabbatic rest.

9. That at the end of this millennial Sabbath the last rebellion shall be quashed, the wicked dead, who shall all continue in Hades until that time, shall be raised and judged, and Satan, Death, Hades, and all antagonisms to good, delivered over to eternal destruction. And—

10. That, under these wonderful administrations, the earth is to be entirely recovered from the effects of the fall, the excellence of God's righteous providence vindicated, the whole curse repealed, death swallowed up, and all the inhabitants of the world thenceforward forever restored to more than the full happiness, purity and glory which Adam forfeited in Eden.

Such is my learning of the Scriptures, and such is my solemn belief upon these momentous themes. Some may be disposed to brand it as the old heresy of Cerinthus; some may classify it with the doctrines of the seditious Anabaptists of Luther's day; and not a few may stigmatize it as "Millerism." But, call it what you please, with my present light it is my faith; and I propose to show you that such was the faith of the universal orthodox church in the purest periods of its history. But, lest it should be derided with names which it does not deserve, let me make an observation or two with regard to the parties just named.

Cerinthus was the contemporary of the Apostle John. It

is a question now, among learned men, whether he ever did teach the carnal notions which are ascribed to him. It is recorded of him, however, that he "falsely pretended to wonderful things, as if they had been shown him by angels, asserting that after the resurrection there would be an earthly kingdom of Christ, and that *the flesh*, (or man again united with flesh,) again inhabiting Jerusalem, would be subject to desires and pleasures;" that, "being an enemy of the divine Scriptures, he said there would be a space of a thousand years for celebrating nuptial festivals;" that "he taught that Christ would have an earthly kingdom, and, as he was a voluptuary and altogether sensual, he conjectured that it would consist in those things that he craved in the gratification of appetite and lust." If these things are true, which is very questionable, it has been well for Christians that they never permitted themselves to be carried away with such gross and plainly unscriptural carnalities. The kingdom of heaven is not meat and drink, marrying or giving in marriage. The children of the resurrection are never to return to this fleshly and sensual life, but are to have *spiritual bodies*, and inhabit a city "not made with hands," and be kings and priests unto God, blessed and holy forever.*

The Anabaptists were a fanatical and seditious people, with whom no sound Christian can sympathize. Mosheim says, "They gave themselves out for the messengers of heaven, to lay the foundations of a new government, and to destroy and overturn all temporal rule and authority,—all human and political institutions. Having turned all things into confusion and uproar in the city of Münster by this seditious declaration, they began to erect a new republic conformable to their absurd and chimerical notions of religion, and committed the administration of it to *John Bockholt*, a tailor by profession!" Milner says, "They taught the people to despise their lawful rulers, and the salutary regulations by which all communities

* See Note E, page 335.

exist. Everywhere it was the cry of these enthusiastic visionaries, No tribute; all things in common; no tithes; no magistrates; the baptism of infants is an invention of the devil!" From such delusion, fanaticism and blasphemy may the Lord ever preserve us! And yet with such people we are often classed when we undertake to declare the real gospel doctrine of Christ's coming and kingdom.

The late Mr. Miller, of whom we heard so much a few years ago, was doubtless a simple-minded, honest and pious man. But he was comparatively illiterate, imaginative and enthusiastic. He did not fully grasp the sweep, order, consistency and grandeur of God's purposes as they are presented in the Scriptures. He believed that this world was to be burned up and depopulated of all its present orders of inhabitants. He taught that none were to exist on the earth after Christ's coming but the church of the first-born in their glorified state, who should return to a physical form of life. He also held that the Gog and Magog rebellion at the end of the Millennium refers to the resurrected wicked. He had no consistent views of Christ's reign over the nations, and denied probation after Christ's coming. He was carried away, too, with certain calculations of prophetic dates, upon which he relied too confidently. He was disappointed in some of the leading particulars upon which he gained his notoriety. But neither prophecy nor the students of prophecy are responsible for his mistakes. And to make all deductions from prophecy bear the odium and ridicule excited by the vagaries of uninformed and credulous, men is neither sensible, pious, nor respectful to the word of God. We have nothing to do with the crudities and wild imaginings of a sensual Cerinthus, the fanatical Anabaptist, or the injudicious Father Miller. Our business is with what God has written for our learning and with the interpretations of those who were the least likely to be mistaken in regard to the leading features of God's revelations.

Let us, then, proceed with our task, and endeavor to ascertain the views and teachings of the early Christians with regard to the doctrines of these discourses. What expectations were formed of the Messiah at his first coming, and how Christ and his apostles proceeded respecting those expectations, I have already set forth. In other words, I have given you the inspired Scriptures for every thing that I have thus far said. This alone is, or ought to be, sufficient. But as there is disagreement as to the manner in which those passages are to be understood, I will give you the proof that the best Christian authority is in favor of the interpretations which I have maintained.

The first witness I produce is Barnabas, a Levite of the country of Cyprus, and one of those who sold their possessions and laid the money at the apostles' feet. Luke says that "he was a good man, and full of the Holy Ghost." He was the companion and fellow-preacher with the Apostle Paul. He has left an epistle which learned men think was written before the Epistle of Jude or the writings of John. Some have considered it apocryphal; but Vossius, Dupuis, Cave, Mill, Clarke, Whiston, Wake, and others not incompetent to judge in the case, esteem it the genuine production of Barnabas the Levite, so honorably mentioned in the Scriptures. At all events, it belongs to early Christian antiquity, and is a competent witness as to what were the views then entertained.

In the thirteenth chapter of this epistle we find it written:—"God made in six days the works of his hands, and he finished them the seventh day, and he rested the seventh day and sanctified it. Consider, my children, what that signifies: he finished them in six days. The meaning of it is this: that *in six thousand years the Lord will bring all things to an end. For with him one day is a thousand years, as himself testifieth.* Therefore, children, in six days—that is, in six thousand years—shall all things be accomplished. And what is that he saith, And he rested the seventh day? *He meaneth this: that when his Son shall come, and abolish the season of the wicked one, and judge the ungodly, and shall change the sun, moon and stars,* THEN *he shall gloriously rest in that seventh* day. . . . Behold, he will *then* truly sanctify it with blessed rest, *when we (having received* THE RIGHTEOUS PROMISE, *when iniquity shall be no more,* ALL THINGS BEING RENEWED BY THE LORD) shall be able to sanctify it, being ourselves first made holy."

In these words it is plainly taught:—

1. That Christ is to come again personally to our world at the end of the six thousand years.

2. That the wicked one and his domination will remain in existence until Christ comes.

3. That the seventh thousand years of the world is to be a millennium of holy rest, in which the saints are to inherit their promises and iniquity be done away; and—

4. That this millennium of glory is to be introduced by the personal coming of the Messiah to abolish the empire of the wicked one, judge the ungodly, change the present constitution of things and renew the world.

Such, then, is the testimony of one, said to have been the companion and fellow of the Apostle Paul.

A second witness is Clement, whom Paul mentions among his "fellow-laborers, whose names are in the book of life." In such high repute were his writings held, that they are found included in one of the oldest collections of New Testament writings as a part of the sacred canon. He does not refer to our subject as directly as Barnabas; but there can be no doubt of his having entertained the same views. Dr. Hamilton of Strathblane, in a work against the students of prophecy, puts him down as evidently a millennarian; that is, one who believes in the personal reign of Christ with his saints on earth. He connected "the great and glorious promises" made to the people of God with the promise that "*the whole earth* shall be filled with the glory of the Lord." He taught that "we shall come to judgment in the flesh, and so also in the flesh receive the reward." He also identified the coming of the kingdom of God with "*the day of God's appearing*," and exhorted his readers hourly to expect, wait and pray for it, that they might "enter into his kingdom and receive the promises." And if there is any weight to be attached to his apprehensions of divine truth, it goes decidedly in favor of our doctrines.

The next witness is Papias, the disciple of the Apostle John and a companion of Polycarp. Eusebius speaks unfavorably of his judgment in one place; but elsewhere pronounces him "eloquent and learned in the Scriptures." He himself says that he had most assiduously collected all that could be gathered of the teachings and sayings of Christ and the apostles. He certainly had every opportunity of knowing the truth. And he has recorded it as his belief, and as contained in what he had collected from the fountains of Christian doctrine, that "*there will be a certain millennium* AFTER THE RESURRECTION OF THE DEAD, *when Christ will reign* BODILY *(personally) upon this very earth.*"

We come now to Justin the martyr, who was born ten years before the death of the Apostle John. Mosheim calls him "a man of eminent piety and learning, who, from a pagan philosopher, became a Christian martyr." In his Dialogue with Trypho, he says, "*I*, AND AS MANY AS ARE ORTHODOX CHRISTIANS, *do acknowledge that there shall be a resurrection of the body, and a residence of a thousand years in Jerusalem rebuilt, adorned and enlarged, as the prophets Ezekiel, Isaiah and others do unanimously attest.* . . . Moreover, a certain man among us, whose name was John, *one of the apostles of Christ*, in a revelation made to him, *did prophesy that the faithful believers in Christ shall live a thousand years in the New*

Jerusalem, and AFTER THAT *shall be the general resurrection and judgment.*" Not only does Justin here declare himself a believer in our doctrines, but, as Semisch (in Herzog's Cyclopedia) says, he "distinguishes that belief as the key-stone of orthodoxy."

The testimony of the distinguished Irenæus is also of particular value. He was the disciple of Polycarp, the pupil of the Apostle John. It has justly been said that, "for learning, steadfastness and zeal, he was among the most renowned of the early fathers." Mosheim says that his writings are "the most precious monuments of ancient erudition." His tutor, Polycarp, was one of those "angels" to whom the Savior addressed one of the seven epistles recorded in John's revelation. He was a most diligent collector of all that was to be known of what Christ and his apostles taught. Irenæus regarded him with peculiar veneration, and says of his teachings, "I remember his discourses concerning the conversations he had with John the apostle and others who had seen the Lord; how he rehearsed their discourses, and what he heard them say of our Lord and of his miracles and doctrine." Irenæus, therefore, had good means of knowing what ideas the sacred writers attached to their own writings, and what ideas and hopes the Spirit through them inculcated respecting God's great purposes. Hear, then, what this learned and devout man has said concerning our doctrine:—

"In whatever number of days the world was created, in the same number of thousands of years it will come to its consummation. God, on the sixth day, finished the works which he made; and God rested on the seventh day from all his works. This is a history of the past and a prophecy of the future; for '*the day of the Lord is as a thousand years.*'" Here is a distinct announcement of the millennial Sabbath. As to where it is to be celebrated, he is equally clear. "It is fitting," says he, "that *the just, rising again at the appear-*

ance of God, should, in the renewed state, receive the promise of inheritance which God covenanted to the fathers, and should reign in it; and that then should follow the final judgment. For, in the same condition in which they have labored and been afflicted, and been tried by sufferings in all sorts of ways, it is but just that *in it* they should receive the fruits of their sufferings, so that *where*, for the love of God they suffered death, *there* they should be brought to life again; and *where* they endured bondage, *there also they should reign.* . . . . I say it is becoming that *the creation, being restored to its original beauty,* should, without any impediment or drawback, be subject to the righteous. This the apostle makes manifest in the Epistle to the Romans. . . . . Thus, therefore, as God promised to Abraham *the inheritance of the earth,* and he received it not during the whole time he lived, *it is necessary that he should receive it, together with his seed,* that is, with *such of them as fear God, and believe in him,* IN THE RESURRECTION OF THE JUST. . . . . They will *undoubtedly* receive it at the resurrection of the just: for true and unchangeable is God; wherefore he also said, Blessed are the meek, *for they shall inherit* THE EARTH."

Four things are here asserted: first, that Christ will really appear at the end of the six thousand years; second, that the millennium comes after the Savior's advent; third, that there is to be a resurrection of the just at the beginning of the millennium; and, fourth, that Christ is to reign with his saints in this world. Such is the testimony of Irenæus, the pupil of Polycarp and Papias, the disciples of the Apostle John.

We come now to Tertullian, the eminent contemporary of Irenæus, a man of eloquence and learning, who, with all his faults, had many excellencies. His testimony is equally conspicuous and positive. "We also confess," says he, "that *a kingdom is promised us on earth,* AFTER THE RESURRECTION; *for it will be for a thousand years* in a city of divine workmanship, viz.: Jerusalem brought down from heaven, which city Ezekiel knew, and the Apostle John saw. This is the city provided of God to receive the saints in the resurrection, wherein to refresh themselves with *all spiritual good things*, in recompense of those which in the world we have despised and lost." He also testifies that it was the custom of his times for Christians to pray that they might have part in the first resurrection; thus showing that this was the general and firm belief of his time.

Clement of Alexandria, the contemporary of Tertullian, whom Eusebius designates as an "incomparable master of the Christian philosophy," also refers to the mystic sanctity of the seventh day, as pointing in the estimation of both Hebrews and Greeks to the final revolution of the world and the renovation of all things.

Cyprian, the great bishop of Carthage, who sealed his faith with his blood, also alludes to the subject in a way leaving no doubt that he apprehended the Scriptures in the same manner. "In the divine arrangement of the world," says he, "seven days were at first employed, and in them seven thousand years were included." This implies the doctrine of the millennial Sabbath; and, taking it in connection with his expectation of the future honors of the martyrs, and his declaration that in this world "things evil and adverse shall increase until the end come as foretold," we cannot suppose that he differed on this subject from the distinguished teachers who went before him and whose disciple he claimed to be.

We have now brought down our list of testimonies to the end of the second century after Christ. I have given you the language of the most pious and distinguished Christian teachers who lived during that time. And without one dissenting voice among them, we here have, as their unanimous apprehension of the Scriptures and of what Christ and his apostles taught,—

1. That there is to be a millennial Sabbath at the end of six thousand years from the creation of Adam, in which the world shall joyfully rest from its long week of turmoil and disorder.

2. That the personal and final advent of Christ, and the resurrection of the holy dead, shall occur at the commencement of the millennium.

3. That Christ is to reign with his saints in glorious empire upon this earth. And,—

4. That all sublunary things, embracing the entire lower creation, are to undergo a universal renovation, and be restored to their original excellence and glory.

Nor was there any acknowledged Christian, until The time of Origen, in the middle of the third century, that ever recorded any other faith upon this subject. We may safely challenge all the research of the world to produce one single orthodox opposing testimony prior to the days of Origen, than whom, Milner says, "no man not altogether unsound and hypocritical ever more injured the church of Christ." Indeed, the evidence that these views were a vital and prominent part of the faith of Christians for the first ages is so clear and conspicuous that I do not know that any scholar has ever ventured to contradict the fact. Let me submit to you some statements of learned men upon the subject.

The well-known infidel historian, Edward Gibbon, has this statement:—"The ancient and popular doctrine of the millennium was intimately connected with the second coming of Christ. As the works of the creation had been finished in six days, their duration in their present state, according to a tradition which was attributed to the prophet Elijah, was fixed to six thousand years. By the same analogy it was inferred that this long period of labor and contention would be succeeded by a joyful Sabbath of a thousand years; and that Christ, with the triumphant band of the saints and the elect who had escaped death, or who had been miraculously revived, would reign upon earth. . . . . The assurance of such a millennium *was carefully inculcated* by a succession of fathers from Justin Martyr and Irenæus, who conversed with the immediate disciples of the apostles, down to Lactantius, who was preceptor to the son of Constantine. IT APPEARS TO HAVE BEEN THE REIGNING SENTIMENT OF THE ORTHODOX BELIEVERS."

This Lactantius, to whom Gibbon refers, lived in the early part of the fourth century. Mosheim pronounces him "the most learned of the Latin fathers." He was known in his time as "the Christian Cicero." His sentiments upon this subject deserve to be presented among our testimonies. "When God shall come to judge the world," says he, "and shall restore unto life the just that have been since the beginning, he shall converse among men a thousand years, and rule them with a most righteous government. . . . . And they that shall be raised from the dead shall be over the living as judges. And the Gentiles shall not be utterly extinguished; but some shall be left for the victory of God. . . . . About the same time the prince of devils, the forger of all evil, shall be bound with chains, and shall be in custody all the thousand years of the heavenly empire under which righteousness shall reign over the world." Such, then, according to Gibbon, were "the reigning sentiments of orthodox believers" for more than three centuries of the Christian era.

The celebrated Chillingworth says, "That this doctrine (of the millennium and Christ's personal reign on earth) was by the church of the next age after the apostles held true and catholic, I prove by these two reasons:—first, whatever doctrine is believed and taught by the most eminent fathers of any age of the church, and by none of their contemporaries opposed or condemned, that is to be esteemed the catholic doctrine of the church of those times; but *the doctrine of the millenaries was believed and taught by the most eminent fathers of the age next after the apostles, and by none of that age opposed or condemned; therefore* IT WAS THE CATHOLIC DOCTRINE OF THOSE TIMES."

Mosheim says, "*The prevailing opinion*, that Christ was to come and reign a thousand years among men before the final dissolution of the world, had *met with no opposition previous* to the time of Origen."

Burton says, "It cannot be denied that Papias, Irenæus, Justin Martyr, and all the other ecclesiastical writers, believed, literally, that the saints would rise in the first resurrection, and reign with Christ upon earth previous to the general resurrection."

Munscher says, "How widely the doctrine of millenarianism prevailed in the first centuries of Christianity, appears from this, that *it was universally received by almost all teachers*."

Gieseler says of the first centuries, "Millenarianism became the general belief of the time."

Newton says, "The doctrine of the millennium was generally believed in the three first and purest ages."

Semisch says, "The ancients expected a kingdom in this world, in which Christ, after his coming, should reign with his risen and glorified saints; that he would visibly return in order to establish a terrestrial theocracy as the centre of a dominion over the world; that he would destroy the kingdom of Antichrist, and subjugate such worldly powers as are susceptible of being fashioned for the divine kingdom; that there would be a distinction in the resurrection, first the resurrection of the saints for the divine kingdom, and afterwards the rest of the dead at the final judgment; that there would then be perfect happiness of soul and sense, and the glorified saints reign together over unglorified humanity."

But I will not trouble you with needless repetitions. What

these authors have said is just what multitudes of others equally learned and disinterested have declared. Russel, and Bush, and Lardner, and Whitby, and Neander, and Mede, and Kitto, and Maitland, and Taylor, and Milner, and Barnes, the encyclopedias and reviews, friends and enemies, ancients and moderns, admit and declare the fact, that the church of Christ, for the first two centuries after the inspired apostles, *was universally millenarian*, and that she substantially believed and taught all that I have brought forward in these discourses. I have not been preaching novelties, as some have been disposed to think. I have been giving you only what I find in the blessed Bible,—what those believed and taught who made the Bible,—and what all the true believers in the revelations of God, for more than two hundred years after Christ, accepted as the teaching of that holy book. And if I have not proven to you that the millenarian faith was the orthodox faith of primitive Christianity, there is no weight in testimony. Ask the fathers, and they will show you—the elders, and they will tell you. And if the church of our day is to keep to the simplicities of those early times after which she professes to pattern, she must hold to the personal reign of Christ with his saints on earth as one of her sublimest hopes.

It is a sad fact, however, that from the fourth century until the sixteenth this doctrine gradually lost its hold upon the minds and hearts of professed Christians, and went down into almost absolute neglect. But with it went down the great doctrine of justification by faith, and nearly every thing that is distinguishing in gospel religion. IT FELL ONLY AS POPERY ROSE; and it is only as it rises again that popery shall shrink and quail. So long as men think they see and hear Christ in the pope, and believe that they are worshipping and honoring Christ by serving and obeying hierarchies regarded as *jure livino*, we need never expect them to believe that Christ will ever reign here in person. The two ideas are fundamentally antagonistic. If Christ is himself to reign here in universal empire, he has not given that empire into the hands of a vicar; and if he has made the pope the supreme lord of the world, it is settled that he will never reign here otherwise than by the pope. Either proposition confutes the other. The two cannot live together. And this puts into our hands the key to the true explanation how the church has come to lose sight of the primitive and apostolic faith upon this subject.

The processes by which millenarian doctrine was gradually reduced to disrepute and neglect are at once curious and deplorable. Mosheim says that "its credit began to decline *principally* through the influence and authority of Origen, who opposed it with the greatest warmth, *because it was incompatible with some of his favorite sentiments.*" So, then, there was something sinister in the very root of anti-millenarianism. And yet Origen could not bring himself to renounce the primitive belief altogether. "We do not deny," says he, "the purging fire of the destruction of wickedness and *the renovation of all things*. . . . If any man shall preserve the washing of the Holy Spirit, he shall have his part *in the first resurrection*. . . . Wherefore, let us lay the Scriptures to heart, and make them the rule of our lives; that so, being cleansed from the defilement of sin before we depart hence, we may be raised up with the saints, and have our lot with Christ Jesus." After all, then, it was more the wild caricatures of our doctrine than the doctrine itself upon which the burden of his opposition fell. And just so Augustine says, that the first resurrection and reign of the thousand years "would indeed be tolerable, if it should be believed that *spiritual* delights should redound to the saints in that Sabbath by the presence of the Lord; for *we also ourselves formerly were of that opinion.*" What induced him to change his mind we know not. Perhaps he also had some favorite notions to support! Even Jerome, that "unmerciful scoffer" (as Ward calls him) at our doctrine, is obliged to admit some of its leading features, and acknowledges that *he "durst not condemn it,* because many ecclesiastical persons and martyrs affirmed the same."

There are, as I apprehend, three great causes to which we are to attribute the decline and fall of ancient millenarianism. The first and greatest was that mystical and allegorical method of interpreting the Scriptures which Origen set on foot, and which has done more mischief to the cause of evangelical religion than all the assaults of its enemies. Mosheim says that this "unhappy method opened a secure retreat for all sorts of errors that a wild and irregular imagination could bring forth. Believing it extremely difficult, if not impossible, to defend the sacred writings when interpreted *literally*, according to the real import of the words, he had recourse to the fecundity of a lively imagination, and maintained that the Holy Scriptures were to be interpreted *in the same allegorical way that the Platonists explained the history of the gods.*" Who would have supposed that the boasted spiritualizing method of modern theologians had its origin in paganism and heathen mythology? "Origen alleged that the words of Scripture were, in many places, *absolutely void of sense!* and that the true meaning was to be sought in a mysterious and *hidden sense arising from the nature of things in themselves.*" That is to say, in plain English, we must first form our conclusions from philosophy, or from our preconceptions as to how things ought to be, and then interpret the Scriptures according to these *a priori* conclusions! A beautiful system, truly, for ascertaining the meaning of God's revelations! The results of its adoption may easily be imagined. There are some rich specimens of its operation upon record. One man found hidden meaning enough in the interjection "O!" to serve him for seven sermons! Another argued eighty-two particulars concerning the Bride of Christ from the hroses of

Pharaoh's chariot! Origen himself gives the meaning of the history of Moses thus:—"The king of Egypt is *the devil;* the male and female children of the Hebrews are the rational and animal faculties of the soul; the midwives are the Old and New Testaments. Pharoah's daughter is the church; Moses is the law; the ark and flags in which he was found are the absurd and carnal glosses of the Jews," &c. &c.

I am thus particular in showing what was Origen's allegorical or *spiritual* method, because, as Mosheim says, "it was followed by a prodigious number of interpreters in that and the succeeding ages, and overflowed the church;"—a system which, to this hour, more or less palsies and disgraces our hermeneutics. Well has Dr. Clarke said that "every friend of rational piety and genuine Christianity must lament that a man of so much learning and unaffected godliness should have been led to countenance, much less to recommend, a plan of interpreting the divine oracles, in many respects the most futile, absurd and dangerous that can possibly be conceived; and by which the sacred writings may be obliged to say any thing, every thing, or nothing, according to the fancy, peculiar creed, or caprice of the interpreter." And Milner declares that "a thick mist for ages pervaded the Christian world, supported by Origen's allegorical manner of interpretation. The learned alone were considered as guides, implicitly to be followed; and the vulgar, when *the literal sense* was hissed off the stage, had nothing to do but to follow their authority wherever it might lead them."

This, then, was, the system, "pernicious," "unhappy," "mischievous," "lamentable to every friend of genuine Christianity," injurious beyond every thing else, casting darkness over the whole field of inspired truth, throwing uncertainty over all Christian hope, and, in the hands of its own author, making the Bride of Christ the daughter of the devil! THIS was the system by which the glorious anticipations of the primitive church were declared mere fable! THIS is the system which modern Christians may thank for striking from their creed the sublime hopes of this world's ultimate renovation and Christ's personal reign over it in eternal peace! I should think that the school of spiritualizers have nothing to boast of in the line of their paternity.

But there was another matter relating to this period, the influence of which gradually increased and spread through succeeding ages, prompting men to lay hold of any artifice or device to get rid of the primitive millenarian doctrine. I refer to the conversion of the Emperor Constantine, and the consequent elevation of the church to the patronage of the civil government. "It was the constant and uniform opinion of the church previous to this period," says Brooks, "that Rome would become the seat of *Antichrist;* that the empire would be divided into ten kingdoms; that then Antichrist would be revealed and prosper for a time; and that, after the reigning power should have suffered a signal discomfiture, the dominion should be altogether taken from the Eternal City. Such a notion could not be palatable to the Roman emperor, if known to him; and the less so if it was further understood that some had already mused in their hearts whether the emperor himself were not personally *the Antichrist.* These things must have been very perplexing to those ecclesiastics now mingling with the court who were of a compliant and secular spirit: which may be judged of, when we find an honest, bold and godly man like Lactantius expressing himself on these topics with avowed reluctance. . . . The convenient explication, however, was soon discovered and adopted by many, that *Antichrist was pagan Rome,* and that from the date of Constantine's conversion *the millennium commenced.*" A strange millennium and binding of Satan that, which comprised the rancorous dissensions, bickerings, persecutions and mischievous strifes that originated in the Arian controversy!

Yet able men maintained the foolish idea. Others betook themselves to the work of raising questions to obscure the divine authority of the Apocalypse, in which the doctrine of the millennium is taught. And all to make the Christian creed agreeable to the pride and vanity of a Roman emperor!

After a while, when the Bishop of Rome came to be elevated to the high rank of universal father, the embarrassment became still greater. "The inconvenience of explaining Rome to be the capital city of Antichrist was more sensibly felt than ever, and could not be asserted without giving occasion for the very obvious conclusion that the bishop of Rome would some day apostatize, together with the church of which he was the head. Accordingly, from the time of Justinian, efforts were both openly and clandestinely made to get rid of the doctrine altogether, by removing or corrupting the evidence in its favor, or by affixing to it the stigma of heresy. Pope Damascus endeavored peremptorily to put it down by a decree. And some works of the fathers which were in favor of it were successfully suppressed, and others were altered or interpolated to make them read as was desired." (Brooks' Elements of Interpretation, pp. 48–60.)

You will thus perceive how sycophancy, villany, corruption and vanity combined with Origen's pernicious obscurations of holy writ for the suppression of the primitive and apostolic doctrine of the millennium.

There was yet another particular which was made to contribute materially to the process of cheating the church out of its ancient hopes. Like all other doctrines of the Bible, this respecting the millennium has suffered in the hands of some of its advocates. Some of its early believers spoke of it in a manner liable to perversion, or connected it with fancies or fables which have nothing to do with it. Cerinthus was a heretic; and yet he had advocated the doctrine of Christ's personal reign on earth, and arrayed its scenes in the fancies of his own carnal heart. Here was a fine chance to stigmatize the whole thing as a sensual and heretical dream, which was not suffered to pass unimproved. Irenæus had also put upon record a floating story that the earth, in the millennuim, will be so productive that "a grain of wheat will produce ten thousand heads; and each head will yield ten thousand grains; and each grain will yield ten pounds of flour; and other fruits will yield seeds and herbage in the same proportion!" &c. That the earth will be extraordinarily fruitful in the good days to come, is distinctly declared in the Scriptures. Joel says, "The mountains shall drop down new wine, and the hills flow with milk." Yet the excessive exaggerations of the matter by some enthusiastic persons were precious morsels for those who wished to destroy the millenarian hopes. On other subjects, wild caricatures furnished no ground for their rejection; but upon this no allowances could be made. And then, as now, these innocent extravagances were most unjustly, but still effectively, paraded around by the opposers of our doctrine, to bring it into disrepute, and to defame it as a mere fancy of over-credulous and weak people.

Such, then, were the processes, facilitated by the growing corruptions of the times, by which the doctrines of the primitive church on this subject were suppressed and branded as heresy. Can any man do justice to himself, or to the revelations of his God, and not appeal from a decision thus brought about, and recoil from it with indignation and abhorrence? It was the decision of sycophancy, deceit and unholy degradations and perversions of the law and the testimony. And yet the Christian world, to this day, has not recovered from it.

But God did not leave himself without witnesses. From the times of Origen to Augustin, and down into papal ages, we can still find many distinguished names whose authority was distinctly given in favor of millenarian views. Among these were Apollinarius, Lactantius, Victorinus, many of the members of the Council of Nice, Epiphanius, Paulinus, Crispold, Norbert and others. But the ages of darkness came. Star after star went out, until the world was at its cloudy midnight. And the hope of the millennial reign, with all other great doctrines of the Scripture, slept, until God called Luther, and the light of Christianity's renewal came.

What were this great man's views upon this subject, is nowhere specifically given. Yet he has left enough on record to demonstrate that his sentiments differed materially from those generally prevalent.*

1. His method of interpreting the Scriptures was the millenarian method. On Deuteronomy he says, "I here once more repeat, what I have so often insisted on, that the Christian should direct his efforts towards understanding the so-called *literal sense of Scripture*, which alone is the substance of faith and of Christian theology,—which alone will sustain him in the hour of trouble and temptation,—and which will triumph over sin, death and the gates of hell, to the praise and glory of God. The allegorical sense is usually uncertain, and by no means safe to build our faith upon; for it depends for the most part on human opinion only, on which if a man lean, he will find it to be no better than the Egyptian reed. Therefore, ORIGEN, *Jerome*, and similar of the fathers, *are to be avoided, with the whole of that Alexandrian school which abounds in this species of interpretation.*"

2. He denied that there will be a millennium of universal righteousness and peace before Christ comes. He says, "They (the pope and his rabble) shall be preserved until the coming of Christ, whose most bitter enemies they are and ever have been." He says that "the gospel shall continue to be preached even to the end of time, but not so as that all men shall repent and accept of it; for *this shall never be;* the devil will not suffer things to be brought so far, and the world without him is the enemy of the word, and will not be ad-

* See Note I, page 354.

monished. There shall, therefore, be and remain in the world manifold perversions of faith and religion." And again he says, "The last days shall be days of unmeasured wickedness, as Christ says, 'When the Son of man cometh, shall he find faith on the earth?'"

3. Luther taught that the earth shall be restored to its original excellence, and that it shall be the residence of the glorified saints. On 2 Pet. iii. 13, he says, "God has promised through the prophets, here and elsewhere, that he will make heaven and earth new again. How it shall be, we know not, except that the promise is that heaven and earth shall become such that no sin shall be in them, but righteousness only, and that they shall be the residence of the children of God. . . . . This text teaches that we shall live upon earth, and that the entire heaven and earth shall become a paradise of God."

4 Luther spoke of Christ's kingship in a way which can be justified only on the supposition that he is to reign literally and personally in this world. On the second Psalm he says, "Christ was appointed King upon the holy Mount Zion. This is particularly to be remarked; for the Holy Ghost mentions the *corporeal Zion*, that we may be assured that this king is divinely appointed, and is a real Man. . . . The Person and the place are appointed and made known. The Person is the Son of God, and he is King in Zion; that is, the Son of David, and the heir of David; and he who was promised to David *to be the King over the circumcised people over whom David reigned.* We are, therefore, to expect this man to teach in Zion, and to reveal himself in Zion, because he is appointed of God to be King of Zion. . . . . The eternal Father himself crowned him to be King of Zion, on Mount Zion, *in the city of Jerusalem.* . . . . He is the Son of God, yet born a man corporeally, that he might receive the throne of his father David, and rule in Zion." The present form of Christ's king-

dom he describes as that in which he "reigneth no otherwise than as master of a hospital amongst the sick, poor, and diseased," but as to be followed by another "of glory and absolute felicity, in which sin with its attendants shall trouble man no more."

5. Luther believed that the great purposes of God's mercy would reach their consummation at the end of the six thousand years from the creation, according to the saying of Elias and the belief of the primitive church.

6. Luther believed and taught that this consummation was to be expected every day. On Daniel xii. 7, he says, "I ever keep it before me, and I am satisfied, that the last day must be before the door; for the signs predicted by Christ and the apostles Peter and Paul have all now been fulfilled, the trees put forth, the Scriptures are green and blooming. That we cannot know the day, matters not; some one else may point it out; things are certainly near their end." Again, "We certainly have nothing now to wait for but the end of all things." Again, "Let us not think that the coming of Christ is far off. Let us look up with uplifted heads, and with a longing and cheerful mind expect our Redeemer's coming. Though the signs may seem uncertain, yet no man can despise them without danger." "I persuade myself, verily, that the day of judgment will not be absent full three hundred years more. God will not, cannot, suffer this wicked world much longer."

Melancthon taught in the same style. He insisted that the Mahometan empire and the papacy shall not be destroyed till the time of the resurrection of the dead; that the world would endure six thousand years in its present state, and then enter upon a millennary Sabbath according to the saying of Elias; and that "we may be sure that this aged world is not far from its end."

Thus, with the dawn of renewed Christianity, we see the glimmerings again of the ancient faith upon this subject.

Gradually, slowly, and against various hindrances, it once more came forth to the view of mankind. Many of the English Reformers were decidedly millenarian. In all reformed Christendom various men of God (such as Comenius, Jurieu, Serarius, Poiret, Mede, Burnet, Peterson, Spener, Lange, Bengel, Boos, Oetinger, Stilling, Lavater, Sander and Hofmann) rose up to defend and proclaim the hopes of Justin, Irenæus and Tertullian. Just as men studied the prophecies, and read them as God caused them to be written, the advocates of the ancient faith increased, until now we can number some of the greatest, wisest, holiest and most eloquent men upon earth among the defenders of the sublime hopes of the millenarian creed.

Nor is our doctrine that barren and useless thing which its enemies have represented it to be. Its influence, wherever believed, has been salutary and comforting. Dodwell testifies, "It was one principal cause of the fortitude of the primitive Christians, who even coveted martyrdom in hopes of being partakers of the privileges and glories of the martyrs in the first resurrection." Bishop Newton endorses this statement as "just." Gibbon says that as long as this *error* (as he calls it) was permitted to subsist in the church, it was productive of the most salutary effects on the faith and practice of Christians, who lived in the awful expectation of that moment when the globe itself, and all the various race of mankind, should tremble at the appearance of their divine Judge." Bush, though an enemy to this doctrine, says, "We have no difficulty in supposing the belief in the millenarian error was calculated to produce, and did produce, *results of a most auspicious character, which a different construction of the sacred oracles would have failed to effect.*" Such testimony, from such sources, is sufficient. Grapes do not grow upon thorns, nor figs upon thistles. *"A corrupt tree cannot bring forth good fruit."*

Everywhere the Scriptures refer us to Christ's coming and kingdom as the great motive to repentance, holiness and watchfulness. The Savior commands us to watch and pray, because we know not what hour the Lord cometh. Our moderation is to be made known unto all men, for the reason that "the Lord is at hand." Amid all the calamities and disturbances that howl around us, we are to lift up our heads, and stand unmoved, "for the day of our redemption draweth nigh." And who does not see and feel that if we did really believe the solemn truth that any day we may witness Christ's final appearing, we would be much more circumspect, prayerful and diligent at our posts? The practical effects of such a faith would be like a resurrection to our dead and slumbering churches. It would be like a new Pentecost to the wilted hopes of our degenerate Christianity.

Brethren, there is one thought more to which I must give utterance in this connection. It relates to the difference between primitive and modern faith and hope. It would seem as if the church had quite drifted away from her ancient moorings. The early Christians dwelt upon no subject more than that of the coming and kingdom of the Son of man. But who among the great mass of living professors is looking for that glorious advent which is to consummate all the gracious purposes of God? Who is expecting Christ? Who believes that his appearing is at hand? Who acts now from the great idea of impending judgment? Who is not dreaming of a millennium first? If Christ were now to come, how many of you could look up and say, "This is my Lord; I have waited for him; blessed is he that cometh in the name of the Lord!" Would not such an occurrence rather fill you with dismay, and make you cry out in surprise and despair? Such was not the mental condition of the first Christians, who suffered, looking for the coming of the Savior. They looked for him every day; most of you are not looking for him at all.

They looked for him with desire and hope; most of you never think of his coming but with fear and dread. They thirsted for it, and longed for the scenes it is to reveal; many of you rather wish that Christ might never come, and would be more comfortable if you could think that the whole thing were a fable. They watched every turn in human affairs, in the hope that the next would bring their Redeemer from the heavens and give them the kingdom; but, amid the most wonderful commotions in society that man ever witnessed, people now stand callous and unmoved, as if they had nothing to hope for and no interests to lose! Alas, alas! it would seem as if all the hardness and unbelief of eighteen centuries were accumulating upon this generation. "Ask thy father, and he will shew thee; thy elders, and they will tell thee."

There is but one way of safety left. We must take the gospel—the simple gospel as Christ has given it—and make it reality in our experience and our hopes, or we must take death and everlasting despair. The decree of the Eternal has gone forth, and we must be hid in Christ or perish. We are hemmed in to this, and there is no escape. All other dependence is vain. The very ground beneath our feet is quaking and gliding away. And, unless we plant ourselves firmly and at once upon the Rock of ages, we shall soon find ourselves tossing upon the boisterous flood of a starless and rayless eternity. Behold and wonder; but do not despise and perish. Rise; call upon God. What you do, do quickly. And may Jehovah be our portion, and helper, and everlasting friend! Amen.

"HE LEFT NOT HIMSELF WITHOUT WITNESS."

Still, through decaying ages, as they glide,
Jehovah's faithful witnesses abide;
  Sprinkled along the waste of years,
  Full many a soft green isle appears:
Pause where we may upon the desert road,
Some signal is in sight to cheer us on to God.

ELEVENTH DISCOURSE.

WHEN SHALL CHRIST COME?—THE TIME NOT WHOLLY A SECRET—RELATION OF CHRIST'S COMING, IN POINT OF TIME, TO OTHER THINGS PREDICTED IN THE SCRIPTURES—FIRST METHOD OF COMPUTING THE TIME, OR MILLENNIAL SEPTENARY—SECOND METHOD, OR 1260 YEARS' DOMINANCE OF THE PAPACY—THIRD METHOD, OR THE VIALS OF WRATH.

JAMES v. 8: *Stablish your hearts: for the coming of the Lord draweth nigh.*

IF, then, it is a truth that Christ the Lord shall return again to this world, as the Scriptures so explicitly affirm, and as is acknowledged in all the creeds, confessions and hymnbooks in Christendom, one of the most stirring questions concerning it is, WHEN SHALL HE COME?

This question was again and again asked by the disciples while he was yet on earth, and must ever possess a lively interest to every thoroughly Christian heart. But, of all questions relating to our faith and hope, this is, perhaps, the most difficult to be answered. Nay, so far as respects the precise day or year, it cannot be answered by man or angel. "The times and seasons the Father hath put in his own power."

It is true, however, that we need not remain in such total ignorance on the subject as that that day must needs come upon us unawares. Daniel was indeed directed to "shut up the words and seal the book" of his visions concerning it; but they were to remain "closed up and sealed *till the time of the end" only;* and he assures us that then "the wise shall understand," though "the wicked shall not understand." Jesus himself has described the signs which are to precede it, by which we may as infallibly judge of the nearness of the end as we judge of the proximity of summer by the budding of the trees. Paul says expressly that "the children of light" "are not in darkness, that that day should overtake them as a thief." And in the Apocalypse, which is specially devoted to the portrayal of the grand scenes of Christ's revelation and the events which are to precede and accompany it, the particular promise is given, "Blessed is he that readeth and they that hear the words of this prophecy, and keep those things which are written therein;" which certainly implies the possibility of being able to understand these things with some good degree of certainty if we will only investigate with proper attention and prayerfulness. Hence Luther expressed it as his belief that God would yet raise up some one who should be able to reckon up the times, and with certainty hit upon the very day. I hold, therefore, that, instead of rendering ourselves chargeable with irreverent prying into the secrets of Deity by inquiring *when Christ shall come*, it is our hopeful duty so to inquire; and that, if any man lack wisdom to understand what the Scriptures have said upon this point, he may ask God and expect it to be given him as liberally as upon any other subject. It is noted, in commendation of the prophets, that they "searched what manner *of time* the Spirit of Christ which was in them did signify;" and why should not similar searching be commendable in us? When the disciples asked the Lord, "Tell us when shall these things be, and what shall be the sign of thy coming and of the end of the age," he kindly entertained their request; and now that we are bordering so near upon the time, will he be angry with us for pressing the same inquiry? And when the Pharisees and Sadducees came to him with their tempting skepticism, did he not rebuke them as hypocrites who could "discern the face of the sky," but would not put themselves to the pains to "discern the signs of the times"? Let us beware, then, how we scout this question, lest we "fall through the same example of unbelief;" and let us reverently approach the holy oracles to learn what God has revealed to us, to ascertain our position in the calendar of prophecy and to make ready for the solemn scenes that are before us. May the Lord aid us in our inquiries!

Our question is, WHEN SHALL THE SON OF MAN COME? I propose to consider it, first, *relatively*, by showing in what connections with other predicted events the Scriptures place the coming of Christ; and second, *absolutely*, by showing to what period things are pointing as the time of the Savior's coming.

1. The Son of man shall come in a period of abounding apostasy, unbelief and wickedness. Such was the condition of the world when God sent the flood; and Jesus says, "As the days of Noah were, so shall also the coming of the Son of man be." Peter says, "There shall come in the last days scoffers, walking after their own lusts, and saying, Where is the promise of his coming?" Paul says of the coming of the Lord Jesus, "That day shall not come, except there come a falling away first;" and that "in the last days perilous times shall come, for men shall be lovers of their own selves, covetous, boasters, proud, blasphemers, disobedient to parents, unthankful, unholy, without natural affection, truce-breakers, false accusers, incontinent, fierce, despisers of those that are good, traitors, heady, high-minded, lovers of pleasures more than lovers of God, having a form of godliness, but denying the power thereof." Such statements need no comment. Christ will come in a period of abounding guilt and faithlessness.

2. He shall come in a period of revolutionary troubles,

political perplexities and great national agitations. Jesus says, "There shall be upon the earth distress of nations, with perplexity; the sea and the waves thereof roaring; men's hearts failing them for fear, and for looking after those things that are coming on the earth: for the powers of heaven shall be shaken. And then shall they see the Son of man coming in a cloud, with power and great glory." According to the Revelation of John, the final advent is to be immediately preceded by the outpouring of sundry vials of wrath in quick succession, each one filling nations with trouble, anguish and desperation. The Psalmist says of the same period that God shall speak to the kings and rulers of the earth in his wrath, "and vex them in his sore displeasure." This point is also sufficiently plain and well settled.

3. The Son of man shall come while the ten ultimate divisions or kingdoms of the Roman empire are still standing. This is clearly revealed in Daniel's interpretations of Nebuchadnezzar's dream of "the great image." That image symbolized the four great monarchies that were to exist and succeed each other upon earth. The first was the Babylonian, or golden head of the image, the lion with eagle's wings. The second, or silver breast and arms, was the Medo-Persian, the great-toothed devouring bear. The third, or brazen loins and thighs, was the Macedonian or Alexander's kingdom, the leopard with four wings and four heads. And the fourth, or iron legs and feet, was the Roman empire, the dreadful, terrible and mighty ten-horned beast which devoured and trampled down every thing before it. The ten toes, or ten horns, are the ten kingdoms into which the Roman empire was divided by the barbarian invasions, and which now stand as the representatives of the old Roman empire. And Daniel tells us that "in the days of these kings (denoted by the ten toes and horns) shall the God of heaven set up a kingdom." He says that he beheld until these thrones were cast down,

and the time that the beast was slain was the time when the judgment should sit, and "one like the Son of man came with the clouds of heaven." The same is taught in the visions of John. The ten-horned beast of the thirteenth chapter can be none other than the Roman empire, and its ten horns its ten divisions. And, according to the nineteenth chapter, it continues in existence, persecuting the saints and warring against the Lamb, until destroyed by the personal descent of him whose name is The Word of God, King of kings, and Lord of lords. This point, then, is also sufficiently established.

4. The Son of man shall come before the Jews as an entire people shall be restored to Palestine. There will be a portion of Jacob restored before the Lord comes, but not the entire race. It is expressly said that when God assembles Jacob and gathers the remnant of Israel, "their King shall pass before them, and the Lord on the head of them:" (Micah ii. 12, 13.) "The Lord will go before them, and the God of Israel will be their rearward:" (Isa. lii. 12.) He must therefore be on earth before this general gathering of the Jews takes place. It is further evident from the twelfth of Zechariah, the twenty-eighth and twenty-ninth of Ezekiel, and the eighteenth and nineteenth of Revelation, that Christ is personally present when the terrible destruction occurs to the armies that invade Palestine; whilst it is plain from the sixty-sixth of Isaiah that it is only after that terrific overthrow that the great and triumphant assembling of Israel takes place. It is those who escape that awful destruction that are to go to the nations, Tarshish, Pul, Lud, Tubal, Javan, and the isles afar off, and make known the wonders they witnessed; and only *then* shall the Gentiles bring *all* the children of Israel out of all nations, upon horses, and in chariots, and in litters, and upon mules, and upon swift vehicles, to God's holy mountain Jerusalem, for an offering unto the Lord: (Isa. lxvi. 19, 20.)

It is also explicitly stated that the time of Israel's deliverance is when Christ personally comes; not before. So Paul affirms in Romans xi. 26, which he says is the teaching of the prophets. So the Psalmist says:—"When the Lord shall build up Zion, he shall *appear in his glory.*" And so Zechariah declares, when God shall "pour upon the house of David, and upon the inhabitants of Jerusalem, the spirit of grace and supplication, they shall *look upon him* whom they have pierced." Christ will therefore come before the general restoration of Israel.

5. He will come while the papacy and the Man of sin still live and continue in power. It is now established, as well as any interpretation of prophecy can be, that the "little horn" in Daniel's vision (Dan. vii. 8–24) denotes the papal power. And he says, "I beheld, and the same horn made war with the saints, and prevailed against them, *until the Ancient of days came.*" It must live on, then, until Christ comes—until "the judgment shall sit." That the "Man of sin, the son of perdition," in 2d Thessalonians, is a power closely akin to the pope and his apostasy, is also pretty well agreed by Protestants. But Paul describes him as pressing his work of deceit and blasphemy until "destroyed by the appearing of Christ's own presence." And in John's account of the doings of Jesus in the great day when he shall come forth in his wrath, we find this self-same monster still existing, still arrayed against God, and only taken and destroyed by the administrations of the great day of God Almighty. The Son of man shall therefore certainly come whilst the papacy and antichrist still live.

6. He shall come in a period when a far-sounding cry shall be raised in slumbering Christendom that his advent is at hand. The Savior tells us that *in that period* "the kingdom of heaven shall be likened unto ten virgins who went forth to meet the bridegroom; but while the bridegroom tarried they all slumbered and slept. *And at midnight there was a cry*

made, Behold, the bridegroom cometh; go ye out to meet him." That this parable portrays the condition of the church in the period of the advent, there can be no room for doubt. Christ, in the preceding chapter, was engaged in a description of his coming and the end of the age. And this is but a continuation of that discourse. "THEN," says he,—that is, in the time when what I have said shall be fulfilled,—*then* shall the kingdom of heaven—the community of professing Christians—be like the ten virgins. They shall sleep with regard to this great subject. And while they sleep the announcement shall go forth that the bridegroom is coming. The same thing is set forth in the Apocalypse, where, in connection with the scenes of the last days, the announcement of the blessed Savior is, "*Behold, I come as a thief; blessed is he that watcheth!*" All this shows that in the period of the advent, a cry declaring his coming shall be poured upon the dull ear of Christendom.

7. But, notwithstanding the cry, Christ shall come when but few will at all believe that his advent is near. He says himself, "When the Son of man cometh, shall he find faith on the earth?" "In such an hour as ye think not, the Son of man cometh." "Evil servants shall say in their hearts, My Lord delayeth his coming." Some will scoff and say, "Where is the promise of his coming?" People will be saying "Peace and safety," when sudden destruction shall come upon them. "As in the days that were before the flood, they were eating and drinking, marrying and giving in marriage,"—self-contentedly pursuing the vanities and pleasures of earth,—"and *knew not* until the flood came and took them all away: so shall also the coming of the Son of man be."

From these plain statements of the word of God, two things may be remarked. The first is, that there certainly is to be no thousand years of universal righteousness and peace previous to Christ's coming. The second is, that we need fix upon no other times for Christ's coming than the times in which we live.

I proceed, then, to the second branch of the subject, in which I proposed to bring forward what light can be obtained for a somewhat more direct and categorical answer to the question, When shall Christ come? Nor is there as much barrenness upon this line of inquiry as may be supposed. There are sundry distinct and independent processes by which information may be gathered. And if we should find upon examination that these several processes harmonize in their results, we may take them as mutually corroborative, the one as sustaining the truthfulness of the other, whilst the combined testimony of all, if found to agree, must create a very strong probability in favor of the period to which they point.

The first method of computing the time I will introduce by a quotation from Johnston, a distinguished writer on the prophecies. "Through the whole Scripture, both of the Old and New Testaments," says he, "there is a striking typical representation of some great and important Sabbath, as a great septenary that has not yet taken place, and which evidently appears to be the millenarian septenary, as the great Sabbath of the whole earth. God blessed the seventh day, and hallowed it. In the Decalogue this peculiar distinguishment of the seventh day, or weekly sabbath, was most solemnly renewed. Every seventh year was appointed a sabbatical year. And the commencement of the year of jubilee, which was every fiftieth year, was to be fixed by the running of a septenary of sabbatical years. 'Thou shalt number seven sabbaths of years unto thee, seven years, and the space of the seven sabbaths of years shall be unto thee forty and nine years.' The number seven, because used in Scripture to complete all the sacred divisions of time, was regarded by the Jews as the symbol of perfection, and is used in this sense in Scripture. The question then arises, Is it to be supposed that all these events, which are interwoven with the Mosaic dispensation, which was itself symbolical or typical, and which are introduced into the New Testament, and abound so much in the book of Revelation, have no antetype to correspond to them?—no great sabbatical septenary to which they all point and in which they all shall be accomplished? Is it not highly probable that they are all typical of the seventh millenary of the earth, which is the great Sabbath?" To this I may answer that it is not only probable, but the next thing to absolute certainty.

When we go back into antiquity, whether Jewish, heathen or Christian, we find a general and deeply-seated belief that the world shall endure six thousand years in its secular and toiling state, answering to the six days of the creation; and that then will follow a thousand years of holy rest, peace and joy,—the millennial Sabbath, or golden period of the world. Bishop Russell, of Scotland, says, "It is found in the most ancient of those commentaries of the Old Testament which we owe to the learning of the Rabbinical school;" and that "there is no room for doubt that the notion preceded by several centuries the introduction of the Christian faith." It is given as a tradition of the house of Elias, and thought by many to date back to the great prophet Elijah. Professor Bush, in his book against the millennium, speaks of this tradition, and says, "It is but fair to admit, that, as there is nothing in the Scriptures which directly contradicts it, *it may be well founded.*" According to Plutarch, the Chaldeans had a similar belief. Zoroaster also taught it. Daubuz says that the Tuscans held it, and that it is retained among the Persians to this day. The Magi entertained it. We saw in a previous discourse that it was held and inculcated, as a branch of Christian truth, by Barnabas, Justin Martyr, Papias, Irenæus, Tertullian, Cyprian, and all orthodox Christians for the first centuries of the Christian era. Luther entertained it. Melancthon wrote it on the fly-leaf of the Bible, as a matter not to be disputed. Thousands of divines since his time have received it as part of their faith. And when we come to place together certain statements of the Scriptures, there seems to me to be a weight of testimony in its favor sufficient to warrant us in regarding it as sacred truth. Look at these sentences:—

"*In six days the Lord made heaven and earth.*"

"*On the seventh day he rested and was refreshed.*"

"*One day is with the Lord as a thousand years.*"

"THERE REMAINETH THEREFORE A REST—*σαββατίσμος*, a KEEPING OF SABBATH—TO THE PEOPLE OF GOD."

I have shown that Christ will come before the millennium, not after it. The millennium is the seventh thousand years, or great Sabbath, of the world. Now then, if we can ascertain in what period of the world's age we live, we may form some idea of the time when the Son of man shall come. To ascertain this with certain accuracy is impossible; but we may approximate the truth with some degree of reliability. The holy Book, to which we are indebted for what else we know upon this subject, has not left blank the department of dates. The births and ages of the ancient patriarchs, both before and since the flood, have been so particularly and circumstantially recorded that we can readily measure the period through which they lived by summing the united lengths of time occupied by the several generations. There are also various important records by which to measure the duration of the servitude in Egypt, of the wandering in the wilderness, and of the reign of the Judges, by whom Israel was governed to the institution of the kingdom under Saul. From that on to the Babylonian captivity the name of every king is given in succession, with the length of time each one reigned. And from the time of the captivity to the present, records, both sacred and profane, are such as leave but little room for uncertainty.

The commonly received chronology, which is usually found printed in the margins of our Bibles, is no part of the inspired record. These dates are inserted from a system framed by Archbishop Usher, and others. It is now agreed that it is defective in many particulars. According to that, it would yet be about one hundred and thirty-five years to the end of the sixth thousand. Capellus reduces this *one* year; Kennedy, Bedford, and Ferguson, 3 years; Playfair and Walker, 4; Rheinhold, 16; Pererius and Jarvis, 17; Langius, 37; Spondanus and Torniellus, 47; Salianus, 49; Maimonides and Blancarnus, 54; Riccioli, 58; Chinese Jews, 75; De Pontac, 84; Genebrard, 86; Ribera, 91; Lidyat, 99; Browne, 117; Vignier, Bowen, and Elliott, 124; Shimeall and Saville about 130; and Tynes, Clinton and others reduce the time to still shorter limits. Having looked somewhat into these chronological matters, I am satisfied that it would be wrong to rely with too much confidence upon either of these or any other like reckonings. There is uncertainty about them all. In the general, however, those are in every way the most reliable which leave but little of the six thousand years unexpired. I have been led to believe that we now are, most probably, in the 5994th year of the world since the creation of Adam; which would bring us, at the present, (1863,) *within some seven years of the Sabbatic Millennium and the glorious epiphany of our Lord.* At any rate, we may be pretty confident that we shall reach the consummation before the end of this century.*

We pass, then, to another method of computation on this subject, to see whither it will conduct us.

The "little horn" described in the seventh of Daniel, the prophet declares, "made war with the saints, and prevailed

* See Note K, page 356.

against them, *until the Ancient of days came*, and judgment was given to the saints;" that is, until the coming of Christ. He also tells us the duration of the period in which the saints are thus to be afflicted. "They shall be given into his hand *until a time and times, and the dividing of time*," or three years and a half. These are of course prophetic or symbolical years, in which each day stands for a year; as in Numb. xiv. 13; Ez. iv. 4–6; Rev. ii. 10; Dan. ix. 24; where this matter is sufficiently explained, a day standing for a year. So Melancthon and the Magdeburg centuriators understood them. Professor Stuart says, "The great mass of interpreters in the English and American world have, for many years, been wont to understand the *days* designated in Daniel and the Apocalypse as the representatives or symbols of *years*. I have found it difficult to trace the origin of this *general, I might say, almost* UNIVERSAL *custom*." Professor Bush says, "In taking a *day* as the prophetical time for a *year*, I believe you are *sustained by the soundest exegesis*, as well as fortified by the high names of Mede, Sir Isaac Newton, Faber, Scott, Bishop Newton, Keith, and a host of others. . . . . If the old year-day is wrong, not only has the whole Christian world been led astray for ages by a mere *ignis-fatuus* of false hermeneutics, but the church is at once cut loose from every chronological mooring, and set adrift on the open sea, without the vestige of a beacon, lighthouse, or star by which to determine her bearings or distances from the desired millennial haven to which she had hoped she was tending."

Three years and a half, as men anciently reckoned, contain twelve hundred and sixty days. Twelve hundred and sixty years, then, is the length of the period from the giving of the saints into the hand of the little horn to the judgment and coming of the Ancient of days. Hence, if we can ascertain when the saints were given into the hand of the little horn, we may judge of the time when Christ is likely to come.

I have said that this little horn denotes the papacy. It may have other applications, but this, without doubt, must be included.

The terrible beast on which it grew certainly represents the Roman empire; and the papacy arose upon the Roman empire.

It grew up among ten other horns of this beast, which are ten kings or kingdoms; the papacy sprung into being from among the ten separate but closely-related powers into which the old Roman empire was divided by the barbarian invasions.

Before this little horn, three of the other horns were plucked up; the papacy possessed itself of the Gothic kingdom of Odoacer, which fell in 493, the Ostrogothic kingdom of Theodoric, which fell in 554, and the Lombardic kingdom of Alboin, which fell in 774; and thus, as proclaimed in the bull against Queen Elizabeth, *he subdued three kingdoms.*

This little horn was "diverse from the first," or other ten; the papacy is an ecclesiastico-political establishment, altogether different in its elements from the other kingdoms in which it sprung up.

"In this (little) horn were eyes, like the eyes of a man." The papacy claims to be a universal *overseer,* and is full of cunning, subtlety and far-sighted plans.

It had also "a mouth speaking great things"—"great words against the Most High," and "his look was more stout than his fellows." The papacy has ever been characterized by its pompous, arrogant, sacrilegious and blasphemous assumptions. There never has been a king or potentate on earth who has ventured upon such pretensions as the pope of Rome.

The little horn "thought to change times and laws." Since the times of Julius Cæsar, none but the papacy has ever arrogated the right to regulate the calendar, or to dictate and annul the legislation of the world.

This little horn prevailed against the saints, and wearied them out, and had them in his hand. The papacy is the power from which the humble confessors of Jesus have suffered more than from Nero and Caligula.

In every particular the prophetic description fits the papacy, and must in some sense refer to it.

The giving of the saints into the hands of the papacy was the investiture of the popes with universal jurisdiction, oversight and dominion over the church. Clothing them with such power was most literally and effectually giving the saints into their hand. Let us inquire, then, when this occurred.

History presents two dates, at which different interpreters have thought they could trace the act which gave the saints into the hands of the papacy. The one is the year 533 or 534, when the Emperor Justinian gave the pope precedence of all his episcopal brethren; the other is the year 606, when the Emperor Phocas declared the pope head of all the churches, and sole universal bishop. Newton has mentioned other dates, such as the years 727, when the pope and the Romans finally broke their connection with the Eastern emperor; 755, when the pope obtained the exarchate of Ravenna; 774, when he acquired the kingdom of Lombardy; and 787, when the worship of images was first established, and the pope's supremacy endorsed by the second Council of Nice. But neither of these dates mentioned by Newton answers to the case before us; and Newton himself does not venture to say upon which of them we are to rely. And the earlier date which goes back to the time of Justinian seems equally inadequate to answer to that for which we are inquiring. The truth is, that the papal power was not the product of a single day or year. *It grew.* But the great and effective act which made the pope lord of Christendom, and thus gave the saints into his hand, was the decree of Phocas in A.D. 606. It is to this date that the great mass of the most accredited interpreters refer us in connection with this subject.

Taking this as the date, then, when the papacy obtained its

power, and adding twelve hundred and sixty years, the given period of its dominancy, we are carried down to the year 1866 or 1867 as the time when Christ shall come and the judgment sit,—the exact date which Bowen and others have hit upon by an entirely different process.

The authorities sustaining this computation are very numerous, and include some of the weightiest of names. I will refer to a few.

Baronius, in his ecclesiastical annals, and other Romish historians, have referred to the decree of Phocas in 606, as the first effective official acknowledgment of the pope's supremacy. Mosheim says, "The most learned writers, and those who are most remarkable for their knowledge of antiquity, are generally agreed that Boniface III. engaged Phocas, that abominable tyrant, to take from the bishop of Constantinople the title of *œcumenical* or *universal bishop*, and to confer it upon the Roman pontiff; *and thus was the papal supremacy first introduced.*"

Luther alludes to the year 606 as a notable commencing papal epoch. Osiander, one of his first disciples, has done the same. Flacius, also a pupil of Luther and Melancthon, represented the twelve hundred and sixty days as having commenced in 606, and by consequence as running out in 1866.

Robert Fleming, about one hundred and fifty years ago, in his little book on the Rise and Fall of Papacy, said, "We may justly reckon that the papal head took its rise from that remarkable year, 606, when Phocas did in a manner devolve the government of the West upon him, *by giving him the title of universal bishop.* From which period, if we date the twelve hundred and sixty years, they lead us down (as I said already) to the year 1866."

David Simpson, a divine of the last century, says, "Some begin to reckon (the twelve hundred and sixty years) from the year 606, when the proud prelate of Rome was declared universal bishop. If this be right, (and he seems to be strongly of that opinion,) then the Pope of Rome will be completely destroyed about the year 1866," and Christ of course come; for the papacy is to stand till Christ comes.

Scott, the commentator, says, "The beginning of the twelve hundred and sixty years must be placed subsequent to the four first trumpets, on the subversion of the Western empire in 566. This made way for the pope. He became universal bishop in A.D. 606."

The learned George Stanley Faber, who examined very deeply into these subjects, says, "The year which I have fixed upon for the date of the twelve hundred and sixty years, is the year 606,—a year marked by so singular a combination of circumstances, that I know not how any other can with equal propriety be selected. If, then, I be right in my opinion, we are now removed but little more than sixty years from the commencement of the end of the vintage of God's wrath." This was written in 1805, and fixes 1866 as the time when things shall come to the scenes of their consummation.

But I have not the time to multiply quotations. Chytræus, Pareus, Whiston, Cogswell, Bryant, Elliott, Cumming, Junkin, Berg, and many more, have taken the same dates. This method of computing the time of the end is, therefore, not a mere conceit, but a thing commanding the belief of some of our ablest interpreters, and claiming our particular attention. I will only add the testimony of Luther, who, not long before his death, said, "I persuade myself verily that the day of judgment will not remain absent full three hundred years more;" according to which we are now living in the very period of the judgment. I would not be understood as holding or teaching that Christ will certainly come in three years from the present time. I do not feel authorized to fix upon any one specific date for that great event. But here we have two distinct and independent processes, sustained by the best authorities on the subject, and both of which concur in the representation that the day of Christ's coming is near at hand, and lies within the limits of this present century. Well may we then take up the language of the text and say, "THE COMING OF THE LORD DRAWETH NIGH!"

But there is still another method by which light may be thrown upon this mysterious subject.

In the sixteenth chapter of Revelation we read of seven angels having seven vials of the wrath of God, which they pour out in quick succession upon the inhabitants of the earth. These vials are called "seven plagues," and evidently relate to "the last times." It is under the pouring out of the sixth vial that the coming of Christ is announced. And if we can identify the fulfillment of these plagues, and ascertain under which of them we are now living, we may form some idea of our probable nearness to the time of the Savior's coming. Let us then enter upon this inquiry.

"And the first (angel) went and poured out his vial upon the earth; and there fell a noisome and grievous sore upon the men which had the mark of the beast, and upon them which worshipped his image."

This, and what follows in the vision, is of course symbolic, and is to be interpreted by the laws which apply to symbolic language. "The land or earth, when distinguished from the sea, rivers, fountains and heaven, denotes the population of an empire under a settled government. The ulcer denotes an analogous disease of the mind, a restlessness and rancor of passion exasperated by agitating and noxious principles and opinions, that fill it with a sense of obstruction, degradation and misery, resembling the torture of an ulcerated body." Accordingly, the best interpreters apply this vial to the first or incipient stages of the French Revolution. As Lord remarks, "No symbol can be conceived more suited to represent the restlessness under injury, the ardor of resentment, hate and revenge, the noxiousness and contagion of false principles and opinions, that marked the commencement of the political disquiets and agitations of the European states toward the close of the last century. . . . France received its first and largest tempest. But the angel, scattering a shower on Belgium, Holland and the Valley of the Rhine, crossed the Alps, steeping heights and recesses in the bitter flood, drenched the vales and plains of Italy, swept around over the German empire and the British isles, and finally dashed the vengeful dregs on the peninsula of Portugal and Spain and the distant southern shores of this continent."

"And the second poured out his vial upon the sea, and it became as the blood of a dead man; and every living thing died in the sea."

"This denotes the second great act in the tragedy of the French Revolution, in which the people slaughtered one another in feuds, insurrections and civil wars, and exterminated with the dagger, the bayonet and the guillotine, all the influential ranks,—king, queen, nobles, prelates, civil magistrates, priests, military commanders, soldiers, persons of illustrious descent, of distinguished reputation, of talents, of wealth, and demagogues, political chiefs, who rose to conspicuity and influence by their acts as revolutionists." Every living soul in any way distinguished died in the sea of deadly blood! So Lord, Faber and Cunninghame understand this vial.

"And the third angel poured out his vial upon the rivers and fountains of waters; and they became blood."

"This symbol denotes the vast bloodshed in other Apocalyptical kingdoms in the insurrections and wars which sprung out of the French Revolution. It commenced in Austria in 1792, and soon extended to Holland, Sardinia, Russia, Italy, Spain, England, Prussia, Switzerland, Denmark and Portugal, and continued with little intermission for more than twenty years, in which the blood of millions of the French was poured out on the soil of other kingdoms, millions of other nations in resisting their aggressions, and vast multitudes of both sexes put to death in the violence of revolution, the siege and sack of cities and the repression of insurrections." Lord, Faber, Cunninghame, Keith and Elliott.

"And the fourth angel poured out his vial on the sun; and power was given unto him to scorch men with fire. And men were scorched with great heat, and blasphemed the name of God, which hath power over these plagues, and they repented not to give him glory."

The sun, in the language of symbols, denotes the civil power, or those who exercise government in a kingdom or state. This plague is accordingly interpreted of those oppressions and spoliations which resulted from previous wars and troubles, and with which the revolutionary rulers of France and contemporary authorities of other countries scorched and devoured their subjects. Alison says that a war of plunder, confiscation and slaughter was waged against the rich from mere envy and avarice, and thousands of families were reduced from affluence to beggary. Time would fail for an enumeration of the distresses inflicted by the mad worshippers of reason and liberty, and even by Napoleon himself. History hardly contains a parallel to those times of wo. And yet the people repented not of their sins.—Lord, Faber, Cunninghame, Keith, and others.

"And the fifth angel poured out his vial *on the seat of the beast; and his kingdom was full of darkness;* and they gnawed their tongues for pain, and blasphemed the God of heaven, because of their pains and sores, and repented not of their deeds."

This plague is so much like the first that it can only be applied to similar revolutionary scenes, in which thrones are made to totter, their power obscured and kingdoms thrown into confusion and distress. The mention of the sores and pains of the first vial shows that these plagues overlap and run through each other, and that they have respect, at least for the most part, to the same people. The wild beast is the civil power of the ten kingdoms occupying the place of the old Roman empire. The pouring of the vial on the seat of the beast shows the troubles with which their authority should be assailed, and the extreme peril to which their power should be subjected. And to what could all this more forcibly apply than to those scenes of revolution which, in 1848, jostled every throne and threatened the utter destruction of every government in Europe? Look back and think over that year of wonders. Consider how the spirit of liberty, poisoned and fouled by many sad commixtures, rose up to shake and darken the world. Convulsion rushed upon the heels of convulsion, until it became difficult to keep pace with the swift shiftings of the fearful diorama. The first cry came from the sunny plains of Lombardy. The Milanese were in open rebellion. Sicily next felt the mighty movement. The imbecile and cruel Bourbon King of Naples stood powerless before his indignant subjects. The Dukes of Tuscany, Parma and Modena beheld themselves suddenly shorn of their old authority. Paris saw another revolution, and the dynasty of Orleans went down forever. Stern and formal Germany rocked from one extremity to the other. The throne of the great Frederick seemed to turn to ashes before the driving wind. The imperial crown fell from the old master of Austria before the brave Magyar, and its wearer driven as a fugitive to the mountains of the Tyrol. Rome shook from centre to circumference, and threw off in horror that pontiff who claims to be the vicar of Christ and the lord of all Christendom. England herself was filled with uneasiness, not knowing at what moment her proud fabric might lie level with the dust. Every thing was tossed hither and thither with the black storms of revolutionary fury. The vial of the wrath of God was poured out upon the seat of the beast, and threatened the whole system of European politics with utter destruction.

But the tide soon turned. The time for the end had not yet come. Despotism and tyranny have since entrenched themselves in their former seats in redoubled strength. And disappointed hope lies festering in the bosoms of subdued or exiled revolutionists, whilst they gnaw their tongues in the pains of unvented ire and blaspheme God for their sores and want of success. The fifth vial, then, has been entirely and but recently fulfilled.

"And the sixth angel poured out his vial upon the great river Euphrates; and the water thereof was dried up, that the way of the kings of the east might be prepared."

Numerous expositors apply this to the Turkish empire, and the gradual disappearance of that persecuting power. If this be true, the prophecy is most rapidly fulfilling. Isaac Taylor says, "Mahometan empire is decrepit, Mahometan faith is decrepit; and both are ready to vanish away." Lamartine says, "Turkey is perishing for want of Turks." Lieutenant Lynch, from what he saw there, says, "The dispassionate observer can already predict the downfall of the Ottoman empire. The handwriting is on the wall, and it needs not a Daniel to interpret it." Cumming has collected a great number of most remarkable testimonies to the same effect.

But it seems to me that this is not the correct application of this prophecy. The river here mentioned is connected with the mystic Babylon, just as the literal Euphrates was related to the literal Babylon that was built upon it. The mystic Babylon is the combination of nationalized hierarchies or churches; and the mystic Euphrates must therefore refer to the popular support from which these establishments derive their sustenance and riches, just as the literal Euphrates was the source of the supplies of the literal Babylon. And as ancient Babylon was destroyed by the kings of the

East by diverting the Euphrates from its proper channel, so these state-church establishments shall be destroyed by the diversion and withdrawing — *drying up* — of their present supports. It is in this sense that Lord, Winthrop and others understand this prophecy; and I see no reason to dissent from them. If this, then, be the true application of this vial, the evidences are before us, and increasing every day, that it is beginning to be fulfilled. The withdrawment of a large body of ministers and people from the Scotch national church, the extensive secessions from the Romish churches of Germany, the resignations of many ministers in Switzerland, are recent events which accord exactly with this symbol. Thousands upon thousands are coming out of these establishments every year by immigration to our own country. Thousands in Ireland are relinquishing the old system and embracing the simple gospel. In Italy and parts of Germany, the great mass of the population is literally infidel, and ready at any moment to murder every priest and to rifle every church. Sardinia is in arms against the ecclesiastical exactions under which she has suffered. In Mexico, government has turned its hand to seize upon the hoarded wealth of the church. Every day the ranks of secessionists and dissenters are growing and swelling in France, in Scotland, in England, in parts of Germany. Taxation for the support of lordly and lazy bishops who revel on their thousands per annum is beginning to grind hard upon men who cannot believe that such luxurious parasites are the exclusive successors of the makers of tents and the menders of nets. Church hierarchies and state religious establishments are falling into less and less repute every day. The waters of the Euphrates are drying up; they are turning from their channel, and soon shall the destroyers enter this den of spiritual harlotry, and great Babylon shall fall to rise no more.

The first part of this vial, therefore, is fulfilling. Upon

the second part I am not so confident. John says, "I saw three unclean spirits, like frogs, come out of the mouth of the dragon, and out of the mouth of the beast, and out of the mouth of the false prophet. For they are *πνευματα δαιμόνων*—*demon-spirits,*—working miracles, which go forth unto the kings of the earth and of the whole world, to gather them to the war of that great day of God Almighty."

This evidently refers to some new and strangely-successful turn in the affairs of the kingdom of darkness. Wonders are to be wrought. Demons are to be the agents. The movement is to combine the elements of paganism, European politics, and the false religion of the papists. Its effect shall be to marshal the powers of the world for their last conflict. And it is not at all improbable that we have the beginning of all this in the strange, infatuating, and widely-spreading abomination called "SPIRITUALISM." Paul most solemnly assures us that "*The Spirit* (*of God*) *speaketh expressly, that* IN THE LATTER TIMES *some shall depart from the faith, giving heed to seducing spirits, and διδασκαλίαις δαιμονίων*—TEACHINGS OF DEMONS—speaking lies in hypocrisy:" (1 Tim. iv. 1, 2.) I cannot dwell upon this now; but I am convinced that a careful investigation of this system of *demonism* will show many and strong points of correspondence to what Paul and John have here written. It is yet in its incipiency. Time will reveal the truth. But enough is plain to show that we are now living in the period of the sixth vial. The fifth reached its acme eight years ago. The sixth certainly has begun. And it is in connection with this sixth vial that Jesus says, "BEHOLD, I COME."*

My brethren, look at it, and put not the solemn truth away from you. Here are three wholly different and independent methods of ascertaining something as to the period when our blessed Lord shall come; and each of the three, according to our very best information on the subject, gives forth the

* See Note L, page 362.

distinct and firm testimony that *we are at this moment treading the very margin of the great consummation.*

There is still another method of learning when the final advent is near, the presentation of which I will reserve for another discourse. But, look in whatever direction we may, we shall only find the evidence thickening that the time has wellnigh come.

> "The tide of pomp
> That beats upon the high shore of this world,"

is ebbing fast. Soon shall those great solemn words be spoken,—"IT IS DONE!"

> "Six thousand years of sorrow have wellnigh
> Fulfilled their tardy and disastrous course
> Over a sinful world; and what remains
> Of this tempestuous state of human things
> Is merely as the working of the sea
> Before a calm that rocks itself to rest.
> . . . . The world appears
> To toll the death-bell of its own decease,
> And by the voice of all its elements
> To preach the general doom!"

And after gathering together all the light within my reach, I say to you, in all seriousness and honesty, that I believe there are some listening to me now who will never taste of death till they see the Son of man coming in the clouds of heaven with power and great glory. You may consider me beside myself if you will. You may take heed to my announcement, or you may despise it as folly. You may be wise, and prepare to meet God, or you may take the opiates of unbelief, and say, "No danger! no danger!" But, in the name of that Jesus whom I believe to have sent me to you as his ambassador, I declare to you that "THE COMING OF THE LORD DRAWETH NIGH!"

What, then, is to be done? Shall we turn aside from our

avocations and give ourselves up to dejection or the silly conceits of wild enthusiasts? No, no, no. We must only stand the firmer to our posts. The command of Jesus is, "OCCUPY TILL I COME." We must keep steadfastly to the duties of our places, and do with our might what our hands find to do, and work and wait, and wait as we work, until Christ shall call to us from the heavens, "Well done, good and faithful servants; enter ye into the joy of your Lord!" He never meant that the promise of his coming should frighten us, or depress us, or make us unhappy. He meant it for the comfort of his people in their trials, to inflame their zeal, to inspire their hopes, and to serve as a sort of present compensation for their toils and sufferings. Instead of being discomfited, then, as we see the time drawing near, let us rather be joyful, and lift up our heads, and press for the crowns that are drawing so close. The faithless and the impenitent may well be alarmed and be moved to cry for mercy; but for those who have laid up their treasures in the world to come, the scenes at hand are full of gladness.

The admonition of the text is, "*Stablish your hearts.*" That is, we are to grasp firm hold of the exceeding great and precious promises of Jesus, and rest confidently upon God's sublime covenant of mercy, and make up our minds to stand or fall clasping the cross, and we shall be safe. We must settle our souls upon Him who is able to save to the uttermost, and give ourselves fully up to be his followers and servants, and he will not disown us in that great day. Though we may have been slumbering long upon Delilah's lap, if we will only rouse up and keep to our duty in Christ Jesus we shall have strength against all our foes and all our dangers.

Let me exhort you, then, by the stirring solemnities of this theme, to be up and doing. "Awake, thou that sleepest, and arise from the dead, and Christ shall give thee light." If you have been prayerless hitherto, begin at once to call upon that

Savior who has never yet despised the cry of a sincere suppliant. If you have never avowed yourself a disciple of Jesus, do it at once, and put yourself within the range of that proffered grace which God has declared to be sufficient for you. "*Be not afraid; only believe.*" And if you are depressed, burdened, or cast down at the prospect before us, listen to the sweet voice of the Savior, as he tenderly says to you and to all, "COME UNTO ME, ALL YE THAT LABOR AND ARE HEAVY LADEN, AND I WILL GIVE YOU REST. TAKE MY YOKE UPON YOU, AND LEARN OF ME, AND YE SHALL FIND REST UNTO YOUR SOULS."

WAKE! AWAKE!

Wake! awake! the call is flying,
From watchmen on the ramparts crying,
Awake! awake! Jerusalem!
While the midnight is prevailing,
These voices clear all souls are hailing:
Virgins, where are ye, virgins pure?
The Bridegroom comes! awake!
The wise their torches take!
HALLELUIA!
Haste to prepare
The feast to share;
The time has come to meet him there!

Zion hears the watchmen singing,
Their hearts with joy and rapture springing.
She wakes, she boundeth from her gloom.
Comes her friend from heaven all-glorious,
In grace, how strong! in truth victorious;
Her Star ascends, her Light is come!
Appear, thou crowned One,
Jesus, God's only Son!
SAVE US, O LORD!
We follow thee
Till heaven we see,
And at thy banquet sup with thee.

PHILIP NIKOLAI, 1597.

TWELFTH DISCOURSE.

RECAPITULATION — FOURTH METHOD OF ASCERTAINING WHEN CHRIST SHALL COME, OR THE SIGNS OF THE TIMES — THE SENTIMENTS OF DISTINGUISHED MEN RESPECTING THE NEARNESS OF THE END—THE INTENSE DESIRABLENESS OF THE SAVIOR'S COMING—CONCLUSION.

LUKE xxi. 28: *And when these things begin to come to pass, then look up, and lift up your heads: for your redemption draweth nigh.*

IT is now three months since I commenced discoursing to you upon the holy prophecies concerning "The Last Times." And though I have announced this as my last discourse in this series, I find that I have not uttered the half that I originally contemplated. I have presented only some fragments of the grand system of God's purposes, as I think I see it revealed in his holy word. I regret that I have not been able to say more and to say it better. Nevertheless, under the divine blessing, what I have said may not be in vain. It may serve to set you upon trains of thought and investigation, and thus conduct you to a knowledge of what is coming on the earth, which perhaps you would not otherwise have reached. I thank God that he has preserved my life and health to pursue these studies thus far, and that so many have given me their serious attention, notwithstanding the obstacles interposed by a winter of unwonted severity. The pleasure and profit which these efforts have given me more than repay for the toils they have cost, whilst I have the further comfort of knowing that they have been blest to the good of immortal souls. Prophecy was "written for our learning, that we through patience and comfort of the Scriptures might have hope;" and in fulfillment of this end have I thus been engaged upon it. I preach for no other purpose than to render you wiser, better and happier. I stand here only to help you to become more heavenly in your thoughts, more angelic in your affections and more Christ-like in your character. And if ever I should lose sight of this great aim of my office, I should fear that my tongue would cleave to the roof of my mouth.

It is, perhaps, the greatest failing of the Christians of this generation that they are too speculative and imitative in their religion. We are too easily satisfied with floating notions of what the Scriptures teach, without searching and verifying for ourselves. We are too prone to think it enough to comply with popular religious customs, and to assent indefinitely to the belief current among those around us. We do not draw our ideas and our hopes with sufficient directness from the fountains of truth, nor bring the teaching of revelation home to our hearts with the proper practical earnestness. We are orthodox enough, but too undevout. We assent to the revealments of God, but we do not drink them in, and imbed them in our souls, and wrap them up in the warm embrace of our affections, as we should. Dr. Chalmers once said, "I have all my life viewed the truths of Christianity too much in the way of speculation, and as if at a distance. I have not closed with them; I have not laid hold of them; I have not apprehended them. I have been persuaded of the truth of the promises, but not embraced them. With the exception of an occasional gleam of light and comfort from the freeness of the gospel, I have had no steady, habitual, personal sense of that freeness. I have abundantly acknowledged it, but have not used it."

This is a sad confession, and a statement too true of many

modern Christians even of the more reputable sort. What we need is a new baptism in the faith which appreciates the power of divine truth and sees and feels its reality. We need some spiritual solvent to reduce our knowledge to wisdom and our intellectual assent to a hearty consent. We need a more vivid and abiding apprehension of what God hath said, that we may live more in and upon his word. Nor is this anywhere more needed than upon the thrilling themes we have been considering. Though there is not a doctrine of our holy Christianity more largely treated in the Scriptures, more definitely asserted in all the creeds, more touchingly celebrated in our sacred songs, or more constantly acknowledged in our sermons and our prayers, than the coming again of Christ; yet there is hardly another article of faith so coldly, remotely, indefinitely and fruitlessly apprehended. Though it involves all our sublimest hopes, and is the basis of our most precious expectations, how few ever advert to it as a reality, or have any clear conceptions of it! Though it is the culmination of human hope and destiny, to how many is it a mere dead letter, awakening no emotion, exciting no concern and making no impression! Though nobody disputes it, yet who feels it or lays hold of it as a literal truth? As a vital thing, it has wellnigh dropped out of the creed. Its practical influences upon men's hearts and lives have become so feeble as to be almost imperceptible. When Christianity was pure, this doctrine was among the most vivifying of the faith. Men believed it, and it quenched the fear of death and made martyrdom a thing to be coveted; but now it stands upon our books like a superannuated fable. Then it beamed forth a light and life which lifted the soul up in sublime and joyous anticipations; but now it has become like the mute letters in the spelling of certain words, which, for all practical purposes, might as well be omitted as retained. These are deplorable facts. They speak badly for our experience in divine things, and tell a mournful tale for modern Christianity. Who, then, can mistake the plain duty of a faithful minister in such a case? The subject is too momentous to be trifled with. Our responsibilities are too solemn for us to be unconcerned. Hence, in much weakness, but with honesty of purpose, I have endeavored to raise my voice in serious warning, and made it my studied aim to give no "uncertain sound." Firmly believing that "He that shall come will come, and will not tarry," I have labored hard to advise you of his approach, and to have you wide awake, that that day may not overtake you unawares.

I have accordingly gone back to the original fountains of information upon the subject. I have tried to show where and how it is presented in the Scriptures. I have called your attention especially to Christ's own great predictions respecting it, and endeavored to brush away some of the cobwebs of a perverted erudition with which modern commentation has obscured and defaced it, and shown that the Savior means exactly what he says.

I have proven to you, in the second place, that Christ's coming is not to be a thousand years hence, at the end of a fancied millennium of universal righteousness, liberty and peace; that sin, oppression and antichristianism shall prevail in the world until he comes; and that only his personal presence and administrations on earth will make the millennium, or impart to this lower creation the redemption for which it sighs.

In the third place, I showed that the prevailing notion that when Christ comes it will be to depopulate, destroy and annihilate the earth, is the mere dream of poets, without foundation in the word of God. This earth shall endure forever, and in the light of its sister worlds roll on to all eternity. It will be changed in its fashion, but not destroyed. It will be renovated, but not depopulated. It will be restored, not annihilated. It will yet be the bright dwelling-place of righteousness and peace. The will of God shall yet be done here as it is in heaven. It will be the perpetual home of a saintly population, reflecting the glory of its Maker and rejoicing forever in his smiles. All that is vile in principle or impure in effect will be purged away; but its firm substance, its splendid scenery, and its impressive images of the Creator's power and the Redeemer's love, shall never end. After Christ shall come and set up his throne here, as Chalmers says, "There will be a firm earth, as we have at present, and a heaven stretched over it, as at present; and it is not by the absence of these, but the absence of *sin*, that the abodes of immortality will be characterized. There will be both heavens and earth in the next great administration, with only this specialty to mark it from the present one, that it will be a heavens and earth wherein dwelleth righteousness."

I next explained the resurrection, showing that the resurrection for which we are to aim and hope is an eclectic resurrection,—a resurrection of them that sleep in Jesus *from among* the dead at Christ's coming, and that "the rest of the dead" shall not live again until the thousand years are finished.

I have also exhibited the Scriptural evidences of the great fact that the Messiah's reign is to be in this world in a universal and eternal kingdom of bliss and glory.

I have endeavored to expound to you the mysterious doctrine and administrations of the coming judgment: how it now exists, how it will be manifested at Christ's coming, and how it will affect the various classes concerned.

I have unfolded to you the destiny of the Jewish race: their restoration, their sanctification, their blessed condition in the millennium, and the good that is yet to come to the world through them.

I have placed before you something of *the world to come*, where Christ's sovereign and personal rule is to be revealed,—

that *new earth*, in which the entire creation shall again return to its pristine loveliness, and where, as Heber sings,

> "On David's throne shall David's offspring reign,
> And the dry bones be warm with life again,
> Ten thousand harps attune the mystic song,
> Ten thousand thousand saints the strain prolong,—
> 'Worthy the Lamb! Omnipotent to save,
> Who died, who lives, triumphant o'er the grave!'"

I have further shown you that these are no mere dreams, now for the first time broached, or found only in the rhapsodies of enthusiastic minds. I have proven to you that such were substantially the hopes of the church before Christ came as the child of Mary; that Jesus and his inspired apostles spoke of these hopes as deeply founded in the purposes and promises of God; that they were entertained, preached and gloried in by those who received their instructions from apostolic lips, and by the Luthers, and Arndts, and Paleys, and Baxters, and Wesleys, and Halls, and Edwardses and Chalmerses of the first three hundred years of the Christian church; that no Christian ever disputed them previous to the time of Origen; and that they are now held and proclaimed by hundreds and thousands among the purest, the most eloquent, the most learned, and the most useful of the children of God on the face of the earth. How the church came to lose sight of these hopes I have also indicated. It was popery that obscured them and cast them into darkness. First came Origen's fanciful method of interpreting the Scriptures, casting uncertainty upon the clearest statements, and introducing a way of exposition which all men unite in lamenting and condemning. Then came the desire to render the Christian faith palatable to a Roman emperor, and then to the papal usurper, leading to a repudiation of a part of the Bible and the mutilation and interpolation of the writings of the fathers. And thus, as the joint work of Origen's vagaries and the sycophantic spirit and corrupt principles of some who came after him, a disposition was made of these great anticipations from which every good man should recoil with horror. It was a stroke of Satan to cheat the Bride of Jesus out of her sublimest dowry. To this day the church is more or less under the influence of that deception. Nor can we do duty to ourselves or to the truth of God, and yet patiently acquiesce in a decision brought about in a way so unchristian and unwarrantable. Nay, I feel confident that when once we have fairly examined this whole matter, the pure millenarian doctrine will be held and preached as one of the most glorious articles of our most holy faith.

But I have gone further than all this. I have not only maintained that Christ will come again to this world to judge, subdue, renovate and reign in it forever, but that he will come *very soon*. I have ventured to proclaim my fixed belief that his coming is near at hand. I do not know the day or the year; but I have shown you, as I think, that God does not mean that we should remain in total ignorance of the period of his coming. In every other great event that he has brought about in human affairs, he has given pre-intimations of the time when it would be; and we cannot suppose that the time of the great consummating event of all is shrouded in such perfect secrecy as that we can know nothing till it comes. We accordingly find various dates and signs described in the Scriptures, from which we may learn enough to prevent our being surprised by it.

In my last I gave three different methods by which light may be thrown upon this subject. First, the Scriptures furnish a system of septenaries, or sevens, from which we learn that Christ will come at the end of six thousand years from the creation of man; which period, according to our best information, will run out within the next twenty or forty years. We next find the duration of the papal dominancy, which is to be destroyed only when Christ comes, limited to twelve hundred and sixty years, which term must needs expire within ten or twenty years from the present date. In the third place, we find a description of the seven last plagues, in connection with the sixth of which Christ's coming is announced, and all of which up to the sixth have clearly been fulfilled, whilst we are now entering upon the sixth. These three processes of computation, independent but harmonious, unconnected yet mutually corroborative, are sufficient to prove to us that we are treading close upon the time when all God's purposes shall be fulfilled.

There is, however, still another method of gaining information upon this point, to which I will direct your attention. The Scriptures very minutely describe certain signs which are to precede the final advent, and direct us to look for those signs, and assure us that "when these things begin to come to pass" we may know that the great event is near, even at the door. Let us then trace some of these signs, and look to see whether they have as yet appeared or not.

1. The Scriptures very distinctly tell us that the period of Christ's coming shall be a period of abounding apostasy, skepticism and wickedness. I need not again repeat the passages on this point. "As the days of Noe were, so shall it be also in the days of the Son of man." As Milton says, "the first peculiar sign (of the second advent) is an extreme recklessness and impiety, and an almost universal apostasy." And what a distressing agreement to this do we find in the characteristics of the present times! Look at Christendom itself. About one-half of those who profess and call themselves Christians are wrapped up in the foul embrace of Popery, where it is the fashion, if not the law, to put aside the Scriptures as dangerous, to trust to the word of the priest for forgiveness, to pray to Mary as the great intercessor, to adore the pope as the vicegerent of God, to hold for doctrines the mere

commandments of men, and to look for admission into heaven through human works. The millions in the Greek and Oriental churches are scarcely any better in regard to what concerns the vital matters of evangelical godliness. Look even at Protestantism,—how fearfully corrupt in some of its branches! How divided and torn by the low bickerings of sect and schism! What vast numbers are in our churches as well as in papal churches who are nothing more than baptized infidels! How many who commune at our altars are not half persuaded of the truth of the professions which they make! Look at the moral and religious condition of the nations at large, even those the most enlightened and Christian. See how crime flourishes and infidelity vaunts itself. What are our secular newspapers but registers of depravity, avarice, ambition, lawlessness and sin? See the inefficiency of law or gospel to restrain the violence of passion, or to keep under the brazen iniquity which rears its head aloft on every side. Behold your crowded infidel clubs, your besotted revolutionary combinations, and your hardened and daring propagandists of falsehood, treason and all forms of social disruption. See with what popular favor the basest of men set themselves up as God's oracles, claiming inspiration from heaven whilst preaching death to the church and to the state, and listened to with admiration by thousands who still wish to be considered virtuous and even Christian. See with what readiness people reputed intelligent take up with the lowest delusions, and stand forth as the abettors and defenders of some of the foulest emissions of hell. Behold how even great men, professed theologians, editors, professors, lecturers and men in high places of influence, adopt, advocate and preach theories of pretended science and philosophy which unsettle the very foundations of piety and faith. What contempt for Christianity, and disrespect for its ministers, and callousness to its great truths, do we everywhere encounter! And may we not conclude, with the great Luther, that "God will not, cannot, suffer this wicked world much longer?"

2. Another sign of the Savior's coming is to be found in great revolutionary troubles, political perplexities and vast national agitations. The Savior himself, and all the prophets, have taught us this. And never have the universal political heavens been so shaken as in our day. When were human politics so confused, contradictory, perplexing and threatening as now? Look at them from one end of the world to the other. Who among the great ones of the earth can tell where he stands? Behold the strange alliances, the deep, sudden and mysterious antipathies, the unforeseen combinations of events, and the unknown tendencies of mighty inscrutable movements, which have been manifesting themselves all over the world in these last days. Who can tell what shall be next? If it is war, who knows where it will end? If it is peace, who is sure that it will not prove as disastrous as war? In either case, mighty dangers everywhere threaten. Democracy, republicanism, autocracy and military despotism have about equal chances; and neither has any rational hope. As things now are, no conceivable human arrangements can steer clear of the mighty maelstrom which seems to have drawn all the nations within the circle of its awful whirl. Men of wisdom, men of Ahithophel astuteness, are at their wits' end, and the prudent and the far-sighted are growing wild with amazement and fear. With all that can be done, things refuse to bend to any mortal control. The ship answers no more to the helm. There is not a government on earth that is not quaking with commotion. Every thing is moving, but whither politicians cannot tell.

3. A third sign of the nearness of the end is a stir and inquiry among many respecting the subject, leading to the conviction that Christ is at hand. This is set forth in two passages, the one in Daniel, the other in the Lord's prophecy

in the twenty-fifth of Matthew. The passage in Daniel is, "O Daniel, shut up the words, and seal the book, *even to the time of the end; many shall run to and fro, and knowledge shall be increased.*" That is, in the period of the end, as Michaelis interprets, "many shall give their sedulous attention to the understanding of these things;" or, according to a marginal note in an old English Bible, "many shall run to and fro to search the knowledge of these mysteries." Dr. Gill thus explains the passage:—"Towards the time of the end appointed, many shall be stirred up to inquire into these things delivered in this book, and will spare no pains or cost to get a knowledge of them; and, with the blessing of God upon them, the knowledge of this book of prophecy will be increased, things will appear clearer and plainer the nearer the accomplishment of them." Luther's rendering of it is as follows:—"And now, Daniel, shut up these words, and seal this book, until the last times; when many shall come over it, and find great understanding." Coke, Clarke, Henry and Duffield understand the passage in the same way. It is about equivalent to that other declaration in the same chapter and concerning the same period of the end,—"*The wise shall understand.*" And as the result of all this inquiry and enlightenment on the subject of prophecy, the Savior tells us that "*then* shall the kingdom of heaven be likened unto ten virgins which went out to meet the bridegroom, and *there was a cry made, Behold, the bridegroom cometh; go ye out to meet him.*"

And how evidently and significantly has this mark of the end been manifesting itself within the last fifty years! Though the multitude still turn from prophecy as from a sealed book, yet what a stir, anxiety and study has it awakened in many earnest minds! I have counted more than one hundred authors who have written and published nearly twice as many volumes on the subjects of unfulfilled prophecies since the present century began, and most of whom have advocated and proclaimed substantially the same views presented in these discourses. Many of them differ with each other; but they differ mostly as the clocks of the same city,—only in minutes, not in hours. Their leading conclusions are the same. In every denomination, and in every Christian country, the subject is being studied and agitated. Everywhere there are men of God proclaiming the great doctrine of Christ's speedy coming to reign with his saints upon the earth. In England, in Scotland, in France, in our own country, in Germany, in Norway, in Russia, in India, in the isles of the sea, the cry has been raised, "BEHOLD, THE BRIDEGROOM COMETH; GO YE OUT TO MEET HIM!" Never, never, since the days of the early Christians, has there been so much earnest longing, expecting, preaching, believing and praying upon the subject of the nearness of Christ's coming. The interest, the study and the faith are by no means as general as they should be, but general and intense, enlightened and earnest enough to warrant us in saying that this sign of the end has appeared.

4. Another indication to which the Scriptures refer upon this subject is the general shaking and crumbling of social order. "In the last days perilous times shall come." There shall be "dreamers who despise dominion, and speak evil of dignities, and of those things which they know not." God says, "I will shake all nations, and the Desire of nations shall come." "Yet once more I shake not the earth only, but also heaven." "I will overturn, overturn, overturn it, until he come whose right it is; and I will give it him."

And how manifestly are these signs fulfilling! What is now the leading watchword that is convulsing the whole earth from the equator to the poles? *Reform, reform, reform!* The church must be reformed; government must be reformed; every thing must be reformed. Nothing is any longer right or adequate for dotard humanity. Laws, creeds, politics, theology, worship, venerable customs, all are found fault with by the restless spirit that is abroad, and must be revised, changed, recast, and reconstructed on other models which cannot be agreed upon. The fathers of old have become mere infants; the intellectual giants of other times have dwindled into dwarfs; the great emancipators of the world have degenerated into dreaming schoolboys, who knew nothing of humanity's wants, and never comprehended the will of God or the good of man. Suddenly it has been discovered that our domestic institutions are wrong, that our marriage-laws are wrong, that our entire legislation is wrong, that the wisest cabinets are composed of fools, that our church arrangements are imbecile, that old-fashioned religion is mere hypocrisy and cant, and that whatever is, is wrong. Protestantism must needs have a new foundation, and men are tinkering to effect it. Catholicism must have an addition to its creed, and a special convention was just called to inaugurate the miserable absurdity. And we must have new recensions, and new liturgies, and new interpretations, and new distributions of powers in church and state, and even new gospels, until every thing rocks and totters in the throes of approaching dissolution. Young America, and young England, and young France, and young Italy, and young China, and the ruling spirit even where things have been stagnant for ages, now cry, "Down with the world's old props! Down with the rickety régime of other days!" And everybody is in the intensest earnest. As Carlyle says, "The age of shams is past." Every sect, party, clique, club and faction, and every individual man, seems to be determined that his own way shall carry. There is no yielding, no compromise, no ear open to the counselings of moderation or entreaty. All is being unsettled, canvassed, distracted and rendered impotent, except in that direction in which the wave may for the moment dash. Never before were such mighty conflicting forces at work in our world. Never before has there been such a deep and universal agitation upon all that respects the interests of man. Governments the most powerful, ideas the most potent and customs the most firmly rooted are becoming mere playthings in the hands of remorseless and determined revolution. Surely the signal for the end has come. This loud cry from every quarter for reform, change and something new, only proves that "SOCIETY IS SICK" and nearing its dissolution, and yet, like the sick man, imagines that if its bed were changed it would be well. Alas, alas, for the projects and dreamy hopes of modern reformers!

"The world is grown old, and her pleasures are past;
The world is grown old, and her form may not last;
The world is grown old, and trembles for fear,—
For sorrows abound, and *judgment is near!*

The sun in the heavens is languid and pale,
And feeble and few are the fruits of the vale,
And the hearts of the nations fail them for fear,—
For the world is grown old, and JUDGMENT IS NEAR!

The king on his throne, the bride in her bower,
The children of pleasure, all feel the sad hour;
The roses are faded, and tasteless the cheer,—
The world is grown old, and JUDGMENT IS NEAR!"

Only look abroad, my brethren, and see how thrones, powers, governments, superstitions, and all the old stabilities, are creaking, shaking, crumbling, dying. Behold how vain the help of man is. Consider how implacable is human dissatisfaction. Mark how the mind of the world is expecting some great, speedy, mysterious change, such as has never yet been. And is it not certain that—

"the old
And crazy earth has had her shaking fits
More frequent, and foregone her usual rest,
And nature seems with dim and sickly eye
To wait the close of all"?

I have read somewhere, in a very sagacious writer, that when happy changes are contemplated most people erroneously turn to the quarters of light for the signs of its approach. This has ever been man's mistake when looking for the fulfillment of God's great purposes, and is the mistake of many now. People are looking for the setting up of Christ's kingdom, and the introduction of millennial glory by reforming and rebaptizing present modes of effort and thought. But so it will not be. God's method of progress is to make darkness the way to light, death the prelude to life, despair the introduction to salvation, and corruption and confusion the road to order and glory. It is not in what seems hopeful, but in what seems gloomy and untoward, that we are to look for the signs of the speedy forthcoming of God's wonder-working goodness. It is the stirring upon the face of the dark waters that gives prognostic of the breaking forth of light, life and beauty. The bursting glories of spring come directly out of the bleak winter. It is from the corrupting seed that we obtain the harvest. The darkest hour is said to be that which immediately precedes the day. The period most hopeful is that when the apparent motives for despondency are most overwhelming. The stress of the controversy between hope and fear always falls upon the eve of triumph. Those dim hours of dismay to the scattered followers of Christ at his crucifixion were but the preludes to the bringing in of light and immortality for man. The bloody persecutions under the Roman emperors which threatened the extinction of Christianity were the immediate precursors of its victory over even the throne of the Cæsars. And so the Scriptures teach that it will be in the ushering in of the great consummation. The sun must darken and the moon withhold her light, and then shall the Sun of righteousness arise with healing in his wings.

People think they see signs of promise in the movements of reform. They think to give the church a better shape, and the state a better government, and the world a freer Bible, and that thus the millennium will come. I have no confidence in any such hopes. I see more of promise in the darkest features of the times than in all these pious and patriotic dreams. I look around me, and find men uniting, oft unconsciously, in pronouncing past experiments inadequate to accomplish what was expected of them. Once it was thought that Protestantism would soon regenerate the world; and yet so little progress has it made in two hundred years that some of its own distinguished children, in every department of it, are proclaiming in many ways that it will not do without mending. Some thought that the great Bible, Tract, Sunday-school and missionary movements would soon win the nations to faith in Jesus; and yet the world is perhaps more wicked now than it has been since Noah's flood. Skeptics in the church, and skeptics out of the church, are rising up to pronounce all our boasted efforts a failure. Many are losing confidence in the Bible and that simple evangelism in which they hoped, and are going back to Rome, to unbelief, to "spiritualism," or to some other low ism of natural or Satanic religion. I deplore the facts, and mourn that people should have so little faith, and reason so illogically. And yet in this very darkness I read the promise of coming light. In this very misgiving, desperation and gloom, I see the argument for the speedy springing forth of glorious and unfading hopes, not as human reason calculates, but as God purposes. I behold in it the rapid winding up of the present dispensation to give place to that better state of things of which the prophets all have spoken. Statesmen and churchmen see in it the unmistakable evidences of unprecedented changes, though they widely differ as to what those changes are to be. I go to the "sure word of prophecy," and there I find the mystery explained. That holy book which is the world's great light on so many important things does not fail me here.

Sir Robert Peel has said, "Every aspect of the present times, viewed in the light of the past, warrants the belief that we are on the eve of a universal change." Dr. Arnold, in his Lectures on History, says, "Modern history appears to be not only a step in advance of ancient history, but *the last step;* it appears to bear marks of *the fullness of time*, as if there would be no future history beyond it. . . . We have the full amount of earth's resources before us, and they seem inadequate to supply life for another period of human history." Professor Robinson says, "Before another half-century shall have rolled away, there will be seen revolutions in the Oriental mind, and the world, of which no one now has any foreboding. The time is short: the crisis rushes on." The London Quarterly says, "The long pent-up winds are beginning to break loose; and the sudden bursts of tempest that have swept over Europe these few years past are precursors of the world's last desolating storm." Bishop Chase asks, "Are not these signs and prognostics of the speedy coming of our Lord to judgment?" And when I look at all these things:—the six thousand years nearing their close; the period of Popery's dominancy expiring; the sixth vial pouring out; the earth exhibiting all the features that are to characterize the last days; the nations distressed and their leaders tremulous with fear; history closing up; all the old landmarks of society invaded and simultaneously giving way more or less before resistless innovation; the predicted cry, *Behold, he cometh,* ringing through every land; the whole world becoming like a magazine, where a single spark may produce a universal explosion that must carry all existing things to desolation; our great men, and devout men, and nearly all thinking men, proclaiming the presence of some unknown change; and the book of God, which I have taken as my guide, telling me that when these things begin to come to pass my Savior and his kingdom are at hand:—would I not deserve to be classed with infidels and scoffers if I did not believe, and merit the condemnation of a hypocritical and faithless watchman if I did not declare, that so it is, and that "THE END OF ALL THINGS IS AT HAND"?

That many will give neither heed nor credit to these statements, is to be expected. It was so in Noah's day. When Lot warned Sodom, "he seemed as one that mocked." And Christ and his prophets have foretold that it will be so again. But, if people will not examine into these things, and, as a consequence, are found unready when the Savior comes, they will have themselves to thank for their calamities. For my own part, I will believe and preach that the Day of the Lord is at hand, and would rather encounter the sneers and vulgar taunts of all mankind and be found ready when my Savior comes, than to be accounted the most sober of theologians and enjoy the fame of the most revered favorite of popular laudation, and have that day find me unfaithful to my duty and unprepared for my change. I have been unable to fix upon any precise time. Some profess to know it; I do not. Christ may come in three, seven, or ten years; or not so soon. A few developments may make the matter certain. But I wish to bear my distinct testimony, that I believe his coming is at hand, and that we ought to be ready and expecting it any and every day.

Nor am I alone in these convictions. "The Lord cometh!" says Krummacher. "Never did the church witness such a constellation of signs of the near coming of Christ as now." That "ripe scholar and profound student of prophecy," Dr. Elliott, says, "We are come so near to the day of the Son of man, that the generation now living shall very possibly not have passed away before its fulfillment; yea, that perhaps our own eyes may witness, without the intervention of death, that astonishing event of the consummation." Pym says, "Upon us the ends of the world are come; and this generation shall witness the advent of the Lord in glory to introduce the millenary reign of righteousness and peace." Cunninghame says, "All the events of our own times,—the growing disorders of the body politic,—the fears and expectations of men,—the deep persuasion of an impending convulsion inrooted in every thinking mind,—the solemn and awakening declarations of Scripture,—the clear and unequivocal voice of prophecy,—every sign, every promise, every testimony,—unite in announcing his (Christ's) approach." Habershon says, "The time undoubtedly is near at hand when the redemption of the body shall be experienced, and when these bodies of our humiliation shall be fashioned like unto his glorious body." "It is reasonable to conclude," says Faber, "that the time is not very far distant when the personal Word shall begin to tread the winepress of the fierceness and wrath of Almighty God." Cumming says, "We are led from all signs to infer that the meeting-place of all the lines of God's providential work on earth is very near. . . . It is very remarkable that all the great times and dates of prophecy meet and mingle about the year 1864–6. . . . I do feel, that if that be not the close of the age that now is, and the commencement of a better one, it will be a time unprecedented since the beginning." Brooks says, "The signs of the second advent in the state of the world at large are such as to impress my own mind with a deep persuasion that we are on the eve of events of immense—*immense* importance to mankind." "From whatever dates we reckon," says Bickersteth, "we cannot but consider that the time of the end is drawing near, and that awful events of judgment and mercy are before us." "The happy hour is not far hence," says Taylor. "It is near, and hasteth greatly. . . . This generation and century will witness his glorious epiphany!" "Almost all writers on prophecy," says Cox, "who have studied its mystic numbers, make them terminate at periods towards which we are rapidly approaching. However different these views and schemes, they agree in this, that within a few years from the present time some of the greatest events ever witnessed will take place." I might give many more such statements.

Let it not be said that these are fanatic ravings, or loose vociferations of ignorant people. They are the deliberately-formed conclusions of our most competent, most pious, and most profound investigators of God's holy revelations. Men of the highest order of mind, scholars of the profoundest erudition, Christians of the most enlightened piety, after years and years of patient, laborious, prayerful, and independent study, and in the face of a speedily-appearing Judge, have thus solemnly proclaimed to the world that we are now standing upon the very eve of the Savior's coming. And he who can rise up and pronounce their testimony false, must, under the circumstances, assume a daring, assurance and responsibility at which a pious heart should be appalled.

Neither is it a useless or unimportant thing to have the solemn truth distinctly and pointedly brought before the people of both the church and the world. The subject of the speedy coming again of the Lord is one of the intensest practical value and of comfort to the believing heart. It need effect no one but for good. It may be awful to think of it; but it will be vastly more awful to have to encounter those scenes unprepared. Nor can there be any just reason for any one to dread the subject. It is the master-theme of the gospel and the final chorus in which all the harmony of the Scriptures concentrates and combines. People regard it as only terrific, whereas the Scriptures commingle with it the fulfillment of all man's sublimest joy. Jesus says, "*When these things begin to come to pass, then* LOOK UP AND LIFT UP YOUR HEADS: FOR YOUR REDEMPTION DRAWETH NIGH." Hear and consider, O ye of little faith. "Are you so enamored of sickness that you have no longing for the resurrection-body and the beauteous robes of incorruption and immortality?

Are you so enamored of aches, and ills, and losses, and bereavements, and pains, and battles, and famine, and plague, and pestilence, that you do not wish them to be done with? Why, every statement in this blessed book leads us to the otherwise-delightful conclusion that the nearer the great issue comes the happier God's people should feel. The sound that rings sweet and audible from the skies amidst the crash of nations, the overturning of thrones, the dissolution of dynasties, and wars and rumors of wars, is, *Lift up your heads,—your redemption is near!* And if I should be able only to point out a few weeds floating upon the sea that indicate we are approaching the great continent of glory,—if I should be able only to give an Alpine flower here and there, however fragile, yet a sweet messenger of the coming spring,—every true Christian ought to rejoice and be glad that there are tokens of a day when a *genesis* shall pass upon the earth better and brighter than the first, and a paradise come in as the coronal of time more glorious than that which was its dawn." So discourses one who, from Covent Garden, is warming more hearts with these momentous themes than any other living man. And many have expressed themselves to the same effect.

Luther once held in his hand a necklace of agates, and said, "I would readily eat up this to-day for the judgment to come to-morrow." "Blessed consummation of this weary and sorrowful world!" says the eloquent Irving; "I give it welcome,—I hail its approach,—I wait its coming more than they that watch for the morning. Over the wrecks of a world I weep,—over broken hearts of parents,—over suffering infancy,—over the unconscious clay of sweet innocents,—over the untimely births that have never seen the light, or have just looked upon it and shut their eyes until the glorious light of the resurrection-morn. O my Lord, come away! Hasten with all thy congregated ones! My soul desireth to see the

King in his beauty, and the beautiful ones whom he shall bring along with him." "Come forth out of thy royal chambers, O Prince of all the kings of earth!" says England's greatest poet. "Put on the visible robes of thy imperial majesty. Take up that unlimited sceptre which thy Almighty Father hath bequeathed thee. For now the voice of thy Bride calls thee, and all creatures sigh to be renewed.". "How cheering the hope," says Cox,—"how cheering the hope, amidst the din of war, the shouts of false joy, the yell of idolatry and the groans of creation, that a period is hastening when peace shall stretch its shady wings over the sons of men, when rivers of joy shall water this vale of tears, when cherubim to cherubim shall cry, HOLY, HOLY, HOLY IS THE LORD GOD OF HOSTS; THE WHOLE EARTH IS FULL OF HIS GLORY!" "Oh that Christ would remove the covering, draw aside the curtains of time and rend the heavens and come down!" says Rutherford. "Oh that shadows and night were gone, that the day would break, and that He who feedeth among the lilies would cry to his heavenly trumpeters, Make ready, let us go down and fold together the four corners of the earth!" "Hasten, O my Savior, the time of thy return," says Baxter. "Send forth thine angels, and let that dreadful joyful trumpet sound. Delay not, lest the living give up their hopes; delay not, lest earth should grow like hell and thy church be crumbled to dust. . . . Oh, hasten that great resurrection-day, when the seed that thou sowest corruptible shall come forth incorruptible, and graves that received but rottenness and retain but dust shall return thee glorious stars and suns. Thy desolate Bride saith, *Come.* The whole creation saith, *Come, even so, come, Lord Jesus!*" And why should not every believing heart look up and respond with rapture, "AMEN, AND AMEN"? View the untold glories which Christ shall bring with him for every waiting soul. Consider the sublimities of happiness which that great consummation shall spread forever upon this smitten world. And why should we start back from the conviction that it is near?

> "Thrice blessed hope,
> If home like this await the weary soul!
> Look up, thou stricken one! Thy wounded heart
> Shall bleed no more at sorrow's stern control."

When the blessed Savior was about to leave this world, he said, "I go to prepare a place for you. And, if I go and prepare a place for you, *I will come again* and receive you unto myself; that where I am there ye may be also." And hardly had he reached the threshold of his Father's sublime and holy habitation until he shouted back, "SURELY I COME QUICKLY." Nor does the church enter into the rapture of her hopes until she brings herself to respond with John, "AMEN; EVEN SO, COME, LORD JESUS!" Therein lies our highest joy. All that is dear and precious is linked with that glorious coming. And when He who is our life shall appear, then shall we also appear with him in glory. Then all wrongs shall be righted, the long-severed united and long-deferred hope be fulfilled. Every thing now is disjointed, depressed, sickly and sad. We are surrounded with funerals, graves, diseases, crimes and tears. There is no home so happy, and no heart so joyous, but it has in it the deep undertones of sorrow and trouble.

> "There is no flock, however watched and tended,
> But one dead lamb is there;
> There is no fireside, howsoe'er defended,
> But hath one vacant chair.
> The air is full of farewells of the dying,
> And mournings for the dead;
> The heart of Rachel for her children crying
> Will not be comforted."

But when the expected Savior comes, these woes and griefs shall have an end. Then shall the buried babe and slumbering boy of promise awake from the cold dark sleep of years, no more to writhe under fierce disease, or to be torn from parental love. Then shall those loved forms on which the clods are pressing, and over whose damp resting-places many a winter's snow has lain and many a summer's flower bloomed, come forth to light and life never again to fall under the power of corruption. Then shall the broken and scattered household be regathered to separate no more. Then shall be the coronation-day for them that have labored and suffered for Jesus. Then shall the martyr receive his crown and the saint his ineffable portion. Then shall tears cease to flow and sadness to depress. Then shall the exile reach his happy home and the toiling pilgrim find his everlasting rest. Then shall the worshipper look upon the face of his God and the faithful servant receive the transporting commendation and welcome of his Lord. Then shall earth's long-predicted sabbath come and the eternal jubilee of the redeemed begin. Then shall the mystery of divine compassion be consummated, and this prodigal orb of ours, restored once more to her Father's smiles, take her place in the sisterhood of unfallen worlds, reflecting in richer lustre and celebrating in grander songs the praises of Him who made it and the mercies of Him that redeemed it with his blood.

No, no, no; the doctrine of the Savior's speedy coming is not a thing of gloom and sadness. It is *gospel*,—pure gospel, —nothing but GOOD NEWS. If it has any thing distressing in it, you yourself must put it there by your hard-heartedness, your prayerlessness and unforsaken sin. If you have fixed your heart and faith on Jesus as your prophet, priest and king, you have naught to fear and every thing to hope. They that put their trust in him shall never be put to confusion. As the mountains are round about Jerusalem, so the Lord encampeth round about them that fear him. Hath he not said, "He that confesseth me before men, him will I also confess before my Father, and before his holy angels"? Is not the immutable covenant made and sealed, pledging all the sublime attributes of God for the believer's safety? If he spared not his own Son, but delivered him up freely for us all, will he not with him also freely give us all things? The only question is, *Have you submitted to Christ?* Have you given up to do all your duty as he enjoins it? Have you accepted of him as your Savior and your hope? Have you identified yourself with him in the fellowship of his church? Is he your alpha and your omega?—your all in all? Then fear not. Only be faithful a little longer, and the day will come which will be to you a gladder day than ever you thought it possible for you to see. And as you behold the fig leaves putting forth as the heralds of its approach, "look up and lift up your head; for your redemption draweth nigh."

But God forbid that I should cry peace where there is no peace, or encourage hope where there is no hope. If any of you are yet prayerless, without submission to Christ, loving self or the world more than God, and standing aloof from the gospel-way of life, you may well be alarmed and tremble at what is before you. The day of the Savior's revelation will be a day of fearful vengeance upon them that know not God and obey not the gospel of his Son. And better, a thousand times better, that you should now be filled with all Belshazzar's terror, if it will lead you to repentance, than to go on in carnal comfort and meet your coming Judge with hearts unreconciled and sins unforgiven. And yet you need not tremble with utter despair. You are not where the rich man called for help but found it not. The door of salvation still is open. The proclamation of forgiving mercy still rings in your ears. Wicked and negligent as you have been, you may yet come and share in the sublimest joys Christianity has to give. Your injured and weeping Redeemer still stretches out to you his hands and bids you *Come*. The Spirit and the Bride say

Come. And whosoever will, let him come. Oh, how great is the mercy which some of you have abused, and the compassion and privileges which you have set at naught! Nevertheless, here I am to-day, with authority from God in heaven to offer to you a free forgiveness and eternal life, if you will but accept the gift upon the plain and easy terms therewith annexed:—"*Turn yourselves and live.*" Will you do it? *You*, prayerless, careless father, mother, child, reviler, prodigal, blasphemer, scoffer, neglecter of God, will you do it? Your time is growing short. Your day of grace will soon be over. Your summer-time of hope will soon have passed away. Will you now start to be a child of God and heir of heaven? There is room enough; will you come and occupy it? The robes, and palms, and harps and crowns of righteousness and life are soon to be distributed; will you come and put in your application? Oh, let those stiff necks bend, those hard hearts relent, those stubborn wills surrender; and send up your prayers to the mercy-seat *now* ere it is changed to an inexorable judgment-throne. Gracious God! pity poor sinners, and spare them yet a little, and plead mightily with them that they may repent and live! Oh, suffer them not to perish forever; but so move them by thy good Spirit that they may seek thy face and come with all thy saints into the joys of that nearing world for which we long and wait. And then and there we will ever sing, "UNTO HIM THAT LOVED US, AND WASHED US FROM OUR SINS IN HIS OWN BLOOD, AND HATH MADE US KINGS AND PRIESTS UNTO GOD, TO HIM BE GLORY AND DOMINION FOREVER AND EVER. AMEN."

The grace of our Lord Jesus Christ, the love of God, and the fellowship of the Holy Ghost, be with you all, now, henceforth, and evermore. Amen.

The New Jerusalem.

O MOTHER dear, Jerusalem,
  When shall I come to thee?
When shall my sorrows have an end?—
  Thy joys when shall I see?
O happy harbor of the saints!
  O sweet and pleasant soil!
In thee no sorrows can be found,—
  No grief, no care, no toil.

In thee no sickness is at all,
  No hurt, nor any sore;
There is no death, nor ugly sight,
  But life for evermore.
No dimming cloud o'ershadows thee,
  No cloud nor darksome night;
But every soul shines as the sun,
  For God himself gives light.

There, lust and lucre cannot dwell,
  There, envy bears no sway;
There is no hunger, thirst, nor heat,
  But pleasures every way.
Jerusalem! Jerusalem!
  Would God I were in thee!
Oh that my sorrows had an end,
  Thy joys that I might see!

No pains, no pangs, no grieving grief,
  No woful night, is there;
No sigh, no sob, no cry is heard—
  No well-a-day, no fear.
Jerusalem the city is
  Of God our King alone;
The Lamb of God, the light thereof,
  Sits there upon his throne.

O God! that I Jerusalem
  With speed may go behold!
For why? the pleasures there abound
  Which here cannot be told.

Thy turrets and thy pinnacles
With carbuncles do shine,
With jasper, pearl, and chrysolite,
Surpassing pure and fine.

Thy houses are of ivory,
Thy windows crystal clear,
Thy streets are laid with beaten gold—
There angels do appear.
Thy walls are made of precious stone,
Thy bulwarks diamonds square,
Thy gates are made of Orient pearl—
O God, if I were there!

Within thy gates nothing can come
That is not passing clean;
No spider's web, no dirt, no dust,
No filth, may there be seen.
Jehovah, Lord, now come away,
And end my grief and plaints;
Take me to thy Jerusalem,
And place me with thy saints.

Who there are crown'd with glory great,
And see God face to face;
They triumph still and aye rejoice—
Most happy is their case.
But we that are in banishment
Continually do moan;
We sigh, we mourn, we sob, we weep,
Perpetually we groan.

Our sweetness mixed is with gall,
Our pleasures are but pain,
Our joys not worth the looking on—
Our sorrows aye remain.
But there they live in such delight,
Such pleasures and such play,
That unto them a thousand years
Seem but as yesterday.

O my sweet home, Jerusalem!
Thy joys when shall I see?

Thy King sitting upon his throne,
  And thy felicity?
Thy vineyards and thy orchards,
  So wonderfully rare,
Are furnish'd with all kinds of fruit,
  Most beautifully fair.

There David stands, with harp in hand,
  As master of the choir;
A thousand times that man were bless'd
  That might his music hear.
There Mary sings "Magnificat,"
  With tunes surpassing sweet;
And all the virgins bear their part,
  Singing about her feet.

"Te Deum," doth St. Ambrose sing,
  St. Austin doth the like;
Old Simeon and Zacharie
  Have not their songs to seek.
There Magdalene hath left her moan,
  And cheerfully doth sing,
With all blest saints whose harmony
  Through every street doth ring.

Jerusalem! Jerusalem!
  Thy joys fain would I see;
Come, quickly, Lord, and end my grief,
  And take me home to thee!
Oh, paint thy name in my forehead,
  And take me hence away,
That I may dwell with thee in bliss,
  And sing thy praises aye!

Jerusalem, the happy home—
  Jehovah's throne on high!
O sacred city, queen, and wife,
  Of Christ eternally!
O comely queen, with glory clad,
  With honor and degree,
All fair thou art, exceeding bright,
  No spot there is in thee.

I long to see Jerusalem,
  The comfort of us all;
For thou art fair and beautiful,—
  None ill can thee befall.
In thee, Jerusalem, I say,
  No darkness dare appear;
No night, no shade, no winter foul,—
  No time doth alter there.

No candle needs, no moon to shine,
  No glittering stars to light;
For Christ, the King of righteousness,
  Forever shineth bright.
A Lamb unspotted, white, and pure,
  To thee doth stand in lieu
Of light,—so great the glory is
  Thine heavenly King to view.

He is the King of kings, beset
  In midst his servants' sight;
And they, his happy household, all
  Do serve him day and night;
There, there the choir of angels sing;
  There the supernal sort
Of citizens, which hence are rid
  From dangers deep, do sport.

There be the prudent prophets all,
  The apostles six and six,
The glorious martyrs in a row,
  And confessors betwixt.
There doth the crew of righteous men
  And nations all consist;
Young men and maids that here on earth
  Their pleasures did resist.

The sheep and lambs that hardly 'scap'd
  The snare of death and hell
Triumph in joy eternally,
  Whereof no tongue can tell;
And though the glory of each one
  Doth differ in degree,
Yet is the joy of all alike
  And common as we see.

There love and charity do reign,
  And Christ is all in all,
Whom they most perfectly behold
  In joy celestial.
They love, they praise,—they praise, they love;
  They "Holy, holy," cry;
They neither toil, nor faint, nor end,
  But laud eternally.

Oh, happy thousand times were I,
  If, after wretched days,
I might with listening ears conceive
  Those heavenly songs of praise
Which to the eternal King are sung
  By happy wights above,—
By saved souls and angels sweet,
  Who love the God of love.

Oh, passing happy were my state,
  Might I be worthy found
To wait upon my God and King,
  His praises there to sound.
O mother dear, Jerusalem,
  When shall I come to thee?
When shall my sorrows have an end?—
  Thy joys when shall I see?

Yet once again I pray thee, Lord,
  To quit me from all strife,
That to thy hill I may attain,
  And dwell there all my life,
With cherubims and seraphims,
  And souls of holy men,
To sing thy praise, O God of hosts,
  Forever, and amen.

David Dickson.

Notes and Additional Observations.

Note A. First Discourse, P. 10.

OPINIONS OF DISTINGUISHED MEN AS TO THE TIMES IN WHICH WE LIVE.

Luther, in his lifetime, said, "I am persuaded that verily the day of judgment is not far off; yea, will not be absent three hundred years longer. The voice will soon be heard, 'Behold the Bridegroom cometh!'" (See Chap. I. of his *Table-Talk*.) Luther died in 1546.

Archdeacon Browne, of England, in 1835, said that he was "strongly impressed with the conviction that our lot has fallen under the solemn period emphatically designated in Daniel as the time of the end!"

Dr. Duff, of Scotland, recently said, "Surely the present crisis is constraining us to arise, and that with our whole heart. Surely it looks as if in response to the sighing of the whole creation groaning in uneasiness and pain, through long bygone ages, for the times of the restitution of all things,—surely in answer to the plaintive cry of the myriad martyrs from under the altar, who age after age have been uttering their longing cry, 'How long, O Lord, how long?'—He who is seated on the throne on high is now indicating, by no ordinary signs, that he is to arise and assume his great power, and to manifest himself as really King and Governor among the nations. Surely, in the language of one of old, the great Messiah is about to come forth from his royal chamber,—about to put on the invisible robes of his imperial majesty, and to take up the unlimited sceptre which his Father hath bequeathed to him. Even now, in the ear of faith, and almost in the ear of sense, we may hear the distant noise of the chariot-wheels of the mighty Saviour-King, coming forth conquering and to conquer, amid the shaking of the nations from pole to pole. Every nation has of late been upheaving from its ancient settled foundations; and there will be mightier upheavings still, and that right speedily,—all preparing the way for the new heavens and the new earth, in which righteousness will forever dwell !"

Macaulay, the essayist, wrote, in 1831, "Many Christians believe that the Messiah will shortly establish a kingdom on the earth and reign visibly over all its inhabitants. Whether this doctrine be orthodox or not, we shall not inquire. The number of people who hold it is very much greater than the number of Jews residing in England. Many of those who hold it are distinguished by rank, wealth, and ability; it is preached from pulpits both of the Scottish and of the English Church. Noblemen and members of Parliament have written in defence of it,—who expect 'that before this generation shall pass away, all the kingdoms of the earth will be swallowed up in one Divine Empire.' "—*Essays on the Jews.*

Dr. N. L. Rice says, "The world is now rapidly approaching another great epoch, the most important in the history of our world." "We live in an eventful day." "The time cannot be distant when great changes are to take place among the nations. It is our wisdom, therefore, both to examine carefully and prayerfully the prophecies whose fulfilment is yet future, and to watch passing events, which throw light upon these prophecies. It is a great misfortune to mistake the character of the age in which we live, and to fail to understand the signs which God gives, that his people may act with him their part."—*Signs of the Times.*

Rev. Hollis Read, author of "God in History," says, "We are living in a very remarkable period of the world's history. A very general impression obtains in all reflecting minds that we are on the confines of another of those signal crises which mark the history of our race. The signs of the times are strangely significant." "There is a feeling in the human breast that despotism, bloodshed, fraud, oppression, and unbridled lust, have, in defiance of Heaven, rioted long enough, and that a righteous God will soon rise in his wrath and make a short work. This prophetic yearning for deliverance—this instinctive prophecy of the human heart—is not peculiar to the Christian: the Hindoo, the Mohammedan, the Papist, feels it. The world waits the coming change."—*The Coming Crisis of the World.*

Dr. Stephen H. Tyng says, "Whatever may be the will of God, who keeps the times and seasons in his own power, in prolonging the days, of which we can know nothing, we may, and must, still say, that all the lines of prophecy meet in this designated year 1868, as the time of the glorious coming of the Son of man,—the manifestation of the Lord Jesus in the glory of his kingdom, according to the testimony of Scripture."—Articles on *The Kingdom of God.*

Dr. Baird, in Rochester, 1852, remarked that "no well-informed man can look upon the world as it is, without coming to the conclusion that some great consummation is about to take place."

Dr. Hitchcock, of Amherst, says, "In a very short time—far shorter than we imagine—all the scenes of futurity will be to us a thrilling reality!"—*The Future Condition and Destiny of the Earth.*

Dr. G. B. Cheever writes, "It is impossible to look upon a more sublime spectacle than that which rises to the mind of a spiritual observer at the present crisis. A voice like the archangel's trumpet is crying, 'Cast up, cast up the highway; gather out the stones; lift up a standard to the people!' Event rolls on after event. As the purposes of God are advancing nearer to their completion, ten thousand significant events sweep onward in the train. The convergency of all things to the point becomes more and more rapid. Meaning begins to appear in events before shrouded in mystery. An omnipotent plan, it is manifest, is in operation, and the trains laid with Divine wisdom are fast completing."—*Grant's Nestorians*, p. 360.

Prof. George Bush says, "If we take the ground of right reason, we must believe that the present age is one expressly foretold in prophecy, and that it is just opening upon the crowning consummation of all prophetic declarations."

Dr. Bogie said, in 1839, "Reflect what mighty changes have occurred in Europe in less than thirty years; what rapid revolutions have taken place within the last six years; changes which no one ten years ago could have imagined he would live to see. The next generation will behold more wonderful things, and may see the commencement of the thousand years."—*Crisis*, p. 309.

These are the declarations of *Christians*. The *Jewish* mind has been brought to like convictions and anticipations. Rabbi Carillon, of Jamaica Island, affirms that "there is every reason to believe that the latter days are not far off: let us, therefore, be on the watch and in continual prayer." It is said by a European writer, that "Jews who never before thought of a Messiah begin now to say, 'These are the days of travail which precede His coming.'" Solomon Herschel, Rabbi of the chief synagogue of the Jews in London, is represented as saying that his people, after close investigation of the subject, think, with him, that the Messiah's advent cannot be delayed beyond 1863. And it was announced in the public journals in 1852 that there were then thousands of Jews in Jerusalem all anxiously expecting the Messiah.

And what *divines* have uttered as their learning of the Scriptures, *statesmen and philosophers* have also declared as their reading of the indications of events.

Hon. Rufus Choate remarked, in 1851, "It has seemed to me as if the prerogatives of crowns, and the rights of men, and the hoarded-up resentments and revenges of a thousand years, were about to unsheath the sword for a conflict, in which blood shall flow, as in the Apocalyptic vision, to the bridles of the horses, and in which a whole age of men shall pass away, in which the great bell of Time shall sound out another hour, in which society itself shall be tried by fire and steel, whether it is of nature and nature's God or not."

Sir Robert Peel said in Parliament, in 1842, "Every aspect of the present times, viewed in the light of the past, warrants the belief that we are on the eve of a universal change."

Louis Kossuth not long ago said, "I say this prophetically. I have already read it in the book of Providence, which is made to be a revelation to mankind. The destiny of mankind has come to the turning-point of centuries. There is a cry of alarm upon the ostensible approach of universal danger. The despotic governments of Europe feel their approaching death. The decisive struggle is near. It will be the last in mankind's history."

Dr. Arnold observes, "Modern history appears to be not only a step in advance of ancient history, but the last step; it appears to bear marks of the fulness of time,—as if there would be no future history beyond it. My sense of the evils of the times that are coming, and of the prospects to which I am bringing up my poor children, is overwhelming."—*Modern History*, p. 38.

The Living Age says, "We stand at a great starting-point in the history of the world. Old things are about to pass away, and we know not what shall be the new. The continent of Europe, startled by the warning trumpet of 1848, has cowered into silence; all faces gather blackness, and men's hearts fail them for fear of what is coming on the earth."

And the spirit of *the Press generally* is to the same effect.

The Presbyterian Expositor says, "We live in a day of unprecedented excitement and agitation; and the minds of all intelligent men are looking for great events. No wonder that some are expecting the second coming of the Son of God to subdue to himself all kingdoms and reign on earth a thousand years. Beyond a question, we are on the eve of great events."

The New York Evangelist, in 1848, remarked, "Had the present state of Europe been prophesied fifty years ago, would any have credited the prophecy? We believe that in this year we have seen the beginning of the end."

The Christian Luminary says, "This truly is an age of wonders, changes, and revolutions. No thinking man can open his eyes upon the great events that are passing before us, without being impressed with the signs of the times, and constrained to admit that important scenes are about to be opened to the view of an astonished world. The seals are opening; the trumpets are sounding; the nations are shaking; signs are seen in the heavens and on earth."

A writer in *The Christian Review* says, "I am strongly persuaded that the present generation of men stand upon the very eve of the mightiest revolution that the annals of time record." "A silent, rapid, irresistible preparation has been making,—making, perhaps, for a sudden, subversive, and universal change. What will it be?"

And *The Scientific Mechanic* affirms, "No man now living has ever witnessed, nor has any historian recorded, so interesting a position of the world and the nations thereof, as is presented at the present time. . . . Men are looking upon the present convulsed state of the world as portending great political reforms; but, in view of certain facts which cannot be disputed, we think it reasonable that faithful Christians should look for something more important. The world is now just about six thousand years old Viewing the fact in connection with the unprecedented tempests, inundations, earthquakes, and famines which have occurred within the last few years, and the present extraordinary perplexity and commotions among the nations, we cannot avoid the anticipation of events incomparably more important than any that have been prognosticated by the secular press."

Church of England Quarterly Review.—"We live in times when the Christian and the Infidel, the statesman and the divine, seem to agree in the expectation that some great crisis is at hand. The public mind, both at home and abroad, is held in the calm of a feverish suspense. New and strange blasphemies are coming to the birth; the foundations of the State are loosing, and the Church of God is beset and assailed on every side. . . . All eyes are fixed with an eager gaze upon the dark and coming future."

Lord Shaftesbury, at a recent meeting for promoting Christianity among the Jews, said, "The signs of the times are really unparalleled and most wonderful. And I think it does not proceed from any spirit of fanaticism, if we say that we really believe they are tending to some final consummation."

Note B. First Discourse, p. 29.

ON THE MEANING OF γενεα ("GENERATION") IN MATT. XXIV. 34.

Both the Syriac and the German versions render the word γενεα, in this place, by terms which signify a continuous *race*, rather than the people living within one limited period of time.

The annotators in the Berlenberg Bible also understand it to refer to "des Jüdischen Volks, die Nachkommen mitgerechnet."—*in loc.*

Flacius Illyricus takes the Savior's declaration as equivalent to "gentum Judaicam non interituram prorsus."—*Scrip. Clav., art. Generatio.*

Joseph Mede, one of the most learned men of his age, says, "γενεα signifies not only *ætas*, but *gens, natio progenies;* and so ought to be here taken, viz.: that *the nation of the Jews should not perish till all these things were fulfilled.*"

Dr. Clarke renders the phrase, Matt. xxiii. 36, "*Επι την γενεαν ταυτην, upon this race of men*, viz.: *the Jews.*" On Matt. xi. 16, he renders the same phrase the same way, and says, "so the word γενεα is often to be understood in the Evangelists." On Matt. xii. 39, he says, further, that this word should be taken as denoting *a race of people*, and that so it "should be translated in most other places in the Gospels; for our Lord, in general, uses it to point out *the Jewish people.* This translation is the key to unlock some very obscure passages in the Evangelists." And in the passage in question he explains the Savior's declaration to mean that "*this race*, i.e. *the Jews*, shall not cease from being a *distinct people*, till all the counsels of God relative to *them* and the *Gentiles* be fulfilled. Some translate *η γενεα αυτη, this generation,* meaning the persons who were then living, that they should not die before these signs, &c. took place; but . . . I think it more proper not to restrain its meaning to the few years which preceded the destruction of Jerusalem; but to understand it of the care taken by Divine Providence to preserve them as a *distinct people,* and yet keep them out of their own land and from their temple-service."

Edward King remarks, "*γενεα*, in its true etymological signification, means surely much rather *this race of mankind*, or *this mode of men's existing upon earth in the present life*, than *this one particular generation*, according to the vulgar acceptation."—*Morsels of Criticism*, vol. i. p. 405.

"The expression, *this generation*," says Dr. Auberlen, "which has caused so much discussion, means here, not *this present generation*, but *this unbelieving Jewish people*. For it has not only been proven with much erudition by Dorner (in his *Dissertatio de Oratione Christi eschatologica*) that the expression γενεα may be also used of a people; but, even taking the word literally, Christ often uses it with somewhat of an undercurrent of reproach. It is impossible to think that the expression refers to the term of human life."—*On Daniel & Rev.*, p. 354.

Dr. Stier finds a parallel in Matt. xxiii. 36, where, he says, "not merely the then present, last, generation was meant, but, including *backwards* the entire race as one stock and lineage, the entire people who are judged in the last generation; so the term here has the same signification pointing *forwards*. Just because the children are like the fathers, γενεα passes beyond the *species* into the idea of the γενος, and *this is the proper sense of this expression when it is used concerning Israel*. . . . What further reference, then, does γενεα include, if not the wondrous *continuance of Israel* even to the end for which it is spared?"—*in loc.*

Dorner has stated the conclusion of his learned investigation of the subject in these words: "Quare omnes reor concessuros, vocem γενεα, si eam vertas ætas, multas easque plane insuperabiles ciere difficultates, contextum vero et orationes progressum flagitare significationem *gentis, nempe Judæorum*."—*Stier*, iii. 291.

Calovius also understands the reference here to be to the Jewish nation.—*Lange, in loc.*

Dean Alford refers to Jer. viii. 3 in LXX.; Matt. xxxiii. 36, 35; Matt. xii. 45; Luke xvii. 25; Matt. xvii. 17; Luke xvi. 8; Acts ii. 40; Phil. ii. 15; and says, "In all these places γενεα is equivalent to γενος, or nearly so; having, it is true, a more pregnant meaning, implying that the character of one generation *stamps itself upon the race*, as here in this verse also. . . . The continued use of παρερχομαι in verses 34, 35, should have saved the commentators from the blunder of imagining that the then living generation was meant, seeing that the prophecy is by the next verse carried on to the end of all things, and that, as a matter of fact, the apostles and ancient Christians did continue to expect the Lord's coming after that generation had passed away."—*Greek N. Test., in loc.*

The same interpretation of this word in this passage is given also by Pareus, Jansenius, Wolfius, Du Veil, Dr. Sykes, Towers, Barnes, Buck, and Ryle. It is without doubt the true interpretation. And, if so, it entirely does away with the alleged necessity of applying the discourse in which it occurs, to the destruction of Jerusalem, and shows that the great burden of the prophecy relates to the last times, and the proper coming of Christ at the great consummation.

Note C. Second Discourse, p. 57.

THE AUGSBURG AND HELVETIC CONFESSIONS AGAINST THE MODERN IDEAS OF THE MILLENNIUM.

The words referring to the subject, in *the Augustana*, are found in the Seventeenth Article:—"Item, hie werden verworffen etliche jüdische Lehre, die sich auch jtzund eräugen, das vor der Auferstehung die Toden, eitel heilige, fromme ein weltlich Reich haben, und alle gottlosen vertilgen werden." The Latin version reads, "Damnant et alios, qui nunc spargunt judaicas, quod ante resurrectionum mortuum pii regnum mundi occupaturi sint, ubique oppressis impiis." A very good translation is given in Hall's "*Harmony of Confessions*," in these words:—"They condemn others also, which spread abroad Jewish opinions, that, before the resurrection of the dead, the godly shall get the sovereignty in the world, and the wicked be brought under in every place."

With this harmonizes exactly the eleventh chapter of *the Latter Confession of Helvetia*, where it is written, "Moreover, we condemn the Jewish dreams, that before the judgment there shall be a golden world in the earth, and that the godly shall possess the kingdoms of the world, their wicked enemies being trodden under foot; for the evangelical truth, Matt. xxiv. and xxv., and Luke xxi., and the apostolic doctrine in the Second Epistle to Timothy iii. and iv., are found to teach far otherwise."

These quotations give the highest Confessional authority in modern Christendom, and they are clearly against the doctrine of a Millennium of universal triumph for Christianity and the Church *previous to* the coming of Christ and the resurrection of the dead.

NOTE D. SECOND DISCOURSE, p. 57.

DOES THE AUGSBURG CONFESSION CONDEMN CHILIASM?

IT has been asserted by many, that the quotation in the preceding note condemns all Chiliastic or Millenarian teachings. (Vide Knapp, *Theol.* 2, p. 637; Schmid, *Dogmatic*, p. 520; Schott, *Aug. Conf.* p. 109; Schmucker, *Manual*, p. 196; Moehler, *Symbolism*, p. 430; et cetera.) It is a statement, however, which has been made without the proper discrimination, and which cannot be maintained. That there is *a kind* of Chiliasm which is condemned by the Augsburg Confession, is admitted. That those are in error, who say that a *temporal kingdom* (weltlich Reich) will be possessed by the saints and the godly, and that *by them* the ungodly will be rooted out of the earth, or subdued to servitude, we sincerely believe. With equal heartiness do we refuse to assent to those who teach that the partakers of the first resurrection shall spend their millennial reign upon earth in all sorts of corporeal gratifications. There have also been people, who have been more or less identified with Chiliastic teachings, whose views on other subjects, and whose manner of life, have been so reprehensible that we can by no means acknowledge fellowship or sympathy with them. From such notions and teachers the Confessors thought it necessary to separate themselves in this article, in which we fully subscribe to their testimony. But *that all Chiliasm*, or that Chiliasm *per se*, is here condemned, we do not believe, and urge in support of our view the following considerations :—

1. Chiliasm, or Millenarianism, is not at all named in the Confession, nor anywhere in the Lutheran symbols. This, we suppose, will not be disputed. By name, therefore, it certainly is not condemned.

2. The description of the opinions condemned does not

describe proper Millenarianism. It is no doctrine of Millenarians that the pious are to have a separate kingdom to themselves "BEFORE *the resurrection of the dead.*" The kingdom and administrations for which they look and hope are AFTER the resurrection. The Millennium and personal reign which Papias taught the Church to expect, he distinctly put "AFTER *the resurrection.*" (Euseb. Hist. 3, cap. 39, p. 126.) Justin Martyr said there must *first* be a rising from the dead at the return of Christ. (Semisch's Life and Times of Justin, 2, p. 371.) Irenæus expressed himself plainly to the same effect. (Dodgson's Tertullian, Oxford, Note D, p. 121.) Tertullian wrote, "We do indeed confess that a kingdom on earth is promised us, before the time of heaven, but *in another state*, because in a city the work of God, Jerusalem brought down from heaven, AFTER *the resurrection.*" (See Greswell on Parables, 1, p. 306.) Lactantius says, "When God shall come to judge the world, *and shall restore unto life the just* that have been since the beginning, he shall converse among men a thousand years, and rule them with a most righteous government. . . . And *they that shall be raised from the dead* shall be over the living as judges." And so all Chiliasts in all ages, who can in any reason be classed with those members of the Church to whom that designation properly belongs, have believed and taught, viz., that an essential preliminary to the instalment of the saints in their future blessed kinghood and priesthood is, their resurrection from the grave to immortality, and that it is only AFTER the resurrection that they are to reign with Christ. Either, then, the Confessors knew not about what they were speaking, or Chiliasm, as such, and as set forth by its only acknowledged teachers, is not the subject of condemnation in this article.

3. It is plain from the words themselves, that the Confessors here referred to a class of errorists living and active at the time the Confession was made. These were evidently

the Anabaptists, who are named in another part of the Article, and who well deserved all the censure that was thus passed upon them. But they were not *Millenarians*, at least in the sense that the Church Fathers were. Chiliastic doctrines were professed by some of them at first, but they were soon merged in enthusiastic and wicked extravagances, which presently extinguished them altogether. They denied the sufficiency of the Bible for man's spiritual enlightenment, claimed to be inspired, and put their utterances on a footing with the teachings of prophets and apostles. They taught, indeed, the speedy setting up of a kingdom, which they called the kingdom of Christ, but assigned it a character of outwardness and earthiness, and other features, as much at variance with Millenarians as with spiritualizers. They repudiated all human laws and magistrates, and set themselves to subvert all existing institutions, in order to realize the kingdom of their dreams, which can in no case be laid to the charge of Church Chiliasts. Instead of leaving to Christ to establish his own kingdom in his own time and superhuman way, as we teach, they themselves undertook to establish it with fire and sword, and took a certain tailor, John Buckholdt, and set him up as "King of Zion," in the name and place of Jesus, regarding him as the representative of God himself, the Lord of all the earth, by whose administrations all worldly powers were to be rooted up, the wicked exterminated, and a kingdom of saints established in this world, without having to wait the time of "the resurrection of the just." (Vide Mosheim, *Ch. Hist.*, vol. i. p. 78; Ranke, *Hist. Reform.*, 3, chap. 1; Hardwick, *On Reform.*, pp. 273–280; Milner, *Ch. Hist.*, 2, pp. 341, 409–441, 532; Mœhler, *Symbolism*, pp. 429–444; Knapp, *Theol.*, art. 15, sec. 154; Walch, *Luther's Works*, 15, pp. 2366–2367; also, vol. 5, p. 1400.)

That these were the people whose teachings and doings the Confessors meant to condemn, is shown by the terms they use, and all the surroundings of the case. That of which they meant to purge themselves and warn mankind was *Munster Anabaptism*,—a base furor of designing or deceived people, with which Christian Chiliasm has less in common, perhaps, than Mormonism with the teachings of Jesus, or Mohammedanism with the Church of Christ.

4. The best authorities on the subject also lead us to believe that it was the seditious and infamous Judaizing doctrines, and the perverted ideas of the kingdom of God, held and disseminated by the Anabaptists, which the Confessors here intended to disown and condemn, and these alone.

The very highest authority is, of course, *Luther* himself. His understanding of the matter has been very well reproduced in a work called *Lutherus Redivivus*, published in 1697, which professes to give authentically the opinions of Luther upon every Article of the Augsburg Confession. On page 384, he is thus made to speak upon the points before us:—"As no one can better say than myself what the Augsburg Confession means by *Jewish doctrines*, in that I myself made the first draft of this Confession, I here give you this account: The Jews desire nothing more of their Messiah than that he should be a *Chocab* and worldly king, who will slay us Christians and heathen, divide the earth among the Jews, and make them lords and princes, and finally, also, die like other kings, as also his children after him. For so says a Rabbi, 'Thou art not to imagine that it will be different, or go otherwise, in the times of the Messiah, than as has been arranged from the beginning of the world;' that is, there will be day and night, years and lunations, summer and winter, seeding and harvests, rearing of children and dying, eating, drinking, sleeping, growing, digesting, &c., every thing as it is now, except that the Jews are to be the rulers, possess the gold and goods, joy and pleasure of the world, whilst we Christians are to be their slaves."

And as to these notions being put forth again at the time the Confession was written, he is made to say, further, "The celestial prophets, against whom I have written, also teach and hold, that they are to reform Christianity, and rebuild it after this fashion: they are to strangle all princes, and the ungodly, in order to make themselves lords upon earth, and live upon earth among none but saints. Such things, and much more, have I myself heard from them. *And as, at the time, among other calumnies, this blame was also cast upon us, as though the gospel taught and encouraged rebellion and undutifulness towards authorities, we had, by these words of the Confession, to free ourselves of such imputations.*"

The passages referred to in Luther's works as authority for putting these words into his mouth are (Altenburg edition) Tom. VIII. fol. 268 *b*, IX. fol. 306 *b*, 1511 *b*, III. fol. 52 *a*, V. fol. 745 *b*. We have referred to these passages, and have found them in every important particular nearly word for word as connected in the above extract.

The next highest authority in the case is *Melancthon*, who was the writer of the Confession as it was finally presented. He certainly should be presumed to know what was intended by the words in question. Referring, then, to his *Variata* of 1531, we find an explanatory amplification of this Article, in which he presents two propositions as containing the whole truth over against the errors therein condemned. They are these: first, that *Christians are bound to be obedient to the government under which they live;* and second, that *the Church in this life is never to attain to a position of universal triumph and prosperity, but is to remain depressed, and subject to afflictions and adversities, until the period of the resurrection of the dead.**

* "Scimus enim quod pii debeant obedire præsentibus magistratibus, non eripere eis imperia, non dissipare politias per seditionem, quia Paulus precipit, Omnis anima magistratui suo subdita sit. Scimus item, quod

The first of these propositions was denied by the Anabaptists; but, so far from being rejected by Millenarians, it is held and taught by them in common with all true Christians; and the second is a characteristic element of the Millenarian faith over against the vast majority of their opponents. According to Melancthon, therefore, the subject of condemnation in this Article is not Millenarianism at all, but rather the views of its modern opposers, and that which has no sort of connection with it.

A concurrent account of the meaning of this article of the Confession is also given by Dr. Semisch, in Herzog's Encyclopedia, where he says that, although it may be taken as preclusive, yet, *properly, it rejects as Jewish dreams only that caricature of true Chiliasm put forth by the Anabaptists*, who abrogated the magistracy and the ministry, and set up a Zion of their own, with community of goods and wives. (Vide Art. *Chiliasmus*, p. 663.) The same author affirms that *the Church never did reject Chiliasm in its* (Grundgedanken) *essential ideas, but only in its Ebionistic or Judaic perversions.*

It is ably maintained also by a recent writer (*Das Tausendjährige Reich gehört nicht der Vergangenheit, sondern der Zukunft an:* Gütersloh, 1860) that the Symbolical Books of the Lutheran Church do not condemn Chiliasm properly so called, but rather *antichiliasm* of every sort. Floerke, too, (in his *Lehre vom tausendjahrigen Reiche*, Marburg, 1859,) takes the same ground, and remarks, that the Confession itself limits its condemnation on this point by the words *qui* NUNC *spargunt;* so that no Chiliasm is symbolically condemned but *that only* which was putting itself forth at the time, and with which we have no part.—See pp. 4–9.

Ecclesia in hoc vita subjecta sit cruci, et primum post hanc vitam glorificabitur, sicut Paulus inquit, Oportet nos similes fieri imaginis filii Dei; Quare Anabaptistarum amentiam et diabolicum furorem damnamus et execramur."—*Corpus Reformatorum* (*Melanch. Op.*), vol. 26, p. 361.

5. It is also a fact, which is not without considerable bearing upon the point, that some of the most intelligent, pious, and conscientious theologians of the Lutheran Church, who were sworn by their ordination vows to every Article of the Augsburg Confession, and who claimed to be faithful to those vows to the end of their lives, were Millenarians, and preached, published, and defended Millenarian doctrines.

Pre-eminent among these was that distinguished prelate and scholar, *John Albert Bengel*, one of the clearest-minded critics that the Church has produced, who was a most decided Millenarian, and who not only claimed to be true to the Confessions on this point, but says, in his preface to his *Gnomon*, "No one as yet has called my orthodoxy in question."

In the same list belongs the revered name of Doctor *Philip Jacob Spener*, "the Protestant Fenelon," to whose piety and teachings the Lutheran Church in this and all other countries owes much, and who, though severely assailed by dogmatists for his cherished expectations of the better times to come, maintained, to the satisfaction of his judges, that he taught nothing contrary to the Confession which he subscribed, and that what the Confessors condemn as Jewish dreams did in no way include what he preached as the glad hope of the Church in these its days of affliction.

Another was the excellent *Christian Augustus Crusius*, Professor and Primarius of Theology in the University of Leipsic, who wrote the *Hypomnemata ad Theol. Propheticam*, in which Hengstenberg and Delitzch find so much to admire and commend.

Another was the great Swabian theosophist, *Frederick Christoph Oetinger*, whom Auberlen characterizes as a profound thinker, and concerning whom Schubart has said that an academy of learning and science expired with him.

Still another was the pious *Magnus Frederick Roos*, whom

Delitzch speaks of as "the great investigator of Scripture, full of quiet depth."

And to the same class belong *Philip Frederick Hiller*, one of the most prolific and admired of Germany's sacred poets; *Joachim Lange*, the able theologian of Halle; and *Dr. J. G. Schmucker*, one of the most pious and learned divines of the Lutheran Church of this country, whose work on the Apocalypse, setting forth the twofold resurrection, and the personal reign of Christ on the earth, also bears the recommendation of *Drs. Helmuth*, *Lochman*, and *D. Kurtz*, who were among the most learned, pious, and devoted Lutherans on this continent.

With these also might be named numbers still living, eminent as Christians, theologians, and adherents to the Confessions of the Church, who yet hold and teach Millenarian doctrines.

It is hard to presume that such men and scholars were so foolish as not to know to what they subscribed as their creed, or so hypocritical as to profess to hold to what they did not receive,—one or the other of which we are bound to believe if the Augsburg Confession condemns Chiliasm.

6. And then, again, who can conceive of the blessed Reformers and Confessors as sitting in judgment upon Barnabas, and Papias, and Justin Martyr, Irenæus, Tertullian, Clement of Alexandria, Cyprian, Lactantius, and at least the great body of the orthodox Church for hundreds of years, and condemning them all as errorists of a class with the Zwickau and Munster prophets? Though refusing, as all Christians should refuse, to be bound in their faith to any thing but the inspired word, they still held the ancient fathers in high esteem as witnesses to the truth, and encouraged the careful study of them. (Vide Walch's *Luther,* vol. 22, p. 2050, vol. 14, p. 420.) Even with reference to some who lived much later than those named, Luther averred that he would rather die

first, yea, that the day of judgment itself must come, before he would reject or condemn them. (*Ibid.* vol. 16, p. 2638.) And as the ancient Fathers, with others who succeeded them, certainly were Millenarians, we are forced either to assign to the Confessors the absurd position of holding those to be pious and worthy Christians whom they at the same time denounce as pernicious heretics, or to conclude that it was not Millenarianism, as such, that they here meant to condemn.

Upon these considerations, we hold it to be a mistake to say that Chiliasm of all forms has been rejected by the Augsburg Confession. It is a mere *assumption*, made without proper discrimination in the first place, and repeated by the enemies of Millenarian doctrine without proper scrutiny. We have sought in vain for adequate vouchers for its truth, and have not seen the first tittle of evidence that it is any thing more than a prevalent misapprehension.

NOTE E. FIFTH DISCOURSE, p. 119.

MILLENARIAN VIEWS OF THE SPIRITUALITY OF CHRIST'S KINGDOM.

IT is sometimes insinuated to the discredit of Millenarians that they deny the spiritual reign of Christ over the heart, and look only for a carnal heaven and a sensual paradise. As they insist upon the interpretation of the Holy Scriptures in a plain, every-day manner, it is presumed that they ignore the proper spirituality of religion, and that their anticipations for the future must necessarily exclude the idea of spiritual good as the leading characteristic of the kingdom to come. So Origen, and Jerome, and Augustine after him; and so Corrodi, Seyffarth, and many of the modern writers and preachers against our doctrines. But nothing could be more uncandid and unjust. Though it may evince wit, it displays very little of that quality of mind and heart which is most to be coveted in view of the solemn judgment to come. We do not deny that there may have been some fanatical and carnal people who have taught certain forms of Millenarian doctrine, as there have been such to accept, caricature, and disgrace the doctrines of every school of religious belief. But it is very questionable whether, as a class of Christian believers in the Church, there has ever lived a more earnest, spiritual-minded, and devout body of men, or any who have more uniformly and stringently insisted on repentance, conversion, and real heart-obedience to the Savior, than Millenarians.

Irenæus speaks of the saints who are to "reign in the earth" as "growing by the sight of the Lord," and "habituated to receive the glory of God the Father," and that they "shall in the kingdom receive a conversation and communion and unity of *spiritual things with the holy angels.*" He says, further, that they shall "truly be practised for incorruption, and shall be enlarged and strengthened in the periods of the kingdom, so as to become capable of receiving the glory of the Father," and in the new heaven and new earth "shall abide ever new, and having intercourse with God."

Justin Martyr says, "They from every nation, slaves or free, *who believe in Christ*, and know the truth in his words and in those of his prophets, know that they shall be with him, and shall inherit things eternal and incorruptible;" and that "*they who repent not* shall inherit nothing in the holy Mount; but the Gentiles *which have believed in him, and repented of their sins, these* shall inherit with the patriarchs, and the prophets, and the righteous who are sprung from Jacob. *They* shall inherit *the holy inheritance of God.*"

It is written of *Melito*, Bishop of Sardis, an acknowledged Millenarian, that, so far from being a carnal man, indulging himself with carnal dreams, "*he had his whole conversation in the Holy Ghost.*"

Tertullian distinctly locates the joys of the children of the resurrection in *all spiritual good things.* Speaking of the glorious city, he says, "This, we say, is provided by God for receiving the saints upon the resurrection, and refreshing them with the abundance of all spiritual good things, in compensation for those which in the world we have either despised or lost."

Dr. Greswell remarks, "If I can form any reasonable conjecture about the sentiments of the advocates of the Millennium, in ancient times, from such of their writings as have come down to us,—if I know any thing of the opinions of the most rational and sober-minded of its supporters still,—and, in particular, if I am not altogether ignorant of my own views and expectations concerning it,—I cannot hesitate to affirm that they are very greatly mistaken, or very grossly pervert and misrepresent our conceptions of the nature and purposes of this dispensation, who charge us with entertaining a sensual and carnal idea of the kingdom of Christ, and attempt to raise a prejudice against us on that account."

And who that has himself any practical acquaintance with the spirituality of religion will ever think of charging Mede, or Spener, or Bengel, or Roos, or Durant, or Farmer, or Lange, or Goodwin, or Bickersteth, with denying that grace must rule in the heart, or with teaching that the world to come is to have its joys made up of eating and drinking and carnal gratifications, because they anticipated a future manifestation of the kingdom on the earth, to which all that has been thus far is merely preparatory? Nor would it be difficult to name scores, if not hundreds, of men now living, who are acknowledged to be among the most faithful, pure, and useful Christians on the face of the earth, to whom the Millenarian faith presents the dearest hopes they cherish.

It was once remarked by Thomas Hartley that, "Among the many arts practised in order to bring any truth into discredit, none is more popular than that of exhibiting it to public view joined with the absurd tenets of some that have espoused it, and which is not improperly called dressing up truth in a fool's coat on purpose to make it appear ridiculous; and this often succeeds with the undiscerning vulgar, who judge only by the outward appearance of things." It is this art which has been practised for the most part by the enemies of Millenarian doctrine, and that, too, with a goodly degree of success. It is to be hoped that the time is at hand when men will deal with the subject with some degree of that candor which it really deserves.

NOTE F. FIFTH DISCOURSE, p. 121.

ON THE DECLARATION OF THE SAVIOR (JOHN xvii., 36) THAT HIS KINGDOM IS NOT OF THIS WORLD.

THERE is no passage more dwelt upon by anti-Millenarians in opposition to our doctrines than this. Indeed, it is about the only text on which any show of scriptural objection can be raised. But it is, after all, nothing but *show*. If they take it to prove that the kingdom of Christ is within,—a reign over the heart by the Holy Spirit,—we maintain this equally with themselves. If they take it to prove that the kingdom of Christ is not of earthly derivation, or of an earthly nature, this, too, we hold with unyielding firmness, insisting that it is neither derived, constituted, nor administered after the fashion of the kingdoms of this world. If they take it to prove that the kingdom of Christ is confined and limited to the Spirit's rule in men's hearts, and that it consequently is and always will be without outward manifestation and visible form, we dispute that there is any thing of the sort in the passage, and insist that they have the Scriptures everywhere against them.

That kingdom even now embraces the organized Church, which is a visible assembly, with outward sacraments and bonds of union, and with external manifestations as real as any of this world's kingdoms. And if they take it to prove that the kingdom of Christ is not *located* on earth, they undertake to make it prove a manifest falsehood. Take the kingdom spoken of in what sense we please, whether as Christ reigning in the heart by his Spirit, or as Christ operating for the salvation of men through the administrations and ordinances of his Church, *its location is in this world,* and in none other. Nor do the Savior's words imply, by any fair, grammatical construction, that his kingdom ever will be located otherwise than upon the earth. It may not be without service to quote here a few authorities on the subject.

Tholuck makes this criticism:—"He does not contradict the assertion that he has a kingdom; nay, he speaks of his kingdom and of his servants. If we are to affirm any thing with regard to the kingdom of Christ, we must not content ourselves with merely saying that the kingdom of Christ is *not of this world;* we must add that, although his kingdom is not *of* this world, yet it is nevertheless *in* this world, and will advance more and more in this world. Yes, God be praised! we can say, with joy, that although the Lord's kingdom is not of this world, still it is in this world, *and, so long as the world exists,* IT WILL NEVER PASS OUT OF IT."—*Light from the Cross,* p. 171, *in loc.*

Stier has this observation:—"This renunciation is by no means to be put in opposition to the true prophecies of the kingdom of the Son of man, to whom *already* power is given, and whose kingdom *finally* will bring all other power to naught: it is very far from renouncing the world, and all external and earthly manifestation and confirmation of his heavenly power. *It does not,* as superficial expositors dream, (here and verse 37,) *refer the kingdom of Christ to the in-*

visible region of the heart. Had he not said already before Caiaphas, 'From this time forth ye shall see him coming in his power'? The observation of Von Gerlach is good, that a purely internal dominion which did not control and subordinate to itself the external, would be no true kingdom, and would have none of the reality of dominion."—*Words of Jesus, in loc.*

So, too, Krummacher:—"He does not deny that he came to establish a kingdom: he only repels the groundless suspicion of his having intended to overthrow the existing authorities and to establish a new political state. He does not say that his kingdom makes no claim eventually to the government of the whole world, or he would have denied more than was consistent with the truth. He only asserts that his kingdom was not of *this* world, and clearly intimates, by laying the emphasis on the word 'this,' that another αἰων than the present would certainly see his delegates seated on thrones, and his word and gospel the *magna charta* of all nations."—*Suffering Savior*, p. 248.

Trench also describes the point of meaning to be, "not the unfolding of any powers which already existed in the world,—a kingdom not rising, as those other kingdoms, '*out of the earth*,' but a new power brought into the world from above." *On the Parables*, p. 160.

Alford also interprets the declaration as conveying "no denial that this kingdom is *over* this world,—but that it is to be established by this world's power."

"Christus sagt nicht: Mein Reich ist nicht hienieden, sondern: Nicht von dannen."—*Lutherus Redivivus*, p. 386.

Edward King says of this declaration of the Savior, "It might be translated, or at least should be paraphrased, *My kingdom is not derived from any powers or authority* in this world."—*Morsels of Crit.*, vol. 1, p. 421.

NOTE G. SEVENTH DISCOURSE, p. 179.

THE PERSONAL ANTICHRIST—IS IT LOUIS NAPOLEON?

THAT there is to be some great, blaspheming, despotic military power, under which the Roman Empire is to be in some sense revived, which is to exercise a most cruel tyranny over the whole civilized world, and which is to lead forth the combined armies of nations to a scene of unprecedented disaster in connection with the reappearance of Christ, is plainly taught in the prophecies of Daniel, Paul, and John, and held by all the best interpreters of the prophetic word. It is this power which is styled by eminence "*The* Antichrist, that denieth the Father and the Son." It is also the growing belief of expositors that this power is the Napoleonic headship of the Roman dominion, especially as that headship has been revived in the present Emperor of the French, Napoleon III. The general grounds upon which this belief rests may be stated somewhat as follows:—

1. He answers to the description which makes this great blaspheming power the septimo-eighth head of the seven-headed and ten-horned beast of the great Roman dominion. The seven heads of this beast were not only "seven mountains," upon which the centre of Roman dominion was seated, but also "seven *Kings*" or regencies. These seven regencies are the seven distinct forms under which the Roman dominion was embodied and administered. These were kings, consuls, dictators, decemvirs, military tribunes, and emperors. Of these, "five" had "fallen" when John wrote; one *was*, and one was "not yet come." That which then was, was the Roman imperial, which in one way or another, as history shows, continued down to Francis II. of Austria, A.D. 1806, when the power of Europe was seized by Napoleon Bonaparte, and the old imperial succession was destroyed. In this Napo-

leon, then, a new and distinct head was set up, whilst there was yet such an assumption by him of the old iron crown, and such an acknowledgment of his authority by the Pope of Rome in his coronation, that it was still to be regarded as the same old Roman dominion simply passed to another form or head. He was, therefore, that seventh head which was to come. "And when he is come," said the angel, "he must continue *a short space.*" The period of Napoleon's imperial rule was *eleven years,* when he was overthrown, and his empire destroyed forever, as it appeared. But it was not effectually destroyed. He is described in the vision as "the beast that was, and is not, *and yet is.*" Though "as it were wounded to death, his deadly wound was healed." The Napoleonic headship ceased with the fall of Napoleon I., but it was soon marvellously revived in his nephew, and now *is* again, in the present Napoleon III. He is "*of the seven*" by his relation to the Napoleon family, and by his assumption of the same dynasty and principles represented by Napoleon I.; but the manner of his coming into power, and various peculiarities in the constitution of his dominion, present features of distinctness from his uncle's headship, showing that he is in some sense also a headship of his own kind. He is consequently the seventh, and yet in some sense the eighth, so answering to the description of a septimo-eighth head or embodiment of the great Roman dominion, which was to be the Antichrist. (See Faber's *Napoleon III.*)

2. Napoleon III. corresponds also with the prophetic portrait of the Antichrist in his prowess, ambition, and military power. In Rev. xiii. 3, 4, as soon as the beast's wounded head is healed, he appears as the wonder and astonishment of the world; which has been very remarkably verified in the surprise and amazement which the career of Louis Napoleon has excited since 1852. And with 750,000 trained troops, furnished with the best arms in the world, with a fleet

of iron-clad war-steamers inferior perhaps to none now afloat, and with his deep and inscrutable policy and ambition, it may very well be said of him, at this moment, "Who is like unto the beast? Who is able to make war with him?" Nor is it difficult to anticipate, from the present condition of the world, and his position in it, that it would not take any great length of time to fulfil the words of the prophet, in which it is said that "power was given him over all kindreds, and tongues, and nations."—(Rev. xiii. 7.) His rapid ascension to power and dominion have startled the world, and his influence and authority are augmenting still in all quarters of the globe. He is at this moment the most daring, the most ambitious, the most powerful, and the most dangerous man on earth. The Crimean War put him at the head of European affairs. His interference in the war of Austria and Sardinia shows with what a controlling hand he is competent to dispose of the disputes of nations. His annexation of Savoy and Nice to France is another illustration of his growing pre-eminence. The recent war with China, and the French occupation of Syria, have planted his power in Asia. The north of Africa is his. Mexico seems ready to fall into his hands. The defeat of his uncle at Waterloo he regards it his solemn destiny to avenge. He is now virtually the possessor of Rome. The prospect is that he will presently have the Jews completely enlisted in his favor. Jerusalem is at this moment stirring throughout its desolations under the influences of his power. Palestine seems as if preparing to open her gates to him. Greece, now in revolution, seems to be ready to accept a member of his family as her king. His monetary resources are greater than those of any power on earth. His desire to interfere in the terrific schism which has occurred in the United States needs only to await the opportunity to put the tottering Republic under his control. All of which would seem to foreshadow, as clearly as may be, the fulfilment to him of what is written in Rev. xvii. 13, 17, xiii. 7; and Dan. xi. 36–39.

3. His name also has peculiarities which appear to fall in very remarkably with the predictions that apply to this last great scourge of the world. It is argued, by some, that the king spoken of in Rev. ix. 11 is also in some sense this wilful king of the last days. And it is there said that "his name in the Hebrew tongue is Abaddon, but in the Greek tongue *Apollyon*,"—which comes nearer to *Napoleon* than many of the New Testament versions of the ancient Scripture names. In Rev. xiii. 18, it is written, "Here is wisdom. Let him that hath understanding count the number of the beast, for it is the number of a man; and his number is six hundred threescore and six." And in Rev. xiii. 17 and xv. 2 this number is further described as "the number of his name;" which is usually taken to mean the number in numerical value of the letters which compose his name. And, giving the name *Louis* in its Latin form, *Ludovicus*, we have, as the total numerical value of the letters, 666. So, too, by putting the name *Napoleon* in its Greek form, as if inscribed upon a monument, *Ναπολεοντι*, the total numerical value of the letters is again 666. Thus:

L	stands	for	50	*N*	stands	for	50
V	"	"	5	*α*	"	"	1
D	"	"	500	*π*	"	"	80
O	"	"	0	*ο*	"	"	70
V	"	"	5	*λ*	"	"	30
I	"	"	1	*ε*	"	"	5
C	"	"	100	*ο*	"	"	70
V	"	"	5	*ν*	"	"	50
S	"	"	0	*τ*	"	"	300
				ι	"	"	10
		Total,	666			Total,	666

It is true that this number can be found in other names, and in some which apply to this beast in some of its earlier forms; but it is very remarkable that this number should be found in both names of the present French emperor, in whom, if these prophecies do apply to him, is to be concentred every form and attribute of all the antichrists which have been before him.

4. The connection of the Antichrist with the apostate Church power, first supporting it, using it, and then despoiling it altogether, also seems to point to Napoleon III. as the man. When yet President of France, in 1849, he sent French troops to support the Pope in Rome, and has not withdrawn them to this day. Yet of late he has been allowing all sorts of damage to befall the papacy, is at present in disagreement with the Church authorities, and in various ways is giving symptoms which look greatly like preparation for that part of prophecy which says that the beast, with his ten subordinate kings, shall "hate the whore, and make her desolate, and naked, and eat her flesh, and burn her with fire." He has also permitted a pamphlet to be issued in which it is proposed that the papal power should be given him, and the political and religious sovereignties united in his own person,—a thing not unlikely to be consummated at no distant day; which would fully invest him with the very attributes which underlie the predictions of Paul in 2 Thess. ii. 8–12.

5. The mysteriousness which characterizes him, his taciturn disposition, his protestations and general policy, and his deep cunning and sagacity, also seem to answer to the predictions made concerning the Antichrist. In Daniel viii. we find a vision of a little horn, which waxed exceeding great,—the Mohammedan power, perhaps, but ultimately the Antichrist,—who (in verses 23–25) is described as "a king of *fierce* (shameless, imperturbable, unawed, impenetrable) *countenance, and understanding dark sentences,*" who "shall

destroy wonderfully, and shall prosper, and practise, and shall destroy the mighty and the holy people," and "through his *policy* also shall cause *craft* to prosper in his hand, and magnify himself in his heart, *and by peace shall destroy many,*" and "shall also stand up against the Prince of princes." He is also described as the king who "shall do according to his will, and shall exalt himself, and magnify himself above every god." Nor can it fail to strike the reader how well this language applies to a man of whom a personal friend of his, who laboriously attempted an analysis of his character, has said, "Frigidly affable, and repulsively polite, he avoided either offence or familiarity, but seemed instinctively to coil up his nature from observation. In phrase and demeanor all that became his birth, still the man was perfectly inaccessible. . . . There was much of peculiarity, much of contrast, abstract yet vigilant, inquisitive in every thing, but studiously incommunicative, diligent in acquiring all men's knowledge, retentive of his own, cold and impassive, but full of latent energy, cautious in decision, but, having decided, prompt, rapid, and impetuous. Almost intuitive in grasping opportunity or detecting weakness; improved by study, steeled by adversity, disciplined for every vicissitude of fortune, he has inestimable qualifications for his own position. . . . Marvellous as his character appears at present, it is, in my judgment, as yet very partially developed. The reserve, however, in which he habitually shrouds himself may not now be violated. . . . Few can see, in the taciturn recluse, the talents, attainments, and accomplishments which he undoubtedly possesses."—(*Phillips on Napoleon III.*) Madden also very pointedly, confirms this well-drawn portrait, and further says that "This man-mystery, the depths of whose duplicity no Œdipus has yet sounded, is a problem even to those who surround him. I watched his pale, corpse-like, imperturbable features, not many months since, for a period of three hours. I saw 80,000 men in arms pass before him, and I never observed a change in his countenance, or an expression in his look, which would enable the bystander to say whether he was pleased or otherwise at the stirring scene that was passing before him on the very spot where Louis XVI. was put to death. He did not speak to those around him except at very long intervals, and then with an air of nonchalance, of ennui, and eternal occupation with self." "Dark, mysterious, impenetrable, inscrutable in his designs," says the author of Armageddon; "concealing every passion of his heart within the innermost depths of his soul; of great personal courage and inflexible will, conjoined with cool deliberation and consummate prudence; entirely devoid, apparently, of any real religion or moral principle; impelled, guided, protected, as he announces himself to be, by his uncle's shade; with the subtlety of that 'more subtle than any beast of the field,' has he hitherto defeated all his opponents, and reached by craft a pinnacle which his uncle could only attain by the sword. Striking not until his quarry be certain, or (as the author of the Last Vials well expresses it) never uncoiling himself to seize his prey until sure of his victim; daily increasing in power and influence over the nations; and bringing the eyes of an astonished world to contrast with wonder his past and present career; all in relation to him seems to be after a superhuman working that none can fathom."

6. His rise from obscurity, the contempt in which all men once held him, the manner of his ascent to the throne and his great dominion, as well as his remarkable control of the precious metals, are also of a character answering to the predictions concerning the Antichrist. He was described in Dan. xi. 21 as "a vile person [one despised], to whom they shall not give the honor of the kingdom; but he shall come in peaceably, and obtain the kingdom by flatteries." . . Also it was further said "he shall have power over the treasures of

gold and silver." And before Napoleon III. obtained the emperorship, there was hardly a man in the world upon whom more contemptuous epithets and opinions were passed than upon him. He was supposed to be without understanding, an idiotic dreamer, as short of brains as he was of friends and means. But from that obscurity and contempt he has risen to imperial power; and the kingdom which no one would have been willing to confer upon him, he yet managed, in the name of liberty and democracy, and with daring adventures in the name of peace and the people, to obtain and hold. It is also a marvellous fact that he has not only succeeded in securing all the money needed for the extraordinary cost of carrying on his government and immense improvements, but in the years 1855, 56, and 57, he coined more gold than both England and the United States together.

7. It would also seem to be impossible for another power, such as the Antichrist is to be, to arise and mature itself in the unexpired time which chronological prophecies place between the present and the great consummation. A dozen different lines of calculation seem to converge and run out within the limits of the next ten years, each of which is supposed to extend to the epoch of the consummation. Seven years, or three and a half years at least, is the period in which the Antichrist, as such, is to continue; which would leave only some half a dozen years for the incoming, establishment, and maturement of the predicted power, of which the earth as yet has no signs apart from Napoleon III.

Without undertaking, therefore, to decide positively that Louis Napoleon is the personal Antichrist of the last days, we have no hesitation in saying that we are strongly inclined, with some of the most sober and learned of prophetic expositors, to believe that he is. Events will very soon show whether this supposition is correct or not. And one of the first tests will be the formation of a league or covenant between Napoleon III. and the Jews, in which they will accept him as their great protector and help in their reinstatement into their land and the restoration of their temple services. When this covenant is once made, it will then be but seven years to the descent of Christ in the clouds of heaven, and the great consummation. (See Dan. ix. 27; xi. 23.) "*Blessed is he that watcheth!*"

Note H. Seventh Discourse, pp. 108, 181.

ON THE TWO STAGES OF THE TRANSLATION.

The opinion that there is to be a duality in the translation of the saints (as also in the resurrection of them that sleep in Christ) seems to me to have strong supports in the Scriptures.

1. In the description of the great woes which are to attend the close of the present dispensation, there is a command given to "watch and pray always," that we "may be accounted worthy to *escape all these things* that shall come to pass, and to stand before the Son of man." It is here implied that there will be persons living when these troubles come, who, by peculiar earnestness in their expectancy of the Lord's return, shall obtain entire exemption from them; and that this exemption will consist in some peculiar introduction into the immediate presence of the Son of man, that is, by being caught up to him in the clouds. Something of the same sort is intimated in Isaiah xxvi. 20, where God's peculiar people are represented as called up into some peaceful pavilion, where they are at rest while the waves of divine indignation are rolling over the world. But in Rev. vii. 9–14 we read of a great multitude of the redeemed, who are represented as having had to suffer these very woes, and as having reached

heaven through them. It is specifically said, "*These are they which came out of the great tribulation,*"—not out of tribulation in general, but some specific and pre-eminent tribulation,—εκ της θλίψεως της μεγαλης, *out of the tribulation, the great one,* —which we find described in Dan. ix. 27, xii. 1; Matt. xxiv. 21, 22; Luke xxi. 24. Now, as some are accounted worthy to escape these things, and escape by their removal to the presence of Christ, and as others only reach their places before the throne of God by passing through the great tribulation, there must needs be two stages in the removal of the Church, that is, two distinct translations.

2. Again, in Rev. xiv. 1–5, we read of a certain number of the "redeemed from among men," who have reached the heavenly state in the presence of the Lamb, and who are called "*the first fruits unto God.*" There is a difference between the *first fruits* and the general harvest, not exactly in kind, but in the order of their gathering, and in the purposes to which they are applied. There is always an interval between the gathering and lifting up of the one, and the general reaping of the other. And, answering in this respect to the first fruits described in the first part of the chapter, we have an account of the reaping of the great harvest in a subsequent part, (verses 15, 16.) Those that constitute the first fruits, of course, cannot be the same as those who constitute the general harvest. The one is a distinct class from the other, and is separated from it especially as to the precise time of the gathering, whilst, nevertheless, the gathering is of the same kind in both. And as both classes are made up of persons redeemed from among men, and "caught up in the clouds to meet the Lord in the air," we must conclude that there is to be a twofold translation.

3. There seems also to be an intimation that even Christ's coming is to possess two distinct stages,—which would again correspond with the idea of a twofold translation. He is to

come "as a thief in the night;" but he is also to come "in the clouds of heaven, with power and great glory," "taking vengeance on them that know not God," and to be "admired in all them that believe." In the one case he is seemingly invisible, removing as by stealth those who are waiting and ready, and fulfilling those words of his, "In that night there shall be two in one bed; the one shall be taken and the other left," &c. In the other case, "every eye shall see him," and he rides forth upon his celestial chariot as a mighty conqueror, crushing down before him all his foes both great and small, and gathering to himself the great totality of them that believe on his name. Both these comings, or stages of his manifestation, cannot occur at one and the same time, and so would involve a twofold translation.

4. To this also agrees the account given in Matt. xxiv. 42–51; where we read of a servant who is "faithful and wise," whom his Lord finds at his post, and at once receives to blessedness; but also of another servant, as really a servant as the first, who is deficient in fidelity and worldly in his temper, and whom his Lord when he comes *severely punishes* (δίχοτομεσω) by assigning him a portion with hypocrites, who are to suffer the great tribulation. The words do not at all imply that the one is saved and the other lost, but simply that the one reaches blessedness at once when the Lord comes, whilst the other, not being prepared by proper watchfulness, is "left," and punished with such temporal judgments as are then to befall the earth, and only saved "so as by fire," at a subsequent period.

5. So, too, the parable of the ten virgins, (Matt. xxv. 1–13.) Those virgins are the whole company of the saints, and are all true Christians and real believers; but only a portion of them go in with Christ to the marriage, whilst the rest are "left" to improve their virtues under the afflictions attending a loss of their place among the first fruits and Church of the

first-born, and to receive their redemption at some later stage of the Savior's manifestation.—See my Discourses on *The Parable of the Ten Virgins.*

6. So, too, in the parable of the pounds, (Luke ix. 11–27,) we have some faithful and industrious servants who improve their trusts well, and who when the Lord returns are at once welcomed into the sublime rewards of their exertions. But there is another class, so timid and unfruitful in their occupancy that, when the Lord comes, they are not honored as the others, but stripped of the trusts they had received, and left to suffer for their unfaithfulness. They are not lost. They are not *slain*, as the malignant "citizens" who would not acknowledge Christ's rule over them. They simply lose their rewards, and their places among those who obtain rulership, and are made to endure the tribulation judgments.

7. To the same effect is the 12th of Revelation. We there read of "the woman's seed," which may be taken first as Christ himself, but, for that reason, as the whole body of his people upon earth. In verse 5, this seed, as intended to "rule the nations," is represented as "caught up unto God, and to his throne." Here, then, is one ascension. But in verse 17 we still read of a "remnant"—λοιποις—*a remaining portion*—of this same woman's seed, which must certainly denote Christian people; for they are such as "keep the commandments of God, and have the testimony of Jesus Christ," and are still upon earth suffering the dragon's wrath. And as all must needs be glorified in due time, there must be a second translation to embrace these. They suffer additional persecutions to their brethren, and so are not taken at the same time with them, but are saved only by passing through the great tribulation, which the more devout and watchful escape by means of an earlier translation. Compare also Matt. xxiv. 28, 31, and Luke xvii. 34, 37.

8. The fourth and fifth chapters of Revelation also evi-

dence the same thing. A scene in heaven is there depicted. The elders and living creatures in that vision must represent saints in the glorified state. They address a song to Christ, in which they say to him, "Thou wast slain, and hast redeemed us to God by thy blood." We know of no redeemed by Christ's blood but men. They were not, therefore, heavenly orders or angels proper, but ransomed human beings from the earth. Nor were they the saints who rose with Christ; for those appear to have been Jews: these are "out of every kindred, and tongue, and people, and nation." They are also already "kings and priests," and have their "crowns,"—which could not be said of the saints of the old dispensation, for they have not yet received the promises. The coronation time is at the coming and consummation. (Heb. xi. 13, 40; 2 Tim. iv. 8; 1 Pet. v. 4; Col. iii. 4). The vision must, therefore, refer to a state of things in the heavenly state of the glorified saints in connection with what is said in 1 Thess. iv. 17. It is remarkable, however, that whilst these are in the heavenly glorified state, and have already received their crowns, the preliminary judgments of the seals are only about to begin. And as the great tribulation occurs only in connection with the opening of these seals, the translation by which they are brought to their rewards must *precede* the great tribulation; whilst, according to Matt. xxiv. 29–31, there is another gathering of the elect "immediately *after* the tribulation;" thus making two stages in the translation. Compare Ps. xxvii. 5, 6, xxxi. 20, xxxii. 6, 7, xlv. 14.

The doctrine of the Scriptures seems to be, that only those who are devoutly looking and waiting for the Savior's return shall be taken at first, whilst all others are left to suffer the great tribulation, which will continue at least three years and a half. See Heb. ix. 28; and Rev. xii. 13, 14, xiii. 5, xi. 3.

NOTE I. TENTH DISCOURSE, p. 253.

LUTHER ON THE MILLENNIUM.

THE authority of Luther is sometimes quoted as decidedly against all expectations of a Millennium yet to come.—(See Dr. Seyffarth's *Chiliasm Critically Examined.*) The evidence relied upon for this representation of the great Reformer is taken from the marginal notes to Luther's German Bible, Rev. x. 2, 3, where he is made to say that "the thousand years must have commenced at the time the Apocalypse was written; mainly because the Turk came a thousand years after that time." Unsatisfactory as this quotation is, it is the only passage from the works of Luther which anti-millenarians have been able to find by which to array the Reformer on their side. The worth of it in such a connection may be estimated from the following observations.

Concerning these marginal notes in general, we have to say, with Fabricius and others, that they have not always been the same in the various editions of Luther's German Bible; that many of them were changed, even by himself; that manifold alterations were made in them before, and still more after, his death; that it is uncertain to what extent they are to be attributed to Luther; and that, whilst some of them furnish much light and information, there are others of which "it must rather be said that they savor of erroneous opinions once held by Luther, which, in justice to him, must be received *with reference to the condition of the times in which they were uttered;* on which account liberty has long ago been taken to alter very materially some of them, as also to muster them out."—See Fabricius's *Centifolium*, pp. 168, 169; also Walch's *Luther*, preface to vol. xii.; also Irmischer's *Luther's Werke*, vol. 64, preface.

As to the particular note to which reference has been made,

whilst it may have come from Luther, we have to say that it was not contained in the edition of 1522, neither in the edition of 1524. Besides, it relates to a department of inquiry in which Luther elsewhere expresses himself as for the most part doubtful. In his preface to his little treatise on Chronology, he says, "It matters nothing to me, indeed, whether this little book shall stand or not. Neither do I inquire with much anxiety whether others shall look with favor upon these reckonings or not."—(See Walch's *Luther*, xiv. 1111.) Whilst at the end of that same treatise he distinctly avows himself a believer in the tradition of the house of Elias, which certainly puts a millennial Sabbath at the end of the six thousand years from the creation of Adam.

Dr. Hengstenberg also pronounces it "an over-estimate of the authority of Luther" to assign this note any value in the direction for which anti-millenarians have cited it. If it really gives Luther's opinion at the time, it was simply *an opinion*, bearing upon its face the plain evidences of having been very loosely made up, and one upon which its author laid no particular stress, grounded no doctrine, placed no confident reliance, and actually contradicted in other portions of his writings.

It does not appear that Luther ever directly took up the subject of the Millennium and its related doctrines in connection. They were not much involved, at least not much brought to the surface, in those controversies and points of exposition which monopolized his attention and energies. His was the sublime work of unchaining the simple word of God, and the establishment of the great doctrines of the right of private judgment and justification by faith. His department was theology and soterology, rather than eschatology and prophecy. And though the greatest of mere men, and next to the apostles in his own sphere, he is about the last man among great theologians to whom to betake ourselves for a guide in the interpretation of the Apocalypse,—a book which he evidently had not at all mastered. The great mass even of his most ardent admirers and followers have long since agreed to surrender his Apocalyptical views as in many points untenable, and as given by himself in a way which deprives them altogether of the weight which attaches to his authority on other subjects. And when we have laid aside this note on Rev. xx. 2, 3, we find his writings generally far more in harmony with the views and spirit of millenarian interpretation than in favor of those who would fain crush us with the majesty of his great name.

NOTE K. ELEVENTH DISCOURSE, p. 269.

THE SCRIPTURE CHRONOLOGY OF THE WORLD.

	YEARS.
From the creation of Adam to the birth of Seth........ "Adam lived one hundred and thirty years, and begat a son, . . . and called his name Seth."—Gen. v. 3.	130
From the birth of Seth to the birth of Enos............ "Seth lived a hundred and five years, and begat Enos."—Gen. v. 6.	105
From the birth of Enos to the birth of Cainan.......... "Enos lived ninety years, and begat Cainan."—Gen. v. 9.	90
From the birth of Cainan to the birth of Mahalaleel. . "Cainan lived seventy years, and begat Mahalaleel."—Gen. v. 12.	70
From the birth of Mahalaleel to the birth of Jared.... "Mahalaleel lived sixty and five years, and begat Jared."—Gen. v. 15.	65

	YEARS.
Brought forward	460
From the birth of Jared to the birth of Enoch	162
"Jared lived a hundred and sixty-two years, and he begat Enoch."—Gen. v. 18.	
From the birth of Enoch to the birth of Methuselah	65
"Enoch lived sixty and five years, and begat Methuselah."—Gen. v. 21.	
From the birth of Methuselah to the birth of Lamech,	187
"Methuselah lived one hundred and eighty-seven years, and he begat Lamech."—Gen. v. 25.	
From the birth of Lamech to the birth of Noah	182
"Lamech lived one hundred and eighty-two years, and begat a son: and he called his name Noah."—Gen. v. 28.	
From the birth of Noah to the flood	600
"Noah was six hundred years old when the flood of waters was upon the earth."—Gen. vii. 6.	
The duration of the flood	1
"It came to pass, in the six hundred and first year, in the first month, the first day of the month, the waters were dried up."—Gen. viii. 13.	
From the flood to the birth of Arphaxad	2
"Shem was a hundred years old, and begat Arphaxad two years after the flood."—Gen. xi. 10.	
From the birth of Arphaxad to the birth of Salah	35
"Arphaxad lived five and thirty years, and begat Salah."—Gen. xi. 12.	
From the birth of Salah to the birth of Eber	30
"Salah lived thirty years, and begat Eber."—Gen. xi. 14.	
From the birth of Eber to the birth of Peleg	34
"Eber lived four and thirty years, and begat Peleg."—Gen. xi. 16.	

	YEARS.
Brought forward....................................	1758
From the birth of Peleg to the birth of Reu........... "Peleg lived thirty years, and begat Reu."—Gen. xi. 18.	30
From the birth of Reu to the birth of Serug........... "Reu lived two and thirty years, and begat Serug." —Gen. xi. 20.	32
From the birth of Serug to the birth of Nahor.......... "Serug lived thirty years, and begat Nahor."—Gen. xi. 22.	30
From the birth of Nahor to the birth of Terah.......... "Nahor lived nine and twenty years, and begat Terah."—Gen. xi. 24.	29
From the birth of Terah to his death..................... "The days of Terah were two hundred and five years."—Gen. xi. 32.	205
From the death of Terah to the covenant with Abraham, "Abraham . . . dwelt in Charran; and from thence, when his father was dead, he removed him into this land, wherein ye now dwell."—Acts vii. 2–4. "Abram was seventy and five years old when he departed out of Haran [Charran]." —Gen xii. 4. Then intervene the events of his life, recorded in Gen. xii. 5 to Gen. xiv. 24; which could not have occupied less than two years. Then comes the Covenant in Gen. xv. 1–21.	2
From the making of the Covenant to the giving of the Law "The Covenant . . . the Law, that was four hundred and thirty years after, cannot disannul." —Gal. iii. 17.	430
From the giving of the Law to the return of the spies.. Compare Exodus xix. 1, and Numbers x. 11.	1

	YEARS.
Brought forward	2517
From the return of the spies to the apportionment of the land	45
Compare Numbers xiv. and Joshua xiv. "And now the Lord hath kept me alive, as he said, these forty and five years, even since the Lord spake this word unto Moses."—Joshua xiv. 10.	
From the apportionment of the land to Samuel the prophet	450
"And after that he gave them judges about the space of four hundred and fifty years, until Samuel the prophet."—Acts xiii. 19, 20.	
From the raising up of Samuel to Saul's death	40
"And afterwards they desired a king; and God gave unto them Saul the son of Cis, a man of the tribe of Benjamin, by the space of forty years."—Acts xiii. 21.	
From the death of Saul to the end of David's reign	40
"And when he had removed him [Saul], he raised up unto them David."—Acts xiii. 22. "And the days that David reigned over Israel were forty years: seven years reigned he in Hebron, and thirty and three years reigned he in Jerusalem."—1 Kings ii. 11.	
From David to the end of Solomon's reign	40
"And Solomon reigned in Jerusalem over all Israel forty years."—2 Chron. ix. 30.	
From Solomon's death to the end of Rehoboam's reign,	17
"So King Rehoboam . . . reigned seventeen years in Jerusalem."—2 Chron. xii. 13.	
From Rehoboam to the end of Abijah's reign	3
"Abijah . . . reigned three years in Jerusalem."—2 Chron. xiii. 1, 2.	

	YEARS.
Brought forward	3152
From Abijah to the death of King Asa	41
"And Asa died in the one and fortieth year of his reign."—2 Chron. xvi. 13.	
From Asa to the end of the reign of Jehoshaphat	25
"He reigned twenty and five years in Jerusalem." —2 Chron. xx. 31.	
From Jehoshaphat to the end of Jehoram's reign	8
"He reigned in Jerusalem eight years."—2 Chron. xxi. 20.	
From Jehoram to the end of Ahaziah's reign	1
"He reigned one year in Jerusalem."—2 Chron. xxii. 2.	
From Ahaziah to the end of Athaliah's usurpation	6
"And he [Joash] was with them hid in the house of God six years: and Athaliah reigned."—2 Chron. xxii. 12.	
From Athaliah's usurpation to the end of Joash's reign,	40
"Joash . . . reigned forty years in Jerusalem."—2 Chron. xxiv. 1.	
From Joash to the end of Amaziah's reign	29
"He reigned twenty and nine years in Jerusalem." —2 Chron. xxv. 1.	
From Amaziah to the end of Uzziah's reign	52
"He reigned fifty and two years in Jerusalem."—2 Chron. xxvi. 1.	
From Uzziah to the end of the reign of Jotham	16
"He reigned sixteen years in Jerusalem."—2 Chron. xxvii. 1.	
From Jotham to the death of Ahaz	16
"Ahaz . . . reigned sixteen years."—2 Chron. xxviii. 1.	
From Ahaz to the death of Hezekiah	29

	YEARS.
Brought forward	3415
"Hezekiah reigned nine and twenty years."—2 Chron. xxix. 1.	
From Hezekiah to the death of Manasseh	55
"Manasseh reigned fifty and five years."—2 Chron. xxxiii. 1.	
From Manasseh to the death of Amon	2
"Amon . . . reigned two years."—2 Chron. xxxiii. 21.	
From Amon to the death of Josiah	31
"Josiah . . . reigned in Jerusalem one and thirty years."—2 Chron. xxxiv. 1.	
From Josiah to the deposition of Jehoahaz	0
"He reigned three months."—2 Chron. xxxvi. 2.	
From the deposition of Jehoahaz to the death of Jehoiachim	11
"Jehoiachim . . . reigned eleven years."—2 Chron. xxxvi. 5.	
From Jehoiachim to the deposition of Jehoiachin	0
"Jehoiachin . . . reigned three months and ten days."—2 Chron. xxxvi. 9.	
From Jehoiachin to the captivity under Zedekiah	11
"Zedekiah . . . reigned eleven years."—2 Chron. xxxvi. 11.	
From the commencement of the Captivity to the decree of Cyrus	70
"These nations shall serve the King of Babylon seventy years."—Jer. xxv. 11: compare 2 Chron. xxxvi. 22, 23.	
From the decree of Cyrus to the birth of Christ	536
Settled by the registers of the reigns of the Chaldean and Persian kings furnished in the royal canon of Ptolemy, as agreed by all our best chronologists.	

	YEARS.
Brought forward	4131
From the birth of Christ to the present	1863
From the creation of Adam to A.D. 1863	5994
Still necessary to complete the period of 6000	6
From the creation of man to the consummation	6000

which, according to this reckoning, will be reached in 1869 or '70, when the great Millennial sabbath, if these dates be correct, is to set in. Other versions of the Scriptures give some of them differently; but the common version, which we have followed, and which is the simple translation of the Hebrew, is quite as likely to be the genuine as any other, and is generally accepted as the true. With our present knowledge of the subject, we are willing to abide by it.

NOTE L. ELEVENTH DISCOURSE, p. 281.

PROBABLE DATES OF THE SEVEN LAST VIALS IN THEIR HISTORICAL FULFILMENT.

VIAL.

I. *The French Revolution*, from the meeting of the States-General to the death of the king:—A.D. 1789–1793.

II. *The Reign of Terror*, from the death of the king to the establishment of the Directory:—A.D. 1793–1795.

III. *The Wars of the Directory*, from the establishment of the Directory of Five to the First Consulship of Napoleon I.:—A.D. 1795–1799.

VIAL.

IV. *The scorching and blasting career of Napoleon I.*, from his appointment as First Consul to his abdication of the empire:—A.D. 1799–1814.

V. *Judgments upon the throne and kingdom of the Beast*, from the overthrow of Napoleon I. to the revolutions of 1848, the overthrow of the Orleans dynasty, and the rise of Napoleon III.:—A.D. 1814–1849.

VI. *Wane of Babylon's resources and supports, and mustering of the nations for their final overthrow*, from the rise of Louis Napoleon to the emperorship to the coming of Christ as the thief to remove the Church of the first-born, or wise virgins, from the earth to meet him in the air:—A.D. 1850—

VII. *The great tribulation, unexampled earthquake, and judgment of the nations*, from the full development of the personal Antichrist—most likely Napoleon III.—to the manifestation of Christ for his final destruction and the binding of Satan; estimated by numerous interpreters to date from A.D. 1865–6—1869–70.

These vials, however, are to have their literal and *complete* fulfilment only within the last months before the descent and manifestation of Christ and his grand saint-army, which ushers in the time of blessedness for those who wait and come to that day—the day for which the earth has been sighing for wellnigh six thousand years.

THE HAPPY DAWN.

LIGHT of the better morning,
  Shine down on me!
Sun of the brighter heaven,
  Bid darkness flee!
Thy warmth impart
To this dull heart:
Pour in thy light,
And let this night
Be turn'd to day
By thy mild ray!
  Lord Jesus, come;
    Thou daystar, shine;
  Enlighten now
    This soul of mine!

Streaks of the better dawning,
  Break on my sight,
Fringing with silver edges
  These clouds of night.
Gems on morn's brow,
Glow, brightly glow,
Foretelling soon
The ascending noon,
Wakening this earth
To second birth,
  When He shall come,
    To earth again,
  Who comes to judge,
    Who comes to reign.

H. BONAR.

Authorities, Books, and References

ON THE SUBJECTS TREATED IN THIS VOLUME,

WITH SOME CRITICAL OBSERVATIONS.

CHAPTER I.

ANALYSIS OF AUTHORITIES FROM THE HOLY SCRIPTURES.

DR. AUBERLEN has remarked that Jesus, and all his prophets and apostles, were *Chiliasts*. He has also said that the doctrine of the Millennial kingdom does not rest, as is often thought, upon an isolated passage in the Apocalypse, but is essential to a right understanding of the entire body of the Old Testament, and is the fundamental idea in the teachings of the New, in which the sum and substance of Messianic prophecy are concentrated. That these are correct representations, the following citations, carefully examined, will help to show :—

1. REFERENCES IN THE TEACHINGS OF CHRIST AND HIS APOSTLES TO THE COMING AGAIN OF THE LORD JESUS IN PERSON TO THE EARTH.

MATTHEW, xvi. 27, 28; xix. 28; xxiii. 39; xxiv. 3, 27, 30–31, 37–39, 42, 44, 48–51; xxv. 6, 10, 13, 19, 31; xxvi. 64. Also, allusions with less specific directness, vi. 10; xiii. 24–30, 37–43, 47–50; xx. 20–23; xxi. 44; xxii. 11, 30, 44; xxvi. 29.

MARK, viii. 38; xiii. 26, 27, 35–37; xiv. 61, 62. Also, by way of allusion, iv. 29; x. 35–40; xiv. 25.

LUKE, ix. 26; xii. 36–40, 43, 45, 46; xiii. 35; xvii. 24, 30; xviii. 8; xix. 12, 13, 15; xxi. 27, 36; xxii. 69. Also, allusions, i. 32, 33; xiv. 10; xix. 38; xx. 18, 35; xxii. 16, 18, 29.

JOHN, xiv. 3, 28; xvi. 16, 22. Also, allusions, i. 51; v. 25, 27, 28; vi. 40, 44, 54; xi. 52; xii. 12, 13; xvii. 24; xxi. 22, 23.

ACTS OF THE APOSTLES, i. 9–11; iii. 19–21. Also, allusions, i. 7; x. 42; xvi. 31; xx. 31, 32; xxiii. 6; xxiv. 15, 25; xxvi. 6. 7.

PAUL TO THE ROMANS, xi. 25, 26. Allusions, v. 2, 9, 17; vi. 8; viii. 17–25; xi. 11, 12; xiii. 11, 12; xvi. 20.

PAUL'S FIRST EPISTLE TO THE CORINTHIANS, i. 7, 8; iv. 5; xi. 26; xv. 23, 24. Allusions, iii. 13; v. 5; vi. 2, 3; xiii. 10, 12; xv. 28, 51, 52.

PAUL'S SECOND EPISTLE TO THE CORINTHIANS, allusions, i. 14; iv. 17, 18; v. 10; xi. 2.

PAUL TO THE GALATIANS, allusions, iii. 29; v. 5.

PAUL TO THE EPHESIANS, allusions, i. 10, 14, 18; ii. 7; iv. 30; v. 27; vi. 18.

PAUL TO THE PHILIPPIANS, i. 6, 10; ii. 16; iii. 20, 21; iv. 5. Allusions, ii. 10; iii. 11, 14.

PAUL TO THE COLOSSIANS, iii. 4. Allusions, i. 5; iii. 24.

PAUL'S FIRST EPISTLE TO THE THESSALONIANS, i. 10; ii. 19; iii. 13; iv. 13–18; v. 1–4, 23. Allusions, i. 3; ii. 12; v. 9.

PAUL'S SECOND EPISTLE TO THE THESSALONIANS, i. 6–11; ii. 1–8; iii. 5. Allusions, ii. 14, 16.

PAUL'S EPISTLES TO TIMOTHY, 1 Tim. vi. 14; 2 Tim. iv. 1, 8. Allusions, 2 Tim. i. 12; ii. 12; iv. 18.

PAUL'S EPISTLE TO TITUS, ii. 13.

PAUL'S EPISTLE TO THE HEBREWS, ix. 28; x. 37. Allusions, i. 13; ii. 5, 7, 8; iv. 9; viii. 10; x. 13, 25, 30; xi. 26, 35; xii. 14, 22, 27, 28; xiii. 14.

JAMES, v. 7, 8. Allusions, i. 18; ii. 5; v. 9.

PETER'S FIRST EPISTLE, i. 7, 13; iv. 13; v. 4. Allusions, i. 3, 5, 11; ii. 7; iii. 15; iv. 5, 7; v. 1, 10.

PETER'S SECOND EPISTLE, i. 16, 19; iii. 10, 11, 14. Allusions, i. 11; iii. 13.

JOHN'S FIRST EPISTLE, ii. 28; iii. 2. Allusions, iv. 17.

JUDE'S EPISTLE, 14–16. Allusion, 24.

JOHN'S REVELATION, i. 7; ii. 25; iii. 3, 11; xvi. 15; xix. 11–16; xx. 11; xxii. 7, 12, 20. Allusions, i. 1, 3, 19; ii. 26, 27; iii. 21; iv. 1; vi. 12–17; xi. 15, 17, 18; xii. 5; xiv. 1–4; xv. 4; xvi. 14; xx. 4; xxii. 10.

2. REFERENCES TO SOME REMARKABLE PASSAGES ON THE SAME SUBJECT IN THE OLD TESTAMENT.

NUMBERS, xxiv. 16–19.

JOB, xix. 25–27.

PSALMS, l. 3–6; xcvi. 10–13; xcviii. 7–9; cii. 16.

ISAIAH, ii. 10–21; viii. 17; xxv. 9; xxvi. 21; xxxv. 4; xl. 10; xlii. 13; lxii. 11; lxiv. 1–4; lxvi. 15.

JEREMIAH, xxiii. 5–7.

EZEKIEL, xxiii. 25–27.

DANIEL, vii. 13, 14; xii. 1, 2.

MICAH, i. 3, 4.

HABAKKUK, iii. 1–19.

ZECHARIAH, ii. 10–13; xiv. 3, 4.

MALACHI, iii. 1, 2.

Sir Isaac Newton has said that "there is scarcely a prophecy in the Old Testament concerning Christ that doth not, in something or other, relate to his second coming."* The above are but a few out of many which refer directly to the subject. The allusions to it are multitudinous.

* "Observations on the Prophecies of Daniel," &c., p. 132.

8. REFERENCES TO THE OBJECTS AND RESULTS OF CHRIST'S RETURN TO THE EARTH.

As regards his true people,—

For the purpose of completing their redemption, Luke xxi. 27, 28; Rom. viii. 19–23; Eph. iv. 30; Heb. ix. 28.

For the purpose of raising them that sleep from their graves, 1 Cor. xv. 22, 23; 1 Thess. iv. 14, 16; Job xix. 25–27.

For the purpose of changing those of them who shall be found living upon the earth from mortal to immortality, 1 Cor. xv. 42–44, 51–54; Phil. iii. 20, 21.

For the purpose of receiving them to himself in some aerial abode in glory, John xiv. 3; 1 Thess. iv. 15–17; 1 John iii. 2; Rev. vii. 15.

For the purpose of investing them with dominion and authority, according to their works, Matt. xvi. 27; 1 Cor. iv. 5; 2 Cor. v. 10; Matt. xix. 28; 1 Cor. vi. 2, 3; Luke xix. 13, 19; Rev. ii. 26, 27; xx. 4; Dan. vii. 21, 22.

As regards his enemies,—

To destroy their power, Isaiah xxiv. 21–23; xxv. 9–12; Rev. vi. 15, 16; Psalm ii. 1–9; Dan. vii. 9, 26; Isaiah xiv. 24–26.

To destroy their armies, Zech. xiv. 3, 12–15; Rev. xvi. 14; xix. 19–21; Isaiah xxxi. 8, 9; Jer. xxv. 33.

To destroy their works, Matt. xv. 13; Jer. xxv. 37, 38.

To hurl their leaders to perdition, Dan. vii. 11; Ezek. xxxviii. 22; 2 Thess. ii. 8–11; Rev. xvii. 11; xix. 20.

To visit terrible retribution on all the disobedient, Luke xix. 27; 2 Thess. i. 8; Jude 15, 16; Rev. i. 7; xvi. 1–21; Isaiah lxiii. 1–4; lxvi. 15, 16; Dan. xii. 1; Joel iii. 9–16; Ps. i. 4, 5.

To destroy utterly some of the great centres of wickedness, with their wicked inhabitants, Rev. xviii. 2, 8, 18; 2 Peter iii. 7.

To bind and shut up Satan in the bottomless pit, Rev. xxx. 1–3.

As regards the Jewish people,—

To deliver them from the power of the armies brought against them, Zech. xiv. 3–5, 12–16; Joel iii. 9–17; Micah iv. 6–13.

To turn them from ungodliness to truth and righteousness, Rom. xi. 26, 27; Isaiah lix. 20, 21; Zech. xii. 10–14; xiii. 1, 2; Ezek. xxxvi. 23–39; Jer. xxxi. 33, 34.

To unite and establish them in their own land, Ezek. xxxvii. 21, 22; xxxiv. 25–31; Isaiah xi. 11–13; lxvi. 6–20; Micah iv. 3, 4.

To make Jerusalem the seat of universal empire, Micah iv. 1, 2; Isaiah lx. 14; Zech. xiv. 16; Luke xxi. 24; Isaiah xxiv. 23; Ps. ii. 6.

To become their king forever, Rev. xi. 15; Isaiah xxiv. 23; ix. 7; Ezek. xxxvii. 24, 25; Luke i. 32, 33; Jer. xxiii. 5, 6; Micah iv. 6, 7.

To make them a blessing to all nations, Gen. xii. 3; xxii. 18; Micah v. 7; Acts iii. 25, 26; Rom. xi. 15.

As regards the world at large,—

To subvert the empire of wickedness, Isaiah ii. 17–22; xxxi. 7; Ps. lxxii. 7, 8; Zech. xiv. 20, 21.

To bring wars and violence to an end, Ps. xlvi. 9; Isaiah ii. 4; lx. 18; Micah iv. 3.

To deliver the suffering creation from the bondage of corruption, Rom. viii. 19–21; Isaiah xxxv. 1, 2, 6, 7, 9; Rev. xxii. 3.

To establish his glorious kingdom upon the earth, Dan. ii. 44; vii. 13, 14; Matt. xxv. 31; Isaiah ix. 7; Ezek. xxi. 27; Zech. xiv. 8; Rev. xi. 15; Matt. vi. 9, 10.

To make all things new, Isaiah lxv. 17–25; lxvi. 22; Matt. xix. 28; Acts iii. 20, 21; 2 Peter iii. 10–13; Rev. xxi. 1–5.

4. REFERENCES TO THE COURSE OF THINGS IN THIS WORLD UNTIL CHRIST COMES.

As to the world in general, showing that wickedness will abound till then, Matt. xxiv. 6–15, 37; Mark xiii. 6–13; Luke xvii. 26–31; 1 Thess. v. 2, 3; 2 Tim. iii. 1–13; 2 Peter iii. 3, 4, 10; Jude 18, 19.

As to the great Gentile and antichristian powers, showing that they shall not be destroyed till then, Dan. ii. 26–45; vii. 1–28; viii. 2–27; xi. 2–45; xii. 1–3; 2 Thess. ii. 3–12; 1 John ii. 18, 19; Rev. xiii. 1–18; xvi. 1–21; xvii. 1–18; xviii. 1–24; xix. 1–21.

As to the professed Church, showing that it will be under the cross and imperfect till then, Matt. xiii. 24–30, 36–42; xxv. 1–13; Mark xiii.; ix. 1–13; Acts xx. 29, 30; 1 Tim. iv. 1–3; 2 Tim. iii. 1–5; 2 Peter ii. 1, 3, 12, 13, 17: Rev. ii. and iii; xiii. 8, 14, 16, 17.

5. REFERENCES TO OUR DUTY WITH REGARD TO THE RETURN OF CHRIST.

We are to watch for it, Matt. xxiv. 43–51; xxv. 13; Mark xiii. 33–37; Luke xii. 35–37; xxi. 34–36; 1 Thess. v. 4–6; Rev. xvi. 15.

We are to pray for it, Matt. vi. 10; Luke xi. 2; Can. viii. 14; Rev. xxii. 20.

We are to wait patiently for it, 1 Thess. i. 10; 2 Thess. iii. 5; 1 Cor. i. 7; Isaiah xxv. 9.

We are to expect it, and look for it continually, Phil. iii. 20; Titus ii. 13; Heb. ix. 28; 2 Peter iii. 12, 14; Rev. i. 7.

We are to love it, and anticipate it with cheerful and fond desire, 2 Tim. iv. 8; Rom. viii. 23; 2 Cor. v. 2; Titus ii. 13.

We are to keep ourselves in constant readiness for it, Matt. xxiv. 44; Mark xiii. 33, 36; Luke xii. 35, 36, 40; xxi. 34; Rom. xiii. 11–14; 1 Thess. v. 6; Rev. xvi. 15.

We are to provide ourselves with oil in our vessels, Matt. xxv. 1–13.

To lay out our talents for the Master, Matt. xxiv. 14–30; Luke xix. 12–17.

To be thoughtful of his afflicted people, Matt. xxv. 31–46.

To have on the wedding garment, Matt. xxii. 11.

6. REFERENCES TO THE SIGNS WHICH ARE TO MARK THE TIMES IMMEDIATELY PRECEDING THE SAVIOR'S RETURN.

The gospel to be universally promulged, Matt. xxiv. 14; xxviii. 19; Luke xxiv. 47; Acts i. 8.

Nominal Christendom to be fearfully apostate, Luke xviii. 8; 2 Thess. ii. 3, 4, 8–12; 2 Tim. iii. 1–5; iv. 3, 4; Matt. xiii. 37–43; xxiv. 37–39; 2 Peter ii. 1–22; iii. 3, 4.

The world to abound with intense wickedness, Matt. xxiv. 37–39; Luke xvii. 26–30; 1 Thess. v. 1–3; 2 Tim. iii. 13; Jude 17–19; Rev. xiii. 1–17.

Great troubles and revolutionary disturbances to oppress the nations, Isaiah ii. 10–22; v. 26–30; xxiv. 1–20; Jer. xxv. 15–29; Ezek. xxi. 24–27; Dan. xii. 1; Haggai ii. 7, 22; Matt. xxiv. 21; Mark xiii. 19, 20; Luke xxi. 10, 25–27; Heb. xii. 27; Rev. viii. 1–13; xix. 1–21; xii. 12.

A wide-spread awakening among Christ's people to the subject of his coming, Dan. xii. 9; Matt. xxv. 6; Hab. ii. 3.

The cessation of the oppressions endured by the Jews, the rebuilding of Jerusalem, and the commencement of the return of the people of Israel to Palestine, Luke xxi. 24; Dan. ix. 27; Rom. xi. 25; Lev. xxvi. 43–45; Isaiah i. 24–28; xi. 11, 12; lxii. 1–12; Jer. xvi. 11–21; xxiii. 3; xxxi. 4–12, 35–40; xxxii. 37–44; xxxiii. 7–11; xlvi. 27, 28; Ezek. xxxvi. 8–36; xxxix. 25–29; Zech. viii. 2–15.

The multiplication of signs and portentous forebodings in nature, Luke xxi. 11, 25, 26, 27, 31; Mark xiii. 8, 25; Acts ii. 19, 20; Micah vii. 15, 16.

Great violence of passion, anger, and blasphemy on the part of nations, Luke xxi. 10; Mark xiii. 8; Ps. ii. 2, 3; Joel iii. 9–12; Rev. xi. 18; xvi. 9, 10, 11.

The devil to manifest himself in the most potent and malignant forms, in the Church and in the world, Matt. xii. 43–46; xxiv. 24; 2 Thess. ii. 7–12; 1 Tim. iv. 1–3; Rev. xii. 12; xiii. 1–18; xvi. 13, 14.

7. REFERENCES TO THE MANNER IN WHICH CHRIST WILL COME.

He will come literally and personally as he ascended, Acts i. 9, 11; Heb. ix. 28; Rev. i. 7.

He will most likely come first invisibly to steal away his waiting and watching saints, when "two shall be in one bed, the one shall be taken and the other left," &c.; at any rate, "as a thief in the night," Matt. xxiv. 43; Luke xii. 39; 1 Thess. v. 2; 2 Peter iii. 10; Rev. xvi. 15; Luke xvii. 34–36.

He will come suddenly, when people generally will not be expecting such a thing, Luke xxi. 34, 35; Mark xiii. 36; 1 Thess. v. 3; Rev. iii. 3.

He will come, as to his visible manifestation, in splendor and great glory, Matt. xvi. 27; xxiv. 30; Luke ix. 26; xxi. 27.

He will come in the clouds, Matt. xxvi. 64; Mark xiv. 62; Acts i. 9; 1 Thess. iv. 17; Rev. i. 7.

He will be revealed from heaven as the lightning shineth, Matt. xxiv. 27; Luke xvii. 24; Zech. ix. 14; 2 Thess. i. 8.

He will be revealed to every one's sight, Rev. i. 7; Numb. xxiv. 17; Job xix. 26, 27; xxxiv. 26; 1 John iii. 2; Zech. xii. 10; Rev. xxii. 4.

He will descend to the earth at the place from which he ascended, Zech. xiv. 4; Ezek. xliii. 2; Acts i. 11, 12.

He will come accompanied with the angel-saints, whom he will raise from among the dead and steal away from among the living for the purpose of having them with him, Jude 14; Matt. xvi. 27; xxv. 31; 1 Thess. iii. 13; Deut. xxxiii. 2; Zech. xiv. 5; Rev. xiv. 4; xix. 14. Compare, also, Matt. xxii. 30.

He will come clothed with irresistible majesty and power, Matt. xxiv. 30; xxvi. 64; Mark xiii. 26; Luke xxi. 27; 2 Thess. i. 7; Ps. cx. 2; Rev. vi. 17; xix. 15, 16.

He will come in connection with some very marvellous heraldic demonstrations, 1 Thess. iv. 16. Compare Exod. xix. 16; xx. 18; Isaiah xxvii. 13; Zech. ix. 14; Matt. xxiv. 31.

8. REFERENCES TO THE TIME WHEN CHRIST WILL COME.

It will be in a period of abounding apostasy and unbelief, Matt. xxiv. 37–39; Luke xviii. 8; 2 Thess. ii. 8; 2 Tim. iii. 1–5; 2 Peter iii. 3, 4.

It will be in a time of revolutionary troubles and political agitations and sufferings, Luke xxi. 25–28; Ps. ii. 1–5; Ezek. xxi. 27; Heb. xii. 26; Rev. xvi. 1–15.

Christ will come while the Roman empire, under its last head, and the ten kings under whom it is to be in a sense revived, are still standing, Dan. vii. 9–14; Rev. xix. 11–20.

He will come before the Jews as an entire people shall return to Palestine, Micah ii. 12, 13; Isaiah lii. 12; lxvi. 15–20; Rom. xi. 26.

He will come when the Man of Sin is still in power, Dan. vii. 8, 24; 2 Thess. ii. 7, 8.

He will come at a time when an awakening cry has gone forth announcing his nearness, Matt. xxv. 6; Mal. iv. 5, 6; Rev. xvi. 15.

He will come when nevertheless there shall be great skepticism and indifference on the subject, Luke xxi. 34, 35; 1 Thess. v. 3; 2 Peter iii. 3, 4; Jude 14, 15, 18.

9. REFERENCES TO THE CONDITION OF THINGS ON THE EARTH AFTER THE SAVIOR'S RETURN.

The world subjected to divine rule, Dan. ii. 44, 45; vii. 13, 14, 26, 27; Matt. xxv. 31, 34; Luke xxi. 31; Rev. xi. 15–18; xx. 4–6; Isaiah xxxii. 1, 17, 18; Jer. xxxiii. 5, 6.

The children of Israel all united again in one permanent nationality, Jer. iii. 18, 19; xxiii. 3–8; xxx. 3–22; xxxiii. 12–26; Isaiah x. 20, 21; xi. 10–13; Ezek. xxxvii. 12–28; Hos. i. 10, 11; Zech. viii. 3–23; ix. 12–17; x. 6–10; xii. 6, 7; Rom. xi. 25–27.

Christ the king, Luke i. 31–33; 2 Sam. vii. 12–16; 1 Chron. xvii. 11–14; Ps. ii. 6–12; lxxxix. 3, 4, 29–37; Isa. ix. 6, 7; Jer. iii. 17; xxxiii. 17, 20, 21; Hos. iii. 5; Ezek. xxxiv. 23, 24; xxxvii. 24, 25; 1 Cor. xv. 25; Zech. xiv. 9; Heb. ii. 6–8.

Satan's power in abeyance, Rev. xx. 1–3; Isaiah xxvii. 1; *and finally destroyed,* Rev. xx. 10.

Israel wholly righteous, and a great blessing in the earth, Jer. xxxi. 33, 34; Ezek. xxxvi. 24–33; xxxvii. 23, 28; Rom. xi. 26, 27; Heb. viii. 10–12; Gen. xii. 2; Isaiah lxvi. 6, 7, 19; Zech. viii. 21, 22; Micah iv. 1, 2.

Jerusalem the glorious metropolis of the world, Isaiah ii. 2–4; xxiv. 23; lx. 1–22; Joel iii. 16, 17, 20; Zech. xiv. 17–21; Ezek. xxxix. 25; xliii. 7.

Christ reigning over all people, Ps. lxxii. 8–19; Micah iv. 1–7; Zech. ix. 10; Rev. xi. 15.

The glorified saints share with him in the administration of his sublime dominion, Exod. xix. 6; Ps. xlvii. 3; xlix. 14; Isaiah xxxii. 1; Dan. vii. 21, 22; Matt. xix. 28; Luke xix. 17, 19; xxii. 29, 30; 1 Cor. iv. 5; vi. 2, 3; ix. 25; 2 Tim. iv. 8; 1 Peter v. 4; Rev. i. 6; ii. 10, 26, 27; iii. 21; v. 10; xx. 4; xxi. 7; xxii. 5.

The knowledge of the Lord fills the world, Isaiah xi. 9; Ps. xxii. 27; Hab. ii. 14; Zech. xiv. 8, 9; Heb. viii. 10, 11.

The curse is repealed, and the suffering creation delivered, Rev. xxii. 3; Rom. viii. 19–23; 1 Tim. ii. 15; Isaiah xi. 6–9; Hosea ii. 17, 18; Zech. xiv. 11, 20, 21.

All things made new, Isaiah lxv. 17–25; lxvi. 22; 2 Peter iii. 10–13; Rev. xxi. 1–5; Matt. xix. 28; Acts iii. 20, 21.

The Lord dwelling with men, Lev. xxvi. 11, 12; Ezek. xxxvii. 27, 28; xliii. 7; xlviii. 35; Rev. xxi. 3.

The earth full of prosperity and blessedness, Ps. lxvii. 6, 7; xcvi. 11–13; Isaiah lii. 9, 10; lv. 12, 13; xxxii. 15–20; xxxv. 1–10; Amos xiii. 15; Joel iii. 18.

Death and all evil finally and completely destroyed, Isaiah xxv. 8; Hosea xiii. 14; 1 Cor. xv. 26; Heb ii. 14, 15; Rev. vii. 16, 17; xx. 14; xxi. 4; xxii. 1–5.

God all in all, 1 Cor. xv. 24, 27, 28.

10. REFERENCES TO THE USES MADE IN THE SCRIPTURES OF THE REVELATIONS CONCERNING THE SECOND ADVENT.

They present it as the great hope of the Church, Titus ii. 13; 1 Peter i. 13; Job xix. 25–27; Isaiah xxv. 9; Col. ii. 4; 2 Tim. iv. 8.

They give it as a motive—

to take up testimony for Christ, Luke ix. 26.

to heavenly-mindedness, Phil. iii. 20.

to moderation, Phil. iv. 5.

to mortification of the flesh, Col. iii. 4, 5.

to faithfulness in God's service, 1 Tim. vi. 14; 2 Tim. iv. 1, 2, 8; 1 Peter v. 4.

to soberness and godly living, Titus ii. 12, 13.

to perseverance, Heb. x. 37.

to patience, James v. 7, 8.

to holy conversation and godliness, 2 Peter iii. 10, 11.

to diligence and activity, Matt. xxv. 14–30; Luke xix. 13; 2 Peter iii. 14.

to hold fast what we have in Christ, Rev. ii. 25; iii. 11.

They give it as a motive—

to carefulness in intercourse with the world, Rev. xvi. 15.

to fraternal affection, 1 Thess. iii. 12, 13.

to abide in Christ, 1 John ii. 28.

They refer to it as a subject of peculiar comfort under bereavement, 1 Thess. iv. 18; 2 Tim. i. 5, 7; ii. 12; Isa. xxx. 18.

They employ it as an encouragement to labor for souls, and as a subject of solemn appeal in the charge to ministers, 1 Cor i. 4–7; 1 Thess. ii. 19, 20; 2 Tim. iv. 1.

They direct attention to it as a corrective of, and support under, censoriousness and judging of others, 1 Cor. iv. 3–5.

They speak of it as a thing which should possess absorbing importance and interest to all who desire to be prepared for the eternal kingdom, Matt. xxiv. 42–51; xxv. 13; Mark xiii. 33–37; Luke xxi. 34–36; 1 Thess. v. 4–6.

11. REFERENCES TO THE FUTURE DESTINY OF THE JEWISH PEOPLE.*

They shall be gathered from all places of their dispersion and brought into their own land, Isaiah xi. 11; xxvii. 12, 13; xliii. 5, 6; xlix. 11, 12; lx. 4; Jer. iii. 18; xvi. 14, 15; xxiii. 3; xxxi. 7–10; xxxii. 37; Zech. viii. 7, 8; x. 8, 9, 10.

They shall be helped, carried, and numerously joined by the Gentiles, Isaiah xlix. 22; xiv. 2; lx. 9; lxvi. 18–20; ii. 2–4; Jer. iii. 17; xvi. 19; Ezek. xlvii. 22, 23; Zech. viii. 20–23.

Great miracles shall attend their restoration, Isaiah xi. 15, 16; Zech. x. 11; Micah vii. 15; Isaiah xix. 20; xli. 19, 20; xliii. 19, 20; lxvi. 18–22; Hosea xii. 9, 10; Isaiah xxxv. 4–10; lii. 12; lviii. 8; Hosea i. 10, 11; Micah ii. 12, 13; Malachi iv. 5, 6.

* Mostly from Powel's Concordance, published in 1673.

They shall again be formed into a state, with judges and counsellors as formerly, Christ himself being their king, Isaiah i. 25, 26; lx. 15–22; Jer. xxiii. 4; xxx. 9, 21; Ezek. xxxiv. 23, 24; xxxvii. 24, 25; Hosea iii. 5; Obadiah 21; Zech. xiv. 5, 9.

They shall have the victory over all their enemies, and the pre-eminence of all the nations, Isaiah xli. 14–16; xlix. 23; lx. 8–14; Joel iii. 7, 8, 19, 20; Obadiah 17, 18; Micah iv. 6–13; v. 5–7; vii. 16, 17; Zech. ii. 12, 13; ix. 13, 17; x. 5, 6; xii. 6–9.

Once restored, they shall live peaceably, and no more be divided into two nations, Isaiah xi. 13, 14; Jer. l. 4; Ezek. xxxvii. 19, 22; Hosea i. 11.

They shall be numerous and multiply greatly, Isaiah xxvii. 6; xliv. 3, 4; xlix. 18–21; liv. 1–3; lxi. 9; Jer. xxiii. 3; xxx. 18–20; xxxiii. 10, 11; xxxvi. 37, 38.

They shall have great peace, safety, and prosperity, Isaiah xxxii. 16–18; xxxiii. 24; liv. 13–17; lx. 18–22; Jer. xxiii. 3–6; xxx. 10–22; xxxi. 34–40; xxxiii. 6–9; l. 19, 20; Zeph. iii. 13; Zech. iii. 9, 10.

They shall be very glorious, and a blessing to the whole earth, Isaiah xix. 24, 25; lxi. 9; Jer. xxxiii. 9; Ezek. xxxiv. 26; Zeph. iii. 19; Zech. viii. 13; xii. 8; Rom. xi. 15.

Judea shall be made extraordinarily fruitful and attractive, Isaiah xxix. 17; xxxv. 1–9; li. 3, 16; liv. 12, 13; lx. 13–17; lxv. 25; Ezek. xxxiv. 26, 27; xxxvi. 36; Joel iii. 18; Amos ix. 13, 14.

Jerusalem shall be rebuilt, and after the restoration of all the tribes shall never be destroyed, nor infested with enemies any more, Isaiah ii. 1–3; lii. 1; xxvi. 1, 2; lx. 10–20; Jer. xxxi. 38–40; Joel iii. 17.

Immediately preceding, and in connection with, their establishment in Palestine, and especially their conversion, there shall be great wars, confusion, and desolation throughout the earth, Isaiah xxxiv. 1–17; Jer. xxx. 17–10; Joel iii. 1–10; Ezek. xxviii. 24–26; Haggai ii. 21–23; Zeph. iii. 8; Zech. xiv. 2, 3, 12–15.

Their general restoration and conversion not to take place till after the return of Christ, Zech. xii. 7; Isaiah xi. 1–16; lii. 12; lxvi. 1–24; Micah ii. 12, 13; Zech. xii. 1–14; xiv. 1–21; Rom. xi. 26; Ezek. xxxvii. 1–28; Ps. cii. 16.

Previous to the return of Christ, just one year-day week, many of them will make a compact with the Antichrist, in some sense accepting him as their protector and Messiah, Dan. ix. 27; xi. 23; Matt. xxiv. 24.

Their land to be invaded, and their city to be once more partially destroyed, immediately before the revelation of Christ on Mount Olivet, Zech. xiv. 2, 12; Dan. xi. 41–45; Ezek. xxviii. 8–23; Isaiah lxvi. 18; Joel iii. 9–17; Rev. xvi. 14; Zech. xii. 9.

Their general conversion to be effected by the personal appearance of Christ, Zech. xii. 10; Rom. xi. 26. Allusion to this seems also to be contained in 1 Tim. i. 16. Paul's conversion was by the personal manifestation of Christ, Acts ix. 3–5; 1 Cor. ix. 1.

12. REFERENCES TO THE ANTICHRIST OF THE LAST DAYS.

His names, 2 Thess. ii. 2, 8; Isaiah xiv. 4, 25; Ezek. xxviii. 2, 12; Dan. xi. 21; viii. 9, 23; Matt. xxiv. 15; Rev. ix. 11; xiii. 18.

His character for deceit and subtlety, Isaiah xiv.; Ezek. xxviii. 3–17; Dan. xi. 32; 2 Thess. ii. 9–11; Matt. xxiv. 24.

Is to utter marvellous things against the Most High, and deny the Father and the Son, Dan. xi. 36; 1 John iv. 3; 2 John 7; Rev. xiii. 13.

Is to establish himself in Jerusalem, Dan. xi. 45; Ezek. xxviii. 2, 14; Matt. xxiv. 15.

Is to appropriate Divine honors and establish idolatry, Ezek. xxviii. 2; Dan. xi. 36; Isaiah xiv. 13, 14; 2 Thess. ii. 4; Rev. xiii. 15.

Is to take away the restored daily sacrifice of the Jews, Dan. viii. 10–12; ix. 27; xi. 31.

Is to destroy and persecute the holy people, Dan. viii. 24; Rev. xii. 13, 17; xiii. 7, 15, 16, 17; xx. 4.

Is to unite the armies of the earth in an expedition into Palestine, Isaiah xiii. 4, 5; xvii. 12–14; Dan. xii. 1; Joel iii. 2; Matt. xxiv. 21; Rev. xvi. 16; perhaps, also, Ezek. xxxviii. 8–19.

Is to be destroyed by the revelation of Christ in Palestine, Isaiah xiv. 10–25; Ezek. xxviii. 7, 8; xxxviii. 21, 22; Dan. xi. 25; 2 Thess. ii. 8; Rev. xix. 11–20.

His greatness and fall specially described, Ezek. xxxi. 2–18; Isaiah xiv. 4–25.

His rule and principal depredations as the Antichrist to continue only about three and a half years, Dan. vii. 25; ix. 27; Rev. xi. 3; xii. 6; xiii. 5.

Irenæus has this observation :—"When Antichrist, reigning three years and six months, shall have laid waste all things in this world, and have sat in the temple of Jerusalem, then shall the Lord come from heaven, in the clouds, in the glory of his Father, casting him and those that obey him into the lake of fire."

13. REFERENCES TO THE GENERAL ORDER OF EVENTS.*

When the times of the Gentiles are passing away, (Luke xxi. 24, 25; Rom. xi. 25–32,) the Jews are recalled (Dan. ix. 27; Ezek. xx. 32–44; Isaiah xlix. 9–12) and replaced in their own land, Ezek. xxxvi. 1–38; xxxvii. 20–23; Isaiah

* Mostly from Bickersteth's "Practical Guide to the Proph.," pp. 209–212.

xi. 11, 12; lxii. 4; Jer. xxxi. 1–6; Deut. xxx. 4–6; xxxii. 43.

The apostate Gentiles under Antichrist come against them, Isaiah lxvi. 1–4; Jer. xxx. 1–9; Isaiah x. 20–27; Dan. ix. 27; Isaiah xxxi.; xxxiii. 1–10; Ezek. xxxviii. 1–16; Dan. xi. 41, 45; Joel ii. 1–20; Micah iv. 8–10; Dan. xii. 1, 2.

The signs in the sun, moon, and stars are manifested, Matt. xxiv. 20–29; Luke xxi. 24–26; Heb. xii. 26–28; Hag. ii. 6, 7; Isaiah xiii. 9–11; xxxiv. 1–4; Joel iii. 12–15; ii. 31–32; Mal. iv. 1–6.

The sign of the Son of man appears in the darkened heavens, Matt. xxiv. 29, 30; Luke xxi. 27, 28; Isaiah xviii. 3–7; xi. 12–14; xxxi. 6–8; Dan. vii. 13–14; Matt. xxiii. 39; Luke xvii. 24.

He raises the great company of the sainted dead, and changes the great company of the sainted living, all of whom ascend to him in the air, Matt. xxiv. 31; Rev. xi. 15–18; 1 Cor. xv. 51–54; 1 Thess. iv. 15–17; 2 Thess. i. 7; Isaiah xxvii. 12, 13; Rev. iii. 10; Isaiah xxvi. 19–21; Mal. iii. 17, 18; Rev. xiv. 16.

The beast, the kings of the earth, and their gathered armies, in their rage, enmity, and blindness, propose to make war against the Lord, and the armies which follow him, Matt. xxiv. 30; Rev. xi. 18; xvi. 14; Isaiah viii. 8–10; x. 24–26; xxiv. 21, 22; xxvii. 4; xxxi. 4; liv. 15; lxvi. 18; Joel iii. 1, 2; Micah iv. 11–13; Zeph. iii. 9; Zech. xii. 2–5; xiv. 1–5; Rev. xix. 19.

Christ pours his judgments on Antichrist and his adherents, pleading with all flesh by fire and sword, Matt. xxiv. 36–39; Rev. xv. 1; xvi. 1; Dan. ix. 27; Isaiah x. 24, 26; xiv. 24–26; xxiv. 21–23; xxxiv.; lxiii.; Rev. xix. 10–21; Joel iii. 11–16; Nahum i. 9–15; Isaiah xxxiii. 27–33; Ezek. xxxviii. 17–23; Dan. vii. 9–14; Mal. iv. 1–3; Matt.

iii. 12; 2 Thess. i. 8; ii. 8; Rev. xix. 15–20; Isaiah lxi. 16.

The character of the dispensation, discriminating, punishing, and purifying, 1 Cor. iii. 12, 13; Mal. iii. 3; Zech. xiii. 9; Mark ix. 42, 50; Jer. xx. 9; xxiii. 29; Psalm xcvii. 3; 1 Peter iv. 12; 2 Peter iii. 10–13; Rev. iii. 18.

Every man's work made manifest, for the day shall declare it, because it shall be revealed by fire, the progress of which accomplishes the predicted passing away of the heavens and the earth into the new heavens and earth, and which, like the Jewish tribulation, seems to have a crisis in the beginning (Ezek. xxxviii. 22; xxxix. 6; Isaiah lxvi. 15, 16) and another at the close (Rev. xx. 9) of the Millennial kingdom, Matt. xxiv. 21; Luke xxi. 22–24; Dan. xii. 1; Jer. xxx. 7; Rev. xix. 20; xx. 9.

The Lord descends visibly on Mount Olivet, with his glorified saints, (Acts i. 11; Zech. xiv. 4, 5; Isaiah lxiv. 1; lxvi. 15; lx. 13; Ezek. xliii. 7–9,) in the sight of his people Israel, Isaiah lxvi. 18, 19; Zech. xii. 10–14; Isaiah xxv. 9; Matt. xxiii. 29; Rom. xi. 26; Isaiah lix. 20; Zech. ii. 10–12.

These, humbled at length by their great affliction, and brought to penitence by beholding their pierced Savior, welcome his return, Zech. xii. 10–14; Jer. xxxi. 8–12; Acts iii. 19–21; Isaiah xii. 2–4; Psalm cvii.; cviii.; Rev. xix. 1, 3, 4, 6.

Satan is then bound, and our Lord proceeds to reward all his faithful servants for every loss and sacrifice made for him, begins his glorious Millennial reign with his saints over the nations who have escaped those awful judgments which have consumed his foes, Isaiah xxxii. 1; Dan. vii. 18, 27; xii. 4; Luke xxii. 28–30; John i. 51; Rev. xi. 18; xx. 4–6.

But, though the spiritual blessedness of this reign far exceeds that of any former dispensation, and the new heavens and the new earth begin in the heavenly reign of the saints, and the glory of the land of Israel, (Isaiah lxv. 17–19,) yet the spirit of rebellion still secretly lurks among the nations, (Zech. xiv. 17–19,) which, after ripening for a time, is permitted to display itself, by the loosing of Satan for a little season, that it may then be put down forever, Rev. xx. 9.

Our Lord reigns till he shall have completely put all enemies under his feet; Satan himself is cast into the lake of fire; the final judgment of "the rest of the dead" takes place, and death and hell, and whosoever is not found written in the book of life, are cast into the lake of fire, Rev. xx. 10–15.

The new heavens and the new earth being now perfected, and there being no more sea, (Rev. xxi. 1,) the holy city descends, and the state of highest happiness arrives, when God is all in all, and his saints reign for ever and ever, Rev. xxi.; xxii. 1–5.

14. REFERENCES TO THE DUTY AND IMPORTANCE OF AN EARNEST AND DEVOUT STUDY AND HANDLING OF THESE THINGS.

No scripture is useless, 2 Tim. iii. 14–17.

It is well to study prophecy, 2 Peter i. 19.

Special blessings are for those who attend to these revelations, Hab. ii. 2, 3; Acts xvii. 11, 12; 1 Peter i. 10–12; 1 Cor. ii. 9, 10; Rom. xv. 4; Dan. x. 11, 12; Rev. i. 1–3; xxii. 7; Luke xi. 28.

It is a special command to give attention to these things, 2 Peter iii. 1–3; Jude 17, 18; Acts xx. 25–27.

Solemn responsibilities are placed upon the ministers of Christ with reference to these things, Ezek. xxxiii. 1–7; Rev. xx. 8–10, 18, 19.

Participation in the honors of the kingdom are made dependent on the manner in which we are affected toward the Savior's coming, Matt. xxiv. 42–51; xxv. 1–13; Heb. ix. 28; 2 Tim. iv. 8; Phil. iii. 20; 1 Thess. i. 9, 10; Titus ii. 11–13; 2 Peter iii. 11, 12; Matt. v. 17–20.

There is great danger of being drawn into a skeptical behavior with reference to these matters, 2 Tim. iii. 4; 2 Peter iii. 1–4; implied also in the many commands to "watch."

CHAPTER II.

REFERENCES TO THE OPINIONS AND WORKS OF THE FATHERS ON THESE SUBJECTS.

THE APOSTOLIC FATHERS, or those Christian teachers and writers who immediately succeeded the apostles, have left but little that has come down to us. But, even in that little, there are evidences that they thought upon these subjects in substance as taught in this volume. We have definite knowledge of but five of them; all of whom appear to have been Millenarians.

1. BARNABAS, quoted at p. 237, was the earliest. He is referred to in Acts iv. 36, 37, and ix. 24. He wrote about A.D. 71. We have from him an epistle, called "The Catholic Epistle of St. Barnabas," consisting of twenty-one chapters; in the 15th of which he refers to the Millennium, the coming of Christ to abolish the wicked one, the judgment of the wicked, the renewal of all things, and the introduction of a new order into the world. There can be no doubt, from this chapter, that he understood the predictions of the Scriptures in the Millenarian sense. For a translation of this Epistle, see Wake's *Apostolic Fathers*, pp. 196–219; or *Apocryphal New Testament*, pp. 90–104. For the original, see Hefele's *Patrum Apostolicorum Opera*, pp. 1–51.

2. CLEMENT, quoted at p. 238, was Bishop of Rome about A.D. 91–93, and is supposed to be the same referred to in Phil. iv. 3. We have from this father an epistle, called "The First Epistle to the Corinthians," consisting of sixty paragraphs or chapters, (in the *Apocryphal N. T.*, 23,) in which we find statements, exhortations, and allusions which have satisfied many that his views accorded with those of Barnabas and were decidedly Millenarian. See Wake's *Apostolic Fathers*, or Hefele's *Pat. Apos. Op.*, Clement's First Epistle, latter part of XXIII. with XXIV., XXXIV., XXXV., L.

What is called the Second Epistle of Clement is referred to a much later period, and is supposed to have been written by a very different hand. It is thought to belong to the fourth century. But, whenever written, or by whomsoever, it is Millenarian in its tone and general conceptions. See Wake's Fathers, Second Epistle of St. Clement, VII., IX., XII.; or Hefele's *Patrum Apostolicorum Opera*, pp. 142, 144, 148.

3. HERMAS, generally allowed to be the same alluded to in Rom. xvi. 14, is supposed to have written his work entitled "The Shepherd" about A.D. 100. That he was a Millenarian is evinced in various parts of the book. In Vision I., latter part of section 3, in Wake's Fathers, the doctrine of the reign of the saints in the renovated world seems clearly to be taught. Vision IV. seems also to be framed, in divers particulars, to Millenarian anticipations. For the original, see Hefele, pp. 325, 342–344.

4. IGNATIUS, surnamed *Theophorus*, received his Christian training under John and Peter, succeeded Peter at Antioch, and died an illustrious martyr under Trajan, A.D. 107. He has left seven epistles which have come down to us. He nowhere touches with much definiteness upon any points from which his views on the Millennium might manifest themselves. But his letters contain nothing in conflict with our doctrines,

and refer frequently to the nearness of Christ's anticipated return in a manner much more after the spirit of Millenarian teaching than any other. See his Epistle to Polycarp, paragraph III., Wake's Fathers; or Hefele, pp. 236–239.

5. POLYCARP, also one of the disciples of John, and the Bishop of Smyrna, supposed to be the person referred to in Rev. ii. 8–11, lived to a great age, and died, a martyr, A.D 167. There remains to us from him but one brief letter, called "The Epistle of St. Polycarp to the Philippians," where he incidentally alludes to the resurrection, and the reign of the saints with Christ after his return, and to the kingdom to be inherited by the truly pure, in a way which seems as if he had conceived of these matters only as Millenarians do. See Wake's Fathers, Polycarp's Epistle, V., XII., or Hefele's *Patrum Apost. Opera*, pp. 262, 271.

THE PRIMITIVE FATHERS, or those who constituted the next several generations after those who enjoyed the personal instructions of the apostles, have, for the most part, given very decided evidence of their earnest belief of Millenarian doctrines.

1. PAPIAS, Bishop of Hieropolis, quoted on p. 239, was the most ancient of them. Indeed, Irenæus asserts that he was one of St. John's hearers, and a personal friend of Polycarp. He is supposed to have written about A.D. 116. His five books, entitled "An Explication of the Oracles of the Lord," have been lost, with the exception of a few fragments preserved by Eusebius. But enough remains to show unmistakably that he was a decided Millenarian, and that he claimed to have received his opinions on this subject from those elders who had been taught by the apostles themselves. See Eusebius's *Ecc. History*, III. 39; or Routh's *Reliquiæ Sacræ*, I. pp. 7–14; or Lardner's *Credibility of the Gospel History*, vol. 2, p. 107. Greswell's remarks in connection

with the testimony of Papias to the Millennium are much to the point. See his *Parables*, vol. 1, pp. 273–284.

2. JUSTIN *the Martyr*, quoted on p. 239, the next in the order of time, was born A.D. 89, and martyred A.D. 163. He was the cotemporary of Papias and Polycarp, and was a learned and admirable Christian writer. Several works from his pen still survive. He was not only a decided Millenarian, but claimed that all orthodox Christians, and such as were in all points right-minded, believed as he did on the subject; thus also attesting the Millenarianism of Polycarp, with whom he was cotemporaneous for about seventy years. See Semisch's *Life, Writings, and Opinions of Justin Martyr*, vol. 2, cap. 7, where full citations of this distinguished father's words are given. See particularly Justini Martyris *Dialogus cum Tryphone Judæo*, cap. 80; Migne's *Patrologiæ*, vol. 6, col. 664–667. There is a translation of this *Dialogue* into English, by Henry Browne, 2 vols. 8vo, London, 1755.

3. TATIAN, a writer of numerous works, only one of which, his "Oration against the Greeks," remains. There is nothing in this from which to ascertain his views on the subject of the Millennium. But, as he was one of the disciples of Justin Martyr, who regarded Millenarianism as a test of orthodoxy, it is to be presumed, until evidence to the contrary is produced, that he believed and taught upon this subject the same as his preceptor.

4. MELITO, Bishop of Sardis, was also a cotemporary of Justin Martyr, and is to be included among those orthodox Christians to whose Millenarianism Justin testifies. He died about A.D. 170, and was one of the most eminent bishops of his time. He was distinguished for holiness, eloquence, and learning. He is supposed by some to have been the person addressed in Rev. iii. 1–6. Among a large number of works, he wrote one on Prophecy and another on the Apocalypse. None of his writings remain; but Guennadius, (*De Dogm.*

Eccles. c. 52,) who seems to have been familiar with them, quotes him as a Millenarian; and the annotator of the Oxford translation of Tertullian, on the authority of Guennadius, classes him with "the maintainers of the Millennium," (pp. 124, 125.) Jerome is also given as authority that he was a Millenarian, (Taylor's *Voice of the Church*, p. 66,) and there cannot be much doubt of it.

5. IRENÆUS, the eminent Bishop of Lyons, born about A.D. 140, to whom reference is made on p. 240, was also a decided Millenarian. Having been a disciple of Polycarp, he was an earnest promulgator of the same views which his teacher held. His great work "Against the Heretics" consists of five books. The original Greek, with the exception of a few fragments, has been lost, but the contents have been preserved in an ancient Latin translation. The whole of the fifth book of this work, from chapter 25 to the end, (see Migne's *Patrologiæ*, vol. 7, col. 1120–1224,) relates to the subject of the unfulfilled prophecies in the book of Revelation, Daniel, &c., and supplies the clearest intimations that, in the expectation of a kingdom of Christ yet to come in this world, his opinions agreed with those of Papias and Justin Martyr. Refer especially to cap. 33, secs. 3, 4, (Migne, col. 1213, 1214.) A good translation of this passage is given by Greswell *On the Parables*, vol. 1, pp. 289, 290.

6. CLEMENS ALEXANDRINUS, referred to on p. 242, was also a distinguished teacher and writer in the early Church, who flourished about A.D. 192. His works do not furnish any thing very decided on the subject, but numerous expressions occur which intimate that he was a Millenarian on some points at least. And as he was for many years cotemporary with Justin Martyr, and was always regarded by the ancients with great respect, the presumption is fair that he was one of those right-minded and orthodox Christians all of whom Justin declares to have been believers in the Millenarian under-

standing of sacred prophecy. He connected the belief of a general renewal of the world with the seventh thousand years from the creation of man, and believed that the kingdom of heaven was to be introduced with judgments; which necessarily involves some of the most important points of the Millenarian faith.

7. TERTULLIAN, quoted at p. 241, was born about A.D. 160. He was bred for the profession of the law, and was a man of rare genius as well as fervent and active piety. Spanheim assigns him "a place in the first rank of the Fathers, in erudition, acumen, and eloquence." He wrote an entire work on the subjects involved in Millenarianism, entitled "*De Spe Fidelium*," which has been lost. He himself gives an account of it, and elsewhere informs us what was the nature of the doctrines which he therein elaborated more at large. See his work *Adversus Marcionem*, lib. 3, cap. 24; Migne's *Opera Tertulliani*, tom. 2, col. 355–358. A good translation of this passage is given by Greswell *On the Parables*, 1, pp. 305–307. He here evinces his full accord with his distinguished cotemporary Irenæus. The same views are also presented in other portions of his works. See his *Apologeticus*, cap. 48, Migne's *Oper. Ter.*, tom. 1, col. 520–527; *De Spectaculus*, cap. 30, Migne's *Op. Ter.*, tom. 1, col. 660–662; *De Oratione*, cap. 5, Migne's *Op. Ter.*, tom. 1, col. 1158, 1159; *De Baptismo*, cap. 19, Migne's *Op. Ter.*, tom. 1, col. 1222; *Adversus Judæos*, cap. 14, Migne's *Op. Ter.*, tom. 2, col. 638–642; *De Anima*, cap. 37, Migne's *Op. Ter.*, tom. 2, col. 713–715; *De Resurrectio Carnis*, cap. 22, 25, 35, Migne's *Op. Ter.*, tom. 2, col. 824–5, 831, 844–5.

There are some valuable remarks on Tertullian's testimony on this subject, by Greswell, *Parables*, vol. 1, pp. 300–309.

APOCRYPHAL WRITINGS OF THE PRIMITIVE CHURCH.—Of course we do not refer to apocryphal works as *authorities*, for authorities they are not; but, as witnesses to the fact that certain doctrines were actually current in the times of their authors, no reasonable objection can be raised against them. The doctrine of the Millennium we receive upon the testimony of the Scriptures alone; but the manner in which those Scriptures were understood at the time certain apocryphal books were composed may be learned as well from such apocryphal books as any other. They are a part of the history of the Church. The references given below are not in proof of the correctness of Millenarian views, but simply as corroborations of the fact that those views were held by the primitive Christians, and by themselves proclaimed as part of their faith.

1. THE BOOK OF ENOCH. This is an apocryphal production, often referred to by the Fathers, but which was supposed to be lost, until Bruce brought it from Abyssinia, where he found it still existing in an Ethiopic version. It was translated by Dr. Laurence into English, and published first in 1821, (3d edition, Oxford, 1838.) There is also a German version, by A. G. Hoffmann, entitled *Das Buch Henoch in volständiger Uebersetzung, mit Commentar, Einleitung und Excursen;* 2 Abth., Jena, 1833–38. It was written some time during the first century. Lücke places it in the time of the Jewish war, probably after the destruction of Jerusalem; Credner, in about the same time the Apocalypse was written; and Greswell, between the Jewish war under Vespasian and that under Hadrian. Christian elements certainly are contained in it. The doctrine of a personal reign of Christ on earth, and of a state of things analogous to what may be expected under the Millennium, occurs in various parts of it. In the first chapter there is a plain allusion to the second coming of Christ with the holy angels; and in the 24th, to the personal residence of God on earth, whilst the saints

enjoy authority and great peace. See chap. x. 20–29; xxiv.; xxxviii.; xxxix. 1; xlv.; lxi. 11–18.

2. THE SECOND BOOK OF ESDRAS. This apocryphal production has been preserved through the Latin vulgate and an Arabic version, the Greek original having been lost. An English version of it is frequently bound in at the end of the Old Testament, with other ancient non-canonical writings. A critical edition of it was published by Dr. Laurence in 1820. Laurence and Merkel fix the time of its composition about a quarter of a century before the birth of Christ; but Corrodi, Lücke, Gfröfer, Wieseler, and Greswell, with more reason, argue that it was written, by a Christian hand, about A.D. 96. It exhibits great familiarity with the writings of the New Testament, and in some parts is but little more than a reproduction of them. Its visions, predictions, and declarations are largely of a Millenarian type. It tells of the return of the hidden tribes of Israel in the time of the end, of great commotions and tribulations preceding that restitution, of an infidel antichristian contest at the end of this dispensation, of a first resurrection, and of the reign of Christ with his saints, or what is equivalent to it. See chap. ii. 10–24, 26–48; vi. 8, 9, 18–28; vii. 26–35, 42–44; viii. 50–52, 61–63; ix. 3–13; xiii. 3–14, 23–58; and indeed the whole book.

3. THE SIBYLLINE ORACLES. (*Sybillinorum Oraculorum*, Servatius Gallæus. Amst. 1689, 4to.) The exact origin of this production is not known. Some consider it a purely Christian work, written in the time of the Emperor Hadrian, and some regard it as a purely Jewish effusion, composed in the second century before Christ. Others, again, consider it of Jewish origin, but subsequently modified, interpolated, and enlarged by some Christian hand. Bleek thinks that the oldest portions of it date back two hundred years before Christ, and that the latest of them originated four hundred years after Christ. We are safe in referring the great mass

of what are now known as the Sibylline Oracles to primitive Christianity, written in all probability within twenty or thirty years of the Revelation of St. John. It is just such a composition as would be likely, above all other writings of the time, to gather up and set forth what were the expectations and doctrines of the primitive Christians with respect to the future, and to those events which are yet to happen before the end of time. It has, of course, suffered much in its transmission to us, and bears the appearance of a very ill-sorted and ill-connected composition; but still it contains a variety of allusions sufficiently intelligible to bear witness to the fact that the Millenarian faith existed at the times in which it was written, and that this faith was a part of the common Christian creed as then received and held. See especially lib. 3, pp. 327, 465, 466–469, 473; lib. 2, pp. 289–293; lib. 5, pp. 561, 592–593, 602–605, 618, 620, 621, 673, 674.

The reader will find these passages cited in full, with able criticisms upon them, in Greswell *On the Parables*, (vol. 5, part 2, pp. 176–236,) where the remark is made that there is nothing extant of primitive Christian antiquity, either apocryphal or non-apocryphal, and belonging strictly to this period, in which the truth of the genuine Millenarian doctrines is not illustrated and confirmed, and in which the same belief is not, in one way or another, recognized.

Bishop Russell also testifies that "so far as we view the question in reference to the sure and certain hope entertained by the Christian world that the Redeemer would appear on earth, and exercise authority during a thousand years, there is good ground for the assertion of Mede, Dodwell, Burnet, and other writers on the same side, that down to the beginning of the fourth century the belief was universal and undisputed." (Discourse on the Millen., p. 236.) Eusebius, too, who flourished about A.D. 300, in what he says of Papias, and his declarations concerning what he had heard from the apostles, acknowledges that there were πλεῖστοι ὅσοι—VERY MANY—*Church writers* who expected that there would be a thousand years after the resurrection of the dead, when Christ would reign personally on the earth. (*Euseb. Ecc. Hist.*, lib. 3, cap. 39.) Upon which Greswell very justly observes, "This admission virtually implies that the belief in the future Millennium was the orthodox or catholic notion in the second and third centuries." See other authorities on pp. 244, 245.

THE LATER FATHERS.—The fact that the primitive Church was thoroughly, if not universally, Millenarian, must go very far towards establishing the presumption that these doctrines were derived from the apostles and Christ himself, as Papias testifies that they were. The testimony of later teachers can add nothing to the force with which this conclusion urges itself upon an honest mind. We refer to the later Fathers, not in the way of proof of the correctness of our doctrines, but as additional human testimonies, and as belonging to the ancient literature of the subject.

1. HIPPOLYTUS, Bishop of Porto, flourished about A.D. 222, was in early life a disciple of Irenæus, and was evidently a believer in the views so earnestly inculcated by his teacher. Most of his works have been lost, and some directly on the subject of the Millennium, the prophecies of Daniel and John, the Resurrection, &c. Some fragments from his pen, however, remain. His tract "De Antichristo," which is admitted to be genuine, is thoroughly Millenarian in its methods of interpretation and in many of its statements. Citations to this effect are given by Greswell *On the Parables*, (1, pp. 331, 376;) and in Elliott's *Horæ Apocalypticæ* (4, pp. 283, 284.) See Hippol. *Opera*, pars II., 13, 14, capp. 19, 20. There are also some sentences from his exposition of Daniel preserved in the British Museum, in Syriac, a translation of some of which is given in *The Journal of Sacred Literature*, N. S.,

vol. 8, pp. 348–354. In these sentences the succession of worldly empires is regularly traced down to Antichrist, and his destruction by the personal appearance of Christ, and the setting up of "the kingdom of heaven" in their place, which is to be enjoyed by all "them that are worthy." See also Photius, cap. 202, where Hippolytus is represented as a Millenarian.

2. CYPRIAN, referred to on p. 242, flourished about A.D. 248. He had the very highest regard for Tertullian and his writings, and had no hesitation in ranking himself as one of his disciples. He must therefore be regarded as a Millenarian, as his works also indicate that he was. See his *Epistles*, lviii. 8; lxi. 3; lxiii. 15, 16, (Oxford ed.;) Migne's Cypriani *Opera Omnia*, col. 355, 388, 389; also *Epist.* 59, (Oxford ed.,) and especially "De Exhortatio Martyrii," latter part, where he shows his accordance with Barnabas, in referring the consummation of all things to the seventh Millennium from the creation.

3. COMMODIAN, a cotemporary of Cyprian, and a poet, wrote about A.D. 270. Clarke (*Sacred Literature*, p. 194) says of him that "he received the docrine of the Millennium, which was the common belief of his time."

4. VICTORINUS, Bishop of Pettau, flourished about A.D. 290. In the fragment of his "Tractatus de Fabrica Cœli," his concurrence with the primitive Church in the expectation of a reign of Christ with his elect upon earth for a thousand years, is amply manifest. A translation of it is given by Greswell, *On the Parables*, vol. 1, p. 333. See Routh's *Reliquiæ Sacræ*, 3, pp. 455–461, 462; also Elliott's *Horæ Apocalypticæ*, 4, pp. 286–295.

5. METHODIUS, Bishop of Tyre, flourished about the same period. Neander says of his *Symposium* that it exhibits "a decided leaning to Chiliasm," (Ec. Hist. 1, p. 721,) and refers in proof to *Orat.* 9, 75. So also, in his "Feast of the

Ten Virgins," ninth discourse, he follows the Fathers generally in making the seventh day of the creation a type of the Millennial sabbath, to enjoy which there is to be a literal resurrection of the saints, to be followed not by the annihilation of the world, but by its purification.

6. NEPOS, an Egyptian bishop, also of the third century, was another decided defender of Millenarian doctrines. He wrote a book, entitled "A Confutation of the Allegorists," which was specially directed against the school of Origen, which explained the Millennium figuratively. This work has not come down to us, but it is admitted to have been a work of eloquence and ability, and decidedly Millenarian. Cave pronounces Nepos a man skilled in the Holy Scriptures, a poet, and a Millenarian. Even Whitby admits that he taught that there shall be a kingdom of Christ upon earth a thousand years after the resurrection, in which the saints are to reign with their Redeemer. And Mosheim states that the book in which Nepos set forth these opinions was specially admired, and excited great interest and pleasure. (Historic. Comment. 2, pp. 249, 250.)

7. LACTANTIUS, referred to on p. 244, flourished about A.D. 300. He was a very eloquent and accomplished Christian teacher, from whom we have more on this subject than from any other of the Fathers. The clearness and decidedness of his views on the Millennium render it very probable that Arnobius, from whom he had his Christian instruction, was also of this way of thinking. See especially his *Divin. Institu.* De Vita Beata, lib. vii. 14, (Lactanti *Opera Omnia*, Lipsiæ, 1698, pp. 524–532.) Refer also to lib. iv. 7, 12, 26; lib. vii. 2, 15; and Epitome.

8. APOLLINARIUS, Bishop of Laodicea, who flourished in the first half of the fourth century, is also known to have been an advocate of Millenarianism. The testimony of Epiphanius (I. 1031, A. B. Dimœritæ, 26) on this point is con-

clusive. Jerome also puts him down as believing, with Tertullian, Lactantius, and Victorinus, that there is to be a personal reign of Christ upon the earth, (III. 952, ad prin. in Ezech. xxxvi.) See Greswell *On the Parables*, I. pp. 334–336, where the passages are quoted and translated.

9. THE COUNCIL OF NICE, A.D. 325, composed of about three hundred bishops of the Church from all sections of the world, has also expressed itself upon this subject, in those forms or models of doctrine which it set forth for the use of the clergy, much in the way of the Homilies published in the reign of Edward VI. Mede (Works, p. 813) gives an extract from one of these forms on the doctrine of the resurrection, as it is recorded by Gelassius Cyzicenus, in his history of the Acts of the Council of Nice, which explains the Scriptures in favor of the Millennium, or a happy, triumphant state of the Church on earth, in which the saints are to have a blessed inheritance and reward under the reign of Christ our Savior. The extract is also given in an English translation, by Thomas Hartley, (*Paradise Restored*, pp. 225, 226,) who observes upon it that it is to be seen from it that "THIS DOCTRINE [OF THE REIGN OF CHRIST WITH HIS SAINTS ON EARTH] STANDS UPON THE SAME AUTHORITY AS DOES THAT OF THE NICENE CREED; and that this Council interprets that promise of our Savior, that the meek shall inherit or possess the earth, into a confirmation of, and identity of sense with, the same prophetical declarations to be found in many places of the Psalms and Prophets. See, in particular, Ps. xxxvii. 11; lxix. 36, 37; cxlvii. 6; cxlix. 4; Isaiah xi. 4; xxvi. 6; xxix. 19."

10. SULPICIUS SEVERUS, who lived about the middle of the fourth century, also believed in the same doctrine, as may be inferred from his *Sacræ Historiæ*, (ii. 4,) where he recounts Nebuchadnezzar's dream respecting the little stone. Jerome also, in the passage referred to above, alludes to a

book from him, called *Gallus*, in which he reports him as teaching on this subject the same as Lactantius, Irenæus, and Apollinarius. See Greswell *On the Parables*, vol. 1, pp. 335, 336.

11. AUGUSTINE, the distinguished Bishop of Hippo, who flourished about the end of the fourth century, by his own confession was also once a decided Millenarian, though he subsequently somewhat modified his views. See his work *De Civitate Dei*, liber 22, cap. 7. And a careful examination of his opinions will show that he never wholly relinquished his Millenarian ideas. See his *De Civ. Dei*, lib. 20, capp. 5, 14, 16; *Homilies*, vol. 1, pp. 43, 70, 83, 252, 358, (Oxford ed.) He is usually rated as an anti-millenarian, as he doubtless was, in some particulars, in the latter part of his life; but his views do not harmonize at all with the doctrine of the conversion of the world and a millennium of peace and righteousness before Christ comes.

12. JEROME, even, held that the world would reach its consummation in six thousand years, and that Christ would come at the end of that period, though he looked for no reign on the earth. See his Letter (139) to Cyprian, on Psalm xc. 4; also his comment on Micah iv. Nor could he rid himself of certain misgivings in refusing to accept the doctrine of a literal Millennium, but on several occasions declared that he did not dare to condemn it, because of the high authorities by which it is supported. See his Preface to Isaiah lxv.; and his comment on Jer. xix. 10.

From the days of Jerome and Augustine, however, but little is heard of the doctrine of the Millennium and the personal reign of Christ with his saints on earth. As remarked by Professor Bush, "through the dreary tract of the ages of darkness, scarcely a vestige of Millenarian sentiment is to be traced." But this is a consideration which makes much more in its favor than against it. During that same period there was hardly a doctrine of the gospel which did not suffer a like eclipse. The Church had become corrupt and vastly apostate, and the peculiarities which were most prominent in the primitive faith were all overlaid and thrust out of sight. It is enough to know that the doctrine of the Millennium and personal reign was the orthodox and catholic persuasion of the primitive Church; that it held its ground as a vital part of the faith until heathen elements began to affect and mould the persuasions of certain prominent Christian teachers; that it only began to wane as men began to Platonize, allegorize, and explain away the Scriptures, and to reject such portions as spurious which could not be made to harmonize with the new philosophy; and that the days of its greatest darkness and depression were the days when Popery reigned, and which all men have agreed to consider "the dark ages."

We close this chapter with a quotation from one of the Lord Bishops of Bristol, who says, "The doctrine of the Millennium was generally believed in the three first and purest ages; and this belief, as the learned Dodwell has justly observed, was one principal cause of the fortitude of the primitive Christians: they even coveted martyrdom, in hopes of being partakers of the privileges and glories of the martyrs in the first resurrection. Afterwards the doctrine grew into disrepute, for various reasons. Some both Jewish and Christian writers have debased it with a mixture of fables; they have described the kingdom more like a sensual than a spiritual kingdom, and thereby they have not only exposed themselves, but (what is infinitely worse) the doctrine itself, to contempt and ridicule. It hath suffered by the misrepresentations of its enemies, as well as by the indiscretions of its friends: many, like Jerome, have charged the Millenarians with absurd and impious opinions which they never held; and, rather than they would admit the truth of the doctrine, they have not scrupled to call in question the genuineness of the book of Revelation. It hath been abused even to worse purposes: it hath been made an engine of faction; and turbulent fanatics, under the pretence of saints, have aspired to dominion and disturbed the peace of civil society. Besides, wherever the influence and authority of the Church of Rome have extended, she hath endeavored by all means to discredit this doctrine; and indeed not without sufficient reason, this kingdom of Christ being founded on the ruins of the kingdom of Antichrist. No wonder, therefore, that this doctrine lay depressed for many ages, but it sprang up again at the Reformation, and will flourish together with the study of the Revelation."—Bishop Newton's *Dissertations on the Prophecies*, Analysis of the Rev., chap. xx. p. 527.

For authorities on the Millenarianism of the early Church, consult the following:—

CHILLINGWORTH, *An Argument drawn from the Doctrine of the Millenaries against Papal Infallibility*. See his *Works*, Phila. ed., 1844, pp. 729–734.

MUNSCHER, DR. W., *Handbuch der christliche Dogmengeschichte*, Marburg, 1817, pp. 408–434.

MOSHEIM, DR. J. L., *Historical Commentaries*, New York, 1856, vol. 2, pp. 244–250.

HAGENBACH, DR. K. R., *History of Doctrines*, New York, 1861, vol. 1, pp. 213–217.

SEMISCH, C., *Herzog's Encyclop.*, Art. *Chiliasm*. This article is much abridged and enfeebled in Dr. Bomberger's translation: hence see the original. Also *The Life, Writings, and Opinions of Justin Martyr*, Edinburgh, 1843, vol. 2, pp. 364–387.

CORRODI, *Kritische Geschichte des Chiliasmus*, Frankfurt and Leipzig, 1781–3, 3 vols. 12mo. This work contains much curious information, but is sarcastic, uncandid, and unsatisfactory. It was written to expose Chiliasm, and to exhibit it in the most unfavorable light possible. It may, however, be read with profit; though we dissent entirely from the rationalistic spirit and principles contained in it.

WHITBY, DR. D., *Treatise on the Millennium, &c.* A strong effort to weaken the evidence that the early Christians were Millenarians, which, however, fails; as the author admits, upon the testimony of Justin and Irenæus, that there were among the ancients "three sorts of men: 1. *The Heretics*, denying the resurrection of the flesh and the Millennium. 2. THE EXACTLY ORTHODOX, ASSERTING BOTH THE RESURRECTION AND THE KINGDOM OF CHRIST UPON EARTH. 3. *The believers* who consented with the just and yet endeavored to allegorize and turn into metaphor all those scriptures produced for a proper reign of Christ, and *who had sentiments rather agreeing with those heretics who denied*, than those exactly orthodox who maintained, *this reign of Christ on earth*." Chap. I. 61.

GRESWELL, DR. E., *Exposition of the Parables*, Oxford, 1834, vol. 1, pp. 273–411. This is one of the fairest and clearest presentations of the views and testimony of the Fathers on this subject that we have anywhere seen.

KITTO'S Cyclopedia, Art. *Millennium*, furnishes some valuable references to the subject.

BROOKS, J. W., *Elements of Prophetical Interpretation*, chapter 3, contains a very full statement.

TAYLOR, D. T., *Voice of the Church on the Coming and Reign of the Redeemer;* revised by Hastings, Phila., 1856.

TILLOTSON, DR. J., *Works*, London, 1820, vol. 10, pp. 392–403.

BUCK, D. D., *Harmony and Exposition of Matt. xxiv.* Buffalo, 1853, pp. 439–442.

DODGSON, REV. C., *Tertullian Translated*, Oxford, 1854, vol. 1, Note D, pp. 120–131.

CHAPTER III.

CLASSIFIED REFERENCES TO MORE RECENT WRITERS AND WRITINGS ON THESE SUBJECTS.

1. COMMENTARIES OF MILLENARIAN COMPLEXION.

DIE BERLENBURGER BIBEL, 1726, Four large folio-volumes, embracing an original German translation of the entire Scriptures, with copious notes and comments, by pious and learned German theologians of the time. A very valuable work, except in its taint of fanaticism. It has contributed largely to subsequent German commentaries.

GILL'S *Exposition of the Old and New Testaments*, six thick large 8vo vols. Valuable, more especially for the extensive acquaintance of the author with Rabbinical learning.

ALFORD, *Greek Testament, with Prolegomena, and a Critical and Exegetical Commentary*, 4 vols. thick 8vo. One of the most thorough and satisfactory works of the kind that has been issued, especially the latest edition.

BENGEL, *Gnomon of the New Testament.* This is an old standard, which still holds its place. The English translation, by Fausset, is published in 5 vols. 8vo, by Smith, English & Co., Philadelphia.

OLSHAUSEN, *Biblical Commentary on the New Testament.* Best edition in English is that edited by Dr. Kendrick, published by Sheldon, Blakeman & Co., New York.

STIER, *The Words of the Lord Jesus*, 8 vols. 8vo, German and English. A learned and highly approved work.

GRESWELL, *Exposition of the Parables, and of other parts of the Gospels*, 5 vols. 8vo.

KEACH, *Exposition of the Parables of our Lord*, in four books, 1 thick vol. royal 8vo.

COCCEIUS, JOHN, Commentaries on most of the books of Holy Scripture, contained in his *Opera Omnia*, 12 vols. folio, 1701, particularly the first six volumes. A man of great distinction as a scholar, and "continually quoted and applauded by Vitringa for his piety, learning, and ability as an expositor of prophecy."

JARCHI, *Commentarius Hebraicus*, 5 vols. 4to, 1710.

KIMCHI, DAVID, Commentary on Isaiah, Jeremiah, Ezekiel, and the twelve minor prophets. A Spanish Jew, of great erudition, who lived in the thirteenth century.

ABRABANEL, *Commentarius in quatuor priores libros prophetarum*, Lug. Bat. 1686.

CUMMING, JOHN, *Foreshadows: Lectures on our Lord's Miracles;* also on *Parables;* also *Readings* on various books of Scripture.

BONAR, A., *Commentary on the Book of Leviticus*, small 8vo; also *Commentary on the Psalms*, 8vo.

TAIT, WILLIAM, *Meditationes Hebraicæ:* A Doctrinal and Practical Exposition of the Epistle to the Hebrews, in a series of Lectures. 2 vols. 8vo.

STUART, MOSES, *Commentary on the Apocalypse*, 2 vols. 8vo. In some of his writings (vide *Hints on Interp. of Proph.*) a violent and bitter opponent of Millenarian views, but in these volumes he concedes so much to them (particularly with reference to the twofold resurrection, the literal resurrection of the martyrs at the commencement of the Millennium, and the orthodoxy of Millenarianism with the early Christians) as to entitle his work to be placed in this list. The exposition is learned and able, the fruit of much study, but not generally successful.

RYLE, J. C., *Expository Thoughts on the Gospels.* Plain, practical, impressive, and good.

SEISS, J. A., *The Gospel in Leviticus*, 1 vol. 12mo. Also, *Lectures on the Epistle to the Hebrews*, 1 vol. 8vo. Also,

The Parable of the Ten Virgins, in six discourses, 1 vol. 12mo. Also, *A Lecture* on 2 Peter iii. 3–14, 12mo.

JONES, JUDGE JOEL, *Notes on Scripture*, 1 vol. large 8vo, 1861. A valuable book from the pen of the editor of *The Literalist.*

LILLIE, JOHN, *Lectures on the Epistles to the Thessalonians*, 8vo, 1860. An able and instructive production.

SCHMUCKER, J. G., *Prophetic Hist. of Christian Church;* or, Exposition of the Revelation of St. John; 2 vols. 12mo, 1817–21. Very clear on the doctrine of the Millennium, but fanciful in his reckoning of dates. A pious and amiable Lutheran divine.

DAUBUZ, CHARLES, *A Perpetual Commentary on the Revelation of St. John;* best edition by P. Lancaster, London, one vol. 4to, 1730. An elaborate and very useful work, to which later writers have been much indebted.

KOPPIUS, or KOPPE, J. B. I., *Com. in Epist. ad Thessalonienses*, at the end of which is an *Excursus* concerning the kingdom of Christ. Latin. Also an English translation in *The Investigator of Prophecy*, Vol. II.

ALTINGIUS, JACOBUS, *Com. in Jeremiam Prophetam*, fol., Amst., 1688. Also *Spes Israelis;* or Com. Eccles. in cap. 11 ad Rom., etc., 1 vol. 4to, 1676.

FRY, JOHN, Explanatory and Practical on Epist. to the Romans, 8vo, 1816; also *Canticles*, new translation with notes, &c., 8vo, 1811; also *Lyra Davidis*, a new translation and exposition of the Psalms, 8vo, 1842.

SIRR, DR. J. DE ARCY, Notes on the Gospel of St. Luke, 1843.

WELLS, DR. ED. The Book of Daniel Explained, &c., 8vo, Oxford, 1716. Also, *A Commentary on the Book of Revelation*, 4to, 1717.

BURROUGHES, JEREMIAH, *Exposition of the Prophesie of Hosea;* new ed., with notice of the author, by Sherman, imperial 8vo, 1843.

PISCATOR, JOHN, *Commentarii in omnes libros Veteris et Novi Testamenti;* 5 vols. in 3, Herb., 1646. A learned divine, once a Lutheran, afterwards a Calvinist.

CARYL, JOSEPH, *Exposition, with Practical Observations on the Book of Job*, 12 vols. 4to, London, 1647–66. "A rich fund of critical and practical divinity."

GOUGE, WM., *A learned and very useful Commentary on the whole Epistle to the Hebrews*, &c., being the substance of 30 years' Wednesday's lectures, 2 vols. folio, London, 1655.

LANGE, JOACH., *Commentatio de Vita et Epistoli Pauli*, 4to, Halæ, 1718.

PASSAVANT, J. C., *Versuch einer prakt. Auslegung des Briefes Pauli an die Philipper*, Basel, 1834; also, *Auslegung des Briefes Pauli an die Epheser*, Basel, 1836.

SPENER, PH. J., *Pauli Epistolæ ad Romanos et Corinth, homiletica paraphrasi illustr.;* Francof., 1691.

COKE, THOMAS, LL.D., *Commentary on the Old and New Testaments*, 6 vols. 4to, London, 1803.

DEMAREST, JOHN T., *A Translation and Exposition of the First Epistle of Peter*, New York, 1851.

DELITZSCH, DR. FRANZ, *Die Genesis ausgelegt;* Leipzig, 1853. *Das Hohenlied untersucht und ausgelegt*, Leipzig, 1851.

NEWTON, SIR ISAAC, *Observations upon the Prophecies of Daniel and the Apocalypse of St. John;* Opera Omnia, vol. 5, p. 297; also separate, 4to, London, 1733.

EBRARD, DR. J. H. A., *Die Offenbarung Johannes erklärt;* Königsberg, 1853; also his comments on other portions of the New Testament, in continuation of Olshausen's *Biblisches Commentar.*

LISCO, FRIED. GUSTAV., *Das Neue Testament*, mit Erklärungen, Einleitungen, &c. Berlin, 1835; especially the appendix, *Vom Reich Gottes.*

SKEEN, ROBERT, *The Unsealed Prophecy:* Lectures on the Revelation of St. John, small 8vo, London, 1857.

HALDANE, ROB., ESQR., *Exposition of the Epistle to the Romans;* reprinted, New York, 1860.

2. COMMENTARIES DEVOTED MORE PARTICULARLY TO THE EXHIBITION OF MILLENARIAN DOCTRINES.

MEDE, JOSEPH, *Clavis Apocalyptica*, Latin and English. Also, *Exposition on Peter.* "One of the profoundest Biblical scholars of the English Church," died 1638. His Expositions have been considered "invaluable, deserving and repaying the closest study."

BRIGHTMAN, THOMAS, *A most comfortable Exposition of the last and most difficult part of the Prophecie of Daniel*, 4to, 1644. Also, *A Revelation of the Apocalypse*, containing an Exposition of the whole Book of St. John, 4to, 1644. A Puritan divine, who "obtained a high character for learning, piety, and sweetness of temper."

BENGEL, JOHN ALBERT, *Exposition of the Apocalypse*, containing a new version, with a running Commentary, prefaced with an Introduction giving a general view of the whole prophecy, and followed by an Appendix of seven sections, embracing—1. A table of the Chronology, (very peculiar.) 2. An attempt to determine more accurately the times of the Beast. 3. Characteristics of genuine interpretation. 4. An account of men's expectations from age to age in reference to prophecy. 5. Prophetic exposition with respect to its influence on men's actions. 6. Examination of some other prophecies. 7. Salutary advices. Most of this work was translated into English by John Robertson. A very full analysis of it is given in Burk's Memoir of the Life and Writings of Bengel.

Also, *Sixty Practical Addresses (Reden für's Volk.) on the Apocalypse*, with various Appendixes or Gleanings.

Bengel was a Lutheran theologian "of profound critical judgment, extensive learning, and solid piety," born 1687, died 1752. He was one of the greatest of Apocalyptic writers.

GOODWIN, THOMAS, *An Exposition upon the Revelation*, 1679, contained in the second volume of his *Works*, 5 vols. folio, London, 1681. A celebrated Dissenter, member of the Assembly of Divines, and one of the two men whom Wood calls "the two Atlases and Patriarchs of Independency."

LANGE, JOACHIM, *Apokalyptisches Licht und Recht;* 1 vol. fol., 1735. Theological Professor at Halle, and one of the fathers of the Pietistic school of Lutheran divines.

AUBERLEN, *The Prophecies of Daniel, and the Revelation of St. John*, viewed in their mutual relation, with an exposition of the principal passages, German and English, 1 vol. 12mo.

ELLIOTT, E. B., *Horæ Apocalypticæ:* A Critical Historical Com. on the Apocalypse, 4 vols. 8vo. A learned and useful exposition, characterized by Cumming as "a noble and precious work." There is appended to 4th vol. a very valuable and thorough "Sketch of the History of Apocalyptic Interpretation."

LORD, DAVID N., *An Exposition of the Apocalypse*, 1 vol. 8vo. An able work from the editor of the *Theological and Literary Journal;* contains a valuable presentation of the laws of symbolization.

BUCK, D. D., *An Original Harmony and Exposition of Matt. xxiv.*, 1 vol. 8vo, 1853. A clear and forcible book, richly rewarding the reader.

CUMMING, JOHN, *Apocalyptic Sketches:* Lectures on the Book of Revelation; 3 vols. 12mo. Eloquent and full of interest.

FRERE, JAMES HATLEY, ESQ., *A combined view of the Prophecies of Daniel, Esdras, and St. John*, showing that all the prophetic writings are formed upon one plan. Also *A minute Explanation of the Prophecies of Daniel;* 1 vol. 8vo, 1815. Also *Notes on the Interpretation of the Apocalypse*, 1 vol. 8vo, 1850.

PITCAIRN, DAVID, *Zion's King:* The Second Psalm Expounded in the Light of History and Prophecy; 1 vol. small 8vo, 1851.

BLOOMSBURY LECTURES, 3d Series, (by error called 4th in the preface,) 1845. *Duties and Privileges of Christians in Connection with the Second Advent*, as unfolded in the First Epistle of St. Paul to the Thessalonians.

CARLETON, H., *Analysis of the 24th Chapter of Matthew*, Windsor, Vt., 1851.

WAPLE, ARCHDEACON E., "*Book of Revelation Paraphrased*," 4to, 1715.

WOODHOUSE, DR. J. C., *The Apocalypse*, or the Revelation of St. John, translated, with Notes, critical and explanatory, royal 8vo, London, 1805.

WICKES, THOMAS, *An Exposition of the Apocalypse*, 12mo, New York, 1851.

BLISS, SYLVESTER, *A Brief Commentary on the Apocalypse*, 18mo, Boston, 1853.

ROOS, MAG. FRED., *An Exposition of the Prophecies of Daniel, and a comparison of them with the Revelation of St. John;* (German,) Leipsic, 1770; second ed., 1795. The same, translated into English by Dr. E. Henderson, 8vo, London, 1811. Also, *Plain and Edifying Discourses on the Revelation of St. John*, 1788. Also, *A Familiar Exposition of the Revelation of St. John*, 8vo, 1789. "A great investigator of Scripture," says Delitzsch.

SANDER, FRED., *An Attempt at an Exposition of the Revelation of St. John;* Stuttgart, 1829 (German).

KOHLER, DR. AUG., *Die Weissagungen Haggais erklärt;* Erlangen, 1860.

3. MISCELLANEOUS WORKS SETTING FORTH MILLENARIAN DOCTRINES, ALPHABETICALLY ARRANGED, ACCORDING TO THE NAMES OF THEIR AUTHORS.*

ABBADIE, DR. J., *Sur la règne glorieux de Jésu Christ sur la terre.* Sermons.

ABDIEL'S ESSAYS *on the Advent*, &c., 12mo, London, 1834.

ADVENT, SECOND, *The Words of Scripture concerning the*, London.

—— *Connected View of some of the Scriptural Evidences of*, &c., 12mo, Lond.

—— *Review of Scripture in Testimony of Truth of*, &c. By a Layman, 8vo, 1819.

—— *The True Hope of Believers*, Dublin, 1833.

ADVENT TRACTS, 2 vols. 18mo, Boston, containing short papers from various authors, including Miller, Himes, Brock, Haldane, Stewart, and others in Europe and America.

ALABASTER, WM., D.D., *Ecce Sponsus venit;* seu tuba pulchritudinis, etc., 1 vol. 4to, London, 1633. Also, *Aparatus in Rev. Jesu Christi;* 4to, Antw., 1607.

ALLEINE, WM., *The Mystery of the Temple and City in the nine last chapters of Ezekiel* unfolded, &c., London, 12mo, 1677.

ALSTEDIUS, J. H., *The Beloved City;* or, *The Saints' Reign on Earth a thousand years asserted and illustrated*, from sixty places of Holy Scripture, besides the judgment of holy, learned men. Likewise thirty-five objections against this truth answered; faithfully Englished (from the Latin) by W. Burton; 4to, London, 1643.

---

* The asterisk [*] prefixed to names or works in this list is meant to designate authors or publications which, in small space and popular form, give the best presentations of the subject, and which are particularly commended to those who are beginners in the study, or who have not the time or means to go into it more extensively. The main questions will be found very clearly discussed in either of the authors or writings so marked.

AMELOTE, PÈRE, *Notes sur l'Apocalypse;* a French Catholic writer.

ANDERSON, WM., *Apology for the Millennial Doctrine* in the form in which it was entertained by the primitive Church. Two parts, 1830–31, 1842. Also *A Letter* to the author of "Millenarianism Indefensible," 8vo, 1834. "An able writer."

APOCALYPSIS RESERATA; or, *The Rev. of St. John Explained:* in three parts; (German,) 8vo, Christianopoli, 1653.

ARCHER, JOHN, *The Personall Reigne of Christ upon Earth,* showing that there shall be such a kingdom; the manner of it; the duration of it; and the time when it is to begin; 1 vol. 4to, 1643. Scarce.

ARMAGEDDON; *or, A Warning Voice from the Last Battle-Field of Nations;* by a Master of Arts of the University of Cambridge; 3 vols. 8vo, London, 1858. A diffuse but able work, containing much information.

ATLAS OF PROPHECY, being the Prophecies of Daniel and St. John, with a simple Exposition, and a series of fourteen maps and charts exhibiting their fulfilment; 4to, 1849, London.

BAUER, FR., Der sogenannte Chiliasmus; Einwort zur Verständigung für unsere Zeit; Nordlingen, 1860.

BAXTER, REV. M., *Louis Napoleon, the destined Monarch of the World, and Personal Antichrist;* 12mo, Philadelphia, 1863. Also several smaller works.

BAXTER, ROBERT, ESQR., *Prophecy the Key of Providence;* large 12mo, London, 1861.

BAYFORD, JOHN, ESQ., *Messiah's Kingdom;* or, a brief inquiry concerning what is revealed in Scripture relative to the fact, the time, the signs, and the circumstances of the Second Advent; Lond., 8vo, 1820; also, *Reply* to Rev.

J. E. Jones on *Modern Millenarianism*, 8vo, London, 1824.

*BEGG, JAMES, Connected view of Scripture Evidence of the Redeemer's personal return and reign, 12mo, 1831; *Letters to a Minister* on Matt. xxiii., xxiv., xxv., 12mo, 1831; *Argument for the Coming of the Lord at Commencement of Millennium*, 12mo, 1844; *The First Resurrection*, 12mo, 1832.

BEN EZRA (LACUNZA), *La Venida del Mesias en Gloria y Magestad;* 4 vols. 8vo, 1816 (Spanish); also in English, translated by Edward Irving, 2 vols. 8vo, 1827.

BEVERLY, THOMAS, *Pamphlets*, thirty in number, mostly on prophetic subjects, 4to, 1670–1699; also, *Scripture Line of Time* drawn in brief from the Lapsed Creation to the Restitution of all Things, 4to, 1684.

*BICKERSTETH, ED., *Practical Guide to the Prophecies*, 12mo, London, 1835. Also, *The Restoration of the Jews*, 12mo, 1841. Also, *The Signs of the Times in the East*, &c., 12mo, 1845. Also, *The Promised Glory of the Church*, 12mo, 1844. A learned man, of a most amiable, candid, and devout spirit. His writings are very useful.

BIENCHO, JAMES, *The Signs of the Times*, in two parts, 8vo, 1792–4; *The Restoration of the Jews, the Crisis of all Nations*, &c., 8vo, 1800.

BIRKS, T. R., *First Elements of Sacred Prophecy*, 12mo. *The Four Prophetic Empires*, 8vo. Also other works. An attractive and able writer.

BLISS, SYLVESTER, *Analysis of Sacred Chronology*, &c. Boston, 18mo, 1840.

BLOOMSBURY LENT LECTURES, 10 vols. 12mo, London. First Series, 1843: *The Second Coming, the Judgment, and the Kingdom of Christ*, by Villiers, Pym, Goodhart, Dalton, Brooks, Birks, Dallas, Freemantle, Bickersteth, and Stewart; with a preface by Bickersteth.

Second Series, 1844: *The Second Coming of Christ*

practically considered, by Auriol, Pym, Hoare, Birks, Brock, Grimshawe, Marsh, Bates, Bickersteth, Philpot, and Villiers; with a preface by Villiers.

Third Series, 1845: *The Hope of the Apostolic Church; or the Duties and Privileges of Christians in connection with the Second Advent, &c.*, by Bickersteth, Woodrooffe, Niven, Goodhart, Bates, Lillingston, Barker, Birks, Brock, Villiers, Marsh, and Dibdin; with preface by Birks.

Fourth Series, 1846: *Israel's Sins and Israel's Hopes*, by Bickersteth, Goodhart, Birks, Dalton, Freemantle, Fisk, Dallas, Brock, Pym, Lillingston, Villiers, and Stewart; with preface by Dr. Marsh.

Fifth Series, 1847: *Good Things to Come*, by Dallas, McCaul, Dibdin, Freemantle, Bickersteth, Pym, Cadman, Birks, Stewart, Goodhart, Lillingston, and Villiers; with preface by Pym.

Sixth Series, 1848: *Lift up your Heads. Glimpses of Messiah's Glory*, by Goodhart, Dallas, Stewart, Cadman, Wilson, Freemantle, Pym, Noel, Philpot, Bickersteth, Birks, and Villiers; with preface by Dallas.

Seventh Series, 1849: *The Priest upon his Throne*, by Freemantle, Auriol, Stewart, McNeile, Hoare, Goodhart, Birks, Bickersteth, Philpot, Brock, Pym, and Villiers; with preface by Stewart.

Eighth Series, 1850: *God's Dealings with Israel*, by Freemantle, Goodhart, Reichardt, Villiers, Harrison, Hoare, Holland, Wigram, Birks, McNeile, Nolan, and Cadman; with preface by Dalton.

Ninth Series, 1851: *Popish Darkness and Millennial Light*, by Cadman, McNeile, Ryle, Harrison, Hoare, Goodhart, Nolan, Freemantle, Birks, Dallas, Pym, and Villiers; with a preface by Dalton.

Tenth Series, 1852: *The Millennial Kingdom*, by Pym, Cadman, Birks, Stewart, Brock, Philpot, Goodhart, Hoare,

Woodrooffe, Freemantle, Harrison, and Villiers; with preface by Freemantle.

*BONAR, A. A., *Redemption draweth nigh*, 12mo, London, 1847. *Development of Antichrist*, 12mo, London, 1853.

*BONAR, H., *Coming of the Lord Jesus*, small 8vo, 1849; *Prophetical Landmarks*, 12mo, 1859; *Apostolicity of Chiliasm.*

*BROOKS, J. W., Elements of Prophetical Interpretation, 12mo, 1836. ABDIEL'S ESSAYS *on the Kingdom of Christ*, 12mo, 1834. A calm, impressive, and instructive writer.

*BRYANT, ALFRED, *Millenarian Views, with reasons for receiving them*, &c., New York, 1852. "Excellently adapted to remove misconception, disarm prejudice, and conciliate faith."

BURGH, W., *Lectures on the Second Advent*, &c., 12mo, 1835; and various discourses and expositions.

BURROUGHES, J., *Jerusalem's Glory breaking forth in the world, &c. immediately before the Second Coming of Christ;* small 8vo, Lond., 1675. A member of the Westminster Assembly, and an eminent divine.

CHRIST'S SPEEDY RETURN IN GLORY, &c., London, 4th ed., 1831.

CLAYTON, BISHOP ROBERT, *Dissertation on the Prophecies*, &c., 8vo, Lond., 1749; also *An Inquiry into the Time of the Coming of the Messiah*, 8vo, Lond., 1751. An author deeply versed in Rabbinical learning.

COLEMAN, J. N., *Sermons, Doctrinal and Practical*, elucidating the doctrine of the Trinity, the Sovereignty of God, the Power of the Devil in the world, the Duty of studying Prophecy, the Intermediate State, the Knowledge of each other in the Life to Come, the Millennial Reign of Christ on Earth, &c., 8vo, 1827.

COMENIUS, JNO. AMOS, *Lux e Tenebris*, etc., 4to, 1665.

COOPER, ED., *The Crisis*, &c., 8vo, London, 1825.

COSTA, DR. ISAAC DA, *Israel und die Völker*, Frankfort, 1854; written originally in Hollandish; translated also into English, and published by Nesbit & Co., London, under the title of *Israel and the Gentiles*. A converted Jew, of many rich gifts.

COX, JOHN, *The Millenarian's Answer*, to which is added a brief History of Millenarianism, London, 1832; *Thoughts on the Coming and Kingdom of Christ*, 1836; *The Future*, &c., 12mo, 1862.

CRESSENER, DR. DRUE, *The Judgments of God*, &c., 4to, 1689; *Protestant Applications of the Apocalypse*, 4to, 1690. A writer much commended.

CROOL, RABBI JOSEPH, *Restoration of Israel*.

CUMMING, JOHN, *The End*, 1 vol. 12mo; *The Great Preparation*, 2 vols. 12mo; *The Great Tribulation*, 2 vols. 12mo; *Voices of the Day*, and of *the Night*, 2 vols. 12mo; and various other works. A prolific author, very eloquent and impressive, but not always accurate and self-consistent.

CUNNINGHAME, W., ESQ., *Dissertation on the Seals and Trumpets*, 8vo, 1832; *Conversion and National Restoration of Israel*, 8vo, 1822; *Scriptural Argument for the pre-Millennial Advent*, &c., 12mo, 1833; *Political Destiny of the Earth as Revealed in the Bible*, 12mo, 1834; and various other works. An able and voluminous writer on the prophecies.

DARBY, J. N., *The Hopes of the Church of God*, &c., 12mo, London, 1849.

DAS TAUSENDJAHRIGE REICH gehört nicht der Vergangenheit, sondern der Zukunft an., Gütersloh, 1860.

DAVIS, WOODBURY, *The Beautiful City and the King of Glory*; Philadelphia, 1860.

DRUMMOND, HENRY, ESQ., *Dialogues on Prophecy*, 2 vols. 8vo, London, 1828. Contain the sentiments of various eminent modern writers on Prophecy, as delivered in private discussion or in their published works; also, *Defence of the Students of Prophecy*, in answer to the attacks of Dr. Hamilton, 8vo, London, 1828. Somewhat crude and unsatisfactory in some of the presentations.

*DUFFIELD, DR. GEORGE, *Dissertation on the Prophecies relative to the Second Coming of Jesus Christ*, 12mo; *Millenarianism Defended*, 12mo; *Reply to Stuart*, 12mo, 1843. A writer of ability and earnestness.

DURANT, JOHN, *The Salvation of the Saints by the Appearances of Christ*, &c., 8vo, 1653. "A delightful Millenarian writer."

EIGHT LECTURES ON PROPHECY, 12mo, Dublin; no date.

ELLIOTT, DR. E. B., *Destinies and Perils of the Church as predicted in Scripture*, London, 8vo.

ENOCH, A small volume without name of the author, London, 1849.

ENQUIRY, AN, *into the Second Coming of our Savior*, &c., 8vo, London, 1795. Also, by the same author, *Further Considerations on the Second Advent of Christ*, &c., 8vo, London, 1796.

EXTRACTS ON PROPHECY, chiefly the approaching Advent and Kingdom of Christ, from Burgh, Anderson, Noel, Cunninghame, Irving, Begg, Mede, &c., 12mo, Glasgow, 1835. A good volume on the subject.

EYRE, JOSEPH, *Observations on the Prophecies relating to the Restoration of the Jews;* 8vo, London, 1797.

FABER, GEORGE STANLEY, *Dissertation on the Prophecies*, 2 vols. 8vo, 1806; also, *Sacred Calendar of Prophecy;* 3 vols. 8vo, 1828. A writer of much learning, pious and able; his works are valuable, but not Millenarian on all points.

FARMER, JOSEPH, *A Sober Inquiry;* or, Christ's Reign with his Saints modestly asserted from the Scriptures. A small volume, published in 1660; republished, New York, 1843. "The spirit of this little piece of antiquity is admirable, calm, candid, and Christian."

FIRST RESURRECTION, *The Nature of, and the Character and Principles of those that shall partake of it,* with an appendix. London, 8vo, 1819.

FLEMMING, ROBERT, JR., *The First Resurrection,* Lond., 1708; also other works bearing on Millenarian questions.

FLOERKE, W., *Die Lehre vom Tausendjäriche Reiche,* Marburg, 1859.

FOX, JOHN, the famous martyrologist, *Christus Triumphans: Comœdia Apocalyptica;* Basel, 1556, London, 1672. A very curious production, but very decided in its Millenarian sentiments.

FRERE, JAMES HATLEY, ESQR., *The Revolution—the Expiration of the Times of the Gentiles,* 8vo, 1848; *The Harvest of the Earth,* 12mo, 1846.

FREY, JOS. S. C. F., *Judah and Israel;* or the Restoration and Conversion of the Jews and the Ten Tribes, 12mo, New York, 1841. Also, *Joseph and Benjamin;* a Series of Letters, 2 vols. 12mo, ninth ed., 1842.

FRIDAY EVENING: *An Attempt to demonstrate that we are now living late in the Sixth Day of the Millenary Week,* &c., 8vo, London, 1822.

FRIEDERICH, PASTOR, OF WINGERHAUSEN, *A Look into the Times of Antichrist,* &c. (German).

FRY, JOHN, *Second Advent, or the Glorious Epiphany of our Lord Jesus Christ,* &c., 2 vols. 8vo, 1822. "Full of useful thoughts."

GASPARIN, MADAME DE, *The Near and the Heavenly Horizon;* New York, 1862.

GAUSSEN, M., *Les Juifs evangelisés enfin, et rétablis;* a Discourse; Toulouse, 1855.

GILFILLAN, GEO., *Christianity and our Era;* a book for the times, 8vo, Edinburgh, 1857.

GILL, DR. JOHN, *Sermon on the Glory of the Church of the Latter Day;* 1752.

GIRDLESTONE, HENRY, *The Hope of Israel*, 12mo, London.

GREGG, DR. T. D., *The Mystery of God Finished*, &c., 8vo, London, 1861.

GUERS, E., *Israël aux derniers jours de l'économie actuelle*, ou Essai sur la restauration prochaine de ce peuple, suivi d'un fragment sur le Millenarisme; Paris, 1856. Also in German, Leipzig, 1860, entitled *Israels Zukunft.*

HABERSHON, MATTHEW, ESQR., *An Historical Dissertation on the Prophetic Scriptures of the Old and New Testament*, &c., 8vo, 1840. Also *Pre-Millennial Hymns*, 18mo, 1841.

HAHN, J. M., *Briefe und Lieder über die Offenbarung.* Works, vol. 5, Tübingen, 1820.

HALES, W., *New Analysis of Chronology and Geography, History and Prophecy, upon Scriptural and Scientific Principles*, &c., 4 vols. 8vo, 1830.

HALLET, JOSEPH, *A free and impartial study of the Holy Scriptures recommended;* being Notes on some peculiar texts, with discourses and observations on various subjects, 3 vols. 8vo, London, 1729–36. "An able work."

HARKNESS, REV. J., *Messiah's Throne and Kingdom*, &c. 12mo, New York, 1855.

HARTLY, THOMAS, *Paradise Restored;* or a testimony to the doctrine of the blessed Millennium, small 8vo, London, 1764. This book was endorsed by John Wesley: see his *Works*, vol. 6, p. 743.

HASTINGS, H. L., *Signs of the Times*, 12mo, Boston, 1862.

HATHERELL, DR. J. W., *The Signs of the Second Advent of our blessed Lord*, 12mo, 1858.

HAWTREY, C. S., *The Nature of the First Resurrection*, &c., 8vo, London, 1815.

HEATH, D. J., *The Future Kingdom of Christ; or*, Man's Heaven to be this Earth. A solution of the Calvinistic and other chief difficulties in theology, by distinguishing the saved nations from the glorified saints; 8vo, London, 1852.

HENSHAW, BISHOP J. P. K., *Lectures on Second Advent;* 12mo, 1842.

HESS, JNO. JACOB, *Vom Reich Gottes;* Ein Versuch über den Plan der göttlichen Anstalten und Offenbarungen; 2 vols. 8vo, 1774; also other works. One of the most eminent and learned divines of the Swiss Reformed Church.

HOFFMAN, DR. W., *Maranatha:* Predigten und Betrachtungen über die Weissagungen des neuen Bundes, 8vo, Berlin, 1858.

HOFMANN, DR. J. CH. KON.; *Weissagung und Erfüllung im Alt. und Neu. Test.*, 2 vols. 8vo, Nördlingen, 1841–4.

HOLGATE, J. B., *Conversations on the Present Age of the World in connection with Prophecy*, small 8vo, Albany, 1853.

HOMES, NATHANIEL, *The Resurrection Revealed;* or, the Dawning of the Daystar, &c.; folio, London, 1654. Also, *Ten Exercitations:* 1. That Chiliasm rightly stated is no error. 2. The manner and measure of the burning world. 3. Touching Gog and Magog. 4. Concerning Covenants, Adamic, Jewish, and Christian. 5. About the Liberty of Man's Will. 6. Of the Two Witnesses. 7. The Character of Antichrist. 8. Touching Hell. 9. The Groaning of the Creature. 10. Scripture prognostics of the future state of the Church. Folio, London, 1661. A learned author, who elucidates Scripture with great ability. A revised edition of both these works, omitting matter thought unimportant, was published by the editor of *The Investigator of Prophecy*, in 1 vol. 8vo, London, 1833.

HOOPER, JOHN, *The Doctrine of the Second Advent, briefly stated*, 12mo, London, 1829; also, *The Present Crisis*, considered in relation to the blessed hope of the glorious appearing, &c., 12mo, Lond., 1831; also, *The Revelation of Jesus Christ Explained*, &c., 8vo, London, 1846; new ed., including Exposition of Daniel, 1847.

HORT, ROBERT, *Sermon on the Glorious Kingdom of Christ upon Earth, or the Millennium;* reprinted, Dublin, 1748; new ed., 8vo, 1821.

HUSSEY, JOSEPH, *The Glory of Christ Unveiled;* 4to, London, 1706. "An author of some distinction."

ILLUSTRATIONS OF PROPHECY, &c., first published in 1799; the edition of 1828 is by Rev. W. Vint. It contains valuable extracts from various authors.

IMBRIE, C. K., *The Kingdom of God;* a Discourse, 1850. Candid and forcible.

INGLIS, JAMES, *The Destiny of the Earth under its Coming King*, 12mo, New York, 1854.

INVESTIGATOR OF PROPHECY, or 4ly Expositor, 4 vols. 8vo, London, 1831–5.

*IRVING, ED., *The Last Days*, &c., with preface by H. Bonar, large 12mo, London, 1850. A work of marked ability, "stamped throughout with irrepressible genius, yet breathing everywhere the spirituality and fervor of the man of God." Also, *The Coming of Messiah in Glory and Majesty*, translated from the Spanish of J. J. Ben Ezra, *alias* Emanuel Lacunza, a Spanish Jesuit, said to have been a converted Jew; 2 vols. 8vo, 1827. A work which throws much light on the subject of unfulfilled prophecy.

JANEWAY, DR. J. J., *Hope for the Jews*, &c., New Brunswick, 1853.

JERRAM, CHARLES, *An Essay to show the ground contained in Scripture for expecting a Restoration of the Jews*, 8vo, 1796.

JEWISH REPOSITORY, afterwards *Expositor and Friend of Israel*, 8vo, Lond., 1813–31.

JEWS, *The Destiny of*, &c., in a course of Lectures at St. Bride's, Liverpool, by several clergymen; 12mo, 1841.

JOURNAL, THE, THEOLOGICAL AND LITERARY, Edited by David N. Lord, and published by Franklin Knight, New York, 13 vols. 8vo, 1849–61. A valuable Review, devoted mostly to prophecy.

JUKES, ANDREW, *The Mystery of the Kingdom of God*, London.

JURIEU, PETER, *L'accomplissement des Prophéties*, ou la délivrance prochaine de l'Église, 2 vols. in one, 12mo, Roter., 1686. Also the same in English, 8vo, London, 1687.

KEITH, DR. ALEX., *The Land of Israel according to the Covenant*, 12mo, Edinburgh, 1843. *The Signs of the Times*, &c., 2 vols. 12mo, 1847. *The Harmony of Prophecy*, &c., 12mo, New York, 1851.

KING, EDWARD, *Morsels of Criticism*, tending to illustrate some few passages in the Holy Scriptures, &c., Lond., 4to, 1788; reprinted in 3 vols. 8vo, Lond., 1800; also *Remarks on the Signs of the Times*. A learned antiquarian.

KINGDOM OF CHRIST, *here on Earth with his Saints, Survey of;* 12mo, London, 1699.

KIRKWOOD, ROBERT, *Lectures on the Millennium*, 12mo, N. York, 1856.

KLETTWICH, SIMON PHIL., *How long the present world will continue*, &c., (German), Mühlhaus. 1699. Also, *Useful*

Information concerning Pietism; or a statement of the real faith and doctrine of the so-called Pietists, (German,) 4to, 1700; and sundry Tracts against Giblehr and Eilmar.

KNIGHT, DR. JAMES, *On the Conflagration and Renovation of the World*, from 2 Peter iii. 10–13. London, 1734, 8vo; reprinted, 1736.

LABAGH, I. P., *Twelve Lectures on the Great Events of Unfulfilled Prophecy*, &c., New York, 1859. A good presentation to the common reader of the subjects treated.

LAMBERT, LE PÈRE, *Expositions des prédictions et promesses faites à l'Église pour les derniers temps de la Gentilité;* 2 vols. 12mo, Paris, 1806; also translated into German, by Von Mayer, at Frankfort. "A striking testimony to the premillennial advent, restoration of the Jews, and reign of Christ, by a French Roman Catholic."

LANCASTER, P., *Interpretation of the Seventy Weeks of Daniel*, 4to, 1722. Also, *Dictionary of Prophetic Symbols*, 8vo, 1842, edited by Habershon.

LANGE, DR. JOACHIM, *Gloria Christi et Christianism., etc.*, folio, Amst. et Lips., 1740.

LAVATER, JNO. C., *Aussichten in die Ewigkeit*, in Briefen an Joh. Geo. Zimmerman, 3 vols. small 12mo, Zurich, 1773.

LEUTWEIN, C. F. P., Die Nähe d. grossen allg. Versuchung, u. der sichtbaren Ankunft unseres Herrn zur Errichtung seines sichtbaren Reiches auf Erden. Tübingen.

LEWIS, SETH, ESQR., *The Restoration of the Jews*, with the political destiny of the nations of the earth, &c., New York, 1851. A writer of strong sense, candor, and reverence for God's word.

LILLIE, JNO., *The Perpetuity of the Earth*, with Notes on the Millenarian Controversy, 18mo, N. York, 1842. A clear and forcible argument.

LITCH, JOSIAH, *Messiah's Throne and Millennial Glory*, Boston, 1855, 12mo.

*LITERALIST, THE, 5 vols. 8vo, Philadelphia, 1840–1841; edited by Judge Jones, and consisting of republications from Brooks, Woodward, McNeil, Noel, Bickersteth, Anderson, Cunninghame, Cox, Thorpe, Habershon, Sirr, and others. A collection of Millenarian works of great value.

LOADER, THOMAS, *The Millennium*, or Joy and Salvation to the World for 1000 Years; 8vo, London, 1812.

LOOKER-ON, *A View of the late momentous events as connected with the Latter Days*, &c., 8vo, London, 1830.

*LORD, D. N., ESQR., *The Coming and Reign of Christ*, 12mo, New York, 1858. An able work.

LORD, N., *The Improvement of the Present State of Things*, a Discourse to the Students of Dartmouth College; Hanover, 1853. Also *The Millennium*, an Essay read to the General Convention of N. Hampshire; Hanover, 1854.

MAITLAND, CHARLES, M.D., *The Apostles' School of Prophetic Interpretation*, &c., 8vo, London, 1849.

MANCHESTER, THE DUKE OF, *The Finished Mystery*, &c., 8vo, London, 1847; also other works. A learned and able investigator.

MANFORD, ——, *Apology for Millenarianism;* small 8vo, 1809, 1843.

MARSH, DR. W., A few plain thoughts on Prophecy, &c., 8vo, Colchester, 3d ed., 1843.

MATHER, INCREASE, *A Discourse concerning faith and fervency in prayer, and the glorious kingdom of Jesus Christ on earth, now approaching*, 12mo, Boston, 1710.

MATON, ROBERT, *Israel's Redemption*, or the prophetical history of our Savior's kingdom on earth, &c., 12mo, London, 1642. This work was assailed by Alexander Petrie, which elicited from the author another work of much greater magnitude, entitled, *Israel's Redemption Redeemed,* or the Jews' general and miraculous conversion to the faith of the gospel and return to their own land, and our Savior's personal reign on earth, clearly proved out of many plain prophecies of the Old and New Testaments; and the chief arguments that can be alleged against those truths fully answered; of purpose to satisfy all gainsayers, and in particular Mr. Alexander Petrie; in two parts, 4to, London, 1646. An able and acute writer.

MAYWAHLEN, DR. V. U., *Intermediate State,* or Christ among the dead, the twofold Resurrection, and the twofold coming of Christ; German; also in English; 12mo.

McCAUL, DR. A., *The Old Paths,* &c., 8vo, London, 1837. *The Conversion and Restoration of the Jews,* two sermons, 8vo, London, 1837. *Plain Sermons* on subjects practical and prophetic, 12mo, London, 1840. *The Messiahship of Jesus,* &c., 8vo, London, 1852.

McNEILE, REV. HUGH, *The Times of the Gentiles,* London, 1828; *Prophecies relating to the Jewish Nation,* 12mo, London, 1840; *Sermons on the Second Advent of the Lord,* 12mo, London, 1842. "Eloquent and pious; one of England's most gifted divines."

MEJANEL, PIERRE, *Miniature Sketch of the Millennium,* &c., 24mo, Edinb., 1831.

MILLENNIAL CHURCH; *or, Christ's Personal Reign upon Earth,* &c., by Clericus Dorcestriensis, 12mo, London. Also, by the same, *Christ's Coming to Judgment,* 12mo, London, 1834.

MILLENNIUM, A TENET OF; *or, The First Resurrection to the Reign of Christ upon the Earth,* by E. L., 8vo, Lond., 1813.

MILLER, WILLIAM, *Evidence from Scripture and History of the Second Coming of Christ,* &c.; a course of Lectures, small 12mo, Boston, 1842.

*Molyneux, C., *The World to Come*, 8vo, 1853. *Israel's Future*, crown 8vo, 6th ed., 1860.

Multum in Parvo; *or Jubilee of Jubilees*, &c., 8vo, 1732.

Newton, Wm., *Lectures on the First Two Visions of the Book of Daniel*, Phila., 1859.

Noel, Hon. & Rev. G. T., *An Inquiry into the Prospects of the Church of Christ, in connection with the Second Advent;* 8vo, London, 1828.

Nolan, Dr. F., *The Chronological Prophecies*, &c., Warburtonian Lectures, 8vo, London, 1837.

Ogilvy, ——, *Popular Objections to the Premillennial Advent considered*, 12mo. Also, other works.

Pagani, John Baptist, *The End of the World;* or, The Second Coming of our Lord and Savior Jesus Christ, 18mo, London, 1855. A valuable testimony, by a Roman Catholic priest.

Paradise Regained; or, *The Scripture Account of the Glorious Millennium*, &c., printed for J. Buckland, 1772.

Penn, Granville (grandson of the founder of Pennsylvania), *A Christian survey of all the primary events and periods of the world from the commencement of History to the conclusion of Prophecy;* small 8vo, Lond., 1812; also, *The Prophecy of Ezekiel concerning Gog*, small 8vo, Lond., 1814.

Perry, W., *Glory of Christ's Visible Kingdom*, 12mo, 1721. "Plain and practical."

Peterson, Dr. Jno. Wm., *A Scriptural exposition and demonstration of the Millennial Reign and the First Resurrection to the Kingdom connected therewith;* (German) 4to, Franckf., 1692. Also, *Warheit des herrlichen Reiches Jesu Christi*, 1693; and many other publications.

PIRIE, REV. ALEX., *An Inquiry into the Prophecies* relating to the conversion and restoration of the Jews; also Sermons and Lectures on prophetic topics; *Works*, 6 vols. 12mo, Edinb., 1805. An acute writer.

POIRET, PIERRE, *The Divine Œconomy;* or an universal system of the works and purposes of God towards men demonstrated; written originally in French, 6 vols. 8vo, London, 1713.

PRE-MILLENNIALISM, *Proofs of, &c.*, with an *Introduction* by Dr. R. Newton, Philadelphia, 1862. A clear and convincing little book.

PURDON, REV. ——, *Last Vials;* 16 small annual volumes, published in monthly and semi-monthly tracts since 1846, London. Still continued.

PURVES, JAMES, *Observations on the Visions of the Apostle John*, compared with other sacred Scriptures; 2 vols. Edinb., 1793.

*PYM, WM. W., *Thoughts on Millenarianism*, 12mo, Lond., 1829; corrected and enlarged, 1831. "Contains, in a small compass, much valuable argument and extracts from the Fathers." Also, *Restitution of all things*, 12mo.

QUARTERLY JOURNAL OF PROPHECY, 1849–1855, London, 7 vols. 8vo. Among the contributors are Elliott, Keith, Kelly, Forster, Hengstenberg, Cumming, &c.

*RAMSEY, DR. WM., *Messiah's Reign*, or the Future Blessedness of the Church and of the World; small 8vo, Philadelphia, 1857. An able, calm, and exegetical treatment of the subject. Also, *Second Coming of Christ*, &c.

RANEW, NATH., *Account concerning the Saints' Glory after the Resurrection*, &c., 4to, Lond., 1670.

READ, HOLLIS, *The Coming Crisis of the World;* or the

Great Battle and the Golden Age, &c., with an Introduction by Dr. S. H. Tyng, Columbus, 1861, 12mo.

REIGN OF CHRIST ON EARTH *noways repugnant to the Spirituality of his Kingdom*, 4to, Lond., 1677.

REVIEW OF SCRIPTURE, in testimony of the truth of the Second Advent, the First Resurrection, and the Millennium, with an *Appendix* on the Restoration of the Jews. By a Layman, 8vo, 1819.

ROACH, R., *The Great Crisis*, &c., 8vo, London, 1825; also, *The Imperial Standard of Messiah Triumphant*, &c., 8vo, Lond., 1727.

RUDD, SAYER, M.D., *An Essay towards a new explication of the doctrine of the Resurrection, Millennium, and Judgment;* with three dissertations on 2 Peter 10–13; Rom. viii. 19–23; Rev. xxi. 24; 8vo, Lond., 1734. Also, other works.

SAVILLE, B. W., *First and Second Advent*, or *the Past and the Future*, &c., 8vo, 1858.

SCHAEFFER, JNO. DAV., *The Everlasting Gospel*, or the doctrine of the Millennium and Reign of Christ and his Saints, &c., 8vo, 1725; also in Latin, *Doctrina de Regno Millennario Christi*.

SCHULTZE, GOTTLOB, *Drei Lebensfragen;* Dresden, 1860. A well-arranged little book, containing much useful exegetical and historical matter.

SCOTT, JAMES, *A Catechism upon the Prophetical System of Scripture*, &c., 12mo, Edinburgh, 1847.

SECOND COMING OF THE LORD, THE, the true Hope of Believers and only Triumph of the Church, &c., Dublin, 1833.

SEISS, J. A., *The Threatening Ruin*, &c., 12mo, Phila., 1861.

SERGENT, FRED., ESQR., *An Essay on the personal and premillennial Advent of the Messiah;* Lond., 1833, small 8vo.

SEVEN, *An Essay* on this number, Lond., 8vo, 1754.

SHADOWS OF THE NEW CREATION, by W. S.

SHERWIN, WM., *Προδρομος, the forerunner of Christ's peaceable Kingdom upon Earth*, Lond., 4to, 1665. *Ειρηνικον, or a peaceable consideration of Christ's peaceable Kingdom to come upon the Earth in the* 1000 *years*, &c., Lond., 4to, 1665; *Supplement* to the same; also, *The Times of the Restitution of All Things*, Lond., 4to, 1675; also, *The True News of the Good New World shortly to come*, &c., Lond., 4to, 1671–2. "A zealous writer on prophecy, a hard student, and of an unblamable life."

SHIMEALL, REV. R. C., *Our Bible Chronology, Historic and Prophetic*, critically examined, &c., royal 8vo, N. York, 1860. Also, *Age of the World*, &c.

SILLIMAN, ANNA, *The World's Jubilee*, N. York, 12mo, 1856.

*SIRR, DR. J. D'ARCY, *The First Resurrection Considered* in a series of Letters; 12mo, 1834. A strong argument, with many useful observations, and written in a good spirit. Also other productions.

SOBER INQUIRY, *or Christ's Reign with his Saints a thousand years*, modestly asserted from the Scripture; 8vo, 1660.

SPENER, PHIL. JAC., *A Defence of the Hope of Better Times to come*, &c., (German,) 12mo, Frankf., 1693.

SPES FIDELIUM, *or the Believer's Hope;* a dissertation proving the thousand years' Reign of Christ; by a presbyter of the Church of England; supposed to be Dr. Grabe, or Dr. Lee; 8vo, 1774.

STERRY, PETER, *The Clouds in which Christ comes*, 4to, 1643; also, *Rise, Race, and Royalty of the Kingdom of God*, 4to, 1683.

STEWART, JAMES HALDANE, *Practical View of the Redeemer's Advent*, 8vo, 1828. Also, *Sermons to strengthen Faith*, &c., 8vo, London, 1828.

STILLING, JOHN HENRY JUNG-, *Siegsgeschichte der christ-*

liche Religion, 8vo, Nuremberg, 1798; also, *Nachtrag*, 1806; also parts of *Der graue Mann*, a periodical.

STRANGE, JUDGE TH. L., *The Light of Prophecy*, 8vo, 1850; also, *Observations on Mr. Elliott's Horæ Apocalypticæ.*

TASK, THE; *or, Scripture Texts connected with the Glorious Advent and Millennial Reign;* 18mo, London, 1847.

*TAYLOR, D. T., *The Voice of the Church on the Coming and Kingdom of the Redeemer;* or a History of the Doctrine of the Reign of Christ on Earth; 12mo, Phila., 1856. A work containing much useful information.

THEOPOLIS, *or the City of God, New Jerusalem,* &c., 8vo, Lond., 1672; Philadelphia, 1808.

THOMAS, J., M.D., *Elpis Israel:* an Exposition of the Kingdom of God, with reference to the end of time and the Age to come; 8vo, N. York, 1851.

THOMPSON, JNO., M.D., *The Judgment* in Matt. xxv. conclusive of Messiah's Personal Advent and his Millennial Kingdom, 4to.

THORPE, WM., *The Destinies of the British Empire,* &c., 8vo, London, 1831.

TILLINGHAST, JOHN, *Generation - Work;* or a brief and seasonable word, offered to the view and consideration of the saints and people of God, &c., First Part, small 8vo, London, 1655.

Generation - Work; the Second Part, wherein is shewed what the designs of God abroad in the world may in all likelihood be, &c., small 8vo, Lond., 1655.

Generation - Work; or an Exposition of the Prophecies of the Two Witnesses, &c., small 8vo, 1655.

Knowledge of the Times, &c., small 8vo, 1654.

Eight Last Sermons, small 8vo, Lond., 1656. "A superior writer, both in practical and evangelical sentiment, and in prophetical knowledge."

Time of the End, *A Prophetic Period*, &c., small 8vo, Boston, 1856, edited by Himes. A collection of matters which will well repay perusal.

Towers, J. L., *Illustrations of Prophecy*, 2 vols. 8vo, 1796.

Tyso, Joseph, *An Inquiry after Prophetic Truth, relative to the Restoration of the Jews and the Millennium*, &c., with various and beautiful maps and engravings; 8vo, London, 1831. "The work contains a clear exposition of the eleven concluding chapters of Ezekiel, the fourteenth of Zechariah, and many other parts of the Old and New Testaments generally considered obscure."

Tyson, Joseph, *A Defence of the Personal Reign of Christ*, 12mo, London, 1841.

Way, Rev. L., *Thoughts on the Scriptural Expectations of the Christian Church*, 8vo, pp. 115; also a poem, entitled *Palingenesia*.

Whiston, Wm., *A New Theory of the Earth, from its original to the consummation of all things*, 8vo, London, 1755; also, *An Essay on the Revelation of St. John*, 4to, Cambridge, 1706; also, *The Accomplishment of Scripture Prophecies*, (Boyle Lecture,) 8vo, Camb., 1708; also, *The Literal Accomplishment of Scripture Prophecies*, &c., London, 1724. A divine of great learning and abilities, but eccentric, and advocating some very peculiar opinions.

*White, Hugh, *Practical Reflections on the Second Advent*, 12mo, Dublin, 1836; N. York, 1843.

White, Jerem., *Restoration of all Things*, 8vo, Lond., 1779, and 1809. "A loving and wise-hearted man," and "a most excellent book."—*Hartley*.

Whowell, T., *Epistles to the Christian Church on the Eve of the Millennium*, &c., 2 vols. 8vo, 1830.

Wilson, John G., *Discourses on Prophecy*, 8vo, Phila., 1858.

WINCHESTER, ELHANAN, *Lectures on the Prophecies that remain to be fulfilled,* 4 vols. 8vo, Helston, 1813.

WINTHROP, ED., Lectures on the Second Advent, 12mo, 1843; also, *Premium Essay on Prophetic Symbols,* 12mo, 1854; also, *Letters on Prophecy,* N. York, 1850.

WITHERBY, WM., ESQ., *A Review of Scripture in testimony of the truth of the Second Advent, the First Resurrection, and the Millennium;* with an *Appendix;* 8vo, Lond., 1818. Also, *Hints to Commentators,* &c., 8vo, Lond., 1821.

WOOD, LEUT. G. H., *The Believer's Guide to the Study of Unfulfilled Prophecy;* containing the Scripture testimony respecting the Gentile apostasy, the Second Advent of Christ, his personal reign on the earth with all his saints, the restoration of the Jews, &c., with the testimony of the Fathers and Reformers; Lond., 1831, 8vo.

WOOD, WALTER, *The Last Things,* London, 1852, 8vo.

WOODWARD, H. W., *Essays on the Millennium.*

ZIPPLE, J. G., *The World's Crisis, and the Restitution of all Things,* 12mo, London, 1854. A Moravian writer.

4. MISCELLANEOUS WORKS WHICH INCIDENTALLY SET FORTH MILLENARIAN DOCTRINES.

AMBROSE, ISAAC, Sermon *on Doomsday; Works,* p. 408.

BENSON, DR. G., *Notes* on Ps. xcvi. 10–13, and xcviii. 4–9.

BONAR, H., *The Eternal Day,* 18mo, London, 1844. Also, *Man—His Religion and his World,* 18mo, London, 1851. Also, *Hymns of Faith and Hope,* 2 vols. 12mo, New York, 1862.

BAUMGARTEN, MICH., *History of the Apostolic Church.*

BLISS, SYLVESTER, *Memoirs of Wm. Miller,* Bost., 12mo, 1853.

BROWN, REV. CH., *Abstract of the New Testament,* 1753, pp. 136, 163.

BURNET, THOMAS, *Sacred Theory of the Earth;* Books III. and IV., especially the latter. Burnet was a writer of great literary excellence, but imaginative and erroneous in his philosophical theories.

BURK, JNO. C. F., *Memoir of the Life and Writings of John Albert Bengel,* translated into English by Walker, 8vo, London, 1837.

CHALMERS, DR. THOMAS, *On the New Heavens and the New Earth,* Sermon on 2 Pet. iii. 13; *Works,* Phila., 1833, p. 411. Also, *Sabbath Scripture Readings.*

CROSBY, THOMAS, History of English Baptists, vol. 2, Appendix 85.

CHARNOCK, DR. STEPHEN, *Discourses on the Existence and Attributes of God,*—Discourse VI., On the Immutability of God, p. 195.

COWPER, WM., *Task,* Book VI.

CLARKE, RICHARD, *The Gospel of the Daily Service of the Law, preached to Jew and Gentile,* &c., 8vo, London, 1767.

CLAYTON, WM., *Rural Discourses,* 2 vols., London, 1814.

CARLYLE, DR. J., *First and Second Advent;* also, *Latter-day Pamphlets.*

DELITZCH, DR. F., *Biblisch-Prophetische Theologie.*

DORNER, *Lehre von d. Person Christi,* i. p. 240, seqq., note.

ELIZABETH, CHARLOTTE, *Judah's Lion,* London, 8vo.

FLÈMING, ROBERT, JR., *Rise and Fall of the Papacy;* also, *Christology,* vol. iii, 8vo, 1708.

FLETCHER, REV. JOHN, *Works,* vol. x.; especially his *Letter on the Prophecies,* dated 1775.

GILFILLAN, G., *Alpha and Omega,* vol. ii., chaps. 20, 21, pp. 331–370; also, *Bards of the Bible,* pp. 345–351.

GILL, DR. JOHN, *Complete Body of Divinity; Prophetical Sermons;* and *Commentary.*

GAUSSEN, M., *Daniel le Prophète,* 3 vols. 2d edition, 1850. An able writer, according very nearly with Elliott. Also, *Lectures on Popery.*

GLASS, JOHN, *Works,* Edinburgh, 1761, vol. 2, pp. 425–430.

HURD, DR. RICHARD, *Introduction to the Study of the Prophecies,* (Warburton Lectures,) vi., pp. 129–163.

HEBER, BISHOP R., *Poetical Works,* small 8vo, London, 1842, especially his *Hymns.*

HARLAN, GENERAL J., *A Memoir on India and Afghanistan,* &c., 12mo, Philadelphia, London, and Paris, 1842.

HORT, ROBERT, *Posthumous Works,* 1805.

JOHNSON, REV. SAMUEL, *Thirty-six Select Discourses,* &c., 2 vols. 8vo, London, 1740. Particularly the Preface.

KEBLE, JNO., *The Christian Year,* New York, 1850. For Advent Season, pp. 17–37.

KLING, DR., DEAN OF MARBACH, Article on *Eschatology* in *Herzog's Encyclopedia.*

LUTHERUS REDIVIVUS, oder des führnehmsten Lehrers der Augsb. Confession, &c., 4to, 1697, pp. 386, 389.

LECHLER, ——, *Das Apost. und Nachapost. Zeitalter,* p. 82.

LORD, ELEAZ., *The Messiah in Moses and the Prophets,* 12mo, New York, 1853.

MILTON, JOHN, *Paradise Lost,* III. 333–338; XII. 531–555. *Prose Works,* Conclusion of Essay on *Reformation in England.*

MATHER, DR. COTTON, *The Student and Preacher;* or Directions for a Candidate for the Ministry. Also, his *Life,* pp. 141–144.

NEWTON, BISHOP THOMAS, *Dissertations on the Prophecies*, Diss. 22, 23, 24, 25, especially his *Analysis of Rev.* xx.

NISSEN, J., *Unterredungen über den Kleinen Catechismus Luthers;* Kiel, 1859, pp. 524–533.

OETINGER, FRIED. CHRISTOPH, *Predigten*, 5 vols. 8vo, Stuttgart, 1858; also *Biblisches Wörterbuch*.

OSIANDER, Prof. at Maulbronn, *Lehrbuch*, sec. 66, 67, 76–78.

POPE, ALEXANDER, *The Messiah*. See his *Works*.

PIERS, HENRY, *Three Sermons on Ephesians* ii. 12; 12mo, London, 1748.

PRESBYTERIAN REVIEW, THE, Organ of the Scotch Church, established some twenty-five or thirty years ago.

REICHEL, CARL RUDOLPH, *Predigten über die Sonn- und Festtags-Episteln*, Leipzig, 4to, 1787. Also, *Evangelisches Denk-Sprüche*, &c., Leipzig, 4to, 1783.

REINHARD, DR. FR. VOLKMAR, *Dogmatik*, sec. 189, where he teaches the twofold nature of the Resurrection; also in sec. 191, on the changes to be wrought in the world.

SHERWOOD, MRS., *The Latter Days*. See her *Works*, vol. ii. pp. 289–455, New York ed.

SHARPE, DR. GREGORY, *Defence of Christianity*, 8vo, London, 1775, p. 140.

SPURGEON, C. H., *Sermons*, sixth series, and elsewhere.

SPALDING, JOSHUA, *Lectures*, pp. 45, 51, 214, etc.

SCHLEGEL, FREDERICK VON, *Lectures on the Philosophy of History*, delivered in 1828, at Vienna; translated into English by Robertson, small 8vo, London, 1846.

SPENER, DR. P. J., *Auffrichtige Ubereinstimmung mit der Augsb. Confession*, &c., 4to, 1695, pp. 287–290.

SCHONER, JNO. G., *Predigten über die Evangelien*, 8vo, Nürnberg, 1804.

SPANGENBERG, BISHOP AUG. GOT., *Exposition of Christian Doctrine*, as taught in the Church of the Unitas Fratrum, London, 8vo, 1784, the last chapter. Also, *Idea Fidei*.

TOPLADY, AUGUSTUS M., *Speech at the Queen's Arms*, &c.; also, *Meditation for a New Year's Day; Works*, London, 1861, pp. 428, 448.

TYNG, DR. STEPHEN H., Articles on *The Coming Kingdom;* also, *Lectures on the Five Universal Monarchies of the Earth*, and elsewhere.

THOMASIUS, at Nuremberg, *Manual of Catechetical Instruction*, sec. 33, 38.

TUPPER, MARTIN F., sundry Poems, especially "*The Last Time*."

WATTS, DR. ISAAC, many of his *Hymns* and *Psalms*.

WESLEY, JOHN, *Works*, 7 vols. 8vo, New York ed., vol. v. pp. 726, 727; also vol. vi. p. 743, where he fully endorses Mr. Hartley's book, "*Paradise Restored: a Testimony to the Doctrine of the Blessed Millennium*." Also, his *Notes on the New Testament*.

WESLEY, CHARLES, *Hymns*, 1762; for example, the one beginning, "I call the world's Redeemer mine."

WOGAN, WM., ESQ., *Essay on the proper Lessons appointed by the Liturgy of the Church of England*, 2 vols. 8vo, Derby, 1841; especially on 27th Sunday after Trinity.

THE END.

INDEX.

ABOMINATION OF DESOLATION, 22.
ADVENT, THE, when to occur, 38, 39, 261–282; signs of, 292–299, 371; is near at hand, 301–303; desirableness of, 304–308; the common expectation of the Church, 15; to be expected from considerations of reason, 31; great interest of, 32; first and second, 37; is premillennial, 40–60, 104, 105; the setting up of the kingdom connected with 126–130; practical value of the doctrine of, 256, 257; how regarded by the primitive Church, 257, 258, 287; our duty in view of, 283, 370; too much skepticism and coldness with regard to, 15, 287; to have two stages, 350, 351; references to the teachings of Christ and his apostles on, 365–367; Old Testament on, 367; references on the objects and results of, 368–370; the manner of, 372; uses made of, in the Scriptures, 375.
AGE OF THE WORLD, 268, 269.
αιων, meaning of, 73.
ALFORD, DEAN, 325, 340, 400.
ALLEGORICAL METHOD, Origen's, 248, 249.
ANABAPTISTS, their fanaticism, 235, 236, 329.
ANALOGY, argument from, on the perpetuity of the earth, 71, 72.
ANTICHRIST, THE, 47, 341; is to be a French emperor, 178; to be destroyed by Christ in person, 47–52; probably Louis Napoleon is to be, 341–349; Scripture reference to, 378, 379; referred to in Matt. xxiv. 15, 22.
ANTICHRISTIAN POWERS, when destroyed, 46–52; can be no Millennium while they remain, 46, 47; shall not exist in the millennial world, 222.
ANTIQUITY, importance of, 231, 232.
APOCRYPHAL WRITINGS on the Millennium, 388–392.
APOLLINARIUS, 394.
APOSTASY of last times, 42, 45, 57, 261, 292, 371.
ARNOLD, DR., 391, 320.
AUBERLEN, DR., 324, 365, 405.
AUGSBURG CONFESSORS, 57, 326; do they condemn Chiliasm? 327–335.
AUGUSTINE, 247, 396.
BABYLON, GREAT, 174; her doom, 175–177, 279, 280.
BACON on the nature of prophecy, 17, 18.
BAIRD, DR., 318.
BARNABAS, 237, 238, 383.
BARONIUS, 273.
BAXTER, 306.
BEECHER, CHARLES, 32.
BENEVOLENT SOCIETIES, THE GREAT, have not accomplished what was claimed for them, 300.
BENGEL, DR., 333, 337, 400, 404.
BERG, 127.
BIBLE, THE, only authority in things of faith, 10, 11, 232; how some read it, 26; how it is to be interpreted, 116; will become a new book in the light of fulfilled prophecy, 202; Luther's method of interpreting, 253; much of it ignored by those who refuse to study prophecy, 12; chronology of, 356–362.
BIBLE, THE BURLENBURG, 400.
BICKERSTETH, 303, 409.
BLESSEDNESS of the millennial world, 212–229.
BODY, THE, resurrection of, not impossible with God, 88; believed in by the Jews, 90; identity preserved in, 91, 92; in the glorified state, 218.
BOGIE, DR., 319.
BONAR, H., hymns by, 230, 364, 401, 411, 428.
BROOKS, 117, 250, 303, 399, 411.
BROWNE, ARCHD., 316.
BUCKHOLDT, JOHN, 235.
BURNET, DR. T., 65, 429.
BURTON, 245.
BUSH, 100, 142, 256, 267, 270, 319, 396.

C.

CALMET, 93.
CALVIN, 80.
CARLYLE, 297.
CATHOLICISM, ROMAN, 292, 297.
CELANO, DE hymn by, 159.
CERINTHUS, errors imputed to him, 235; his injury to millenarian doctrine, 251.
CHABBO, 99.

CHALMERS, DR. T., 286, 289, 429.
CHARNOCK, on the restoration of all things, 80, 429.
CHEEVER, DR. G. B., 318.
CHILLINGWORTH, 244, 398.
CHINESE PHILOSOPHERS, 65.
CHOATE, RUFUS, 320.
CHRIST, spiritual or providential coming of, 37, 59; claims of, for the gospel, 110; to reign as a great prince upon earth, 113–131, 204. 212; his reign eternal, 144; the bliss of seeing, 215–217.
CHRIST, THE RETURN OF, certain, 15. 30, 31, 37; importance of, 32; few properly influenced by it, 15, 287; great original prophecy on, 16; hymn on, 136; will be as a thief, 152; importance of being prepared for it, 156; bliss of seeing him, 215–217; when it shall occur. how far made known, 259, 260; the time of. considered relatively. 261; a period of apostasy and revolutionary troubles, 261, 262. 371, 373; before the Jews are entirely restored. 263: while papacy and antichrist continue, 264, 373; at a time of alarm on the subject, 265, 371, 373; but while the multitudes scoff and disbelieve, 265, 373; our duty with reference to, 172, 283. 370; is near at hand, 282, 291, 302. 303; the desirableness of, 131–133, 304–308; want of faith in, 286, 287: how to affect his enemies, 368.
CHRISTENDOM, survey of, 292, 293.
CHRISTIAN, A, no sorrowful thing to be, 111; is safe, 181, 309; is not done with this world when he dies, 221.
CHRISTIANITY not to triumph universally till Christ comes, 53–56; Luther and Melancthon on the subject, 56–58; other testimonies, 57, 58; a spiritual religion, 119. 120.
CHRISTOCRACY, 113.
CHRISTS, FALSE, 19, 20, 23.
CHRONOLOGY, different systems of, 269; of the Bible. 356–362.
CHURCHES, THE, to be thoroughly revolutionized, 170–172; how to regulate our present relations to, 172.
CHURCHES, THE NATIONALIZED, abominations of, 174, 175; the doom of, 176, 177; decay of, 280.
CHURCH, PRIMITIVE, THE, how regarded the advent of Christ, 257, 258. 287; opinion of, on the Millennium, 383–398: Apocryphal writings of, 388–392; authorities on the millenarianism of, 398.
CHURCH, THE, afflicted till Christ comes, 40, 41, 44: Melancthon on this point, 56, 255; Henry and Whitefield on the same, 58; difference between its spirit now and in primitive times, 257; removal of, when Christ comes, 154, 162, 349–353.
CITY, THE HEAVENLY, 207, 219, 311.
CLARKE, DR. A., 323.
CLEMENT, 238, 384.
CLEMENT OF ALEXANDRIA, 242, 387.
COMMENTATORS, on Matt. xxiv., 25–27; poets and painters as, 137.
COMMODIAN, 393.
CONFESSIONS, or creeds, referred to, 15, 57, 58, 287, 326.
CONFLAGRATION, THE, 75–79.
CONSTANTINE, elevation of the Church under him supposed to begin the Millennium, 250; his legalization of the Church the inlet of great evils, 94.
CONSUMMATION, THE, changes to be effected in, 82, 83; joy of 228, 307, 308.
CORONATION OF CHRIST as king of the world, 112.
CORRODI, his work on Chiliasm, 398.
COX, 303, 306. 412.
COXE, hymn by. 182.
CREATION, THE, longing for the consummation, 63, 79, 85.
CRUSIUS, 333.
CRY. THE MIDNIGHT, beginning to go forth, 296.
CUMMING, JOHN, 72, 303, 305, 401, 405, 412.
CUNNINGHAME, 303, 412.
CURSE, THE, to be repealed, 79–81, 226–228.
CYPRIAN, 242, 393.

D.

DANA, 76.
DARKNESS the herald of day, 299, 300.
DAUBUZ, 267.
DAVID. tabernacle of, to be rebuilt. 192.
DAY, often taken for a long period of time, 141, 142.
DAYS. taken for years, 270.
DEAD. THE. resurrection of, 88–92: comfort with reference to, 105–108; the judgment of. 161; "the rest of," Rev. xx.; what is meant by. 95–98.
DEATH, repulsiveness of 105; to what it is reduced under Christ, 106; triumphs over, in the resurrection, 107, 108.
DEMOCRACY, the spirit of the times, would level every thing, 297.
DEMONISM, 281.
DICKSON, hymn by, 311.
DISPENSATIONS, overlap. 150.
DOANE, BISHOP, hymn by, 35.
DODWELL. 256.
DORNER, DR., 324, 429.
DUFF, DR., 316.
DUFFIELD, DR., 413.

E.

EAGLES, the saints compared to, 24.
EARTH, its perpetuity asserted in Scriptures, 68–70: dreams of its destruction, 67; its probable destiny if sin had never touched it, 68.
ELDERS, THE. in Rev. iv. 5, 353.
ELECT, THE. 23.
ELIAS, tradition of the house of, 255, 267.
ELLIOTT, DR., 49, 302, 405, 413.

END OF THE WORLD, THE, what is meant by, 73-75; nearness of, 282; opinions of students of prophecy on the nearness of, 302-304; really to be desired, 304-307.
ENOCH, BOOK OF, 389.
ἐπιφανειά, meaning of, 48.
ERNESTI, 116.
ESDRAS, second book of, 390.
EUPHRATES, drying up of, 279, 280.
EVENTS, general order of, 379-382.
EXPECTATION of Christ's coming a characteristic of the early Church, 257, 287.

F.

FABER, G. S., 270, 274, 303, 342, 413.
FAITH, great want of, 286; shall be feeble and scarce when Christ comes, 42.
FALL, THE, consequences of, 62, 63.
FARMER, JOSEPH, 147, 337. 414.
FATHERS, THE, opinions of, on millenarian doctrine, 237-245; Luther's respect for, 334; references to their opinions and works, 383-398.
FIRES, THE, spoken of by Peter, not universal, 76-79; Christ shall be revealed in, 78.
FIRST-FRUITS, 350.
FLACIUS, 273.
FLEMING, ROBERT, 49, 273, 414, 429.
FLŒRKE, 332, 414.
FLOOD, THE, how it came, 155.
FRENCH REVOLUTION, THE, 275, 276, 362.
FRENCH, THE, Emperor of, to be the personal antichrist, 178.

G.

γη, nowhere said to have an end, 73, 74; is to survive the baptism of fire, 75.
γενεα, meaning of, 28, 323.
GENTILES, THE times of, 187.
GIBBON, ED., 243, 256.
GIESELER, 245.
GŒTHE, his view of nature's ailings, 63.
GOODWIN, DR. T., 148, 405.
GOSPEL, THE, preaching of, to all nations, 20, 371; our only hope, 258; its glorious promises, 109.
GOVERNMENT, good, the greatest desideratum, 131, 134; all present forms of, to be modified or destroyed, 170-172.
GREEK CHURCH, 293.
GRESWELL, DR., 337, 388, 391, 392, 399, 400.

H.

HABERSHON, 303.
HALL, THOMAS, his argument that the Millennium cannot precede the judgment, 57, 58.
HAMILTON, DR., 197. 202.
HARTLEY, TH., 337, 338, 395, 415, 432.
HEBER, BISHOP, 290, 430.
HENGSTENBERG, DR., 355.
HENRY, MATTHEW, on the mixed condition of the world till Christ comes, 58.
HERMAS, 384.
HILLER, P. F., 334.
HINDOSTANEE opinions on the world's future, 65.
HIPPOLYTUS, 392.
HISTORY continually repeating itself, 17; one of the storehouses of wisdom, 231.
HITCHCOCK, DR., 318.
HODY, 101.
HOMES, N., 416.
HOOKER, 116.
HORN, THE LITTLE, 271.
HORT, 65, 417, 430.
HYMNS, "Even so come, Lord Jesus," 35; "Another Admonition," 61; "Waiting for that day," 87; "Wird das nicht Freude seyn," 111; "Maranatha," 136; "Dies Iræ," 159; "Arouse for Duty," 182; "The Day is Coming," 208; "Yet a Little While," 230; "He Left not Himself without Witness," 258; "Wake, Awake," 284; "The New Jerusalem," 311; "The Happy Dawn," 364.

I.

IGNATIUS, 384.
INTERPRETATION, laws of, 116.
IRENÆUS, 240, 241, 252, 336, 387.
IRVING, 305, 417.
ISRAEL, exemptions of, in the judgment times, 167; all to be saved, 187, 188, 189; kingdom to be restored to, 190, 191; to return to Palestine, 193-196; to be thoroughly converted and sanctified, 202, 203; exaltation of, in the Millennium, 223, 224.

J.

JEREMIAH XXV., 163, 164.
JEROME, 247, 396.
JERUSALEM, 197, 199; is to be the metropolis of the world, 204-206, 374; destruction of, 21; a type of the end 17, 18.
JERUSALEM, the heavenly, 207, 311-315.
JEWS, THE, to remain a distinct people till Christ comes, 28, 29. 323; their conceptions of the Messiah, 117. 118; contemned by many, 168; are the living symbols of coming evil. 168, 169; shall be concerned in the last great wars, 178; are to be converted, 183; are to be restored to Palestine, 184; objections answered, 184-186; referred to in the New Testament, 186-192; proofs from the Old Testament, 192-195; historical facts bearing on the question, 196-198; how the return will begin, 199; will be effected only in the judgment period, 201; accompaniments and results of their return, 202-207; future glory of, 223; God's covenant with them, 188. 189; restoration of the kingdom to, 190, 191; their restoration not merely spiritual,

193, 194; survey of their history and condition, 196; their metropolis, 197, 204–206; lines on their restoration, 208; mistaken views of, on Christ's kingdom, 118–120, 330; their estimate of our times, 319; how affected by Christ's coming 369; destiny of, 376, 378.
JOHN xviii. 36 often misquoted, 121; true meaning of, 338–340.
JOHNSTON, 266.
JONATHAN, the Paraphrast, 99.
JUDGE, scriptural conception of a, 139, 140.
JUDGMENT, administrations of, with respect to the dead, 143, 161; as respects the living, 162–167; how they will begin to be felt, 169; general results of, in the world, 170–172; more particular effects, 173–179; how these things should impress us 178, 181.
JUDGMENT, day of not a day of twenty-four hours, 141; stretches through the thousand years, 141–148; will be introduced differently from what is generally supposed 149–156; will have its morning and its evening, 144, 145, 160; admonitions in view of, 157, 158.
JUDGMENT, THE, much misunderstood, 137; certainty of 138; not to be thought of as an assize, 139; is the administration of the Divine government, 141; is progressive, 142, 143; connects with the personal reign of Christ, 141–148; how it will begin, 149–151, 155; hymn on, 159.
JUSTINIAN, 272.
JUSTIN MARTYR, 239, 336, 386.

K.

KARENS, their tradition, 65.
KEBLE, hymn by, 61, 430.
KEITH, DR., 270.
KIMCHI, RABBI, 99, 401.
KINGDOM, the Messiah's, 112; how predicted in the Old Testament, 113–116; the ideas entertained of it by the Jews, 117, 118; how spoken of in the New Testament, 119–125; connected with the second advent, 126–130; is not yet manifested, 132–134; is to be on earth, 120, 121, 124–131, 212, 330, 340; is to be eternal 144; connects with the throne of David, 114–116; is to be a literal kingdom, 122–125, 127, 128, 131; is not from this world, 130, 339, 340; coexists with the world to come, 210; the glory of, 133, 135, 226–228, 290; how spoken of by Luther, 254; the spirituality of, 119, 335–338.
KING, ED., 324, 340, 418.
KINGS AND PRIESTS of the world to come, 218–221.
KINNEY, 76.
KNAPP, 117.
KNOX, JOHN, on the world's reform before Christ comes, 56.
κοσμος, meaning of, 73, 74.
KOSSUTH, LOUIS, 320.
KRUMMACHER, 302, 340.

L.

LACTANTIUS, 244, 394.
LAMBERT, 419.
LAW governing the Divine operations, 71, 72.
LORD, DAVID N., 77, 96, 198, 275, 405, 420.
LUTHER, his conception of the gathering of the eagles to the body, 24; his opinion on the question of the world's conversion before Christ comes, 56; on the restoration, 80, 354; his method of interpreting Scripture, 253; denied that a Millennium of righteousness would come before Christ comes, 253; how he spoke of the kingdom, 254; believed that the end would come in six thousand years from Adam, 255, 355; anticipated the time as near, 255; held that the time was not beyond human knowledge, 260; refers to A.D. 606 as a notable commencing epoch, 273; thought the end would certainly come in about three hundred years, 274, 316; on the desirableness of the end, 305; on the meaning of the 17th Article of the Augsburg Confession, 330, 331; respect for the fathers, 334; on the Millennium, 354–356.
LYNCH, LIEUT., 200.

M.

MACAULAY, 317.
MACDUFF, hymn by, 136.
MAGDEBURG CENTURIATORS, 270.
MAHOMETANISM, 153, 279.
MAN OF SIN, his duration and end, 47–49.
MARTYRS, their resurrection at the commencement of the Millennium, literal, 95, 96 97.
MATON, 115, 420.
MATTER not essentially corrupt, 72.
MATTHEW xxiv. 16, true key to the meaning of 17; an axiom for its interpretation, 25; what it teaches, 30.
MEDE, 66, 142, 148, 270, 323, 337, 395, 404.
MELANCTHON, 49; his opinion on the Church's prospects in this dispensation, 56, 255; on the 17th Article of Augsburg Confession, 331, 332.
MELITO, 336, 386.
MESSIAH, THE, prophecies concerning, 113–116, 122, 129.
METHODIUS, 393.
MILLENARIANS, a summary of their doctrines 233, 234; not Millerites, 236; the fathers were, 237–246; how their doctrines came into disrepute, 246–252, 307; popery the great enemy of, 246, 250, 251, 290; classified references to the writings of, 400–432.
MILLENNIUM, what it means, 38; common views of, criticized, 39; not to be till

Christ comes, 40–60, 104; Scriptures promise no, before the advent, 40; no place for in the great prophetic discourse of Christ before his advent, 44, 45; no acknowledged creed places before the advent, 58; Whitbian theory on, 94; Barnabas on, 237, 238; Papias and Justin Martyr on, 239; Irenæus on, 240; Tertullian on, 241; Cyprian on, 242; Lactantius on, 244; Augsburg and Helvetic Confessions on, 326.
MILLER, WILLIAM, his views, 236, 421.
MILTON, 49, 430; on the Church's prospects till Christ comes, 57; on the signs of the advent, 202; prayer of, for Christ's coming, 306.
MOSHEIM, 235, 240, 245, 248, 273, 398.
MUNSCHER, 245, 398.

N.

NAPOLEON I., poem on return of his remains to France, 208; affliction caused by him, 277, 363; seventh head of the Roman power, 341, 342.
NAPOLEON III., question of his being the antichrist presented, 341; his power, 342, 343; peculiarities of his name, 344; relation to the Church power, 345; his character, 345–347; his rise from obscurity, 347, 348; his resources, 348.
NATIONS, distress of, 169, 170, 262, 294, 371.
NATURE, how reduced and afflicted by sin, 62, 63; beauties of, still remaining, 72, 73; to be renewed, 81–85; illustrations from, on the resurrection, 89, 90; longeth for the consummation, 63, 79, 85; shall give forebodings of the time of the end, 371.
NEANDER, 117.
NEBUCHADNEZZAR, dream of, 262.
NEPOS, 394.
NEWSPAPERS, secular, 293.
NEWTON, BISHOP, 245, 256, 270, 397, 431.
NEWTON, SIR ISAAC, 367, 403.
NICE, COUNCIL OF, 253, 272, 395.
NIKOLAI, hymn by, 284.
NOAH, moral aspect of his times, 45, 155; God's covenant to, 74.

O.

ŒTINGER, F. C., 333, 431.
οἰκουμενη, 210, 211.
OLD TESTAMENT of equal authority with the New, 186.
ORIGEN, 65, 243, 247; his system of spiritualizing described, 248, 249, 290.

P.

PALESTINE, 198, 199, 204, 205.
PAPACY, THE, its commencement and duration, 271–274.
PAPIAS, 239, 385.
PARADISE to be restored, 80.
παρουσία, meaning of, 48.
PEEL, SIR ROBERT, 301.
PHILO, 65.
PHOCAS, 272, 273.
PLATO, 64.
PLUTARCH, 64, 267.
POETS, their foolish dreams, 67; very poor theologians, 137.
POLYCARP, 385.
POUNDS, parable of, 352.
PREPARATION, importance of 33, 34, 156.
PROPHECY, prejudices against the study of, 11; a somewhat difficult subject, 13; is for our enlightenment, 3 ; our duty to study it, 12, 13; a delightful subject, 14; of no private interpretation, 77, 78; nature of, 18.
PROTESTANTISM, 293; hopes concerning, not fulfilled, 300, 297.
PROVIDENCE, all things in the hands of, 180.
ψυχη, meaning of, 95.
PYM, 302, 423.

R.

READ, HOLLIS, 318.
REFORM, the watchword of our times, 296–298.
REIGN OF CHRIST AND HIS SAINTS, 113, 114, 125, 130, 135, 144, 204, 218–220, 374.
RENOVATION OF THE WORLD, by whom expected, 64, 65; to be desired, 72; Luther, and Calvin, and Charnock on, 80; Scripture statements concerning, 80–84; hymn on, 86.
RESURRECTION, THE, not impossible, 88; shadowed in nature, 89; was believed in by the Jews, 90; has actually occurred in certain cases, 90, 91; identity preserved in, 91, 92; twofold character of, 98–104; that of the saints eclectic and invisible, 103, 154.
RESURRECTION, THE FIRST, not figurative, but literal, 93–98; an ancient belief, 98, 99; Scripture reasons for this view, 102–104; joyfulness of, 106–111; will be invisible, 154; a peculiar blessing, 102.
REVELATION XX. 4–6, literal interpretation of, maintained, 93–98.
REVOLUTIONS, 1848 the year of, 278; to connect with Christ's second coming, 32, 261, 262, 294, 371.
RICE, DR. N. L., 317.
ROOS, M. F., 333, 334, 337, 406.
RUSSELL, BISHOP, 267, 391.
RUTHERFORD, 306.

S.

SAINTS THE, compared to eagles, 24; to be raised and translated when Christ comes, 106, 108, 154, 161, 162; are to live a glorified angelic life, 218; are to have high official honors, 218; partake with Christ in his dominion, 219, 374; shall have to do with those who shall

continue to live in the flesh, 220; will not be usually visible to those in the body, 220; their ministrations to be for the general good. 220, 221; how affected when Christ comes, 368.
SCHAFF, DR., 117.
SCHMUCKER, DR. J. G., 334, 402.
SCHUBERT on nature's yearnings. 63. 64.
SCHWEINITZ H. C. VON, hymn by, 111.
SCIENCE. men of, do not stop on account of difficulties 13. 14; what they tell us of the interior of the earth, 75, 76; falsely so called, 293.
SEED. THE WOMAN'S, 113. 352.
SEMISCH, DR.. 240. 245. 332. 398.
SEVENS, system of, in Scripture, 266, 291.
SIBYLLINE ORACLES. 64. 390.
SIGNS of the Lord's coming, 292–300, 371.
SIRR, DR. D'ARCY, 425.
SKEPTICS multiplying, 300.
SOCIETIES, Mission, Bible, Sunday-school, &c., 300.
SPENER. DR., 333, 337, 403, 425, 431.
SPIRITUALISM, 281.
SPIRITUALITY demanded by the gospel, 119.
SPIRITUAL RESURRECTION, 93, 96, 103.
STIER. DR., 324, 339, 400.
STRABO, 65.
STUART. PROFESSOR, 116, 270, 401; on the twofold resurrection, 96, 99, 103, 104.
STUDY. when a pleasure, 14.
SULPICIUS SEVERUS. 395.
SUMMARY of the judgment scenes, 169–171; of millenarian doctrines, 233, 234.

T.

TARES, PARABLE OF THE, 45, 46.
TATIAN, 386.
TAYLOR, D. T., 426.
TEN KINGDOMS, THE. 173, 262.
TERTULLIAN, 232, 241, 387. 388.
THANKFULNESS due for the gospel, 110.
THOLUCK, DR. 339.
TILLINGHAST. his argument on the literalness of Messiah's kingdom 127, 128, 426.
TIME of the return of Christ references to. 373; not entirely and perpetually concealed. 259–261.
TIMES immediately preceding the judgment, 169–172; of the Savior's return 261, 262, 292–294, 371; after Christ's return, 374.
TIMES OUR. aspect of 10, 292, 294; opinions of distinguished men on. 301. 316–322.
TRANSFIGURATION, THE, a picture of the kingdom. 213.
TRANSLATION. THE. when Christ comes. 108, 109, 162; the two stages in, 349–353.
TRENCH. DEAN, 340.
TRIBULATION, THE, 20 22. 23, 24, 25; some escape it, 349; who shall suffer it, 351, 352, 353; when it is to begin, 22.
TRUMPET, the last, 152, 153.
TURKEY, 279.
TYNG, DR. S. H., 318, 424.

U.

UNBELIEF a characteristic of the last times, 42. 43, 261, 265; the spirit of, too prevalent among modern Christians. 286, 300.
UNSANCTIFIED, THE, discomfiture of, in the judgment, 156, 162–168.
USHER, ARCHBISHOP, 49, 78, 269.

V.

VIALS. the seven last, 275–281, 362, 363.
VICTORINUS, 393.
VIRGINS. parable of the ten, 351.
VITRINGA, 116.
VOLCANOES, irruptions of, described, 76

W.

WAITING for Christ's return, 87.
WARNING to the wicked and careless, 157, 369.
WESLEY, JOHN, 432.
WHITBY, 94, 184, 399.
WHITING, PROFESSOR, 101.
WITNESSES, GOD'S. 258.
WOLFFE, DR. JOSEPH, 65.
WORLD, THE, to abound with wickedness till Christ comes, 42; its population to be of good and bad till then. 45, 46; its original estate. 62; its present condition, 63, 132, 134, 166; to be restored, 64, 65, 86, 211; is not to be annihilated 66–70; is to be regenerated. 71, 75; end of how to be understood. 73. 74; is not to be depopulated, 69; Christ's kingdom not from. 121; kingdoms of to be broken, 150; the nations of, how affected by the judgment 151, 170; its present state to endure six thousand years from Adam, 237, 255, 267; present age of 268, 269; will be taken by dismaying surprise when Christ comes, 156; Bible chronology of, 356–362; how affected by Christ's coming. 369.
WORLD TO COME. THE. 210; is the present world in its renewed condition, 211, 212; glory of exhibited on the Mount of Transfiguration, 213; Christ to be present in it. 214–217; to have in it the ministrations of the glorified. 218–221; the powers of evil to be excluded from it. 222. 223; the Jews to have the pre-eminence in, 223, 224; the curse to be repealed, 226–228; lines on, 229, 374, 375.

Y.

YEAR-DAY system explained. 270.
YEARS, the 1260, of the little horn, 271–274.

Z.

ZOROASTER, 267.

THE END.

PULPIT THEMES AND PREACHERS' ASSISTANT. Outlines of Sermons, by the Author of "Helps for the Pulpit." 12mo, cloth, $1.50.

MOSHEIM'S HISTORICAL COMMENTARIES on the State of Christianity during the first 325 years from the Christian Era. Translated by James Murdock, D.D. 2 vols. 8vo, cloth, $4.00.

AIKMAN'S CYCLOPEDIA OF CHRISTIAN MISSIONS; their Rise, Progress, and Present Position. 12mo, cloth, $1.50.

THE WORKS OF NATHANIEL LARDNER, D.D. With a Life, by Dr. Kippis. 10 vols. 8vo, cloth, *net* $15.00, or half calf, *net* $18.00.

FARRAR'S SCIENCE IN THEOLOGY. Sermons preached before the University, Oxford. 12mo, cloth, 85 cents.

TOOKE'S DIVERSIONS OF PURLEY. New Edition, Revised and Corrected, with additional Notes, by RICHARD TAYLOR, F.S.A., F.L.S. 8vo, cloth, $4.00.

LUTHER'S COMMENTARY ON GALATIANS. With Lisher's Life of Luther, Abridged; a Sketch of the Life of Zuingle, and a Discourse on the Glorious Reformation, by S. S. Schmucker, D.D. Small 8vo, cloth, $1.25.

KURTZ'S TEXT BOOK OF CHURCH HISTORY. Vol. I. To the Reformation. Vol. II. From the Reformation. *Each*, $1.50.

MACLAURIN'S WORKS. New and Complete Edition. Edited by the REV. W. H. GOOLD, D.D. 2 vols. crown 8vo, cloth, $4.00.

COLES' PRACTICAL DISCOURSE ON GOD'S SOVEREIGNTY, with other material points derived thence. From the *Forty-third* London Edition. 12mo, cloth, 75 cents.

McILVAINE'S EVIDENCES OF CHRISTIANITY. Exhibited in a course of Lectures. 12mo, cloth, 75 cents.

SEISS ON THE PARABLE OF THE TEN VIRGINS. Six Discourses. And a Sermon on the Judgeship of the Saints. 12mo, cloth, 75 cents.

THE THREATENING RUIN; or, Our Times, our Prospects, and our Duty. A Discourse by JOS. A. SEISS, D.D. Paper, 12 cents, cloth, 25 cents.

THE DAY OF THE LORD: A Lecture by JOS. A. SEISS, D.D. Paper, 12 cents, cloth, 25 cents.

Dr. SEISS

ON THE

PARABLE OF THE TEN VIRGINS.

Opinions of the Press.

These sermons are strikingly original and forcible. Among all the productions of the modern pulpit, we have seen few so likely to command attention; and this, not from sensationalism of style, but from vigor of thought. In doctrine they hold to an orthodox, but tolerant, Lutheranism. —*Episcopal Recorder.*

Some of the interpretations in this interesting volume may startle the reader, as, for instance, that the foolish virgins represent a class of genuine Christians, and were not lost. The scope of the parable is represented as generic, covering the Church on a grand scale, and opening up the mysteries of our Lord's second coming. The positions of Dr. Seiss' book are stated with great clearness, and argued with a force which will carry conviction to many, and will make a deep impression upon those whom it does not convince. While it presents much that stimulates and profoundly interests the reader, it also has another excellence, characteristic of all Dr. Seiss' works: it has practical pungency, and no one can rise from a careful perusal of it without being strengthened in the purposes and energies of Christian duty.—*The Lutheran and Missionary.*

These sermons are written in Dr. Seiss' usual fluent and graphic style. Without endorsing every point of interpretation, we are decidedly pleased with the book, and believe that much good would result from its general circulation. The discussion of the subject is more thorough than we have yet seen in any other work; and, though a practical vein runs throughout, the author has not permitted this to rule out the more solid and learned matter which belongs to the subject.—*German Reformed Messenger.*

The interpretation given to the parable differs from the common one, but is entertained with much firmness by the author, and held by him to be of much importance. The Discourses are in a strain of earnest piety, and contain much interesting matter, both in the line of exegesis, and of practical observations; and we can recommend the book as one profitable to read and examine. Careful and discriminating attention to the author's views and the arguments by which he supports them, will give one a larger knowledge of Scriptural interpretation and enable him to fix more exactly and hold more firmly the precise doctrine of the New Testament on the subject of Christ's second appearing.—*Boston Recorder.*

There is a great deal of original thought in this book, well worthy of being read, even if we do not accept all its conclusions. These discourses were preached in St. John's Lutheran Church, Philadelphia, last winter, and seem to have attracted much attention. They are based on a kind of millennial theory, or a peculiar view of "the world to come," as a new dispensation or order of things on this earth,—a view which, in many respects, is very fascinating. They are very well written.—*Gospel Messenger.*

Dr. Seiss, of the Lutheran Church in this city, has won for himself an honorable and a deserved reputation as a fervid and elegant preacher and writer; as a diligent student of the Word, and of ancient and modern biblical literature; and as a man of devout and evangelical spirit. These characteristics appear in his recently published volume of *Discourses on the Parable of the Ten Virgins*, which is a most readable and, in the main, highly profitable work. His views involve the doctrine of the literal second coming. . . . A sermon on the "Judgeship of the Saints" is added. It is doubtless true that the clergy generally pay too little attention to the eschatology of the Scriptures as an effective element of preaching. Dr. Seiss' book is calculated to stir up their interest on the subject.—*American Presbyterian.*

The views of the Doctor are presented with great clearness and maintained with plausibility and force. He always seems to speak with an honest heart and with a profound reverence for the teachings of the Word. He endeavors to excite in the minds of Christians a deeper interest in the Redeemer's second advent. The discourses are interesting, instructive, and suggestive, and no one can rise from their perusal without being strengthened in his Christian purposes and efforts.—*Evangelical Review.*

www.ingramcontent.com/pod-product-compliance
Lightning Source LLC
LaVergne TN
LVHW021135110826
845150LV00005B/1038

9781425549497